Yii2 Application Development Cookbook

Third Edition

Discover 100 useful recipes that will bring the best out of the Yii2 framework and be on the bleeding edge of web development today

Andrew Bogdanov

Dmitry Eliseev

Based on Yii Application Development Cookbook - Second Edition, written by Alexander Makarov

BIRMINGHAM - MUMBAI

Yii2 Application Development Cookbook
Third Edition

First published: August 2011

Second edition: April 2013

Third edition: October 2016

Production reference: 2100417

Published by Packt Publishing Ltd.
Livery Place
35 Livery Street
Birmingham B3 2PB, UK.

ISBN 978-1-78528-176-1

www.packtpub.com

Credits

Authors

Andrew Bogdanov

Dmitry Eliseev

Reviewer

Maurizio Domba Cerin

Commissioning Editor

Ashwin Nair

Acquisition Editors

Vivek Anantharaman

James Jones

Aaron Lazar

Content Development Editor

Sanjeet Rao

Technical Editors

Bhagyashree Rai

Nidhisha Shetty

Copy Editor

Tom Jacob

Project Coordinator

Judie Jose

Proofreader

Safis Editing

Indexer

Pratik Shirodkar

Graphics

Kirk D'Penha

Production Coordinator

Deepika Naik

Cover Work

Deepika Naik

About the Authors

Andrew Bogdanov is a seasoned web developer from Yekaterinburg, Russia with more than six years of experience in industrial development. Since 2010 he has been interested in Yii and MVC frameworks. He has taken part in projects written in Yii such as a work aggregator for a UK company, high-load projects, real-estate projects, and development of private projects for the government.

He has worked on various CMS and frameworks using PHP and MySQL, which includes Yii, Kohana, Symphony, Joomla, WordPress, CakePHP, and so on. Also, having good hands in integrating third-party APIs such as Payment gateways (Paypal, Facebook, Twitter, and LinkedIn), he is very good in slicing and frontend. So he can provide full information about Yii framework.

He is also well-versed in PHP/MYSQL, Yii 1.x.x, Yii 2.x.x, Ajax, JQuery, MVC frameworks, Python, LAMP, HTML/CSS, Mercurial, Git, AngularJs, and adaptive markup. You can also visit his blog `http://jehkinen.com`.

In his free time he likes to visit and talk with new people and discuss web development problems. He is currently working with professionals `http://2amigos.us`.

Dmitry Eliseev has been a web developer since 2008 and specializes in server-side programming on PHP and PHP frameworks.

Since 2012 he has authored his personal blog, `http://elisdn.ru`, about web development in general and about the Yii Framework particularly. His blog became a well-known resource in the Russian Yii community. He is an active member of a Russian-language forum `http://yiiframework.ru`.

Dmitry is interested in developmental best practices, software architectures, object-oriented programming, and other approaches.

He is an author and a presenter of practical courses about principles and best practices of object oriented programming and the use of version control systems. And also he is an author of webinars, the Yii2 Framework, and common developmental subjects. He practices teaching and counseling by development on frameworks and using of principles of software design and improvements of common code quality. This is his first book.

About the Reviewer

Maurizio Domba Cerin is a frontend and backend web developer with over 24 years of professional experience in computer programming and 13 years in web development. He is an active member of the Yii community. At the moment he is developing intranet web applications for an export-import enterprise and working on other international projects, always trying to help others to improve their code and project usability. When not programming the Web, he is programming his wife and kids, always with a smile on his face, open-hearted and open-minded. He loves climbing, martial arts, meditation, and salsa.

www.PacktPub.com

eBooks, discount offers, and more

Did you know that Packt offers eBook versions of every book published, with PDF and ePub files available? You can upgrade to the eBook version at www.PacktPub.com and as a print book customer, you are entitled to a discount on the eBook copy. Get in touch with us at customercare@packtpub.com for more details.

At www.PacktPub.com, you can also read a collection of free technical articles, sign up for a range of free newsletters and receive exclusive discounts and offers on Packt books and eBooks.

https://www.packtpub.com/mapt

Get the most in-demand software skills with Mapt. Mapt gives you full access to all Packt books and video courses, as well as industry-leading tools to help you plan your personal development and advance your career.

Why Subscribe?

- Fully searchable across every book published by Packt
- Copy and paste, print, and bookmark content
- On demand and accessible via a web browser

Table of Contents

Preface

Yii is a free, open source web application development framework, written in PHP5, that promotes clean DRY design and encourages rapid development. It works to streamline your application development time and helps to ensure an extremely efficient, extensible, and maintainable end product. Being extremely performance-optimized, Yii is a perfect choice for any size project. However, it has been built with sophisticated, enterprise applications in mind. You have full control over the configuration from head-to-toe (presentation-to-persistence) to conform to your enterprise development guidelines. It comes packaged with tools to help test and debug your application, and has clear and comprehensive documentation.

This book is a collection of Yii2 recipes. Each recipe is represented as a full and independent item, which showcases solutions from real web applications. So you can easily reproduce them in your environment and learn Yii2 fast and without tears. All recipes are explained with step-by-step code examples and clear screenshots. Yii2 is like a suit that looks great off the rack, but is also very easy to tailor to fit your needs. Virtually every component of the framework is extensible. This book will show how to use official extensions, extend any component, or write a new one.

This book will help you create modern web applications quickly, and make sure they perform well using examples and business logic from real life. You will deal with the Yii command line, migrations, and assets. You will learn about role-based access, security, and deployment. We'll show you how to easily get started, configure your environment, and be ready to write web applications efficiently and quickly.

What this book covers

Chapter 1, Fundamentals, covers how to install the Yii Framework and different ways to install it. We will introduce you to application templates: basic and advanced and what is difference between them. Then you will learn about dependency injection container. This chapter contains info about model events, which are triggered after some simple actions such as model saving and updating and another. We will learn how to use external code which will include ZendFramework, Laravel, and Sympony in examples. We will also learn how to update your yii-1.x.x based application to yii2 step-by-step. A few more recipes are available at `https://www. packtpub.com/sites/default/files/downloads/4270OS_Chapter1.pdf`.

Chapter 2, Routing, Controllers, and Views, teaches some handy things about the Yii URL router, controllers, and views. You will be able to make your controllers and views more flexible.

Chapter 3, ActiveRecord, Model, and Database, discusses the three main methods to work with databases in Yii: Active Record, query builder, and direct SQL queries through DAO. All three are different in terms of syntax, features, and performance. In this chapter we will learn how to work with the database efficiently, when to use models and when not to, how to work with multiple databases, how to automatically preprocess Active Record fields, and how to use powerful database criteria.

Chapter 4, Forms, covers how Yii makes working with forms a breeze and the documentation on it is almost complete. Still, there are some areas that need clarification and examples.

Chapter 5, Security, discusses how to keep your application secure according to the general web application security principle "filter input, escape output." We will cover topics such as creating your own controller filters, preventing XSS, CSRF, and SQL injections, escaping output, and using role-based access control.

Chapter 6, RESTful Web Services, covers how to write RESTful Web Services using Yii2 and built-in features.

Chapter 7, Official Extensions, explains us how to install and use official extensions in your project. You will learn how to write your own extension and share it for another developers.

Chapter 8, Extending Yii, covers not only how to implement your own Yii extension, but also how to make your extension reusable and useful for the community. In addition, we will focus on many things you should do in order to make your extension as efficient as possible.

Chapter 9, Performance Tuning, teaches some best practices of developing an application that will run smoothly until you have very high loads. Yii is one of the fastest frameworks out there. Still, when developing and deploying an application, it is good to have some extra performance for free, as well as following best practices for the application itself. In this chapter, we will see how to configure Yii to gain extra performance. In addition, we will learn some best practices for developing an application that will run smoothly until we have very high loads.

Chapter 10, Deployment, covers various tips, which are especially useful on application deployment and when developing an application in a team, or when you just want to make your development environment more comfortable.

Chapter 11, Testing, teaches us how to use the best technologies for testing such as Codeception, PhpUnit, Atoum, and Behat. You will be introduced how to write simple tests and how to avoid regression errors in your applicaiton.

Chapter 12, Debugging, Logging, and Error Handling, discusses review logging, analyzing the exception stack trace, and implementing our own error handler. It is not possible to create a bug-free application if it is relatively complex, so developers have to detect errors and deal with them as fast as possible. Yii has a good set of utility features to handle logging and handling errors. Moreover, in the debug mode, Yii gives you a stack trace if there is an error. Using it, you can fix errors faster.

What you need for this book

In order to run the examples in this book, the following software will be required:

- ▸ Web server
- ▸ Database server
- ▸ PHP
- ▸ Yii2

Who this book is for

This book is for developers with good PHP5 knowledge and MVC-frameworks who have tried to develop applications using the Yii 1.x.x version. This book will be very useful for all those who would like to try Yii2, or those who are afraid to move from Yii 1.x.x. to Yii2. If you have still not tried Yii2, this book is definitely for you!

Sections

In this book, you will find several headings that appear frequently (Getting ready, How to do it..., How it works..., There's more..., and See also).
To give clear instructions on how to complete a recipe, we use these sections as follows:

Getting ready

This section tells you what to expect in the recipe, and describes how to set up any software or any preliminary settings required for the recipe.

How to do it...

This section contains the steps required to follow the recipe.

How it works...

This section usually consists of a detailed explanation of what happened in the previous section.

There's more...

This section consists of additional information about the recipe in order to make the reader more knowledgeable about the recipe.

See also

This section provides helpful links to other useful information for the recipe.

Conventions

In this book, you will find a number of text styles that distinguish between different kinds of information. Here are some examples of these styles and an explanation of their meaning.

Code words in text, database table names, folder names, filenames, file extensions, pathnames, dummy URLs, user input, and Twitter handles are shown as follows: "we are defining an alias parameter that should be specified in the URL after /page/."

A block of code is set as follows:

```
'urlManager' => array(
    'enablePrettyUrl' => true,
    'showScriptName' => false,
),
```

When we wish to draw your attention to a particular part of a code block, the relevant lines or items are set in bold:

```
'urlManager' => array(
    'enablePrettyUrl' => true,
    'showScriptName' => false,
),
```

Any command-line input or output is written as follows:

```
./yii migrate up
```

New terms and **important words** are shown in bold. Words that you see on the screen, for example, in menus or dialog boxes, appear in the text like this: "Generate a `Post` model using Gii with an enabled **Generate ActiveQuery** option that generates the `PostQuery` class."

Warnings or important notes appear in a box like this.

Tips and tricks appear like this.

Reader feedback

Feedback from our readers is always welcome. Let us know what you think about this book—what you liked or disliked. Reader feedback is important for us as it helps us develop titles that you will really get the most out of.

To send us general feedback, simply e-mail `feedback@packtpub.com`, and mention the book's title in the subject of your message.

If there is a topic that you have expertise in and you are interested in either writing or contributing to a book, see our author guide at `www.packtpub.com/authors`.

Customer support

Now that you are the proud owner of a Packt book, we have a number of things to help you to get the most from your purchase.

Downloading the example code

You can download the example code files for this book from your account at `http://www.packtpub.com`. If you purchased this book elsewhere, you can visit `http://www.packtpub.com/support` and register to have the files e-mailed directly to you.

You can download the code files by following these steps:

1. Log in or register to our website using your e-mail address and password.
2. Hover the mouse pointer on the **SUPPORT** tab at the top.
3. Click on **Code Downloads & Errata**.
4. Enter the name of the book in the **Search** box.
5. Select the book for which you're looking to download the code files.
6. Choose from the drop-down menu where you purchased this book from.
7. Click on **Code Download**.

Once the file is downloaded, please make sure that you unzip or extract the folder using the latest version of:

▶ WinRAR / 7-Zip for Windows

▶ Zipeg / iZip / UnRarX for Mac

▶ 7-Zip / PeaZip for Linux

The code bundle for the book is also hosted on GitHub at `https://github.com/PacktPublishing/Yii2-Application-Development-Cookbook-Third-Edition`. We also have other code bundles from our rich catalog of books and videos available at `https://github.com/PacktPublishing/`. Check them out!

Downloading the color images of this book

We also provide you with a PDF file that has color images of the screenshots/diagrams used in this book. The color images will help you better understand the changes in the output. You can download this file from `http://www.packtpub.com/sites/default/files/downloads/Yii2ApplicationDevelopmentCookbookThirdEdition_ColorImages.pdf`.

Errata

Although we have taken every care to ensure the accuracy of our content, mistakes do happen. If you find a mistake in one of our books—maybe a mistake in the text or the code—we would be grateful if you could report this to us. By doing so, you can save other readers from frustration and help us improve subsequent versions of this book. If you find any errata, please report them by visiting `http://www.packtpub.com/submit-errata`, selecting your book, clicking on the **Errata Submission Form** link, and entering the details of your errata. Once your errata are verified, your submission will be accepted and the errata will be uploaded to our website or added to any list of existing errata under the Errata section of that title.

To view the previously submitted errata, go to `https://www.packtpub.com/books/content/support` and enter the name of the book in the search field. The required information will appear under the **Errata** section.

Piracy

Piracy of copyrighted material on the Internet is an ongoing problem across all media. At Packt, we take the protection of our copyright and licenses very seriously. If you come across any illegal copies of our works in any form on the Internet, please provide us with the location address or website name immediately so that we can pursue a remedy.

Please contact us at `copyright@packtpub.com` with a link to the suspected pirated material.

We appreciate your help in protecting our authors and our ability to bring you valuable content.

Questions

If you have a problem with any aspect of this book, you can contact us at `questions@packtpub.com`, and we will do our best to address the problem.

1

Fundamentals

In this chapter, we will cover the following topics:

- ▶ Installing the framework
- ▶ Application templates
- ▶ Dependency injection container
- ▶ Service locator
- ▶ Code generation
- ▶ Configuring components
- ▶ Working with events
- ▶ Using external code

Introduction

In this chapter we will cover how to install Yii Framework and about possible techniques of installation. We will introduce you to application templates: basic and advanced and their difference between them. Then you will learn about dependency injection container. This chapter contains info about model events, which trigger after some actions such as model saving, updating and others. We will learn how to use external code which will include ZendFramework, Laravel, or Symfony. We will also be learning about how to update your `yii-1.x.x` based application to `yii2` step-by-step.

Installing the framework

Yii2 is a modern PHP framework provided as a Composer package. In this recipe, we will install the framework via the Composer package manager and configure the database connection for our application.

Getting ready

First of all, install the Composer package manager on your system.

 Note: If you use the OpenServer application on Windows, than the `composer` command already exists in the OpenServer terminal.

In Mac or Linux download the installer from `https://getcomposer.org/download/` and install it globally by using the following command:

```
sudo php composer-setup.php --install-dir=/usr/local/bin
--filename=composer
```

In Windows without OpenServer download and run `Composer-Setup.exe` from the `https://getcomposer.org/doc/00-intro.md` page.

If you do not have administrative privileges on the system then as an alternative you can just download the `https://getcomposer.org/composer.phar` raw file and use the `php composer.phar` call instead of single the `composer` command.

After installation run in your terminal:

```
composer
```

Or (if you just download archive) its alternative:

```
php composer.phar
```

When the installation succeeds you will see the following response:

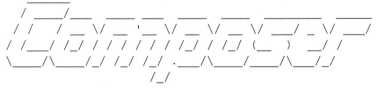

```
Composer version 1.2.0 2016-07-18 11:27:19
```

Right now you can install any package from the `https://packagist.org` repository.

How to do it...

You can install basic or advanced application templates. In order to learn about the differences between the templates see the *Application templates* recipe.

> Note that during installation the Composer package manager gets a lot of information from the GitHub site. GitHub may limit requests for anonymous users. In this case Composer asks you to input your access token. You should just register the `https://github.com` site and generate a new token via the `https://github.com/blog/1509-personal-api-tokens` guide.

Installing a basic project template

Carry out the following steps for installing basic project template:

1. As the first step open your terminal and install **Bower-to-Composer** adapter:

   ```
   composer global require "fxp/composer-asset-plugin:^1.2.0"
   ```

   It provides a simple way to load related non-PHP packages (JavaScript and CSS) from the Bower repository.

2. Create a new application in the new `basic` directory:

   ```
   composer create-project --prefer-dist yiisoft/yii2-app-basic basic
   ```

3. Check that your PHP contains the required extensions:

   ```
   cd basic
   php requirements.php
   ```

   > **Note**: PHP in command-mode and in web-interface mode can use different `php.ini` files with different configurations and different extensions.

4. Create a new database (if it is needed for your project) and configure it in the `config/db.php` file.

5. Try to run application via the following console command:

   ```
   php yii serve
   ```

6. Check in your browser that the application works by the `http://localhost:8080` address:

For permanent working create a new host in your server (Apache, Nginx, and so on) and set the web directory as a document root of the host.

Installing advanced project template

Carry out the following steps for installing advanced project template:

1. As the first step open your terminal install Bower-to-Composer adapter:

```
composer global require "fxp/composer-asset-plugin:^1.2.0"
```

It provides a simple way to load related non-PHP packages (JavaScript and CSS) from the Bower repository.

2. Create a new application in the new `basic` directory:

```
composer create-project --prefer-dist yiisoft/yii2-app-advanced advanced
```

3. The new application does not contains local configuration files and `index.php` entry scripts yet. To generate the files just `init` a working environment:

```
cd advanced
php init
```

During initialization select the **Development** environment.

4. Check that your PHP contains the required extensions:

```
php requirements.php
```

> **Note**: PHP in **command-line** mode and in **web-interface** mode can use different `php.ini` files with different configuration and different extensions.

5. Create a new database and configure it in the generated `common/config/main-local.php` file.

6. Apply the application migrations:

   ```
   php yii migrate
   ```

   This command will automatically create a `user` table in your database.

7. Try to run a frontend application by the following console command:

   ```
   php yii serve --docroot=@frontend/web --port=8080
   ```

   Then run the backend in an other terminal window:

   ```
   php yii serve --docroot=@backend/web --port=8090
   ```

8. Check in your browser that the application works via the `http://localhost:8080` and `http://localhost:8090` addresses:

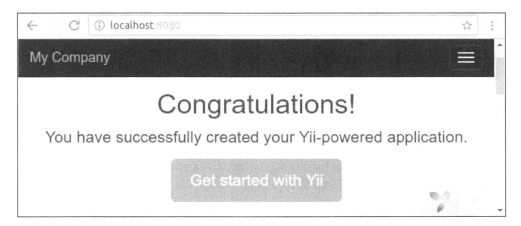

Create two new hosts for backend and frontend application in your server (Apache, Nginx, and so on) and set the `backend/web` and `frontend/web` directories as document roots of the hosts.

How it works...

First of all, we installed the Composer package manager and the Bower asset plugin.

After we installed the application via the `composer create-project` command, the command creates a new empty directory, clones the source code of application template and loads all its inner dependencies (framework and other components) into the `vendor` subdirectory.

If needed, we will initialize application configuration and set up a new database.

We can check system requirements via running the `requirements.php` script in console or browser mode.

And after cloning of the code we can configure our own PHP server to work with the `web` directories as the server's document roots.

See also

- ▸ For more information about installing `yii2-app-basic` refer to, `http://www.yiiframework.com/doc-2.0/guide-start-installation.html`.
- ▸ Refer to, `https://github.com/yiisoft/yii2-app-advanced/blob/master/docs/guide/start-installation.md` for `yii2-app-advanced`.
- ▸ Refer to, `https://getcomposer.org` for the Composer package manager.
- ▸ For creating a GitHub access token for Composer refer to `https://github.com/blog/1509-personal-api-tokens`.

Application templates

Yii2 has two application templates for development: basic and advanced. What is the difference between basic and advanced templates?

The names are confusing. Some people in the end choose basic because advanced may sound repulsive. In this chapter we will look at the differences.

How to do it...

Please refer to the *Installing the framework* recipe's *How to do it...* section to understand and learn how to install different templates.

How it works...

The advanced template has a custom system of configurations. It is developed so that a team can work together on a project but each developer can customize their own configurations for development, testing, and other environments.

Configuration environments can be complicated and normally aren't used when you develop alone.

The advanced template has frontend and backend folders for the frontend and backend parts of the web application accordingly. So you can configure a separate host for each folder and thereby isolate the frontend and backend part.

This is a simple way to organize files into directories and configure the web server. You can easily do the same thing in the basic template.

Neither front/back-end separation nor user management is on its own a good reason to choose the advanced template. It's better to adapt these features to your app—you'll learn more and won't get the difficult config problem.

If you will be working on the project with a team and you might need configuration flexibility, use different environments to develop and in this case a better choice would be the advanced application template. If you will be working alone and your project is simple you should choose the basic application template.

Dependency injection container

Dependency Inversion Principle (**DIP**) suggests we create modular low-coupling code with the help of extracting clear abstraction subsystems.

For example, if you want to simplify a big class you can split it into many chunks of routine code and extract every chunk into a new simple separated class.

The principle says that your low-level chunks should implement an all-sufficient and clear abstraction, and high-level code should work only with this abstraction and not low-level implementation.

When we split a big multitask class into small specialized classes, we face the issue of creating dependent objects and injecting them into each other.

If we could create one instance before:

```
$service = new MyGiantSuperService();
```

And after splitting we will create or get all dependent items and build our service:

```
$service = new MyService(
    new Repository(new PDO('dsn', 'username', 'password')),
    new Session(),
    new Mailer(new SmtpMailerTransport('username', 'password',
    host')),
    new Cache(new FileSystem('/tmp/cache')),
);
```

Dependency injection container is a factory that allows us to not care about building our objects. In Yii2 we can configure a container only once and use it for retrieving our service like this:

```
$service = Yii::$container->get('app\services\MyService')
```

We can also use this:

```
$service = Yii::createObject('app\services\MyService')
```

Or we ask the container to inject it as a dependency in the constructor of an other service:

```
use app\services\MyService;
class OtherService
{
    public function __construct(MyService $myService) { … }
}
```

When we will get the OtherService instance:

```
$otherService = Yii::createObject('app\services\OtherService')
```

In all cases the container will resolve all dependencies and inject dependent objects in each other.

In the recipe we create shopping cart with storage subsystem and inject the cart automatically into controller.

Getting ready

Create a new application by using the Composer package manager, as described in the official guide at http://www.yiiframework.com/doc-2.0/guide-start-installation.html.

How to do it...

Carry out the following steps:

1. Create a shopping cart class:

```php
<?php
namespace app\cart;

use app\cart\storage\StorageInterface;

class ShoppingCart
{
    private $storage;

    private $_items = [];

    public function __construct(StorageInterface $storage)
    {
        $this->storage = $storage;
    }

    public function add($id, $amount)
    {
        $this->loadItems();
        if (array_key_exists($id, $this->_items)) {
            $this->_items[$id]['amount'] += $amount;
        } else {
            $this->_items[$id] = [
                'id' => $id,
                'amount' => $amount,
            ];
        }
        $this->saveItems();
    }

    public function remove($id)
    {
        $this->loadItems();
        $this->_items = array_diff_key($this->_items, [$id
        => []]);
        $this->saveItems();
    }
```

```php
        public function clear()
        {
            $this->_items = [];
            $this->saveItems();
        }

        public function getItems()
        {
            $this->loadItems();
            return $this->_items;
        }

        private function loadItems()
        {
            $this->_items = $this->storage->load();
        }

        private function saveItems()
        {
            $this->storage->save($this->_items);
        }
    }
```

2. It will work only with own items. Instead of built-in storing items to session it will delegate this responsibility to any external storage class, which will implement the `StorageInterface` interface.

3. The cart class just gets the storage object in its own constructor, saves it instance into private `$storage` field and calls its `load()` and `save()` methods.

4. Define a common cart storage interface with the required methods:

```php
<?php
namespace app\cart\storage;

interface StorageInterface
{
    /**
     * @return array of cart items
     */
    public function load();

    /**
     * @param array $items from cart
     */
    public function save(array $items);
}
```

5. Create a simple storage implementation. It will store selected items in a server session:

```php
<?php
namespace app\cart\storage;

use yii\web\Session;

class SessionStorage implements StorageInterface
{
    private $session;
    private $key;

    public function __construct(Session $session, $key)
    {
        $this->key = $key;
        $this->session = $session;
    }

    public function load()
    {
        return $this->session->get($this->key, []);
    }

    public function save(array $items)
    {
        $this->session->set($this->key, $items);
    }
}
```

6. The storage gets any framework session instance in the constructor and uses it later for retrieving and storing items.

7. Configure the `ShoppingCart` class and its dependencies in the `config/web.php` file:

```php
<?php
use app\cart\storage\SessionStorage;

Yii::$container->setSingleton('app\cart\ShoppingCart');

Yii::$container->set('app\cart\storage\StorageInterface',
function() {
    return new SessionStorage(Yii::$app->session, 'primary-
    cart');
```

```
});

$params = require(__DIR__ . '/params.php');

//...
```

8. Create the cart controller with an extended constructor:

```php
<?php
namespace app\controllers;

use app\cart\ShoppingCart;
use app\models\CartAddForm;
use Yii;
use yii\data\ArrayDataProvider;
use yii\filters\VerbFilter;
use yii\web\Controller;

class CartController extends Controller
{
    private $cart;

    public function __construct($id, $module, ShoppingCart
    $cart, $config = [])
    {
        $this->cart = $cart;
        parent::__construct($id, $module, $config);
    }

    public function behaviors()
    {
        return [
            'verbs' => [
                'class' => VerbFilter::className(),
                'actions' => [
                    'delete' => ['post'],
                ],
            ],
        ];
    }

    public function actionIndex()
    {
```

```php
        $dataProvider = new ArrayDataProvider([
            'allModels' => $this->cart->getItems(),
        ]);

        return $this->render('index', [
            'dataProvider' => $dataProvider,
        ]);
    }

    public function actionAdd()
    {
        $form = new CartAddForm();

        if ($form->load(Yii::$app->request->post()) &&
        $form->validate()) {
            $this->cart->add($form->productId, $form-
            >amount);
            return $this->redirect(['index']);
        }

        return $this->render('add', [
            'model' => $form,
        ]);
    }

    public function actionDelete($id)
    {
        $this->cart->remove($id);

        return $this->redirect(['index']);
    }
}
```

9. Create a form:

```php
<?php
namespace app\models;

use yii\base\Model;

class CartAddForm extends Model
{
    public $productId;
```

```php
    public $amount;

    public function rules()
    {
        return [
            [['productId', 'amount'], 'required'],
            [['amount'], 'integer', 'min' => 1],
        ];
    }
}
```

10. Create the `views/cart/index.php` view:

```php
<?php
use yii\grid\ActionColumn;
use yii\grid\GridView;
use yii\grid\SerialColumn;
use yii\helpers\Html;

/* @var $this yii\web\View */
/* @var $dataProvider yii\data\ArrayDataProvider */

$this->title = 'Cart';
$this->params['breadcrumbs'][] = $this->title;
?>
<div class="cart-index">
    <h1><?= Html::encode($this->title) ?></h1>

    <p><?= Html::a('Add Item', ['add'], ['class' => 'btn
    btn-success']) ?></p>

    <?= GridView::widget([
        'dataProvider' => $dataProvider,
        'columns' => [
            ['class' => SerialColumn::className()],

            'id:text:Product ID',
            'amount:text:Amount',

            [
                'class' => ActionColumn::className(),
                'template' => '{delete}',
```

```
            ]
        ],
    ]) ?>
</div>
```

11. Create the `views/cart/add.php` view:

```php
<?php
use yii\helpers\Html;
use yii\bootstrap\ActiveForm;

/* @var $this yii\web\View */
/* @var $form yii\bootstrap\ActiveForm */
/* @var $model app\models\CartAddForm */

$this->title = 'Add item';
$this->params['breadcrumbs'][] = ['label' => 'Cart', 'url' =>
['index']];
$this->params['breadcrumbs'][] = $this->title;
?>
<div class="cart-add">
    <h1><?= Html::encode($this->title) ?></h1>

    <?php $form = ActiveForm::begin(['id' => 'contact-
    form']); ?>
        <?= $form->field($model, 'productId') ?>
        <?= $form->field($model, 'amount') ?>
        <div class="form-group">
            <?= Html::submitButton('Add', ['class' => 'btn
            btn-primary']) ?>
        </div>
    <?php ActiveForm::end(); ?>
</div>
```

12. Add link items into the main menu:

```php
['label' => 'Home', 'url' => ['/site/index']],
['label' => 'Cart', 'url' => ['/cart/index']],
['label' => 'About', 'url' => ['/site/about']],
// …
```

13. Open the cart page and try to add rows:

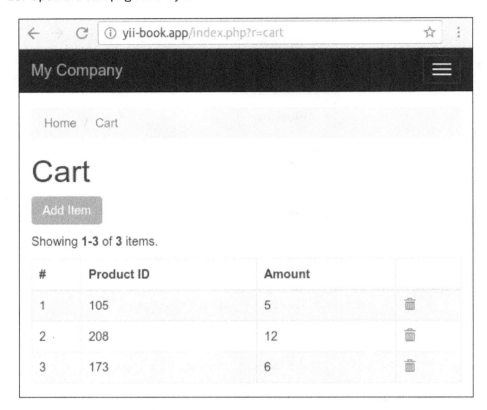

In this case we have the main `ShoppingCart` class with a low-level dependency, defined by an abstraction interface:

```
class ShoppingCart
{
    public function __construct(StorageInterface $storage) { … }
}

interface StorageInterface
{
   public function load();
   public function save(array $items);
}
```

And we have some an implementation of the abstraction:

```
class SessionStorage implements StorageInterface
{
    public function __construct(Session $session, $key) { … }
}
```

Right now we can create an instance of the cart manually like this:

```
$storage = new SessionStorage(Yii::$app->session, 'primary-cart');
$cart = new ShoppingCart($storage)
```

It allows us to create a lot of different implementations such as `SessionStorage`, `CookieStorage`, or `DbStorage`. And we can reuse the framework-independent `ShoppingCart` class with `StorageInterface` in different projects and different frameworks. We must only implement the storage class with the interface's methods for needed framework.

But instead of manually creating an instance with all dependencies, we can use a dependency injection container.

By default the container parses the constructors of all classes and recursively creates all the required instances. For example, if we have four classes:

```
class A {
    public function __construct(B $b, C $c) { … }
}

class B {
    ...
}

class C {
    public function __construct(D $d) { … }
}

class D {
    ...
}
```

We can retrieve the instance of class `A` in two ways:

```
$a = Yii::$container->get('app\services\A')
// or
$a = Yii::createObject('app\services\A')
```

And the container automatically creates instances of the B, D, C, and A classes and injects them into each other.

In our case we mark the cart instance as a singleton:

```
Yii::$container->setSingleton('app\cart\ShoppingCart');
```

This means that the container will return a single instance for every repeated call instead of creating the cart again and again.

Besides, our ShoppingCart has the StorageInterface type in its own constructor and the container does know what class it must instantiate for this type. We must manually bind the class to the interface like this:

```
Yii::$container->set('app\cart\storage\StorageInterface', 'app\cart\
storage\CustomStorage',);
```

But our SessionStorage class has non-standard constructor:

```
class SessionStorage implements StorageInterface
{
    public function __construct(Session $session, $key) { … }
}
```

Therefore we use an anonymous function to manually creatie the instance:

```
Yii::$container->set('app\cart\storage\StorageInterface',
function() {
    return new SessionStorage(Yii::$app->session, 'primary-cart');
});
```

And after all we can retrieve the cart object from the container manually in our own controllers, widgets, and other places:

```
$cart = Yii::createObject('app\cart\ShoppingCart')
```

But every controller and other object will be created via the createObject method inside the framework. And we can use injection of cart via the controller constructor:

```
class CartController extends Controller
{
    private $cart;

    public function __construct($id, $module, ShoppingCart $cart,
    $config = [])
    {
```

```
        $this->cart = $cart;
        parent::__construct($id, $module, $config);
    }

    // ...
}
```

Use this injected cart object:

```
public function actionDelete($id)
{
    $this->cart->remove($id);
    return $this->redirect(['index']);
}
```

See also

▶ For more information about DIP refer to `https://en.wikipedia.org/wiki/Dependency_inversion_principle`

▶ In order to learn more about dependency injection container refer to `http://www.yiiframework.com/doc-2.0/guide-concept-di-container.html`

Service locator

Instead of manually creating instances of different shared services (application components) we can get them from a special global object, which contains configurations and instances of all components.

A service locator is a global object that contains a list of components or definitions, uniquely identified by an ID, and allow us to retrieve any needed instance by its ID. The locator creates a single instance of the component on-the-fly at the first call and returns a previous instance at the subsequent calls.

In this recipe, we will create a shopping cart component and will write a cart controller for working with it.

Getting ready

Create a new application by using the Composer package manager, as described in the official guide at `http://www.yiiframework.com/doc-2.0/guide-start-installation.html`.

How to do it...

Carry out the following steps to create a shopping cart component:

1. Create a shopping cart component. It will store selected items in a user session:

```php
<?php
namespace app\components;

use Yii;
use yii\base\Component;

class ShoppingCart extends Component
{
    public $sessionKey = 'cart';

    private $_items = [];

    public function add($id, $amount)
    {
        $this->loadItems();
        if (array_key_exists($id, $this->_items)) {
            $this->_items[$id]['amount'] += $amount;
        } else {
            $this->_items[$id] = [
                'id' => $id,
                'amount' => $amount,
            ];
        }
        $this->saveItems();
    }

    public function remove($id)
    {
        $this->loadItems();
        $this->_items = array_diff_key($this->_items, [$id
        => []]);
        $this->saveItems();
    }

    public function clear()
    {
        $this->_items = [];
```

```php
        $this->saveItems();
    }

    public function getItems()
    {
        $this->loadItems();
        return $this->_items;
    }

    private function loadItems()
    {
        $this->_items = Yii::$app->session->get($this->sessionKey, []);
    }

    private function saveItems()
    {
        Yii::$app->session->set($this->sessionKey,
        $this->_items);
    }
}
```

2. Register the `ShoppingCart` in service locator as an application component in the `config/web.php` file:

```php
'components' => [
    …
    'cart => [
        'class' => 'app\components\ShoppingCart',
        'sessionKey' => 'primary-cart',
    ],
]
```

3. Create a cart controller:

```php
<?php
namespace app\controllers;

use app\models\CartAddForm;
use Yii;
use yii\data\ArrayDataProvider;
use yii\filters\VerbFilter;
use yii\web\Controller;
```

```php
class CartController extends Controller
{
    public function behaviors()
    {
        return [
            'verbs' => [
                'class' => VerbFilter::className(),
                'actions' => [
                    'delete' => ['post'],
                ],
            ],
        ];
    }

    public function actionIndex()
    {
        $dataProvider = new ArrayDataProvider([
            'allModels' => Yii::$app->cart->getItems(),
        ]);

        return $this->render('index', [
            'dataProvider' => $dataProvider,
        ]);
    }

    public function actionAdd()
    {
        $form = new CartAddForm();

        if ($form->load(Yii::$app->request->post()) &&
        $form->validate()) {
            Yii::$app->cart->add($form->productId,
            $form->amount);
            return $this->redirect(['index']);
        }

        return $this->render('add', [
            'model' => $form,
        ]);
    }

    public function actionDelete($id)
    {
```

```php
        Yii::$app->cart->remove($id);

        return $this->redirect(['index']);
    }
}
```

4. Create a form:

```php
<?php
namespace app\models;

use yii\base\Model;

class CartAddForm extends Model
{
    public $productId;
    public $amount;

    public function rules()
    {
        return [
            [['productId', 'amount'], 'required'],
            [['amount'], 'integer', 'min' => 1],
        ];
    }
}
```

5. Create the `views/cart/index.php` view:

```php
<?php
use yii\grid\ActionColumn;
use yii\grid\GridView;
use yii\grid\SerialColumn;
use yii\helpers\Html;

/* @var $this yii\web\View */
/* @var $dataProvider yii\data\ArrayDataProvider */

$this->title = 'Cart';
$this->params['breadcrumbs'][] = $this->title;
?>
<div class="site-contact">
    <h1><?= Html::encode($this->title) ?></h1>
```

```
<p><?= Html::a('Add Item', ['add'], ['class' => 'btn
btn-success']) ?></p>

<?= GridView::widget([
    'dataProvider' => $dataProvider,
    'columns' => [
        ['class' => SerialColumn::className()],

        'id:text:Product ID',
        'amount:text:Amount',

        [
            'class' => ActionColumn::className(),
            'template' => '{delete}',
        ]
    ],
]) ?>
</div>
```

6. Create the `views/cart/add.php` view:

```php
<?php
use yii\helpers\Html;
use yii\bootstrap\ActiveForm;

/* @var $this yii\web\View */
/* @var $form yii\bootstrap\ActiveForm */
/* @var $model app\models\CartAddForm */

$this->title = 'Add item';
$this->params['breadcrumbs'][] = ['label' => 'Cart', 'url' =>
['index']];
$this->params['breadcrumbs'][] = $this->title;
?>
<div class="site-contact">
    <h1><?= Html::encode($this->title) ?></h1>

    <?php $form = ActiveForm::begin(['id' => 'contact-
form']); ?>
        <?= $form->field($model, 'productId') ?>
        <?= $form->field($model, 'amount') ?>
        <div class="form-group">
            <?= Html::submitButton('Add', ['class' => 'btn
            btn-primary']) ?>
        </div>
    <?php ActiveForm::end(); ?>
</div>
```

7. Add a link item into the main menu:

```
['label' => 'Home', 'url' => ['/site/index']],
['label' => 'Cart', 'url' => ['/cart/index']],
['label' => 'About', 'url' => ['/site/about']],
// …
```

8. Open the cart page and try to add rows:

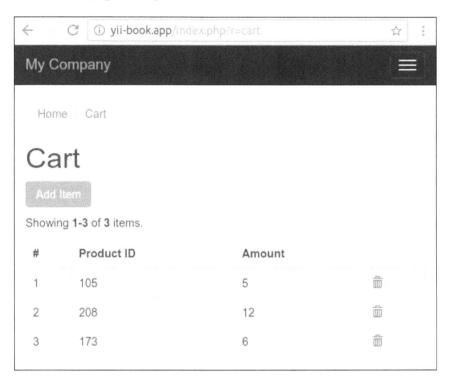

How it works...

First of all we created our own class with a public `sessionKey` option:

```php
<?php
namespace app\components;
use yii\base\Component;

class ShoppingCart extends Component
{
    public $sessionKey = 'cart';

    // …
}
```

Secondly, we added the component definition into the `components` section of the configuration file:

```
'components' => [
    …
    'cart => [
        'class' => 'app\components\ShoppingCart',
        'sessionKey' => 'primary-cart',
    ],
]
```

Right now we can retrieve the component instance in two ways:

```
$cart = Yii::$app->cart;
$cart = Yii::$app->get('cart');
```

And we can use this object in our own controllers, widgets, and other places.

When we call any component such as `cart`:

```
Yii::$app->cart
```

We call the virtual property of the `Application` class instance in the `Yii::$app` static variable. But the `yii\base\Application` class extends the `yii\base\Module` class, which extends the `yii\di\ServiceLocator` class with the `__get` magic method. This magic method just calls the `get()` method of the `yii\di\ServiceLocator` class:

```
namespace yii\di;

class ServiceLocator extends Component
{
    private $_components = [];
    private $_definitions = [];

    public function __get($name)
    {
        if ($this->has($name)) {
            return $this->get($name);
        } else {
            return parent::__get($name);
        }
    }
    // …
}
```

As a result it is an alternative to directly calling the service via the `get` method:

```
Yii::$app->get('cart');
```

When we get a component from the `get` method of service locator, the locator finds needed definition in its `_definitions` list and if successful it creates a new object by the definition on the fly, registers it in its own list of complete instances `_components` and returns the object.

If we get some component, multiplying the locator will always return the previous saved instance again and again:

```
$cart1 = Yii::$app->cart;
$cart2 = Yii::$app->cart;
var_dump($cart1 === $cart2); // bool(true)
```

It allows us to use the shared single cart instance `Yii::$app->cart` or single database connection `Yii::$app->db` instead of creating one large set from scratch again and again.

See also

► For more information about the service locator and about core framework components refer to `http://www.yiiframework.com/doc-2.0/guide-concept-service-locator.html`

► The *Configuring components* recipe

► The *Creating components* recipe in *Chapter 8*, *Extending Yii*

Code generation

Yii2 provides the powerful module Gii to generate models, controllers, and views, which you can easily modify and customize. It's a really helpful tool for fast and quick development.

In this section we will explore how to use Gii and generate code. For example you have a database with one table named `film` and you would like to create an application with CRUD operations for this table. It's easy.

Getting ready

1. Create a new application by using composer as described in the official guide at `http://www.yiiframework.com/doc-2.0/guide-start-installation.html`.

2. Download the Sakila database from `http://dev.mysql.com/doc/index-other.html`.

3. Execute the downloaded SQLs: first the schema then the data.

4. Configure the database connection in `config/main.php` to use the Sakila database.

5. Run your web-server by `./yii serve`.

How to do it...

1. Go to `http://localhost:8080/index.php?r=gii` and select **Model Generator**.

2. Fill out **Table Name** as `actor` and **Model Class** as `Actor` and press button **Generate** at the bottom of page.

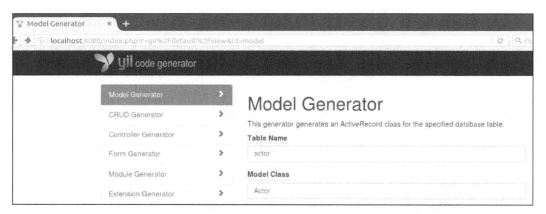

3. Return tothe main Gii menu by clicking the **yii code generator** logo on the header and choose **CRUD Generator**.

4. Fill out the **Model Class** field as `app\models\Actor` and **Controller Class** as `app\controllers\ActorController`.

CRUD Generator

This generator generates a controller and views that implement CRUD (Create, Read, Update, Delete data model.

Model Class

app\models\Actor

Search Model Class

Controller Class

app\controllers\ActorController

View Path

5. Press the **Preview** button at the bottom of page and then press green button **Generate**.

6. Check the result via `http://localhost:8080/index.php?actor/create`.

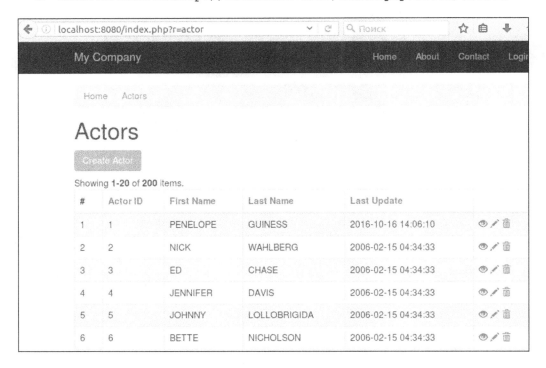

How it works...

If you check your project structure you will see autogenerated code:

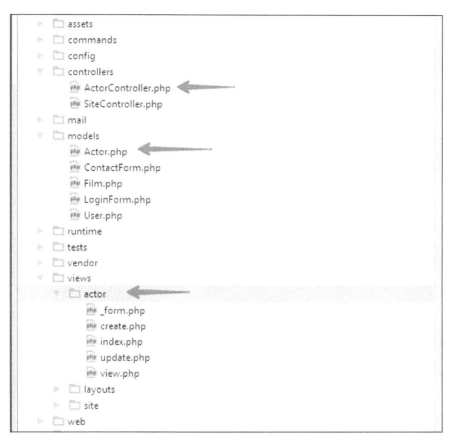

Firstly we've created an `Actor` model. Gii automatically creates all model rules which depends on `mysql` field types. For example, if in your MySQL `actor` table's fields `first_name` and `last_name` have `IS NOT NULL` flag then Yii automatically creates rule for it `required` and sets max length `45` symbols because in our database max length of this field is set up as `45`.

```
public function rules()
{
    return [
        [['first_name', 'last_name'], 'required'],
        [['last_update'], 'safe'],
        [['first_name', 'last_name'], 'string', 'max' => 45],
    ];
}
```

Also Yii creates relationship between models automatically, based on foreign keys you added to your database. In our case two relations were created automatically.

```
public function getFilmActors()
{
    return $this->hasMany(FilmActor::className(), ['actor_id' =>
    'actor_id']);
}

public function getFilms()
{
    return $this->hasMany(Film::className(), ['film_id' =>
    'film_id'])->viaTable('film_actor', ['actor_id'
    => 'actor_id']);
}
```

This relationship has been created because we have two foreign keys in our database. The `film_actor` table has foreign key `fk_film_actor_actor` which points to `actor` table fields `actor_id` and `fk_film_actor_film` which points to `film` table field `film_id`.

Notice that you haven't generated `FilmActor` model yet. So if you would develop full-app versus demo you had to generate `Film`, `FilmActor` models also. For the rest of the pieces, refer to `http://www.yiiframework.com/doc-2.0/guide-start-gii.html`.

Configuring components

Yii is a very customizable framework. Moreover, as in all customizable code, there should be a convenient way to set up different application parts. In Yii, this is provided through configuration files located at `config`.

Getting ready

Create a new application by using the Composer package manager as described in the official guide at `http://www.yiiframework.com/doc-2.0/guide-start-installation.html`.

How to do it...

If you have worked with Yii before, then you have probably configured a database connection:

```
return [
    ...
    'components' => [
        'db' => [
```

```
            'class' => 'system.db.CDbConnection',
            'dsn' => 'mysql:host=localhost;dbname=database_name',
            'username' => 'root',
            'password' => '',
            'charset' => 'utf8',
        ],
        ...
    ],
    ...
];
```

This way of configuring components is used when you want to use a component across all application parts. With the preceding configuration, you can access a component by its name, such as `Yii::$app->db`.

How it works...

When you are using the `Yii::$app->db` component for the first time directly or through an Active Record model, Yii creates a component and initializes its public properties with the corresponding values provided in db array under the `components` section of the application configuration file. In the preceding code, dsn value will be assigned to `yii\db\Connection::dsn`, username will be assigned to `Connection::username`, and so on.

If you want to find out what `charset` stands for or want to know what else you can configure in the db component, then you need to know its class. In the case of the db component, the class is `yii\db\Connection`. You can just open the class and look for its public properties, which you can set from config.

In the preceding code, the `class` property is a bit special because it is used to specify the component class name. It does not exist in the `yii\db\Connection` class. Therefore, it can be used to override a class as follows:

```
return [
    ...
    'components' => [
        'db' => [
            'class' => app\components\MyConnection',
            ...
        ],
        ...
    ],
    ...
);
```

This way, you can override each application component; this is very useful whenever a standard component does not fit your application.

Built-in components

Now, let's find out which standard Yii application components you can configure. There are two application types bundled with Yii:

- ▸ Web application (`yii\web\Application`)
- ▸ Console application (`yii\console\Application`)

Both are extended from `yii\base\Application`, so both console and web applications share its components.

You can get the component names from the source code of the `coreComponents()` application's method.

You can add your own application components (classes extended from `yii\base\Component`) by simply adding new configuration items and pointing their class properties to your custom classes.

See also

- ▸ Both console and web application components are listed in the list at `http://www.yiiframework.com/doc-2.0/guide-structure-application-components.html`
- ▸ For more information on creating your own components see:
    - ❏ The *Service locator* recipe
    - ❏ The *Creating components* recipe in *Chapter 8, Extending Yii*

Working with events

Yii's events provide a simple implementation, which allows you to listen and subscribe to various events that occur in your web-application. For example, you may wish to send a notification about a new article to followers each time you publish new material.

Getting ready

1. Create a new application by using the Composer package manager, as described in the official guide at `http://www.yiiframework.com/doc-2.0/guide-start-installation.html`.

2. Execute the following SQL code on your server to create the `article` table:

```
CREATE TABLE `article` (
`id` int(11) NOT NULL AUTO_INCREMENT,
`name` varchar(255) DEFAULT NULL,
`description` TEXT,
PRIMARY KEY (`id`)
) ENGINE=InnoDB DEFAULT CHARSET=utf8;
```

3. Generate the `Article` model using Gii.

4. Run your webserver by `./yii serve` command.

How to do it...

1. Add an action test to `\controllers\SiteController`:

```
public function actionTest()
{
    $article = new Article();
    $article->name = 'Valentine\'s Day\'s coming? Aw crap!
    I forgot to get a girlfriend again!';
    $article->description = 'Bender is angry at Fry for
    dating a robot. Stay away from our women.
    You\'ve got metal fever, boy. Metal fever';

    // $event is an object of yii\base\Event or a child
    class
    $article->on(ActiveRecord::EVENT_AFTER_INSERT,
    function($event) {
        $followers = ['john2@teleworm.us',
        'shivawhite@cuvox.de',
        'kate@dayrep.com' ];
        foreach($followers as $follower) {
            Yii::$app->mailer->compose()
                ->setFrom('techblog@teleworm.us')
                ->setTo($follower)
                ->setSubject($event->sender->name)
                ->setTextBody($event->sender->description)
                ->send();
        }
        echo 'Emails has been sent';
    });
```

```
    if (!$article->save()) {
        echo VarDumper::dumpAsString($article-
        >getErrors());
    };
}
```

2. Update the `config/web.php` component `mailer` using the following code.

```
'mailer' => [
    'class' => 'yii\swiftmailer\Mailer',
    'useFileTransport' => false,
],
```

3. Run this URL in your browser: `http://localhost:8080/index.php?r=site/test`.

4. Also check `http://www.fakemailgenerator.com/inbox/teleworm.us/john2/`.

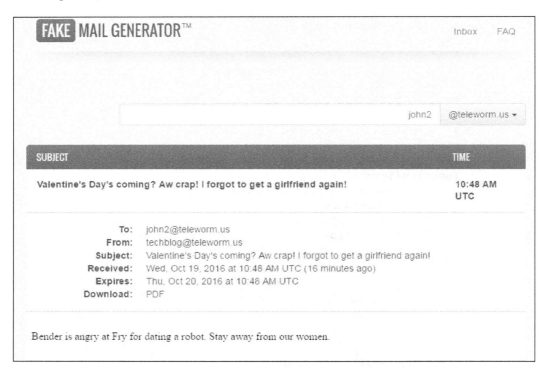

How it works...

We've created an `Article` model and added a handler for the `ActiveRecord::EVENT_AFTER_INSERT` event to our `Article` model. It means that every time we save a new article an event is triggered and our attached handler will be called.

In the real-world, we would like to notify our blog followers each time we publish a new article. In a real application we would have a `follower` or `user` table and with different blog sections not only single blog. In this example, after saving our model we notify our followers `john2@teleworm.us`, `shivawhite@cuvox.de`, and `kate@dayrep.com`. In the last step we just prove that users have received our notifications, particularly `john2`. You can create your own event with any name. In this example we use a built-in event called `ActiveRecord::EVENT_AFTER_INSERT`, which is called after each insert to the database.

For example, we can create our own event. Just add a new `actionTestNew` with the following code:

```php
public function actionTestNew()
{
    $article = new Article();
    $article->name = 'Valentine\'s Day\'s coming? Aw crap! I
    forgot to get a girlfriend again!';
    $article->description = 'Bender is angry at Fry for dating a
    robot. Stay away from our women.
    You've got metal fever, boy. Metal fever';

    // $event is an object of yii\base\Event or a child class
    $article->on(Article::EVENT_OUR_CUSTOM_EVENT, function($event) {
        $followers = ['john2@teleworm.us', 'shivawhite@cuvox.de',
        'kate@dayrep.com' ];
        foreach($followers as $follower) {
            Yii::$app->mailer->compose()
                ->setFrom('techblog@teleworm.us')
                ->setTo($follower)
                ->setSubject($event->sender->name)
                ->setTextBody($event->sender->description)
                ->send();
        }
        echo 'Emails have been sent';
    });

    if ($article->save()) {
        $article->trigger(Article::EVENT_OUR_CUSTOM_EVENT);
    }
}
```

Also add the `EVENT_OUR_CUSTOM_EVENT` constant to `models/Article` as:

```
class Article extends \yii\db\ActiveRecord
{
    CONST EVENT_OUR_CUSTOM_EVENT = 'eventOurCustomEvent';
    ...
}
```

Run `http://localhost:8080/index.php?r=site/test-new`.

You should see the same result and all notifications to followers will be sent again. The main difference is we used our custom event name.

After the save, we've triggered our event. Events may be triggered by calling the `yii\base\Component::trigger()` method. The method requires an event name, and optionally an event object that describes the parameters to be passed to the event handlers.

See also

For more information about events refer to `http://www.yiiframework.com/doc-2.0/guide-concept-events.html`

Using external code

Package repositories, PSR standards, and social coding provide us with lots of high-quality reusable libraries and other components with free licenses. We can just install any external component in project instead of reengineering them from scratch. It improves development performance and makes for higher-quality code.

Getting ready

Create a new application by using the Composer package manager as described in the official guide at `http://www.yiiframework.com/doc-2.0/guide-start-installation.html`.

How to do it...

In this recipe we will try to attach some libraries manually and via Composer.

Installing a library via Composer

When you use NoSQL or other databases without autoincrement primary keys, you must generate unique identifiers manually. For example, you can use **Universally Unique Identifier** (**UUID**) instead of a numerical one. Let's do it:

1. Install `https://github.com/ramsey/uuid` component via Composer:

   `composer require ramsey/uuid`

2. Create a demonstration console controller:

   ```php
   <?php
   namespace app\commands;

   use Ramsey\Uuid\Uuid;
   use yii\console\Controller;

   class UuidController extends Controller
   {
       public function actionGenerate()
       {
           $this->stdout(Uuid::uuid4()->toString() . PHP_EOL);
           $this->stdout(Uuid::uuid4()->toString() . PHP_EOL);
           $this->stdout(Uuid::uuid4()->toString() . PHP_EOL);
           $this->stdout(Uuid::uuid4()->toString() . PHP_EOL);
           $this->stdout(Uuid::uuid4()->toString() . PHP_EOL);
       }
   }
   ```

3. And just run it:

   ```
   ./yii uuid/generate
   ```

4. If successful, you'll see the following output:

   ```
   25841e6c-6060-4a81-8368-4d99aa3617dd
   fcac910a-a9dc-4760-8528-491c17591a26
   4d745da3-0a6c-47df-aee7-993a42ed915c
   0f3e6da5-88f1-4385-9334-b47d1801ca0f
   21a28940-c749-430d-908e-1893c52f1fe0
   ```

5. That's it! Now you can use the `Ramsey\Uuid\Uuid` class in your project.

Installing libraries manually

We can install a library automatically when it is provided as a Composer package. In other cases we must install it manually.

For example, create some library examples:

1. Create the `awesome/namespaced/Library.php` file with the following code:

```php
<?php
namespace awesome\namespaced;

class Library
{
    public function method()
    {
        return 'I am an awesome library with namespace.';
    }
}
```

2. Create the `old/OldLibrary.php` file:

```php
<?php
class OldLibrary
{
    function method()
    {
        return 'I am an old library without namespace.';
    }
}
```

3. Create a set of functions as an `old/functions.php` file:

```php
<?php
function simpleFunction()
{
    return 'I am a simple function.';
}
```

And now set up this file in our application:

4. Define the new alias for the `awesome` library namespace root in the `config/web.php` file (in `aliases` section):

```php
$config = [
    'id' => 'basic',
    'basePath' => dirname(__DIR__),
    'bootstrap' => ['log'],
```

```
        'aliases' => [
            '@awesome' => '@app/awesome',
        ],
        'components' => [
            // …
        ],
        'params' => // …
];
```

or via the `setAlias` method:

```
Yii::setAlias('@awesome', '@app/awesome');
```

5. Define a simple class file path at the top of the `config/web.php` file:

```
Yii::$classMap['OldLibrary'] = '@app/old/OldLibrary.php';
```

6. Configure autoloading of the `functions.php` file in `composer.json`:

```
"require-dev": {
    . . .
},
"autoload": {
    "files": ["old/functions.php"]
},
"config": {
    . . .
},
```

And apply the changes:

```
composer update
```

7. And now create an example controller:

```php
<?php
namespace app\controllers;

use yii\base\Controller;

class LibraryController extends Controller
{
    public function actionIndex()
    {
        $awesome = new \awesome\namespaced\Library();
        echo '<pre>' . $awesome->method() . '</pre>';
```

```
        $old = new \OldLibrary();
        echo '<pre>' . $old->method() . '</pre>';

        echo '<pre>' . simpleFunction() . '</pre>';
    }
}
```

And open the page:

```
←  →  C   ⓘ yii-book.app/index.php?r=library      ☆   ⋮

I am an awesome library with namespace.

I am an old library without namespace.

I am a simple function.
```

Using Yii2 code in other frameworks

If you want to use Yii2 framework code with other frameworks just add Yii2-specific parameters in `composer.json`:

```
{
    ...
    "extra": {
        "asset-installer-paths": {
            "npm-asset-library": "vendor/npm",
            "bower-asset-library": "vendor/bower"
        }
    }
}
```

And install the framework:

`composer require yiisoft/yii2`

Now open the entry script of your application (on ZendFramework, Laravel, Symfony, and many more), require the Yii2 autoloader, and create the Yii application instance:

```
require(__DIR__ . '/../vendor/autoload.php');
require(__DIR__ . '/../vendor/yiisoft/yii2/Yii.php');

$config = require(__DIR__ . '/../config/yii/web.php');

new yii\web\Application($config);
```

That's it! Now you can use Yii::$app instances, models, widgets and other components from Yii2.

How it works...

In the first case we just install a new Composer package in our project and use it, because its `composer.json` file defines all aspects of `autoloading` library files.

But in the second case we did not have Composer packages and registered the files in the autoloading mechanism manually. In Yii2 we can use aliases and `Yii::$classMap` for registering the roots of PSR-4 namespaces and for single files.

But as an alternative we can use Composer autoloader for all cases. Just define an extended `autoload` section in the `composer.json` file like this:

```
"autoload": {
    "psr-0": { "": "old/" },
    "psr-4": {"awesome\\": "awesome/"},
    "files": ["old/functions.php"]
}
```

Apply the changes using this command:

```
composer update
```

Right now you can remove aliases and `$classMap` definitions from your configuration files and ensure the example page still works correctly:

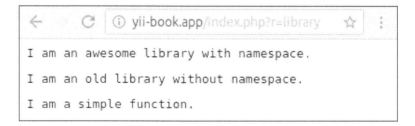

This example completely uses Composer's autoloader instead of the framework's autoloader.

See also

- ▶ For more information about integrating external code in Yii2 and framework code into our projects see the guide at `http://www.yiiframework.com/doc-2.0/guide-tutorial-yii-integration.html`

- ▶ For more on aliases refer to `http://www.yiiframework.com/doc-2.0/guide-concept-aliases.html`

- ▶ For more on the `autoload` section of `composer.json` refer to `https://getcomposer.org/doc/01-basic-usage.md#autoloading`

- ▶ And also you can browse or search any Composer packages on `https://packagist.org`

2
Routing, Controllers, and Views

In this chapter, we will cover the following topics:

- ▶ Configuring URL rules
- ▶ Generating URLs
- ▶ Using regular expressions in URL rules
- ▶ Using a base controller
- ▶ Using standalone actions
- ▶ Creating a custom filter
- ▶ Displaying static pages
- ▶ Using flash messages
- ▶ Using the controller context in a view
- ▶ Reusing views with partials
- ▶ Using blocks
- ▶ Using decorators
- ▶ Defining multiple layouts
- ▶ Pagination and sorting data

Introduction

This chapter will help you to learn some handy things about the Yii URL router, controllers, and views. You will be able to make your controllers and views more flexible.

Configuring URL rules

In this recipe, we will learn how to configure URL rules. Before we begin lets set up an application.

Getting ready

1. Create a new application using the Composer package manager, as described in the official guide at `http://www.yiiframework.com/doc-2.0/guide-start-installation.html`.

2. Create the `@app/controllers/TestController.php` controller with the following code inside:

```php
<?php

namespace app\controllers;

use yii\helpers\Html;
use yii\web\Controller;

class TestController extends Controller
{
    public function actionIndex()
    {
        return $this->renderContent(Html::tag('h2',
            'Index action'
        ));
    }

    public function actionPage($alias)
    {
        return $this->renderContent(Html::tag('h2',
            'Page is '. Html::encode($alias)
        ));
    }
}
```

This is the application controller that we are going to customize URLs for.

3. Configure your application server to use clean URLs. If you are using Apache with `mod_rewrite` and `AllowOverride` turned on, then you should add the following lines to the `.htaccess` file under your `@web` directory:

```
Options +FollowSymLinks
IndexIgnore */*
RewriteEngine on
# if a directory or a file exists, use it directly
RewriteCond %{REQUEST_FILENAME} !-f
RewriteCond %{REQUEST_FILENAME} !-d
# otherwise forward it to index.php
RewriteRule . index.php
```

How to do it...

Our website should display the index page at `/home` and all other pages at `/page/<alias_here>`. Additionally, `/about` should lead to a page with the alias about:

1. Add the following config of the `urlManager` component in `@app/config/web.php`:

```
'components' => [
    // ..
    'urlManager' => [
        'enablePrettyUrl' => true,
        'rules' => [
            'home' => 'test/index',
            '<alias:about>' => 'test/page',
            'page/<alias>' => 'test/page',
        ]
    ],
    // ..
],
```

After saving your changes, you should be able to browse the following URLs:

```
%/home
%/about
%/page/about
/page/test
```

2. Try running the `/home` URL and you will get the following:

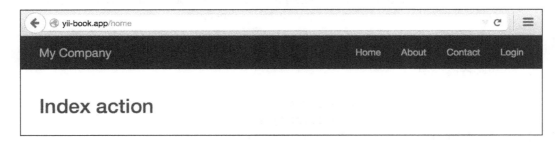

3. Then try running the `/about` page:

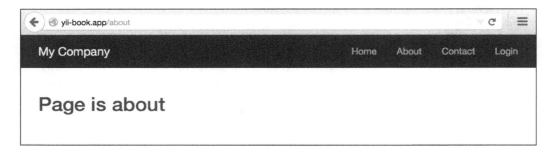

How it works...

Let's review what was done and why it works. We'll start with the right-most part of the first rule:

```
'home' => 'test/index',
```

What is `test/index` exactly? In the Yii application, each controller and its actions have corresponding internal routes. A format for an internal route is `moduleID/controllerID/ actionID`. For example, the `actionPage` method of `TestController` corresponds to the `test/page` route. So, in order to get the controller ID, you should take its name without the Controller postfix and make its first letter lowercase. To get an action ID, you should take the action method name without the action prefix, and again, make its first letter lowercase.

Now, what is home? To understand it in a better way, we need to know, at least superficially, what's happening when we access our application using different URLs.

When we use `/home`, the URL router checks our rules one by one starting from the top, trying to match the URL entered with the rule. If a match is found, then the router gets the controller and its action from an internal route assigned to the rule and executes it. So, `/home` is the URL pattern that defines which URLs will be processed by the rule it belongs to.

There's more...

You can also create parameterized rules using a special syntax. Let's review the third rule:

```
'page/<alias>' => test/page',
```

Here, we are defining an alias parameter that should be specified in the URL after /page/. It can be virtually anything and it will be passed as the $alias parameter to the following:

```
TestController::actionPage($alias).
```

You can define a pattern for such a parameter. We did it for the second rule, as follows:

```
'<alias:about>' => test/page',
```

The alias here should match about, otherwise, the rule will not be applied.

See also

Refer to the following links for further reading:

▶ http://www.yiiframework.com/doc-2.0/guide-runtime-routing.html
▶ http://www.yiiframework.com/doc-2.0/guide-runtime-url-handling.html
▶ http://www.yiiframework.com/doc-2.0/yii-web-urlmanager.html

▶ The *Using regular expressions in URL rules* recipe

Generating URLs

Yii allows you to not only route your URLs to different controller actions, but also to generate a URL by specifying a proper internal route and its parameters. This is really useful because you can focus on internal routes while developing your application, and only worry about real URLs before going live. Never specify URLs directly and make sure that you use the Yii URL toolset. It will allow you to change URLs without rewriting a lot of application code.

Getting ready

1. Create a new application using the Composer package manager, as described in the official guide at http://www.yiiframework.com/doc-2.0/guide-start-installation.html.

2. Find your @app/config/web.php file and replace the rules array as follows:

```
'urlManager' => array(
    'enablePrettyUrl' => true,
    'showScriptName' => false,
),
```

3. Configure your application server to use clean URLs. If you are using Apache with mod_rewrite and AllowOverride turned on, then you should add the following lines to the .htaccess file under your @app/web folder:

```
Options +FollowSymLinks
IndexIgnore */*
RewriteEngine on
# if a directory or a file exists, use it directly
RewriteCond %{REQUEST_FILENAME} !-f
RewriteCond %{REQUEST_FILENAME} !-d
# otherwise forward it to index.php
RewriteRule . index.php
```

How to do it...

1. In your @app/controllers directory, create BlogController with the following code inside:

```php
<?php

namespace app\controllers;
use yii\web\Controller;

class BlogController extends Controller
{

    public function actionIndex()
    {
        return $this->render('index');
    }
}
```

```php
    public function actionRssFeed($param)
    {
        return $this->renderContent('This is RSS feed for
        our blog and ' . $param);
    }

    public function actionArticle($alias)
    {
        return $this->renderContent('This is an article
        with alias ' . $alias);
    }

    public function actionList()
    {
        return $this->renderContent('Blog\'s articles
        here');
    }

    public function actionHiTech()
    {
        return $this->renderContent('Just a test of action
        which contains more than one words in the name') ;
    }
}
```

This is our blog controller that we are going to generate custom URLs for.

2. In your `@app/controllers` directory, create `TestController` with the following code inside:

```php
<?php

namespace app\controllers;
use Yii;
use yii\web\Controller;

class TestController extends Controller
{

    public function actionUrls()
    {
        return $this->render('urls');
    }


}
```

3. In the `@app/views` directory, create the `test` directory and the `urls.php` view file, and place the following code inside:

```php
<?php
    use yii\helpers\Url;
    use yii\helpers\Html;
?>
<h1>Generating URLs</h1>

<h3>Generating a link with URL to <i>blog</i> controller and
<i>article</i> action with alias as param</h3>
<?= Html::a('Link Name', ['blog/article', 'alias' =>
'someAlias']); ?>

<h3>Current url</h3>
<?=Url::to('')?>

<h3>Current Controller, but you can specify an action</h3>
<?=Url::toRoute(['view', 'id' => 'contact']);?>

<h3>Current module, but you can specify controller and action</h3>
<?= Url::toRoute('blog/article')?>

<h3>An absolute route to blog/list </h3>
<?= Url::toRoute('/blog/list')?>

<h3> URL for <i>blog</i> controller and action <i>HiTech</i> </h3>
<?= Url::toRoute('blog/hi-tech')?>

<h3>Canonical URL for current page</h3>
<?= Url::canonical()?>

<h3>Getting a home URL</h3>
<?= Url::home()?>

<h3>Saving a URL of the current page and getting it for re-use</
h3>
<?php Url::remember()?>
<?=Url::previous()?>

<h3>Creating URL to <i>blog</i> controller and <i>rss-feed</i>
action while URL helper isn't available</h3>
```

```
<?=Yii::$app->urlManager->createUrl(['blog/rss-feed', 'param' =>
'someParam'])?>

<h3>Creating an absolute URL to <i>blog</i> controller and <i>rss-
feed</i></h3>
<p>It's very useful for emails and console applications</p>

<?=Yii::$app->urlManager->createAbsoluteUrl(['blog/rss-feed',
'param' => 'someParam'])?>
```

4. Go to the URL `http://yii-book.app/test/urls` and you will see the output.
   (Refer to the full list of methods in the preceding code.):

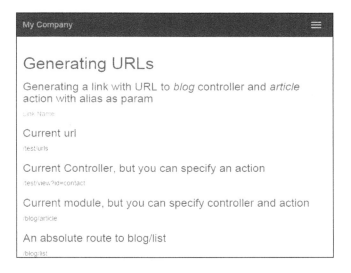

How it works...

We need to generate URLs pointing to the controller actions (RssFeed, Article, List, HiTech) of
`BlogController`.

Depending on where we need it, there are different ways of doing it, but the basics are the
same. Let's list some methods that generate URLs.

What is an internal route? Each controller and its actions have corresponding routes. A format
for a route is `moduleID/controllerID/actionID`. For example, the `actionHiTech`
method of `BlogController` corresponds to the `blog/hi-tech` route.

To get a controller ID, you should take its name without the Controller postfix and make its first letter lowercase. To get an action ID, you should take the action method name without the action prefix and make the first letter in each word lowercase, and separate them with a dash (-) sign (for example, `actionHiTech` will be `hi-tech`).

The `$_GET` variables are the parameters that will be passed to an action with an internal route specified. For example, if we want to create a URL to a `BlogController::actionArticle` that passes the `$_GET['alias']` parameter to it, it can be done as follows:

```
<?= Html::a('Link Name', ['blog/article', 'alias' => 'someAlias']); ?>
```

Relative URLs can be used inside your application, while absolute ones should be used for pointing to locations outside your website (such as other websites) or for linking to resources meant to be accessed from outside (RSS feeds, e-mails, and so on).

You can do it easily with the URL manager. The URL manager is a built-in application component named `urlManager`. You have to use this component, which is accessible from both web and console applications via `Yii::$app->urlManager`.

When you cannot get a controller instance, for example, when you implement a console application, you can use the two following `urlManager` creation methods:

```
<?=Yii::$app->urlManager->createUrl(['blog/rss-feed', 'param' =>
'someParam'])?>
<?=Yii::$app->urlManager->createAbsoluteUrl(['blog/rss-feed', 'param'
=> 'someParam'])?>
```

There's more...

For further information, refer to the following URLs:

- https://en.wikipedia.org/wiki/Canonical_link_element
- http://www.yiiframework.com/doc-2.0/guide-structure-controllers.html
- http://www.yiiframework.com/doc-2.0/guide-runtime-routing.html
- http://www.yiiframework.com/doc-2.0/guide-helper-url.html
- http://www.yiiframework.com/doc-2.0/yii-web-urlmanager.html

See also

- The *Configuring URL rules* recipe

Using regular expressions in URL rules

One of the hidden features of the Yii URL router is that you can use regular expressions that are pretty powerful for handling strings.

Getting ready

1. Create a new application using the Composer package manager, as described in the official guide at `http://www.yiiframework.com/doc-2.0/guide-start-installation.html`.

2. In your `@app/controllers` directory, create `PostController.php` using the following:

```php
<?php

namespace app\controllers;

use yii\helpers\Html;
use yii\web\Controller;

class PostController extends Controller
{
    public function actionView($alias)
    {
        return $this->renderContent(Html::tag('h2',
            'Showing post with alias ' .
            Html::encode($alias)
        ));
    }

    public function actionIndex($type = 'posts', $order =
    'DESC')
    {
        return $this->renderContent(Html::tag('h2',
            'Showing ' . Html::encode($type) . ' ordered ' .
            Html::encode($order)
        ));
    }

    public function actionHello($name)
    {
```

```
        return $this->renderContent(Html::tag('h2',
            'Hello, ' . Html::encode($name) . '!'
        ));
    }
}
```

This is our application controller that we are going to access using our custom URLs.

3. Configure your application server to use clean URLs. If you are using Apache with `mod_rewrite` and `AllowOverride` turned on, then you should add the following lines to the `.htaccess` file under your @web folder:

```
Options +FollowSymLinks
IndexIgnore */*
RewriteEngine on
# if a directory or a file exists, use it directly
RewriteCond %{REQUEST_FILENAME} !-f
RewriteCond %{REQUEST_FILENAME} !-d
# otherwise forward it to index.php
RewriteRule . index.php
```

How to do it...

We want our `PostController` action to accept parameters according to some specified rules and give the `404 not found` HTTP response for all parameters that do not match. In addition, post/index should have an alias URL archive.

Add the following config of the `urlManager` component to @app/config/web.php:

```
'components' => [
    // ..
    'urlManager' => [
        'enablePrettyUrl' => true,
        'rules' => [
            'post/<alias:[-a-z]+>' => 'post/view',
            '<type:(archive|posts)>' => 'post/index',
            '<type:(archive|posts)>/<order:(DESC|ASC)>' =>
            'post/index',
            'sayhello/<name>' => 'post/hello',
        ]
    ],
    // ..
],
```

The following URLs will be successful:

- `http://yii-book.app/post/test`
- `http://yii-book.app/posts`
- `http://yii-book.app/archive`
- `http://yii-book.app/posts/ASC`
- `http://yii-book.app/sayhello`

The following URLs will fail:

- `http://yii-book.app/archive/test`
- `http://yii-book.app/post/another_post`

The following screenshot shows that the URL `http://yii-book.app/post/test` has run successfully:

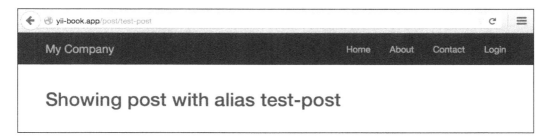

The following screenshot shows that the URL `http://yii-book.app/archive` has run successfully too:

The following screenshot shows that the URL `http://yii-book.app/archive/test` did not run successfully and encountered an error:

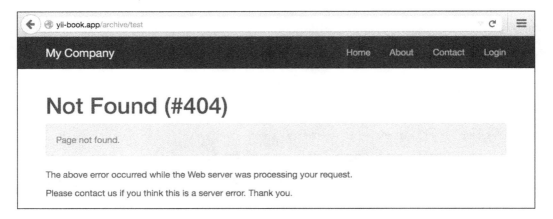

How it works...

You can use regular expressions in both the parameter definition and the rest of the rule. Let's read our rules one by one:

```
'post/<alias:[-a-z]+>' => 'post/view',
```

The alias parameter should contain one or more English letters or a dash. No other symbols are allowed.

```
'posts' => 'post/index',
'posts/' => 'post/index',
```

Both paths lead to `post/index`. The order parameter can only accept two values — DESC and ASC.

```
'sayhello/' => 'post/hello'
```

You should specify the name part but there are no restrictions on what characters are allowed. Note that regardless of the rule used, the developer should never assume that the input data is safe.

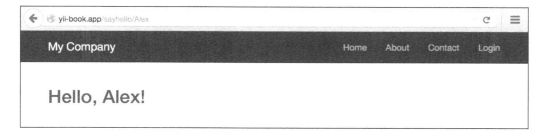

There's more...

To learn more about regular expressions, you can use the following sources:

 ▸ `http://www.php.net/manual/en/reference.pcre.pattern.syntax.php`
 ▸ *Mastering Regular Expressions*, *Jeffrey Friedl* available at `http://regex.info/`.

See also

 ▸ The *Configuring URL rules* recipe

Using a base controller

In many frameworks, the concept of a base controller that is being extended by other ones is described right in the guide. In Yii, it is not in the guide, as you can achieve flexibility in many other ways. Still, using a base controller is possible and can be useful.

Let's say we want to add some controllers that will be accessible only when the user is logged in. We can certainly set this constraint for each controller separately, but we will do it in a better way.

Getting ready

Create a new application using the Composer package manager, as described in the official guide at `http://www.yiiframework.com/doc-2.0/guide-startinstallation.html`.

How to do it...

1. First, we will need a base controller that our user-only controllers will use. Let's create `@app/components/BaseController.php` with the following code:

```php
<?php

namespace app\components;

use Yii;
use yii\web\Controller;
use yii\filters\AccessControl;

class BaseController extends Controller
{
    public function actions()
    {
        return [
            'error' => ['class' => 'yii\web\ErrorAction'],
        ];
    }

    public function behaviors()
    {
        return [
            'access' => [
                'class' => AccessControl::className(),
                'rules' => [
                    [
                        'allow' => true,
                        'actions' => 'error'
                    ],
                    [
                        'allow' => true,
                        'roles' => ['@'],
```

```
                    ],
                ],
            ]
        ];
    }
}
```

This controller has an action map with an error action also.

2. Now, create `TestController` by Gii, but set the value of the base class field as `app/components/BaseController`:

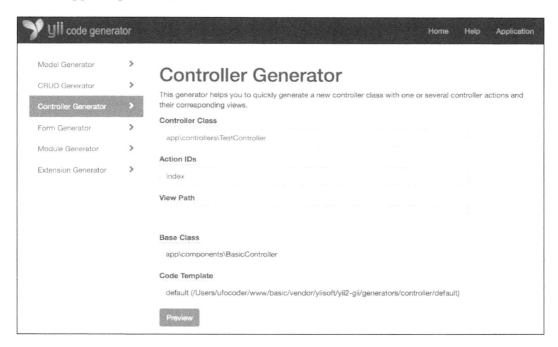

You will get something similar to the following:

```php
<?php
namespace app\controllers;
class TestController extends \app\components\BaseController
{
    public function actionIndex()
    {
        return $this->render('index');
    }
}
```

3. Now, your `TestController` will be only accessible if the user is logged in, even though we have not declared it explicitly in the `TestController` class. You can check it by visiting `http://yii-book.app/index.php?r=test/index` while logged out.

How it works...

The trick is nothing more than a basic class inheritance. If filters or access control rules are not found in `TestController`, then they will be called from `SecureController`.

There's more...

If you need to extend the base controller's method, keep in the mind that it must not be overridden. For example, we need to add a page action to the controller's action map:

```php
<?php

namespace app\controllers;

use yii\helpers\ArrayHelper;
use app\components\BaseController;

class TestController extends BaseController
{
    public function actions()
    {
        return ArrayHelper::merge(parent::actions(), [
            'page' => [
                'class' => 'yii\web\ViewAction',
            ],
        ]);
    }

    public function behaviors()
    {
        $behaviors = parent::behaviors();

        $rules = $behaviors['access']['rules'];
```

```
    $rules = ArrayHelper::merge(
        $rules,
        [
            [
                'allow' => true,
                'actions' => ['page']
            ]
        ]
    );

    $behaviors['access']['rules'] = $rules;

    return $behaviors;
    }

    public function actionIndex()
    {
        return $this->render('index');
    }
    }
}
```

For further information, refer to `http://www.yiiframework.com/doc-2.0/yii-base-controller.html`.

Using standalone actions

In Yii, you can define controller actions as separate classes and then connect them to your controllers. This will help you to reuse some common functionality.

For example, you can move the backend for autocomplete fields to an action and save some time by not having to write it over and over again.

Another example is that we can create all CRUD operations as separate standalone actions. We will write, create, view, and delete operations of the model and view the list operation of models.

Getting ready

1. Create a new application using the Composer package manager, as described in the official guide at `http://www.yiiframework.com/doc-2.0/guide-start-installation.html`.

2. Let's create `post` table. Create migration for this using the following command:

   ```
   ./yii migrate/create create_post_table
   ```

3. Update the just-created migration's methods and list of imported classes as follows:

   ```php
   <?php

   use yii\db\Schema;
   use yii\db\Migration;

   class m150719_152435_create_post_table extends Migration
   {
       const TABLE_NAME = '{{%post}}';

       public function up()
       {
           $tableOptions = null;
           if ($this->db->driverName === 'mysql') {
               $tableOptions = 'CHARACTER SET utf8 COLLATE
                   utf8_general_ci ENGINE=InnoDB';
           }

           $this->createTable(self::TABLE_NAME, [
               'id' => Schema::TYPE_PK,
               'title' => Schema::TYPE_STRING.'(255) NOT
                   NULL',
               'content' => Schema::TYPE_TEXT.' NOT NULL',
           ], $tableOptions);

           for ($i = 1; $i < 7; $i++) {
               $this->insert(self::TABLE_NAME, [
                   'title' => 'Test article #'.$i,
                   'content' => 'Lorem ipsum dolor sit amet,
                   consectetur adipiscing elit. '
                   .'Sed sit amet mauris est. Sed at
                       dignissim dui. '
   ```

```
                        .'Phasellus arcu massa, facilisis a
                            fringilla sit amet, '
                        .'rhoncus ut enim.',
                ]);
            }
        }

        public function down()
        {
            $this->dropTable(self::TABLE_NAME);
        }
    }
```

4. Install all migrations using the following command:

   ```
   ./yii migrate up
   ```

5. Create the Post model using Gii.

How to do it...

1. Create the standalone action @app/actions/CreateAction.php as follows:

   ```php
   <?php

   namespace app\actions;

   use Yii;
   use yii\base\Action;

   class CreateAction extends Action
   {
       public $modelClass;

       public function run()
       {
           $model = new $this->modelClass();

           if ($model->load(Yii::$app->request->post()) &&
           $model->save()) {
               $this->controller->redirect(['view', 'id' =>
               $model->getPrimaryKey()]);
           } else {
   ```

```
                        return $this->controller->
                        render('//crud/create', [
                            'model' => $model
                        ]);
                }
            }
        }
```

2. Create the standalone action @app/actions/DeleteAction.php as follows:

```php
<?php

namespace app\actions;

use yii\base\Action;
use yii\web\NotFoundHttpException;

class DeleteAction extends Action
{
    public $modelClass;

    public function run($id)
    {
        $class = $this->modelClass;

        if (($model = $class::findOne($id)) === null) {
            throw new NotFoundHttpException('The requested
            page does not exist.');
        }

        $model->delete();

        return $this->controller->redirect(['index']);
    }
}
```

3. Create the standalone action @app/actions/IndexAction.php as follows:

```php
<?php

namespace app\actions;

use yii\base\Action;
use yii\data\Pagination;
```

```php
class IndexAction extends Action
{
    public $modelClass;
    public $pageSize = 3;

    public function run()
    {
        $class = $this->modelClass;
        $query = $class::find();
        $countQuery = clone $query;

        $pages = new Pagination([
            'totalCount' => $countQuery->count(),
        ]);
        $pages->setPageSize($this->pageSize);

        $models = $query->offset($pages->offset)
                        ->limit($pages->limit)
                        ->all();

        return $this->controller->render('//crud/index', [
            'pages' => $pages,
            'models' => $models
        ]);
    }
}
```

4. Create the standalone action @app/actions/ViewAction.php as follows:

```php
<?php

namespace app\actions;

use yii\base\Action;
use yii\web\NotFoundHttpException;

class ViewAction extends Action
{
    public $modelClass;

    public function run($id)
    {
        $class = $this->modelClass;
```

```php
        if (($model = $class::findOne($id)) === null) {
            throw new NotFoundHttpException('The requested
            page does not exist.');
        }

        return $this->controller->render('//crud/view', [
            'model' => $model
        ]);
    }
}
```

5. Create the view file `@app/views/crud/create.php` as follows:

```php
<?php

use yii\helpers\Html;
use yii\widgets\ActiveForm;

/*
 * @var yii\web\View $this
 */

?>
<h1><?= Yii::t('app', 'Create post'); ?></h1>
<?php $form = ActiveForm::begin();?>
<?php $form->errorSummary($model); ?>

<?= $form->field($model, 'title')->textInput() ?>
<?= $form->field($model, 'content')->textarea() ?>

<?= Html::submitButton(Yii::t('app', 'Create'), ['class' => 'btn
btn-primary']) ?>

<?php ActiveForm::end(); ?>
```

6. Create the view file `@app/views/crud/index.php` as follows:

```php
<?php

use yii\widgets\LinkPager;
use yii\helpers\Html;
use yii\helpers\Url;

/*
 * @var yii\web\View $this
```

```
 * @var yii\data\Pagination $pages
 * @var array $models
 */

?>
<h1>Posts</h1>
<?= Html::a('+ Create a post', Url::toRoute('post/create')); ?>

<?php foreach ($models as $model):?>
    <h3><?= Html::encode($model->title);?></h3>
    <p><?= Html::encode($model->content);?></p>

    <p>
        <?= Html::a('view', Url::toRoute(['post/view', 'id'
        => $model->id]));?> |
        <?= Html::a('delete', Url::toRoute(['post/delete',
        'id' => $model->id]));?>
    </p>
<?php endforeach; ?>

<?= LinkPager::widget([
    'pagination' => $pages,
]); ?>
```

7. Create the view file @app/views/crud/view.php as follows:

```
<?php

use yii\helpers\Html;
use yii\helpers\Url;

/*
 * @var yii\web\View $this
 * @var app\models\Post $model
 */

?>
<p><?= Html::a('< back to posts', Url::toRoute('post/index'));
?></p>

<h2><?= Html::encode($model->title);?></h2>
<p><?= Html::encode($model->content);?></p>
```

To use standalone actions, we declared it in the action map by overriding the actions method.

8. Run `post/index`:

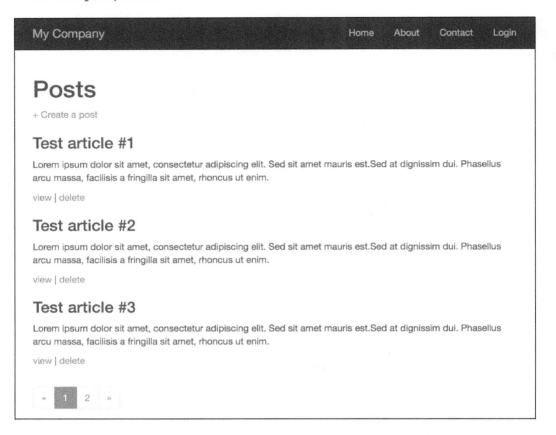

How it works...

Every controller can be built from standalone actions, like a puzzle from pieces. The difference is that you can make standalone actions very flexible and reuse them in many places.

In our actions, we defined the `modelClass` public property, which helps to set up a specific Model class in the `actions` method of `PostController`.

See also

For further information, refer to `http://www.yiiframework.com/doc-2.0/guide-structure-controllers.html#standalone-actions`.

Creating a custom filter

Filters are objects that run before and/or after controller actions. For example, an access control filter may run before actions to ensure that they are allowed to be accessed by particular end users; a content compression filter may run after actions to compress the response content before sending them out to end users.

A filter may consist of a prefilter (filtering logic applied before actions) and/or a postfilter (logic applied after actions). Filters are essentially a special kind of behavior. Therefore, using filters is the same as using behaviors.

Let's assume that we have a web application, which provides a user interface for working only at specified hours, for example, from 10 AM to 6 PM.

Getting ready

Create a new application using the Composer package manager, as described in the official guide at `http://www.yiiframework.com/doc-2.0/guide-start-installation.html`.

How to do it...

1. Create a controller, `@app/controllers/TestController.php`, as follows:

```php
<?php

namespace app\controllers;

use app\components\CustomFilter;
use yii\helpers\Html;
use yii\web\Controller;

class TestController extends Controller
{
    public function behaviors()
    {
        return [
            'access' => [
                'class' => CustomFilter::className(),
            ],
        ];
    }
```

```php
        public function actionIndex()
        {
            return $this->renderContent(Html::tag('h1',
                'This is a test content'
            ));
        }
    }
```

2. Create a new filter, @app/components/CustomFilter.php, as follows:

```php
<?php
namespace app\components;

use Yii;
use yii\base\ActionFilter;
use yii\web\HttpException;

class CustomFilter extends ActionFilter
{
    const WORK_TIME_BEGIN = 10;
    const WORK_TIME_END = 18;

    protected function canBeDisplayed()
    {
        $hours = date('G');

        return $hours >= self::WORK_TIME_BEGIN && $hours <=
        self::WORK_TIME_END;
    }

    public function beforeAction($action)
    {
        if (!$this->canBeDisplayed())
        {
            $error = 'This part of website works from '
                    . self::WORK_TIME_BEGIN . ' to '
                    . self::WORK_TIME_END . ' hours.';

            throw new HttpException(403, $error);
        }

        return parent::beforeAction($action);
    }
```

```
public function afterAction($action, $result)
{
    if (Yii::$app->request->url == '/test/index') {
        Yii::trace("This is the index action");
    }

    return parent::afterAction($action, $result);
}
}
```

3. If you've visited this page outside of the specified time period, you'll get the following:

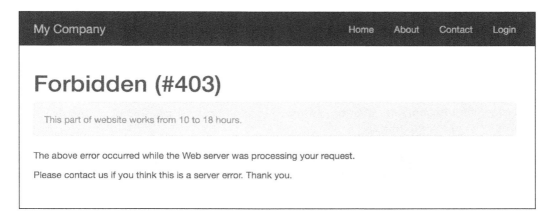

How it works...

At first, we added a piece of code to our controller, which implements our custom filter:

```
public function behaviors()
{
    return [
        'access' => [
            'class' => CustomFilter::className(),
        ],
    ];
}
```

By default, the filter applies to all actions of the controller, but we can specify actions for which it will be applied, or even exclude actions from our filter.

You have two actions inside it—`beforeAction` and `afterActions`. The first one runs before the controller's actions and the next one after.

In our simple example, we defined a condition which doesn't allow access to website if the time is earlier than 10 AM, and in the after method we just run a trace method if the current path is `test/index`.

You can see the result in the debugger, in the `log` section:

| 13 | 17:18 34 289 | trace | application | This is the index action |
| | | | | C:\web\projects\yii-book.loc\components\CustomFilter.php (23) |

In real applications, filters are more complex and also, Yii2 provides a lot of built-in filters, such as core, authentication, content negotiator, HTTP cache end, and so on.

See also

For further information, refer to `http://www.yiiframework.com/doc-2.0/guide-structure-filters.html`.

Displaying static pages

If you have a few static pages and aren't going to change them very frequently, then it's not worth querying the database and implementing page management for them.

Getting ready

Create a new application using the Composer package manager, as described in the official guide at `http://www.yiiframework.com/doc-2.0/guide-start-installation.html`.

How to do it...

1. Create the test controller file, `@app/controllers/TestController.php`, as follows:

```php
<?php

namespace app\controllers;

use yii\web\Controller;
```

```
class TestController extends Controller
{
    public function actions()
    {
        return [
            'page' => [
                'class' => 'yii\web\ViewAction',
            ]
        ];
    }
}
```

2. Now, put your pages into `views/test/pages`, and name them `index.php` and `contact.php`. The content of `index.php` is as follows:

```
<h1>Index</h1>
content of index file
```

Contact.php content is:

```
<h2>Contacts</h2>
<p>Our contact: contact@localhost</p>
```

3. Now you can check your pages by typing in the URL,

4. `http://yii-book.app/index.php?r=test/page&view=contact`:

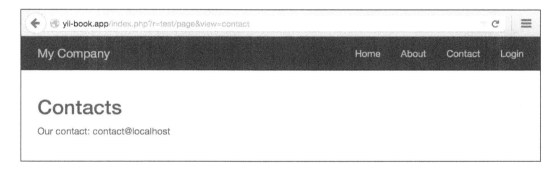

5. Alternatively, you can type in the URL `http://yii-book.app/test/page/view/about`, if you have configured clean URLs with a path format.

How it works...

We connect the external action named `\yii\web\ViewAction`, which simply tries to find a view named the same as the `$_GET` parameter supplied. If it is there, it displays it. If not, then it will give you a `404 not found` page. In case `viewParam` is not set, the `defaultView` value will be used.

There's more...

About ViewAction

There are some useful `\yii\web\ViewAction` parameters we can use. These are listed in the following table:

Parameter name	Description
`defaultView`	The name of the default view when the `yii\web\ViewAction::$viewParam` GET parameter is not provided by the user. Defaults to `'index'`. This should be in the format of `path/to/view`, similar to that given in the GET parameter.
`layout`	The name of the layout to be applied to the requested view. This will be assigned to `yii\base\Controller::$layout` before the view is rendered. Defaults to null, meaning the controller's layout will be used. If false, no layout will be applied.
`viewParam`	The name of the GET parameter that contains the requested view name.
`viewPrefix`	A string to be prefixed to the user-specified view name to form a complete view name. For example, if a user requests `tutorial/chap1`, the corresponding view name will be `pages/tutorial/chap1`, assuming that the prefix is pages. The actual view file is determined by `yii\base\View::findViewFile()`.

Configuring URL rules

The `ViewAction` action provides you a way to minify your controller, but the URLs look like `http://yii-book.app/index.php?r=test/page&page=about`. To make URLs short and more readable, add a URL rule to `urlManager` component:

```
'<view:about>' => 'test/page'
```

If the `urlManager` component configures properly you will get the following:

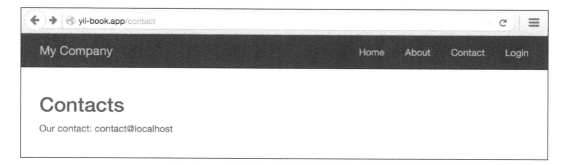

To configure the `urlManager` component, refer to the *Configuring URL rules* recipe.

See also

For further information, refer to the following URLs:

▶ http://www.yiiframework.com/doc-2.0/yii-web-viewaction.html

▶ http://www.yiiframework.com/doc-2.0/guide-structure-views.html#rendering-static-pages

▶ The *Configuring URL rules* recipe

Using flash messages

When you are editing a model with a form, deleting a model, or doing any other operation, it is good to tell users if it went well or if there was an error. Typically, after some kind of action, such as editing a form, a redirect will happen and we need to display a message on the page we want to go to. However, how do we pass it from the current page to the redirect target and clean up afterwards? Flash messages will help us do this.

Getting ready

Create a new application using the Composer package manager, as described in the official guide at http://www.yiiframework.com/doc-2.0/guide-start-installation.html.

How to do it...

1. Let's create a @app/controllers/TestController.php controller as follows:

```php
<?php

namespace app\controllers;

use Yii;
use yii\web\Controller;
use yii\filters\AccessControl;

class TestController extends Controller
{
    public function behaviors()
    {
        return [
            'access' => [
                'class' => AccessControl::className(),
                'rules' => [
                    [
                        'allow' => true,
                        'roles' => ['@'],
                        'actions' => ['user']
                    ],
                    [
                        'allow' => true,
                        'roles' => ['?'],
                        'actions' => ['index', 'success',
                        'error']
                    ],
                ],
                'denyCallback' => function ($rule, $action)
                {
                    Yii::$app->session->setFlash('error',
                    'This section is only for registered
                        users.');
                    $this->redirect(['index']);
                },
            ],
        ];
    }
```

```php
    public function actionUser()
    {
        return $this->renderContent('user');
    }

    public function actionSuccess()
    {
        Yii::$app->session->setFlash('success', 'Everything
            went fine!');
        $this->redirect(['index']);
    }

    public function actionError()
    {
        Yii::$app->session->setFlash('error', 'Everything
            went wrong!');
        $this->redirect(['index']);
    }

    public function actionIndex()
    {
        return $this->render('index');
    }
}
```

2. Additionally, create the `@app/views/common/alert.php` view as follows:

```php
<?php
    use yii\bootstrap\Alert;
?>
<?php if (Yii::$app->session->hasFlash('success')):?>
    <?= Alert::widget([
        'options' => ['class' => 'alert-success'],
        'body' => Yii::$app->session->getFlash('success'),
    ]);?>
<?php endif ?>

<?php if (Yii::$app->session->hasFlash('error')) :?>
    <?= Alert::widget([
        'options' => ['class' => 'alert-danger'],
        'body' => Yii::$app->session->getFlash('error'),
    ]);?>
<?php endif; ?>
```

3. Create the `@app/views/test/index.php` file view as follows:

```php
<?php

/* @var $this yii\web\View */

?>

<?= $this->render('//common/alert') ?>

<h2>Guest page</h2>
<p>There's a content of guest page</p>
```

4. Create the `@app/views/test/user.php` file view as follows:

```php
<?php

/* @var $this yii\web\View */

?>

<?= $this->render('//common/alert') ?>

<h2>User page</h2>
<p>There's a content of user page</p>
```

5. Now, if you go to `http://yii-book.app/index.php?r=test/success`, you will be redirected to `http://yii-book.app/index.php?r=test/index` and a success message will be displayed as follows:

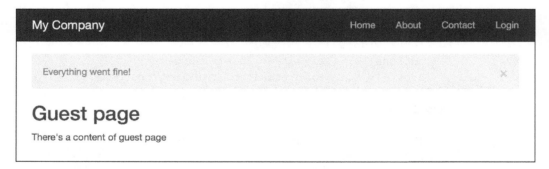

6.   Moreover, if you go to `http://yii-book.app/index.php?r=test/error`, you will be redirected to the same page, but with an error message. Refreshing the `index` page will hide the message:

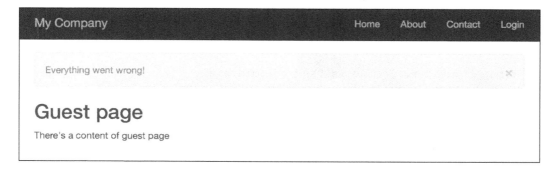

7.   Then try running `http://yii-book.app/index.php?r=test/user`. You will be redirected to `http://yii-book.app/index.php?r=test/index` and an error message will be displayed that executed in the `denyCallback` function:

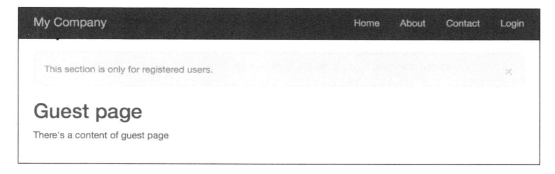

How it works...

We set a flash message with `Yii::$app->session->setFlash('success', 'Everything went fine!')`. Internally, it saves a message into a session state, so at the lowest level, our message is being kept in `$_SESSION` until `Yii::$app->session->getFlash('success')` is called and the `$_SESSION` key is deleted.

The flash message will be automatically deleted after it is accessed in a request.

There's more...

The getAllFlashes() method

Sometimes you need to handle all flashes. You can do it in a simple manner, as follows:

```
$flashes = Yii::$app->session->getAllFlashes();

<?php foreach ($flashes as $key => $message): ?>
    <?= Alert::widget([
        'options' => ['class' => 'alert-info'],
        'body' => $message,
    ]);
    ?>
<?php endforeach; ?>
```

The removeAllFlashes() method

When you need to flush all your flashes, use the following:

```
Yii::$app->session->removeAllFlashes();
```

The removeFlash() method

When you need to remove the `flash` method with a specified key, use the following:

```
Yii::$app->session->removeFlash('success');
```

In this example, we added a very useful callback function, which sets up an error message and does a redirect to the `test/index` page.

See also

For further information, refer to:

- http://www.yiiframework.com/doc-2.0/yii-web-session.html
- http://www.yiiframework.com/doc-2.0/yii-bootstrap-alert.html

Using the controller context in a view

Yii views are pretty powerful and have many features. One of them is that you can use the controller context in a view. So, let's try it.

Getting ready

Create a new application using the Composer package manager, as described in the official guide at http://www.yiiframework.com/doc-2.0/guide-start-installation.html.

How to do it...

1. Create a `controllers/ViewController.php` as follows:

```php
<?php

namespace app\controllers;

use yii\web\Controller;

class ViewController extends Controller
{
    public $pageTitle;

    public function actionIndex()
    {
        $this->pageTitle = 'Controller context test';

        return $this->render('index');
    }

    public function hello()
    {
        if (!empty($_GET['name'])) {
            echo 'Hello, '  . $_GET['name'] . '!';
        }
    }
}
```

2. Now, we will create a `@app/views/view/index.php` with following code:

```
context->pageTitle ?>
Hello call. context->hello() ?>
```

3. In order to test it, you can follow `/index.php?r=view/index&name=Alex`:

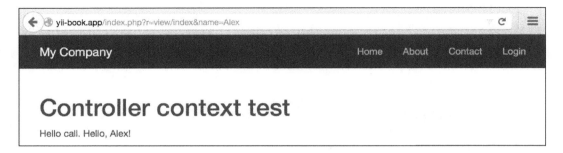

How it works...

We are using `$this` in a view to refer to a currently running controller. When doing this, we can call a controller method and access its properties. The most useful property is `pageTitle`, which refers to the current page title. There are many built-in methods that are extremely useful in views such as `renderPartials` and widget.

There's more...

The `http://www.yiiframework.com/doc-2.0/guide-structure-views.html#accessing-data-in-views` URL contains the API documentation for `yii\web\`

Controller, where you could find out a good list of methods which you can use to access data in `a=your` view

Reusing views with partials

Yii supports partials, so if you have a block without much logic that you want to reuse or want to implement e-mail templates, partials are the right way to go about this.

Imagine that we have two Twitter accounts, one for our blog and another for company activity, and our goal is to output Twitter timelines on specified pages.

Getting ready

1. Create a new application using the Composer package manager, as described in the official guide at `http://www.yiiframework.com/doc-2.0/guide-start-installation.html`.

2. Create Twitter widgets at `https://twitter.com/settings/widgets/` for `php_net` and `yiiframework` users, and find a `data-widget-id` value for each widget created.

How to do it...

1. Create a controller, `@app/controllers/BlogController.php`, as follows:

```php
<?php

namespace app\controllers;

use yii\web\Controller;

class BlogController extends Controller
{
    public function actionIndex()
    {
        $posts = [
            [
                'title' => 'First post',
                'content' => 'There\'s an example of
                reusing views with partials.',
            ],
            [
                'title' => 'Second post',
                'content' => 'We use twitter widget.'
            ],
        ];

        return $this->render('index', [
            'posts' => $posts
        ]);
    }
}
```

2. Create a view file named `@app/views/common/twitter.php` and paste an embed code from Twitter. You will get something like the following:

```php
<?php

/* @var $this \yii\web\View */
/* @var $widget_id integer */
/* @var $screen_name string */

?>
<script>!function(d,s,id){var js,fjs=d.getElementsByTagName(s)
[0],p=/^http:/.test(d.location)?'http':'https';if(!d.
getElementById(id)){js=d.createElement(s);js.id=id;js.
src=p+"://platform.twitter.com/widgets.js";fjs.parentNode.
insertBefore(js,fjs);}}(document,"script","twitter-wjs");</script>

<?php if ($widget_id && $screen_name): ?>
<a class="twitter-timeline"
    data-widget-id="<?= $widget_id?>"
    href="https://twitter.com/<?= $screen_name?>"
    height="300">
    Tweets by @<?= $screen_name?>
</a>
<?php endif;?>
```

3. Create a view `@app/views/blog/index.php` file as follows:

```php
<?php

/* @var $category string */
/* @var $posts array */
/* @var $this \yii\web\View */

?>

<div class="row">
    <div class="col-xs-7">
        <h1>Posts</h1>
        <hr>
        <?php foreach ($posts as $post): ?>
            <h3><?= $post['title']?></h3>
            <p><?= $post['content']?></p>
        <?php endforeach;?>
    </div>
    <div class="col-xs-5">
```

```php
<?= $this->render('//common/twitter', [
    'widget_id' => '620531418213576704',
    'screen_name' => 'php_net',
]);?>
    </div>
</div>
```

4. Replace the `@app/views/site/about.php` file's content with the following:

```php
<?php

use yii\helpers\Html;
/* @var $this yii\web\View */
$this->title = 'About';
?>

<div class="col-xs-7">
    <h1><?= Html::encode($this->title) ?></h1>
    <p>
        This is the About page. You may modify this page.
    </p>
</div>
<div class="col-xs-5">
    <?= $this->render('//common/twitter', [
        'widget_id' => '620526086343012352',
        'screen_name' => 'yiiframework'
    ]);?>
</div>
```

5. Try to run `index.php?r=blog/index`:

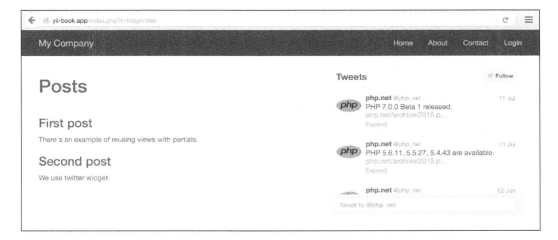

6. Try to run `index.php?r=site/about`:

How it works...

In the current example, two views render `@app/views/common/twitter.php` with additional parameters for forming Twitter widgets inside themselves. Note that views can be rendered in controllers, widgets, or any other place, by calling the view rendering methods. For example, `\yii\base\Controller::render` does the same template processing as `\yii\base\View::render`, except the former does not use layout.

In each view file, we can access two instances of the View class using $this, so any view file can be rendered in an other view by calling the `render` method.

There's more...

For further information, refer to `http://www.yiiframework.com/doc-2.0/guide-structure-views.html#rendering-views`.

Using blocks

One of the Yii features you can use in your views is blocks. The basic idea is that you can record some output and then reuse it later in a view. A good example would be to define additional content regions for your layout and filling them elsewhere.

In the previous version, Yii 1.1, blocks were called clips.

Getting ready

Create a new application using the Composer package manager, as described in the official guide at http://www.yiiframework.com/doc-2.0/guide-start-installation.html.

How to do it...

1. For our example, we need to define two regions in our layout—beforeContent and footer.

2. Open @app/views/layouts/main.php and insert the following code line just before the content output:

```php
<?php if(!empty($this->blocks['beforeContent'])) echo $this->blocks['beforeContent']; ?>
```

3. Then, replace the footer code with the following code:

```php
<footer class="footer">
    <div class="container">
        <?php if (!empty($this->blocks['footer'])):
            echo $this->blocks['footer'] ?>
        <?php else: ?>
            <p class="pull-left">&copy; My Company <?=
                date('Y') ?></p>
            <p class="pull-right"><?= Yii::powered() ?></p>
        <?php endif; ?>
    </div>
</footer>
```

4. That is it! Then, add a new action to controllers/SiteController.php, named blocks:

```php
public function actionBlocks()
{
    return $this->render('blocks');
}
```

5. Now, create a view file, views/site/blocks.php, with the following content:

```php
<?php

use \yii\Helpers\Html;
```

```
/* @var $this \yii\web\View */
?>

<?php $this->beginBlock('beforeContent');
    echo Html::tag('pre', 'Your IP is ' . Yii::$app
    ->request->userIP);
$this->endBlock(); ?>

<?php $this->beginBlock('footer');
    echo Html::tag('h3', 'My custom footer block');
$this->endBlock(); ?>

<h1>Blocks usage example</h1>
```

6. Now, when you open your `/index.php?r=site/blocks` page, you should get your IP just before the page content and a built-with note in the footer:

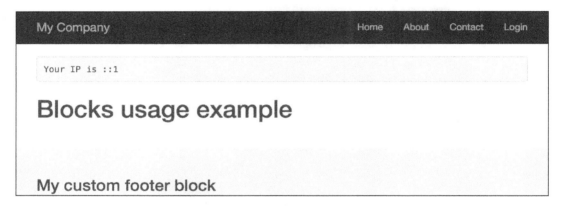

How it works...

We mark regions with the code that just checks for the existence of a specific block, and if the block exists, the code outputs it. Then, we record content for blocks we defined using the special controller methods named `beginBlock` and `endBlock`.

From controller, you can easily access our block's variables via `$this->view->blocks['blockID']`.

- ▶ The *Using the controller context in a view* recipe
- ▶ http://www.yiiframework.com/doc-2.0/guide-structure-views.
  html#using-blocks

Using decorators

In Yii, we can enclose content into a decorator. The common usage of decorators is layout. When you are rendering a view using the render method of your controller, Yii automatically decorates it with the main layout. Let's create a simple decorator that will properly format quotes.

Getting ready

Create a new application using the Composer package manager, as described in the official guide at http://www.yiiframework.com/doc-2.0/guide-start-installation.
html.

How to do it...

1. First, we will create a decorator file, @app/views/decorators/quote.php:

```
<div class="quote">
    <h2>&ldquo;<?= $content?>&rdquo;, <?= $author?></h2>
</div>
```

2. Now, replace the content of @app/views/site/index.php with the following code:

```
<?php

use yii\widgets\ContentDecorator;

/* @var */
?>

<?php ContentDecorator::begin([
        'viewFile' => '@app/views/decorators/quote.php',
        'view' => $this,
        'params' => ['author' => 'S. Freud']
    ]
```

```
);?>
Time spent with cats is never wasted.
<?php ContentDecorator::end();?>
```

3. Now, your **Home** page should look like the following:

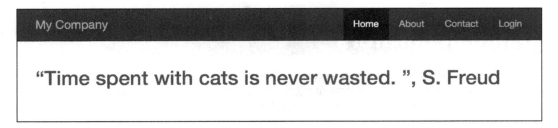

How it works...

Decorators are pretty simple. Everything between `ContentDecorator::begin()` and `ContentDecorator::end()` is rendered into a `$content` variable and passed into a decorator template. Then, the decorator template is rendered and inserted in the place where `ContentDecorator::end()` was called.

We can pass additional variables into the decorator template using a second parameter of `ContentDecorator::begin()`, such as the one we did for the author.

Note that we have used `@app/views/decorators/quote.php` as the view path.

See also

▶ The `http://www.yiiframework.com/doc-2.0/yii-widgets-contentdecorator.html` URL provides more details about decorators:

▶ The *Using the controller context in a view* recipe

Defining multiple layouts

Most applications use a single layout for all their views. However, there are situations when multiple layouts are needed. For example, an application can use different layouts on different pages: two additional columns for blogs, one additional column for articles, and no additional columns for portfolios.

Getting ready

Create a new application using the Composer package manager, as described in the official guide at `http://www.yiiframework.com/doc-2.0/guide-start-installation.html`.

How to do it...

1. Create two layouts in views/layouts: `blog` and `articles`. Blog will contain the following code:

```php
<?php $this->beginContent('//layouts/main')?>
    <div>
        <?= $content ?>
    </div>
    <div class="sidebar tags">
        <ul>
            <li><a href="#php">PHP</a></li>
            <li><a href="#yii">Yii</a></li>
        </ul>
    </div>
    <div class="sidebar links">
        <ul>
            <li><a href="http://yiiframework.com/">
                Yiiframework</a></li>
            <li><a href="http://php.net/">PHP</a></li>
        </ul>
    </div>
<?php $this->endContent()?>
```

2. Articles will contain the following code:

```php
<?php

    /* @var $this yii\web\View */
?>

<?php $this->beginContent('@app/views/layouts/main.php'); ?>
    <div class="container">
        <div class="col-xs-8">
            <?= $content ?>
        </div>
```

```
        <div class="col-xs-4">
            <h4>Table of contents</h4>
            <ol>
                <li><a href="#intro">Introduction</a></li>
                <li><a href="#quick-start">Quick
                    start</a></li>
                <li>..</li>
            </ol>
        </div>
    </div>
<?php $this->endContent() ?>
```

3. Create a view file, `views/site/content.php`, as follows:

```
<h1>Title</h1>
<p>Lorem ipsum dolor sit amet, consectetur adipisicing elit, sed
do eiusmod tempor incididunt ut labore et dolore magna aliqua. Ut
enim ad minim veniam, quis nostrud exercitation ullamco laboris
nisi ut aliquip ex ea commodo consequat. Duis aute irure dolor
in reprehenderit in voluptate velit esse cillum dolore eu fugiat
nulla pariatur.</p>
```

4. Create three controllers named `BlogController`, `ArticleController`, and `PortfolioController`, with index actions in all three. The content of the `controllers/BlogController.php` file is as follows:

```php
<?php

namespace app\controllers;

use yii\web\Controller;

class BlogController extends Controller
{
    public $layout = 'blog';

    public function actionIndex()
    {
        return $this->render('//site/content');
    }
}
```

5. The content of the `controllers/ArticleController.php` file is as follows:

```php
<?php

namespace app\controllers;
```

```
use yii\web\Controller;

class ArticleController extends Controller
{
    public $layout = 'articles';

    public function actionIndex()
    {
        return $this->render('//site/content');
    }
}
```

6. The content of the `controllers/PortfolioController.php` file is as follows:

```
<?php

namespace app\controllers;

use yii\web\Controller;

class PortfolioController extends Controller
{
    public function actionIndex()
    {
        return $this->render('//site/content');
    }
}
```

7. Now try running `http://yii-book.app/?r=blog/index`:

My Company			Home	About	Contact	Login

Title

Lorem ipsum dolor sit amet, consectetur adipisicing elit, sed do eiusmod tempor incididunt ut labore et dolore magna aliqua. Ut enim ad minim veniam, quis nostrud exercitation ullamco laboris nisi ut aliquip ex ea commodo consequat. Duis aute irure dolor in reprehenderit in voluptate velit esse cillum dolore eu fugiat nulla pariatur.

Tags
- PHP
- Yii

Links
- Yiiframework
- PHP

8. Then try running `http://yii-book.app/?r=article/index`:

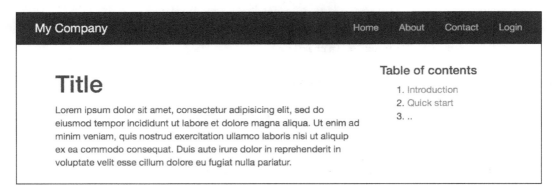

9. Finally, try running `http://yii-book.app/?r=portfolio/index`:

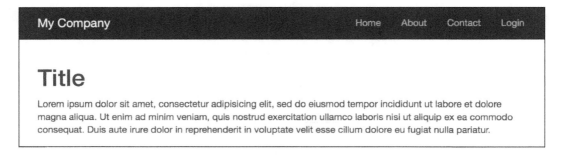

How it works...

We defined two additional layouts for the blog and articles. As we don't want to copy and paste common parts from the main layout, we apply additional layout decorators using `$this->beginContent` and `$this->endContent`.

So, we use a view rendered inside the articles layout as the main layout's `$content`.

See also

- The `http://www.yiiframework.com/doc-2.0/guide-structure-views.html#nested-layouts` URL provides more details about layouts.
- The *Using the controller context in a view* recipe
- The *Using decorators* recipe

Pagination and sorting data

In the latest Yii releases, the focus was moved from using Active Record directly, to grids, lists, and data providers. Still, sometimes it is better to use Active Record directly. Let's see how to list paginated AR records with the ability to sort them. In this section, we would like to create a list of films and sort them by some attributes from a database. In our example, we will sort our films by film title and rental rate attributes.

Getting ready

1. Create a new application using the Composer package manager, as described in the official guide at `http://www.yiiframework.com/doc-2.0/guide-start-installation.html`.

2. Download the Sakila database from `http://dev.mysql.com/doc/index-other.html`.

3. Execute the downloaded SQLs; first schema, then data.

4. Configure the database connection `config\db.php` to use the Sakila database.

5. Use Gii to create the `Film` model.

How to do it...

1. First, you need to create `@app/controllers/FilmController.php`:

```php
<?php

namespace app\controllers;

use app\models\Film;
use yii\web\Controller;
use yii\data\Pagination;
use yii\data\Sort;

class FilmController extends Controller
{
    public function actionIndex()
    {
        $query = Film::find();
        $countQuery = clone $query;
        $pages = new Pagination(['totalCount' =>
            $countQuery->count()]);
        $pages->pageSize = 5;
```

```
            $sort = new Sort([
                'attributes' => [
                    'title',
                    'rental_rate'
                ]
            ]);

            $models = $query->offset($pages->offset)
                ->limit($pages->limit)
                ->orderBy($sort->orders)
                ->all();

            return $this->render('index', [
                'models' => $models,
                'sort' => $sort,
                'pages' => $pages
            ]);
        }
    }
```

2. Now, let's implement @app/views/film/index.php, as follows:

```php
<?php

use yii\widgets\LinkPager;

/**
 * @var \app\models\Film $models
 * @var \yii\web\View $this
 * @var \yii\data\Pagination $pages
 * @var \yii\data\Sort $sort
 */

?>

<h1>Films List</h1>

<p><?=$sort->link('title')?> | <?=$sort->link('rental_rate')?></p>

<?php foreach ($models as $model): ?>
    <div class="list-group">
```

```
                <h4 class="list-group-item-heading"> <?=$model
                    ->title ?>
                    <label class="label label-default"> <?=$model
                        ->rental_rate ?>
                    </label>
                </h4>
                <p class="list-group-item-text"><?=$model
                    ->description ?></p>
        </div>
    <?php endforeach ?>

    <?=LinkPager::widget([
        'pagination' => $pages
    ]); ?>
```

3. Try to load `http://yii-book.app/index.php?r=film/index`. You should get a working pagination and links that allow sorting of list by the film's title or by rental rate:

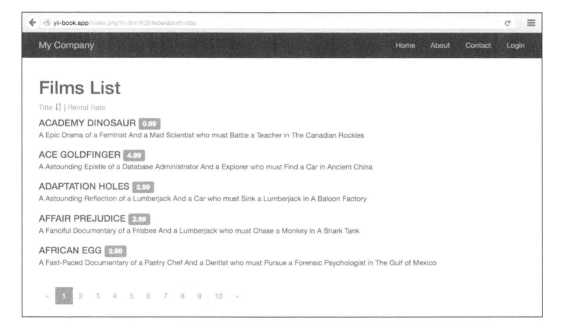

How it works...

First, we got the total models count and initialized the new pagination component instance with it by passing the `totalCount` variable to our `Pagination` instance. Then, we used the `$pages->pageSize` field to set up the page size for our pagination. After that, we created a sorter instance for the model, specifying model attributes we wanted to sort by and applying order conditions to the query by calling `orderBy` and passing `$sort->orders` as a parameter. Then, we called `all()` to get records from the DB.

At this point, we have the models list, pages, and data used for the link pager, and the sorter that we use to generate sorting links.

In a view, we use the data we have gathered. First, we generate links with the `Sort::link` method. Then, we list the models. Finally, using the *LinkPager* widgets, we render the pagination control.

See also

Visit the following links to get more information about pagination and sorting:

- http://www.yiiframework.com/doc-2.0/yii-data-pagination.html
- http://www.yiiframework.com/doc-2.0/yii-data-sort.html
- http://www.yiiframework.com/doc-2.0/guide-output-pagination.html
- http://www.yiiframework.com/doc-2.0/guide-output-sorting.html

3
ActiveRecord, Model, and Database

In this chapter, we will cover the following topics:

- ▸ Getting data from a database
- ▸ Defining and using multiple DB connections
- ▸ Customizing the ActiveQuery class
- ▸ Processing model fields with AR event-like methods
- ▸ Automating timestamps
- ▸ Setting up an author automatically
- ▸ Setting up a slug automatically
- ▸ Transactions
- ▸ Replication and read-write splitting
- ▸ Implementing single table inheritance

Introduction

In this chapter, you will learn how to work with a database efficiently, when to use models and when not to, how to work with multiple databases, how to automatically preprocess Active Record fields, how to use transactions, and so on.

Getting data from a database

Most applications use databases today. Be it a small website or a social network, at least some parts are powered by databases.

Yii introduces three ways to allow you to work with databases. They are as follows:

▸ Active Record
▸ Query Builder
▸ SQL via DAO

We will use all these methods to get data from the `film`, `film_actor`, and `actor` tables and show it in a list. Also, we will compare the execution time and memory usage to determine in which cases we should use these methods.

Getting ready

1. Create a new application using the Composer package manager, as described in the official guide at `http://www.yiiframework.com/doc-2.0/guide-start-installation.html`.
2. Download the Sakila database from `http://dev.mysql.com/doc/index-other.html`.
3. Execute the downloaded SQLs; first schema, then data.
4. Configure the DB connection in `config/main.php` to use the Sakila database.
5. Use Gii to create models for the actor and film tables.

How to do it...

1. Create `app/controllers/DbController.php` as follows:

```php
<?php

namespace app\controllers;

use app\models\Actor;
use Yii;
use yii\db\Query;
use yii\helpers\ArrayHelper;
use yii\helpers\Html;
use yii\web\Controller;
```

```php
/**
 * Class DbController
 * @package app\controllers
 */
class DbController extends Controller
{
    /**
     * Example of Active Record usage.
     *
     * @return string
     */
    public function actionAr()
    {
        $records = Actor::find()
                        ->joinWith('films')
                        ->orderBy('actor.first_name,
                        actor.last_name, film.title')
                        ->all();

        return $this->renderRecords($records);
    }

    /**
     * Example of Query class usage.
     *
     * @return string
     */
    public function actionQuery()
    {
        $rows = (new Query())
            ->from('actor')
            ->innerJoin('film_actor',
            'actor.actor_id=film_actor.actor_id')
            ->leftJoin('film',
            'film.film_id=film_actor.film_id')
            ->orderBy('actor.first_name, actor.last_name,
            actor.actor_id, film.title')
            ->all();

        return $this->renderRows($rows);
    }
```

```php
/**
 * Example of SQL execution usage.
 *
 * @return string
 */
public function actionSql()
{
    $sql = 'SELECT *
        FROM actor a
        JOIN film_actor fa ON fa.actor_id = a.actor_id
        JOIN film f ON fa.film_id = f.film_id
        ORDER BY a.first_name, a.last_name, a.actor_id,
        f.title';

    $rows = Yii::$app->db->createCommand($sql)-
>queryAll();

    return $this->renderRows($rows);
}

/**
 * Render records for Active Record array.
 *
 * @param array $records
 *
 * @return string
 */
protected function renderRecords(array $records = [])
{
    if (!$records) {
        return $this->renderContent('Actor list is
        empty.');
    }

    $items = [];

    foreach ($records as $record) {
        $actorFilms = $record->films
            ? Html::ol(ArrayHelper::getColumn($record-
            >films, 'title'))
            : null;
        $actorName = $record->first_name.' '.$record-
            >last_name;
```

```php
                $items[] = $actorName.$actorFilms;
        }

        return $this->renderContent(Html::ol($items, [
            'encode' => false,
        ]));
    }

    /**
     * Render rows for result of query.
     *
     * @param array $rows
     *
     * @return string
     */
    protected function renderRows(array $rows = [])
    {
        if (!$rows) {
            return $this->renderContent('Actor list is
            empty.');
        }

        $items = [];
        $films = [];

        $actorId = null;
        $actorName = null;
        $actorFilms = null;

        $lastActorId = $rows[0]['actor_id'];

        foreach ($rows as $row) {
            $actorId = $row['actor_id'];
            $films[] = $row['title'];

            if ($actorId != $lastActorId) {
                $actorName = $row['first_name'].'
                '.$row['last_name'];
                $actorFilms = $films ? Html::ol($films) :
                null;
```

```
                    $items[] = $actorName.$actorFilms;
                    $films = [];
                    $lastActorId = $actorId;
                }
            }

            if ($actorId == $lastActorId) {
                $actorFilms = $films ? Html::ol($films) : null;
                $items[] = $actorName.$actorFilms;
            }

            return $this->renderContent(Html::ol($items, [
                'encode' => false,
            ]));
        }
    }
```

2. Here, we have three actions corresponding to the three different methods of getting data from a database.

3. After running the preceding `db/ar`, `db/query` and `db/sql` actions, you should get a tree showing 200 actors and 1,000 films they have acted in, as shown in the following screenshot:

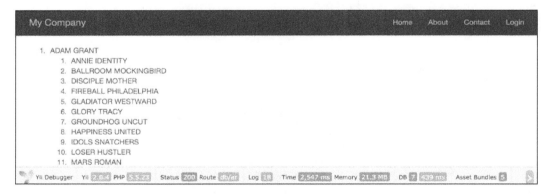

4. At the bottom, there are statistics that give information about the memory usage and execution time. Absolute numbers can be different if you run this code, but the difference between the methods used should be about the same:

Method	Memory usage (megabytes)	Execution time (seconds)
Active Record	21.4	2.398
Query Builder	28.3	0.477
SQL (DAO)	27.6	0.481

How it works...

The `actionAr` action method gets model instances using the Active Record approach.

We start with the `Actor` model generated with Gii to get all the actors, and specify `joinWith => 'films'` to get the corresponding films using a single query or eager loading through relation, which Gii builds for us from `InnoDB` table foreign keys. We then simply iterate over all the actors and for each actor, over each film. Then, for each item, we print its name.

The `actionQuery` function uses Query Builder. First, we create a query for the current DB connection with `\yii\db\Query`. We then add query parts one by one with `from`, `joinInner`, and `leftJoin`. These methods escape values, tables, and field names automatically. The `all()` function of `\yii\db\Query` returns an array of raw database rows. Each row is also an array, indexed with result field names. We pass the result to `renderRows`, which renders it.

With `actionSql`, we do the same, except that we pass SQL directly instead of adding its parts one by one. It's worth mentioning that we should escape parameter values manually using `Yii::app()->db->quoteValue` before using them in the query string:

The `renderRows` method renders the Query Builder.

The `renderRecords` method renders the active records.

Method	Active Record	Query Builder	SQL (DAO)
Syntax	This will do SQL for you. Gii will generate models and relations for you. Works with models, completely OO-style, and a very clean API. Produces an array of properly nested models as the result.	Clean API, suitable for building query on the fly. Produces raw data arrays as the result.	Good for complex SQL. Manual values and keyword quoting. Not very suitable for building a query on the fly. Produces raw data arrays as the result.
Performance	Higher memory usage and execution time compared to SQL and Query Builder.	Okay.	Okay.
Extra features	Quotes values and names automatically. Behaviors. Before/after hooks. Validation. Prototyping selects.	Quotes values and names automatically.	None.
Best for	Update, delete, and create actions for single models (the model gives a huge benefit when using with forms).	Working with large amount of data and building queries on the fly.	Complex queries you want to complete with pure SQL and have maximum possible performance.

There's more...

In order to learn more about working with databases in Yii, refer to the following resources:

- ▶ http://www.yiiframework.com/doc-2.0/guide-db-dao.html
- ▶ http://www.yiiframework.com/doc-2.0/guide-db-query-builder.html
- ▶ http://www.yiiframework.com/doc-2.0/guide-db-active-record.html

Defining and using multiple DB connections

Multiple database connections are not used very often for new standalone web applications. However, when you are building an add-on application for an existing system, you will most probably need another database connection.

From this recipe, you will learn how to define multiple DB connections and use them with DAO, Query Builder, and Active Record models.

Getting ready

1. Create a new application using the Composer package manager, as described in the official guide at http://www.yiiframework.com/doc-2.0/guide-start-installation.html.

2. Create two MySQL databases named db1 and db2.

3. Create a table named post in db1, as follows:

```
DROP TABLE IF EXISTS 'post';
CREATE TABLE IF NOT EXISTS 'post' (
    'id' INT(10) UNSIGNED NOT NULL AUTO_INCREMENT,
    'title' VARCHAR(255) NOT NULL,
    'text' TEXT NOT NULL,
     PRIMARY KEY  ('id')
);
```

4. Create a table named comment in db2, as follows:

```
DROP TABLE IF EXISTS 'comment';
CREATE TABLE IF NOT EXISTS 'comment' (
    'id' INT(10) UNSIGNED NOT NULL AUTO_INCREMENT,
    'text' TEXT NOT NULL,
    'post_id' INT(10) UNSIGNED NOT NULL,
     PRIMARY KEY  ('id')
);
```

How to do it...

1. We will start with configuring the DB connections. Open `config/main.php` and define a primary connection as described in the official guide:

```
'db' => [
    'connectionString' =>
    'mysql:host=localhost;dbname=db1',
    'username' => 'root',
    'password' => '',
    'charset' => 'utf8',
],
```

2. Copy it, rename the db component to db2, and change the connection string accordingly. Also, you need to add the class name as follows:

```
'db2' => [
    'class'=>'yii\db\Connection',
    'connectionString' =>
    'mysql:host=localhost;dbname=db2',
    'username' => 'root',
    'password' => '',
    'charset' => 'utf8',
],
```

3. That is it. Now you have two database connections and you can use them with DAO and Query Builder, as follows:

```
$rows1 = Yii::$app->db->createCommand($sql)->queryAll();
$rows2 = Yii::$app->db2->createCommand($sql)->queryAll();
```

4. Now, if we need to use Active Record models, we first need to create the Post and Comment models with Gii. You can select an appropriate connection for each model. Set the db2 for database connection ID when you create the Comment model, as shown in the following screenshot:

Model Generator

This generator generates an ActiveRecord class for the specified database table.

Table Name

comment

Model Class

Comment

Namespace

app\models

Base Class

yii\db\ActiveRecord

Database Connection ID

db2

5. Now you can use the `Comment` model as usual and create `controllers/DbController.php`, as follows:

```php
<?php

namespace app\controllers;

use app\models\Post;
use app\models\Comment;
use yii\helpers\ArrayHelper;
use yii\helpers\Html;
use yii\web\Controller;

/**
 * Class DbController.
 * @package app\controllers
 */
class DbController extends Controller
{
    public function actionIndex()
    {
```

```
$post = new Post();
$post->title = 'Post #'.rand(1, 1000);
$post->text = 'text';
$post->save();

$posts = Post::find()->all();

echo Html::tag('h1', 'Posts');
echo Html::ul(ArrayHelper::getColumn($posts,
'title'));

$comment = new Comment();
$comment->post_id = $post->id;
$comment->text = 'comment #'.rand(1, 1000);
$comment->save();

$comments = Comment::find()->all();

echo Html::tag('h1', 'Comments');
echo Html::ul(ArrayHelper::getColumn($comments,
'text'));
    }
}
```

6. Run `db/index` multiple times and you should see records added to both databases, as shown in the following screenshot:

Posts

- Post #50
- Post #917
- Post #186
- Post #321
- Post #574
- Post #552
- Post #708

Comments

- comment #344
- comment #922
- comment #602
- comment #563
- comment #461
- comment #336
- comment #200

How it works...

In Yii, you can add and configure your own components through the configuration file. For nonstandard components such as db2, you have to specify the component class. Similarly, you can add db3, db4, or any other component, for example, facebookApi. The remaining array key/value pairs are assigned to the component's public properties, respectively.

There's more...

Depending on the RDBMS used, there are additional things we can do to make it easier to use multiple databases.

Cross-database relations

If you are using MySQL, it is possible to create cross-database relations for your models. In order to do this, you should prefix the Comment model's table name with the database name, as follows:

```
class Comment extends \yii\db\ActiveRecord
{
    //...
    public function tableName()
    {
        return 'db2.comment';
    }
    //...
}
```

Now, if you have a comments relation defined in the Post model relations method, you can use the following code:

```
$posts = Post::find()->joinWith('comments')->all();
```

See also

For further information, refer to http://www.yiiframework.com/doc-2.0/guide-db-dao.html#creating-db-connections.

Customizing the ActiveQuery class

By default, all Active Record queries are supported by `yii\db\ActiveQuery`. To use a customized query class in an Active Record class, you should override the `yii\db\ActiveRecord::find()` method and return an instance of your customized query class.

Getting ready

1. Create a new application using the Composer package manager, as described in the official guide at `http://www.yiiframework.com/doc-2.0/guide-start-installation.html`.

2. Set up the database connection and create a table named `post`, as follows:
   ```
   DROP TABLE IF EXISTS 'post';
   CREATE TABLE IF NOT EXISTS 'post' (
       'id' INT(10) UNSIGNED NOT NULL AUTO_INCREMENT,
       'lang' VARCHAR(5) NOT NULL DEFAULT 'en',
       'title' VARCHAR(255) NOT NULL,
       'text' TEXT NOT NULL,
        PRIMARY KEY ('id')
   );
   INSERT INTO 'post'('id','lang','title','text')
   VALUES (1,'en_us','Yii news','Text in English'),
   (2,'de','Yii Nachrichten','Text in Deutsch');
   ```

3. Generate a `Post` model using Gii with an enabled **Generate ActiveQuery** option that generates the `PostQuery` class.

How to do it...

1. Add the following method to `models/PostQuery.php`:
   ```php
   <?php

   namespace app\models;

   /**
    * This is the ActiveQuery class for [[Post]].
    *
    * @see Post
    */
   ```

```
class PostQuery extends \yii\db\ActiveQuery
{
    /**
     * @param $lang
     *
     * @return $this
     */
    public function lang($lang)
    {
        return $this->where([ 'lang' => $lang ]);
    }
}
```

2. That is it. Now, we can use our model. Create `controllers/DbController.php` as follows:

```php
<?php

namespace app\controllers;

use app\models\Post;
use yii\helpers\Html;
use yii\web\Controller;

/**
 * Class DbController.
 * @package app\controllers
 */
class DbController extends Controller
{
    public function actionIndex()
    {
        // Get posts written in default application
        language
        $posts = Post::find()->all();

        echo Html::tag('h1', 'Default language');
        foreach ($posts as $post) {
            echo Html::tag('h2', $post->title);
            echo $post->text;
        }
```

```
        // Get posts written in German
        $posts = Post::find()->lang('de')->all();

         echo Html::tag('h1', 'German');
         foreach ($posts as $post) {
             echo Html::tag('h2', $post->title);
             echo $post->text;
         }
      }
   }
```

3. Now, run `db/index` and you should get an output similar to the one shown in the following screenshot:

Default language

Yii news

Text in English

Yii Nachrichten

Text in Deutsch

German

Yii Nachrichten

Text in Deutsch

How it works...

We have rewritten the `find` method in the `Post` model and extended the ActiveQuery class. The `lang` method returns ActiveQuery with the specified language value. In order to support chained calls, `lang` returns the model instance by itself.

There's more...

According to the Yii2 Guide, in Yii 1.1, there was a concept called scope. Scope is no longer directly supported in Yii 2.0, and you should use customized query classes and query methods to achieve the same goal.

See also

For further information, refer to the following URLs:

- ► `http://www.yiiframework.com/doc-2.0/guide-db-active-record.html#customizing-query-classes`
- ► `http://www.yiiframework.com/doc-2.0/guide-intro-upgrade-from-v1.html#active-record`

Processing model fields with AR event-like methods

Active Record implementation in Yii is very powerful and has many features. One of these features is the event-like methods, which you can use to preprocess model fields before putting them into the database or getting them from a database, as well as to delete data related to the model, and so on.

In this recipe, we will link all URLs in the post text and list all existing Active Record event-like methods.

Getting ready

1. Create a new application using the Composer package manager, as described in the official guide at `http://www.yiiframework.com/doc-2.0/guide-start-installation.html`.

2. Set up the database connection and create a table named `post`, as follows:

```
DROP TABLE IF EXISTS 'post';
CREATE TABLE IF NOT EXISTS 'post' (
    'id' INT(10) UNSIGNED NOT NULL AUTO_INCREMENT,
    'title' VARCHAR(255) NOT NULL,
    'text' TEXT NOT NULL,
     PRIMARY KEY ('id')
);
```

3. Generate the `post` model using Gii.

How to do it...

1. Add the following method to `models/Post.php`:

```php
/**
 * @param bool $insert
 *
 * @return bool
 */
public function beforeSave($insert)
{
    $this->text = preg_replace('~((?:https?|ftps?)://.*?)(
    |$)~iu',
    '<a href="\1">\1</a>\2', $this->text);

    return parent::beforeSave($insert);
}
```

2. That is it. Now, try saving a post containing a link. Create `controllers/TestController.php` as follows:

```php
<?php

namespace app\controllers;

use app\models\Post;
use yii\helpers\Html;
use yii\helpers\VarDumper;
use yii\web\Controller;

/**
 * Class TestController.
 * @package app\controllers
 */
class TestController extends Controller
{
    public function actionIndex()
    {
        $post = new Post();
        $post->title = 'links test';
        $post->text = 'before http://www.yiiframework.com/
        after';
```

```
$post->save();

return $this->renderContent(Html::tag('pre',
VarDumper::dumpAsString(
    $post->attributes
)));
    }
}
```

3. That is it. Now, run `test/index`. You should get the following result:

How it works...

The `beforeSave` method is implemented in the `ActiveRecord` class and executed just before saving a model. Using a regular expression, we replace everything that looks like a URL with a link that uses this URL and call the parent implementation, so that real events are raised properly. In order to prevent saving, you can return false.

See also

▸ For further information, refer to `http://www.yiiframework.com/doc-2.0/guide-db-active-record.html#active-record-life-cycles`.

▸ The *Working with events* recipe in *Chapter 1, Fundamentals*

▸ The *Automating timestamps* recipe

▸ The *Setting up an author automatically* recipe

▸ The *Setting up a slug automatically* recipe

Automating timestamps

For instance, we have a simple blog application. As in any blog, it has posts, comments, and so on. We would like to populate the timestamps during the create/update events for posts. Let us assume that our post model is named `BlogPost` model.

Getting ready

1. Create a new application using the Composer package manager, as described in the official guide at `http://www.yiiframework.com/doc-2.0/guide-start-installation.html`.

2. Set up the database connection and create a table named `blog_post`, as follows:

```sql
DROP TABLE IF EXISTS 'blog_post';
CREATE TABLE IF NOT EXISTS 'blog_post' (
    'id' INT(10) UNSIGNED NOT NULL AUTO_INCREMENT,
    'title' VARCHAR(255) NOT NULL,
    'text' TEXT NOT NULL,
    'created_date' INTEGER,
    'modified_date'INTEGER,
     PRIMARY KEY  ('id')
);
```

3. Use Gii to create a model for the `blog_post` table.

How to do it...

1. Add the following method to `models/BlogPost.php`:

```php
/**
* @return array
*/
public function behaviors()
{
    return [
        'timestamp'=> [
```

```
                'class' => 'yii\behaviors\TimestampBehavior',
                'createdAtAttribute' => 'creation_date',
                'updatedAtAttribute' => 'modified_date'
        ]
    ];
}
```

2. Create `controllers/TestController.php` as follows:

```php
<?php

namespace app\controllers;

use app\models\BlogPost;
use yii\helpers\Html;
use yii\helpers\VarDumper;
use yii\web\Controller;

/**
 * Class TestController.
 * @package app\controllers
 */
class TestController extends Controller
{
    public function actionIndex()
    {
        $blogPost = new BlogPost();
        $blogPost->title = 'Gotcha!';
        $blogPost->text = 'We need some laughter to ease
        the tension of holiday shopping.';
        $blogPost->save();

        return $this->renderContent(Html::tag('pre',
        VarDumper::dumpAsString($blogPost->attributes)
        ));
    }
}
```

3. That is it. Now, run `test/index`. You should get the following result:

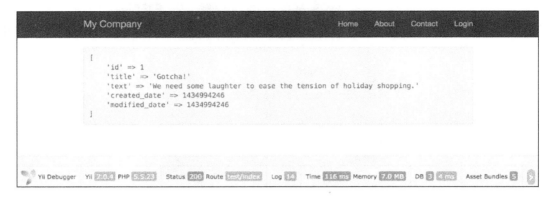

How it works...

By default, the Timestamp behavior populates `created_at` (the timestamp which points to the time when the model was created) and `updated_at` (the time when the model was updated). It's a standard practice to name these fields, but if we would like to make a change, we can specify fields, which will be updated, and model events.

There's more...

For instance, our fields are named `creation_date` and `modified_date`.

Let's configure our model with behavior according to these fields. In addition, we should add our behavior's code to our `Post` model:

```php
<?php

namespace app\models;

use Yii;
use yii\db\BaseActiveRecord;

class Post extends \yii\db\ActiveRecord
{
    // ..
    public function behaviors()
```

```
        {
            return [
                [
                    'class' => 'yii\behaviors\TimestampBehavior',
                    'attributes' => [
                        BaseActiveRecord::EVENT_BEFORE_INSERT =>
                        'creation_date',
                        BaseActiveRecord::EVENT_BEFORE_UPDATE =>
                        'modified_date',
                    ]
                ]
            ];
        }
        // ..
    }
```

In this example, we've pointed to the `creation_date` and `modified_date` attributes before creating and updating our model accordingly by dint of using special ActiveRecord events: `EVENT_BEFORE_INSERT` and `EVENT_BEFORE_UPDATE`.

In addition...

You may want to save the timestamp for custom scenarios. Let's say you want to update the `last_login` field, for example, for a specific controller action. In this situation, you can trigger the timestamp update for your specific attribute using the following:

```
$model->touch('last_login');
```

Be aware that `touch()` can't be used for new models. You will get `InvalidCallException` in this case:

```
$model = new Post();
$model->touch('creation_date');
```

The `touch()` method calls model saving inside itself so you don't need to save the model after calling it.

See also

For further information, refer to `http://www.yiiframework.com/doc-2.0/guide-concept-behaviors.html#using-timestampbehavior`.

Setting up an author automatically

The `Blameable` behavior allows you to update one or more authors' fields automatically. This is primarily used to populate data into the `created_by` and `updated_by` fields. Similar to the Timestamp behavior, you can easily specify some special parameters and essential events for this behavior.

Let us return to the example from the previous section. We also have posts in our blog application. For example, let's assume that our blog model is called `BlogPost`. The model has `author_id`, the field which points to who created this post, and `updater_id`, the field which points to who updated it. We would like to populate these attributes automatically during the create/update model events. Now you can learn how to do it.

Getting ready

1. Create a new application using the Composer package manager, as described in the official guide at `http://www.yiiframework.com/doc-2.0/guide-start-installation.html`.

2. Set up the database connection and create a table named `blog_post`, as follows:
   ```sql
   DROP TABLE IF EXISTS 'blog_post';
   CREATE TABLE IF NOT EXISTS 'blog_post' (
       'id' INT(10) UNSIGNED NOT NULL AUTO_INCREMENT,
       'author_id' INT(10) UNSIGNED DEFAULT NULL,
       'updater_id' INT(10) UNSIGNED DEFAULT NULL,
       'title' VARCHAR(255) NOT NULL,
       'text' TEXT NOT NULL,
       PRIMARY KEY ('id')
   );
   ```

3. Use Gii to create the `BlogPost` model for the `blost_post` table.

How to do it...

1. Add the following `behaviors` method to `models/BlogPost.php`:
   ```php
   <?php

   namespace app\models;

   use Yii;
   ```

```php
use yii\db\BaseActiveRecord;

/**
 * This is the model class for table "blog_post".
 *
 * @property integer $id
 * @property integer $author_id
 * @property integer $updater_id
 * @property string $title
 * @property string $text
 */
class BlogPost extends \yii\db\ActiveRecord
{
    /**
     * @return array
     */
    public function behaviors()
    {
        return [
            [
                'class' =>
                'yii\behaviors\BlameableBehavior',
                'attributes' => [
                    BaseActiveRecord::EVENT_BEFORE_INSERT
                    => 'author_id',
                    BaseActiveRecord::EVENT_BEFORE_UPDATE
                    => 'updater_id'
                ]
            ]
        ];
    }

}
```

2. Create `controllers/TestController.php` as follows:

```php
<?php

namespace app\controllers;

use app\models\BlogPost;
use app\models\User;
use Yii;
```

```php
use yii\helpers\Html;
use yii\helpers\VarDumper;
use yii\web\Controller;

/**
 * Class TestController.
 * @package app\controllers
 */
class TestController extends Controller
{
    public function actionIndex()
    {
        $users = new User();
        $identity = $users->findIdentity(100);

        Yii::$app->user->setIdentity($identity);

        $blogPost = new BlogPost();
        $blogPost->title = 'Very pretty title';
        $blogPost->text = 'Success is not final, failure is
        not fatal...';
        $blogPost->save();

        return $this->renderContent(Html::tag('pre',
        VarDumper::dumpAsString(
            $blogPost->attributes
        )));
    }
}
```

3. That is it. Now, run `test/index`. You will get the following result:

How it works...

By default, the `Blameable` behavior populates the `created_by` and `updated_by` attributes, but we will make a change and set up our behavior according to our own fields.

We also specified model events and fields in the model, so, during the model creation, `author_id` will be populated. Similarly, during the model update, we will populate `updater_id`.

What `Blameable` does is insert the current user id value into the `created_by` and `updated_by` fields during the create/update model events. This is a super-convenient way of doing things. Every time a model gets created or updated, we automatically fill out the essential fields.

This works out really well for little projects such as for large systems, where multiple users are admin and you need to keep track of who is doing what. You can also use this for frontend implementations, for example, if you had a `blog_comment` table and you wanted to use this method to keep track of the author of a comment. Also, you could set the author's fields in the controller, but the behavior helps you to avoid writing unnecessary and additional code. This is a very effective and easy way to implement this thing.

There's more...

Sometimes we need to fill out `author_id` and `updater_id` by an id other than that of the current user. In such a case, we may detach our behavior as follows:

```
$model->detachBehavior('blammable');
```

We can detach any behavior we like in this way.

See also

For further information, refer to `http://www.yiiframework.com/doc-2.0/yii-behaviors-blameablebehavior.html`.

Setting up a slug automatically

On the web, slug is a short text used in a URL to identify and describe a resource. A slug is the part of a URL which identifies a page using human-readable keywords. Sluggable behavior is the Yii2 model behavior that allows us to generate unique slugs.

In this section, we will be guiding you through modifying Yii's default view URL routes for model objects to be more user-friendly and search engine-friendly. Yii provides built-in support for this via its sluggable behaviors.

Getting ready

1. Create a new application using the Composer package manager, as described in the official guide at http://www.yiiframework.com/doc-2.0/guide-start-installation.html.

2. Set up the database connection and create a table named `blog_post`, as follows:

```
DROP TABLE IF EXISTS 'blog_post';
CREATE TABLE IF NOT EXISTS 'blog_post' (
    'id' INT(10) UNSIGNED NOT NULL AUTO_INCREMENT,
    'title' VARCHAR(255) NOT NULL,
    'slug' VARCHAR(255) NOT NULL,
    'text' TEXT NOT NULL,
    PRIMARY KEY ('id')
);
```

3. Use Gii to create a model for the post table.

How to do it...

1. Add the following `behaviors` method to `models/BlogPost.php`:

```php
<?php

namespace app\models;

use Yii;
use yii\db\BaseActiveRecord;

class BlogPost extends \yii\db\ActiveRecord
{
    // ..
    public function behaviors()
    {
        return [
            [
                'class' =>
                'yii\behaviors\SluggableBehavior',
                'attribute' => 'title',
                'slugAttribute' => 'slug',
                'immutable'=> false,
```

```
                        'ensureUnique' => true
                    ]
                ];
        }
        // ..
    }
```

2. Create `controllers/TestController.php` as follows:

```php
<?php

namespace app\controllers;

use app\models\BlogPost;
use Yii;
use yii\helpers\Html;
use yii\helpers\VarDumper;
use yii\web\Controller;

/**
 * Class TestController
 * @package app\controllers
 */
class TestController extends Controller
{
    public function actionIndex()
    {
        $blogPostA         = new BlogPost();
        $blogPostA->title = 'Super Quote title 1';
        $blogPostA->text  = 'The price of success is hard
        work, dedication to the job at hand';
        $blogPostA->save();

        $blogPostB         = new BlogPost();
        $blogPostB->title = 'Super Quote title 2';
        $blogPostB->text  = 'Happiness lies in the joy of
        achievement...';
        $blogPostB->save();

        return $this->renderContent(
            '<pre>' .
```

```
            VarDumper::dumpAsString(
                $blogPostA->attributes
            ) .
            VarDumper::dumpAsString(
                $blogPostB->attributes
            ) .
            '</pre>'
        );
    }
}
```

3. The result will be as follows:

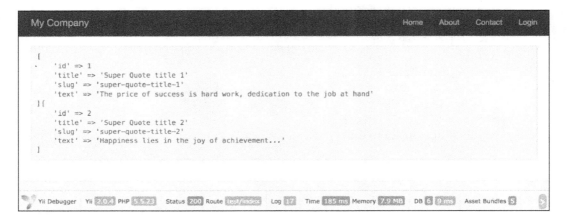

How it works...

▶ Yii offers some nice enhancements to `SluggableBehavior` for useful scenarios.

▶ For example, once a search engine records a slug, you probably don't want the page URL to change.

▶ The immutable attribute tells Yii to keep the slug the same after it's first created—even if the title will be updated.

▶ If users enter messages that overlap in content, the `ensureUnique` property will automatically append a unique suffix to duplicates. This makes certain that each message has a unique URL, even if the message is identical.

► If you go ahead and create another post with the exact same title, you'll see that its slug is incremented to hot-update-for-ios-devices-2.

 Note: If you get an error related to the immutable property, it may be that you need to run a Composer update to get the latest version of Yii.

There's more...

1. Use Gii to generate CRUD for the model class `app\models\Post` and the controller class `app\controllers\BlogPostController`.

2. Add the following action to `controllers/BlogPostController.php`:

```
/**
* @param $slug
*
* @return string
* @throws NotFoundHttpException
*/
public function actionSlug($slug)
{
    $model = BlogPost::findOne(['slug'=>$slug]);

    if ($model === null) {
        throw new NotFoundHttpException('The requested page
        does not exist.');
    }

    return $this->render('view', [
        'model' => $model,
        ]);
}
```

3. That it is. If you run `blogpost/slug` with the slug value as `sluggablebehavior-test`, you will get the following result:

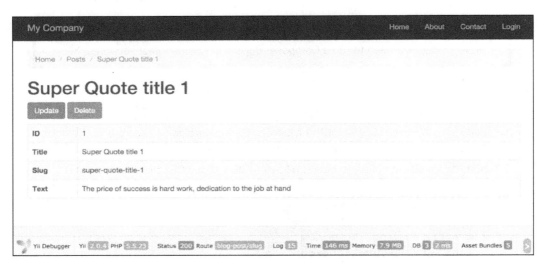

4. It's suggested that the previous slug recipe be successfully completed with a created instance of `Post` model.

5. To beautify the URL, add the following `urlManager` component in `config\web.php`:

```
//..
'urlManager' => [
    'enablePrettyUrl' => true,
    'rules' => [
        'blog-post' => 'blog-post/index',
        'blog-post/index' => 'blog-post/index',
        'blog-post/create' => 'blog-post/create',
        'blog-post/view/<id:\d+>' => 'blog-post/view',
        'blog-post/update/<id:\d+>' => 'blog-post/update',
        'blog-post/delete/<id:\d+>' => 'blog-post/delete',
        'blog-post/<slug>' => 'blog-post/slug',
        'defaultRoute' => '/site/index',
    ],
]
//..
```

6. It's important that the `'blog-post/<slug>' => 'blog-post/slug'` rule is the last in the post URL rule list.

7. Now, if you go to the page using your slug URL, such as `index.php/blog-post/super-quote-title-1/`, you will get a result like similar to that in step 3:

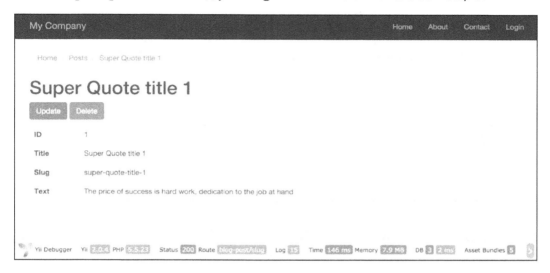

See also

For further information, refer to:

- `http://www.yiiframework.com/doc-2.0/yii-behaviors-sluggablebehavior.html`
- `http://www.yiiframework.com/doc-2.0/guide-runtime-routing.html#url-rules`

Transactions

In modern databases, transactions also do some other things, such as ensuring that you can't access data that another person has written halfway. However, the basic idea is the same—transactions are there to ensure that no matter what happens, the data you work with will be in a sensible state. They guarantee that there will *not* be a situation where money is withdrawn from one account, but not deposited to another.

Yii2 supports a powerful transaction mechanism with savepoints.

A classic example is of transferring money from one bank account to another. To do that, you have to first withdraw the amount from the source account, and then deposit it to the destination account. The operation has to succeed in full. If you stop halfway, the money will be lost, and that is very bad. For instance, we have a recipient account and a sender account. We would like to transfer money from sender to recipient. Let's assume that we have an account model.

Getting ready...

Our account model will be very simple and it will contain only the id and balance fields.

1. Create a new application using the Composer package manager, as described in the official guide at http://www.yiiframework.com/doc-2.0/guide-start-installation.html.

2. Create a migration, which adds an account table, using the following command:

   ```
   ./yii migrate/create create_account_table
   ```

3. Also, update the just-created migration using the following code:

   ```php
   <?php

   use yii\db\Schema;
   use yii\db\Migration;

   class m150620_062034_create_account_table extends Migration
   {
       const TABLE_NAME = '{{%account}}';

       public function up()
       {
           $tableOptions = null;
           if ($this->db->driverName === 'mysql') {
               $tableOptions = 'CHARACTER SET utf8 COLLATE
               utf8_general_ci ENGINE=InnoDB';
           }

           $this->createTable(self::TABLE_NAME, [
               'id' => Schema::TYPE_PK,
               'balance' => ' NUMERIC(15,2) DEFAULT NULL',
           ], $tableOptions);

       }

       public function down()
       {
           $this->dropTable(self::TABLE_NAME);
       }
   }
   ```

4. Then, install migration with the following command:

```
./yii migrate up
```

5. Use Gii to create a model for the account table.

6. Create a migration, which adds some test `Account` models with balance for our table:

```
./yii migrate/create add_account_records
```

7. Also, update the just-created migration using the following code:

```php
<?php

use yii\db\Migration;
use app\models\Account;

class m150620_063252_add_account_records extends Migration
{
    public function up()
    {
        $accountFirst = new Account();
        $accountFirst->balance = 1110;
        $accountFirst->save();

        $accountSecond = new Account();
        $accountSecond->balance = 779;
        $accountSecond->save();

        $accountThird = new Account();
        $accountThird->balance = 568;
        $accountThird->save();
        return true;
    }

    public function down()
    {
        $this->truncateTable('{{%account}}');
        return false;
    }
}
```

How to do it...

1. Add the following rule to the `rules` method, to `models/Account.php`:

```php
public function rules()
{
    return [
        //..
        [['balance'], 'number', 'min' => 0],
        //..
    ];
}
```

2. Let us assume that our balance may be only positive and that it can't be negative.

3. Create `TestController` with success and error actions:

```php
<?php

namespace app\controllers;

use app\models\Account;
use Yii;
use yii\db\Exception;
use yii\helpers\Html;
use yii\helpers\VarDumper;
use yii\web\Controller;

class TestController extends Controller
{

    public function actionSuccess()
    {
        $transaction = Yii::$app->db->beginTransaction();

        try {
            $recipient = Account::findOne(1);
            $sender    = Account::findOne(2);

            $transferAmount = 177;
            $recipient->balance += $transferAmount;
            $sender->balance -= $transferAmount;
```

```
        if ($sender->save() && $recipient->save()) {
            $transaction->commit();

            return $this->renderContent(
                Html::tag('h1', 'Money transfer was
                successfully')
            );
        } else {
            $transaction->rollBack();
            throw new Exception('Money transfer
            failed:' .
            VarDumper::dumpAsString
            ($sender->getErrors()) .
            VarDumper::dumpAsString
            ($recipient->getErrors())
            );
        }
    } catch ( Exception $e ) {
        $transaction->rollBack();
        throw $e;
    }
}

public function actionError()
{
    $transaction = Yii::$app->db->beginTransaction();

    try {
        $recipient = Account::findOne(1);
        $sender    = Account::findOne(3);

        $transferAmount = 1000;
        $recipient->balance += $transferAmount;
        $sender->balance -= $transferAmount;

        if ($sender->save() && $recipient->save()) {
            $transaction->commit();

            return $this->renderContent(
                Html::tag('h1', 'Money transfer was
                successfully')
            );
```

```
            } else {
                $transaction->rollBack();

                throw new Exception('Money transfer
                failed: ' .
                VarDumper::dumpAsString
                ($sender->getErrors()) .
                VarDumper::dumpAsString
                ($recipient->getErrors())
                );
            }

        } catch ( Exception $e ) {
            $transaction->rollBack();
            throw $e;
        }
    }
}
```

4. Run `test/success` and you should get the output shown in the following screenshot:

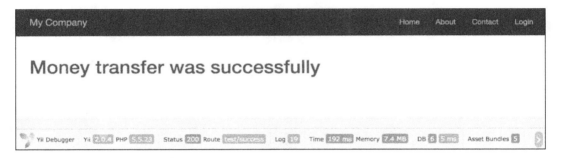

5. In this case, the transaction mechanism will not update the recipient and sender balance if some error occurred.

6. Run `test/error` and you should get the output shown in the following screenshot:

Database Exception – yii\db\Exception

```
Money transfer failed: [
'balance' => [
0 => 'Balance must be no less than 0.'
]
][
```

As you will remember, we added a rule to the `Account` model, so our account balance can be only positive. The transaction will roll back in this case and it prevents a situation where money is withdrawn from a sender's account but not deposited to the recipient's account.

See also

For further information, refer to:

- `http://www.yiiframework.com/doc-2.0/guide-db-dao.html#performing-transactions`
- `http://www.yiiframework.com/doc-2.0/guide-db-dao.html#nesting-transactions`

Replication and read-write splitting

In this recipe we will have a look at how to do replication and read-write splitting. We will see how slave and master servers help us in getting these done.

Getting ready

1. Create a new application using the Composer package manager, as described in the official guide at `http://www.yiiframework.com/doc-2.0/guide-start-installation.html`.

2. Set up the database connection and create a table named `post`, as follows:

```
DROP TABLE IF EXISTS 'blog_post';
CREATE TABLE IF NOT EXISTS 'blog_post' (
    'id' INT(10) UNSIGNED NOT NULL AUTO_INCREMENT,
    'title' VARCHAR(255) NOT NULL,
    'text' TEXT NOT NULL,
    'created_at' INTEGER,
    'modified_at'INTEGER,
     PRIMARY KEY  ('id')
);
```

3. Generate the `BlogPost` model for the table `blog_post`.

4. Configure master-slave replication between your database servers, for example, as in the article at `https://www.digitalocean.com/community/tutorials/how-to-set-up-master-slave-replication-in-mysql/`.

5. Configure the `db` component in `config/main.php`; here's an example of configuration:

```php
'components' =>
    // ..
    'db' => [
        'class' => 'yii\db\Connection',

        'dsn' => 'mysql:host=4.4.4.4;dbname=masterdb',
        'username' => 'master',
        'password' => 'pass',
        'charset' => 'utf8',

        'slaveConfig' => [
            'username' => 'slave',
            'password' => 'pass',
        ],

        // list of slave configurations
        'slaves' => [
            ['dsn' => 'mysql:host=5.5.5.5;dbname=slavedb']
        ]
    ],
    // ..
]
```

How to do it...

1. Create `TestController.php` as follows:

```php
<?php

namespace app\controllers;

use app\models\BlogPost;
use Yii;
use yii\helpers\Html;
use yii\helpers\VarDumper;
use yii\web\Controller;
```

```
/**
* Class TestController
* @package app\controllers
*/
class TestController extends Controller
{
    public function actionIndex(){

        $masterModel = new BlogPost();
        $masterModel->title = 'Awesome';
        $masterModel->text = 'Something is going on..';
        $masterModel->save();

        $postId = $masterModel->id;

        $replModel = BlogPost::findOne($postId);

        return $this->renderContent(
            Html::tag('h2', 'Master') .
            Html::tag('pre', VarDumper::dumpAsString(
                $masterModel
                    ? $masterModel->attributes
                    : null
            )) .
            Html::tag('h2', 'Slave') .
            Html::tag('pre', VarDumper::dumpAsString(
                $replModel
                    ? $replModel->attributes
                    : null

            ))
        );
    }

}
```

2. Run `test/index` and you should get the output shown in the following screenshot:

Slave servers are used for data reading, whereas the master server is used for writing. After the ActiveRecord model is saved at the master server, new records, replicate to the slave server and then `$replModel` finds records on it.

There's more...

The `\yii\db\Connection` component supports load balancing and failover between slaves. When performing a read query for the first time, the `\yii\db\Connection` component will randomly pick a slave and try connecting to it. If the slave is found dead, it will try another one. If none of the slaves are available, it will connect to the master. By configuring a server status cache, a dead server can be remembered so that it will not be tried again during a certain period of time.

See also

For further information, refer to the following URLs:

- `http://www.yiiframework.com/doc-2.0/guide-db-dao.html#replication-and-read-write-splitting`

- `http://dev.mysql.com/doc/refman/5.6/en/replication.html`

- `http://docs.mongodb.org/manual/tutorial/deploy-replica-set/`

- `http://docs.mongodb.org/manual/tutorial/deploy-replica-set-for-testing/`

Implementing single table inheritance

Relational databases do not support inheritance. If we need to store inheritance in the database, we should somehow support it through code. This code should be efficient, so that it should generate as few JOINs as possible. A common solution to this problem was described by *Martin Fowler* and is named **single table inheritance**.

When we use this pattern, we store all the class tree data in a single table and use the type field to determine a model for each row.

As an example, we will implement the single table inheritance for the following class tree:

Car

|- SportCar

|- FamilyCar

Getting ready

1. Create a new application using the Composer package manager, as described in the official guide at `http://www.yiiframework.com/doc-2.0/guide-start-installation.html`.

2. Create and set up a database. Add the following table:

```
DROP TABLE IF EXISTS 'car';
CREATE TABLE 'car' (
    'id' int(10) UNSIGNED NOT NULL AUTO_INCREMENT,
```

```
'name' varchar(255) NOT NULL,
'type' varchar(100) NOT NULL,
 PRIMARY KEY ('id')
);

INSERT INTO 'car' ('name', 'type')
VALUES ('Ford Focus', 'family'),
('Opel Astra', 'family'),
('Kia Ceed', 'family'),
('Porsche Boxster', 'sport'),
('Ferrari 550', 'sport');
```

3. Use Gii to create a Car model for the car table and generate ActiveQuery for the Car model.

How to do it...

1. Add the following method and property to models/CarQuery.php:

```php
/**
 * @var
 */
public $type;

/**
 * @param \yii\db\QueryBuilder $builder
 *
 * @return \yii\db\Query
 */
public function prepare($builder)
    {
        if ($this->type !== null) {
            $this->andWhere(['type' => $this->type]);
        }
        return parent::prepare($builder);
    }
```

2. Create models/SportCar.php as follows:

```php
<?php

namespace app\models;

use Yii;
```

```
/**
 * Class SportCar
 * @package app\models
 */
class SportCar extends Car
{
    const TYPE = 'sport';

    /**
     * @return CarQuery
     */
    public static function find()
    {
        return new CarQuery(get_called_class(), ['where' =>
        ['type' => self::TYPE]]);
    }

    /**
     * @param bool $insert
     *
     * @return bool
     */
    public function beforeSave($insert)
    {
        $this->type = self::TYPE;
        return parent::beforeSave($insert);
    }
}
```

3. Create `models/FamilyCar.php` as follows:

```
<?php

namespace app\models;

use Yii;

/**
 * Class FamilyCar
 * @package app\models
 */
```

```php
class FamilyCar extends Car
{
    const TYPE = 'family';

    /**
     * @return CarQuery
     */
    public static function find()
    {
        return new CarQuery(get_called_class(), ['where' =>
        ['type' => self::TYPE]]);
    }

    /**
     * @param bool $insert
     *
     * @return bool
     */
    public function beforeSave($insert)
    {
        $this->type = self::TYPE;
        return parent::beforeSave($insert);
    }
}
```

4. Add the following method to `models/Car.php`:

```php
/**
 * @param array $row
 *
 * @return Car|FamilyCar|SportCar
 */
public static function instantiate($row)
{
    switch ($row['type']) {
        case SportCar::TYPE:
            return new SportCar();
        case FamilyCar::TYPE:
            return new FamilyCar();
        default:
            return new self;
    }
}
```

5. Add `TestController` with the following code:

```php
<?php

namespace app\controllers;

use app\models\Car;
use app\models\FamilyCar;
use Yii;
use yii\helpers\Html;
use yii\web\Controller;

/**
 * Class TestController
 * @package app\controllers
 */
class TestController extends Controller
{
    public function actionIndex()
    {
        echo Html::tag('h1', 'All cars');

        $cars = Car::find()->all();
        foreach ($cars as $car) {
            // Each car can be of class Car, SportCar or
            FamilyCar
            echo get_class($car).' '.$car->name."<br />";
        }

        echo Html::tag('h1', 'Family cars');

        $familyCars = FamilyCar::find()->all();
        foreach($familyCars as $car)
        {
            // Each car should be FamilyCar
            echo get_class($car).' '.$car->name."<br />";
        }
    }
}
```

6. Run `test/index` and you should get the output shown in the following screenshot:

All cars

app\models\FamilyCar Ford Focus
app\models\FamilyCar Opel Astra
app\models\FamilyCar Kia Ceed
app\models\SportCar Porsche Boxster
app\models\SportCar Ferrari 550

Family cars

app\models\FamilyCar Ford Focus
app\models\FamilyCar Opel Astra
app\models\FamilyCar Kia Ceed

How it works...

The base model `Car` is a typically-used Yii AR model except that it has two added methods. The `tableName` method explicitly declares the table name to be used for the model. For the `Car` model alone, this does not make sense, but for child models, it will return the same car table, which is just what we want—a single table for the entire class tree. The instantiate method is used by AR internally to create a model instance from the raw data when we call methods such as `Car::find()->all()`. We use a `switch` statement to create different classes based on the type attribute and use the same class if the attribute value is either not specified or points to the non-existing class.

The `SportCar` and `FamilyCar` models simply set the default AR scope, so when we search for models with the `SportCar::model()->` methods, we will get the `SportCar` model only.

See also

Use the following references to learn more about the single table inheritance pattern and Yii Active Record implementation:

▶ `http://martinfowler.com/eaaCatalog/singleTableInheritance.html`
▶ `https://blog.liip.ch/archive/2012/03/27/table-inheritance-with-doctrine.html`
▶ `http://www.yiiframework.com/doc/api/CActiveRecord/`

4
Forms

In this chapter, we will cover the following topics:

- ▶ Writing your own validators
- ▶ Uploading files
- ▶ Adding and customizing CaptchaWidget
- ▶ Customizing Captcha
- ▶ Creating a custom input widget
- ▶ Tabular input
- ▶ Conditional validation
- ▶ Complex forms with multiple models
- ▶ AJAX-dependent drop-down list
- ▶ AJAX validation
- ▶ Creating a custom client-side validation

Introduction

Yii makes working with forms a breeze and the documentation on it is almost complete. Still, there are some areas that need clarification and examples. We will describe them in this chapter.

Writing your own validators

Yii provides a good set of built-in form validators that cover the most typical developer needs and are highly configurable. However, in some cases, a developer may need to create a custom validator.

This recipe is a good example of creating a standalone validator that checks the number of words.

Getting ready

Create a new application by using the Composer package manager, as described in the official guide at http://www.yiiframework.com/doc-2.0/guide-start-installation.html.

How to do it...

1. Create a standalone validator at @app/components/WordsValidator.php as follows:

```php
<?php
namespace app\components;
use yii\validators\Validator;
class WordsValidator extends Validator
{
    public $size = 50;
    public function validateValue($value){
        if (str_word_count($value) > $this->size) {
            return ['The number of words must be less than
            {size}', ['size' => $this->size]];
        }
        return false;
    }
}
```

2. Create an `Article` model at @app/models/Article.php as follows:

```php
<?php
namespace app\models;
use app\components\WordsValidator;
use yii\base\Model;
class Article extends Model
{
```

```
    public $title;
    public function rules()
    {
        return [
            ['title', 'string'],
            ['title', WordsValidator::className(), 'size'
                => 10],
        ];
    }
}
```

3. Create @app/controllers/ModelValidationController.php as follows:

```php
<?php
namespace app\controllers;
use app\models\Article;
use yii\helpers\Html;
use yii\web\Controller;
class ModelValidationController extends Controller
{
    private function getLongTitle()
    {
        return 'There is a very long content for current
        article, '.'it should be less then ten words';
    }
    private function getShortTitle()
    {
        return 'There is a shot title';
    }
    private function renderContentByModel($title)
    {
        $model = new Article();
        $model->title = $title;
        if ($model->validate()) {
            $content = Html::tag('div', 'Model is valid.',[
                'class' => 'alert alert-success',
            ]);
        } else {
            $content = Html::errorSummary($model, [
                'class' => 'alert alert-danger',
            ]);
        }
```

```php
        return $this->renderContent($content);
    }
    public function actionSuccess()
    {
        $title = $this->getShortTitle();
        return $this->renderContentByModel($title);
    }
    public function actionFailure()
    {
        $title = $this->getLongTitle();
        return $this->renderContentByModel($title);
    }
}
```

4. Run the `success` action of the `modelValidation` controller by opening the `index.php?r=model-validation/success` URL, and you'll get the following:

5. Run the `failure` action of the `modelValidation` controller by opening the `index.php?r=model-validation/failure` URL, and you'll get the following:

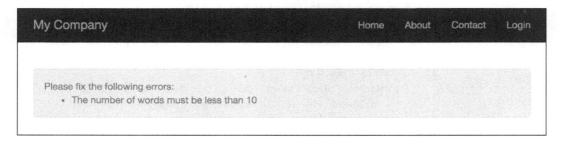

6. Create `@app/controllers/AdhocValidationController.php` as follows:

```php
<?php
namespace app\controllers;
use app\components\WordsValidator;
use app\models\Article;
```

```php
use yii\helpers\Html;
use yii\web\Controller;
class AdhocValidationController extends Controller
{
    private function getLongTitle()
    {
        return 'There is a very long content for current
        article, '.'it should be less then ten words';
    }
    private function getShortTitle()
    {
        return 'There is a shot title';
    }
    private function renderContentByTitle($title)
    {
        $validator = new WordsValidator([
            'size' => 10,
        ]);
        if ($validator->validate($title, $error)) {
            $content = Html::tag('div', 'Value is valid.',[
                'class' => 'alert alert-success',
            ]);
        } else {
            $content = Html::tag('div', $error, [
                'class' => 'alert alert-danger',
            ]);
        }
        return $this->renderContent($content);
    }
    public function actionSuccess()
    {
        $title = $this->getShortTitle();
        return $this->renderContentByTitle($title);
    }
    public function actionFailure()
    {
        $title = $this->getLongTitle();
        return $this->renderContentByTitle($title);
    }
}
```

7. Run the `success` action of the `AdhocValidationController` by opening the `index.php?r=adhoc-validation/success` URL, and you'll get the following:

8. Run the `failure` action of the `adhocValidation` controller by opening the `index.php?r=adhoc-validation/failure` URL, and you'll get the following:

How it works...

First, we created a standalone validator that checks the number of words by using the standard `str_word_count` PHP function, and then demonstrated two validator use cases:

- Using the validator as a validation rule in the `Article` model
- Using the validator as an ad hoc validator

The validator has a size attribute, which sets the maximum value for the number of words.

See also

For further information, refer to the following URLs:

- `http://www.yiiframework.com/doc-2.0/guide-input-validation.html`
- `http://www.yiiframework.com/doc-2.0/guide-tutorial-core-validators.html`

Uploading files

Handling file uploads is a pretty common task for a web application. Yii has some helpful classes built in to do this. Let's create a simple form that will allow the upload of ZIP archives and store them in /uploads.

Getting ready

1. Create a new application by using the Composer package manager, as described in the official guide at http://www.yiiframework.com/doc-2.0/guide-start-installation.html.

2. Create the @app/web/uploads directory.

How to do it...

1. We will start with the model, so create the @app/models/Upload.php model as follows:

```php
<?php
namespace app\models;
use yii\base\Model;
use yii\web\UploadedFile;
class UploadForm extends Model
{
    /**
     * @var UploadedFile
     */
    public $file;
    public function rules()
    {
        return [
            ['file', 'file', 'skipOnEmpty' => false,
            'extensions' => 'zip'],
        ];
    }
    public function upload()
    {
        if ($this->validate()) {
            $this->file->saveAs('uploads/' . $this->file-
            >baseName . '.' . $this->file->extension);
```

```
        return true;
    } else {
        return false;
    }
    }
}
```

2. Now we will move on to the controller, so create `@app/controllers/`
`UploadController.php` as follows:

```php
<?php
namespace app\controllers;
use Yii;
use yii\web\Controller;
use app\models\UploadForm;
use yii\web\UploadedFile;
class UploadController extends Controller
{
    public function actionUpload()
    {
        $model = new UploadForm();
        if (Yii::$app->request->isPost) {
            $model->file =
            UploadedFile::getInstance($model,
            'file');
            if ($model->upload()) {
                return $this->renderContent("File {$model-
                >file->name} is uploaded successfully");
            }
        }
        return $this->render('index', ['model' => $model]);
    }
}
```

3. Finally, you can view `@app/views/upload/index.php` as follows:

```php
<?php
use yii\widgets\ActiveForm;
use yii\helpers\Html;
?>
<?php $form = ActiveForm::begin(['options' => ['enctype' =>
'multipart/form-data']]) ?>
    <?= $form->field($model, 'file')->fileInput() ?>
    <?= Html::submitButton('Upload', ['class' => 'btn-
    success'])?>
<?php ActiveForm::end() ?>
```

4. That is it. Now, run the upload controller and try uploading both ZIP archives and other files, as shown in the following screenshot:

How it works...

The model we use is pretty simple. We define only one field, named $file, and a validation rule that uses the FileValidator file validator, which reads only ZIP files.

We create a model instance and fill it with data from $_POST if the form is submitted:

```
$model->file = UploadedFile::getInstance($model, 'file');
if ($model->upload()) {
    return $this->renderContent("File {$model->file->name} is
    uploaded successfully");
}
```

We then use UploadedFile::getInstance, which gives us access to use the UploadedFile instance. This class is a wrapper around the $_FILE array that PHP fills when the file is uploaded. We make sure that the file is a ZIP archive by calling the model's validate method, then we save the file using UploadedFile::saveAs.

In order to upload a file, the HTML form must meet the following two important requirements:

▸   Method must be set to POST
▸   The enctype attribute must be set to multipart/form-data

It is important to remember that you add the enctype option to the form so that the file can be properly uploaded.

We can generate this HTML using the Html helper or ActiveForm with htmlOptions set. Here, HTML was used:

```
<?= Html::beginForm('', 'post', ['enctype'=>'multipart/form-data'])?>
```

In the end, we display an error and a field for the model's file attribute, and render a submit button.

There's more...

To upload multiple files, Yii2 implements two special methods.

For instance, you have defined `$imageFiles` in your model in the view file in common all will be the same with a little difference:

```
..
<?= $form->field($model, 'imageFiles[]')->fileInput(['multiple' =>
true, 'accept' => 'image/*']) ?>
..
```

To get all file instances, you have to call `UploadedFile::getInstances()` instead of `UploadedFile::getInstance()`:

```
..
$model->imageFiles = UploadedFile::getInstances($model, 'imageFiles');
..
```

Handling and saving multiple files can be done with a simple code snippet:

```
foreach ($this->imageFiles as $file) {
    $file->saveAs('uploads/' . $file->baseName . '.' . $file-
    >extension);
}
```

See also

For further information, refer to:

- http://www.yiiframework.com/doc-2.0/guide-input-file-upload.
  html
- http://www.yiiframework.com/doc-2.0/guide-input-file-upload.
  html#uploading-multiple-files

Adding and customizing CaptchaWidget

Nowadays, on the Internet, if you leave a form without spam protection, you will get a ton of spam data entered in a short time. Yii includes a Captcha component that makes adding such protection a breeze. The only problem is that there is no systematic guide on how to use it.

In the following example, we will add Captcha protection to a simple form.

Getting ready

1. Create a new application by using the Composer package manager, as described in the official guide at `http://www.yiiframework.com/doc-2.0/guide-start-installation.html`.

2. Create a form model, `@app/models/EmailForm.php`, as follows:

```php
<?php
namespace app\models;
use yii\base\Model;
class EmailForm extends Model
{
    public $email;
    public function rules()
    {
        return [
            ['email', 'email']
        ];
    }
}
```

3. Create a controller, `@app/controllers/EmailController.php`, as follows:

```php
<?php
namespace app\controllers;
use Yii;
use yii\web\Controller;
use app\models\EmailForm;
class EmailController extends Controller
{
    public function actionIndex(){
        $success = false;
        $model = new EmailForm();
        if ($model->load(Yii::$app->request->post()) &&
        $model-
        >validate()) {
            Yii::$app->session->setFlash('success',
            'Success!');
        }
        return $this->render('index', [
            'model' => $model,
            'success' => $success,
        ]);
    }
}
```

4. Create a view, `@app/views/email/index.php`, as follows:

```php
<?php
use yii\helpers\Html;
use yii\captcha\Captcha;
use yii\widgets\ActiveForm;
?>
<?php if (Yii::$app->session->hasFlash('success')): ?>
    <div class="alert alert-success"><?=Yii::$app->session-
    >getFlash('success')?></div>
<?php else: ?>
    <?php $form = ActiveForm::begin()?>
        <div class="control-group">
            <div class="controls">
                <?= $form->field($model, 'email')-
                >textInput(['class' => 'form-control']); ?>
                <?php echo Html::error($model, 'email',
                ['class' => 'help-block'])?>
            </div>
        </div>
        <?php if (Captcha::checkRequirements() &&
        Yii::$app->user->isGuest): ?>
            <div class="control-group">
                <?= $form->field($model, 'verifyCode')-
                >widget(\yii\captcha\Captcha::
                classname(), [
                'captchaAction' => 'email/captcha'
                ]) ?>
            </div>
        <?php endif; ?>
        <div class="control-group">
            <label class="control-label" for=""></label>
            <div class="controls">
                <?=Html::submitButton('Submit', ['class' =>
                'btn btn-success'])?>
            </div>
        </div>
    <?php ActiveForm::end()?>
<?php endif;?>
```

5. Now, we have an e-mail submission form, as shown in the following screenshot, which validates the e-mail field. Let's add Captcha:

1. First, we need to customize the form model. We need to add $verifyCode, which will hold the verification code entered and add a validation rule for it:

```php
<?php
namespace app\models;
use yii\base\Model;
use yii\captcha\Captcha;
class EmailForm extends Model
{
    public $email;
    public $verifyCode;
    public function rules()
    {
        return [
            ['email', 'email'],
            ['verifyCode', 'captcha', 'skipOnEmpty' =>
            !Captcha::checkRequirements(), 'captchaAction'
            => 'email/captcha']
        ];
    }
}
```

2. We then need to add an external action to the controller. Add the following code to it:

```php
public function actions()
{
    return [
        'captcha' => [
            'class' => 'yii\captcha\CaptchaAction',
        ],
    ];
}
```

3. In a view, we need to show an additional field and the Captcha image. The following code will do this for us:

```php
...
<?php if (Captcha::checkRequirements() && Yii::$app->user->isGuest): ?>
    <div class="control-group">
        <?=Captcha::widget([
            'model' => $model,
            'attribute' => 'verifyCode',
        ]);?>
        <?php echo Html::error($model, 'verifyCode')?>
    </div>
<?php endif; ?>
...
```

4. Also, do not forget to add the `Captcha` import in the header section of the view:

```php
<?php
    use yii\helpers\Html;
    use yii\captcha\Captcha;
?>
....
```

5. That is it. Now, you can run the e-mail controller and see Captcha in action, as shown in the following screenshot:

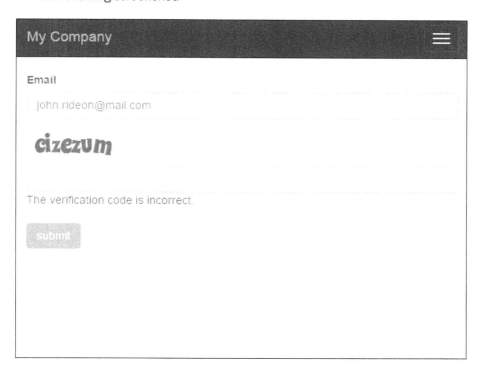

If there are no errors on the screen and no `Captcha` field on the form, most probably, you don't have the GD PHP or Imagick extensions installed and configured. Imagick or GD is required for Captcha because it generates images. We have added several `Captcha::checkRequirements()` checks, so the application will not use Captcha if the image cannot be displayed, but it will still work.

How it works...

In a view, we call the Captcha widget that renders the `img` tag with a `src` attribute pointing to the Captcha action we added to the controller. In this action, an image with a random word is generated. The word generated is a code that the user should enter into the form. It is stored in a user session and an image is displayed to the user. When the user enters the e-mail and verification code into the form, we assign these values to the form model and then validate it. For the verification of the code field, we use `CaptchaValidator`. It gets the code from the user session and compares it to the code entered. If they don't match, the model data is considered invalid.

If you restrict access to controller actions by using the `accessRules` controller method, don't forget to grant everyone access to them:

```
public function behaviors()
{
    return [
        'access' => [
            'class' => AccessControl::className(),
            'rules' => [
                [
                    'actions' => ['index', 'captcha'],
                    'allow' => true,
                ]
            ],
        ],
    ];
}
```

Customizing Captcha

A standard Yii Captcha is good enough to protect you from spam, but there are situations where you may want to customize it, such as the following:

- You face a spam bot that can read image text and you need to add more security
- You want to make it more interesting or easier to enter the Captcha text

In our example, we will modify Yii's Captcha so it will require the user to solve a really simple arithmetic puzzle instead of just repeating the text in an image.

Getting ready

As a starting point for this example, we will take the result of the *Adding and customizing CaptchaWidget* recipe. Alternatively, you can take any form that uses Captcha, as we are not modifying the existing code a lot.

How to do it...

We need to customize `CaptchaAction`, which generates the code and renders its image representation. The code should be a random number and the representation should be an arithmetic expression that gives the same result:

1. Create an `@app/components/MathCaptchaAction.php` action as follows:

```php
<?php
namespace app\components;
use \Yii;
use yii\captcha\CaptchaAction;
class MathCaptchaAction extends CaptchaAction
{
    protected function renderImage($code)
    {
        return parent::renderImage($this->getText($code));
    }
    protected function generateVerifyCode()
    {
        return mt_rand((int)$this->minLength,
        (int)$this->maxLength);
    }
    protected function getText($code)
    {
        $code = (int) $code;
        $rand = mt_rand(1, $code-1);
        $op = mt_rand(0, 1);
        if ($op) {
            return $code - $rand . " + "   . $rand;
        }
        else {
            return $code + $rand . " - " . " " . $rand;
        }
    }
}
```

2. Now, in our controller's `actions` method, we need to replace `CaptchaAction` with our own Captcha action, as follows:

```
public function actions()
{
    return [
        'captcha' => [
            'class' => 'app\components\MathCaptchaAction',
            'minLength' => 1,
            'maxLength' => 10,
        ],
    ];
}
```

3. Now, run your form and try the new Captcha. It will show arithmetic expressions with numbers from 1 to 10 and will require entering an answer, as shown in the following screenshot:

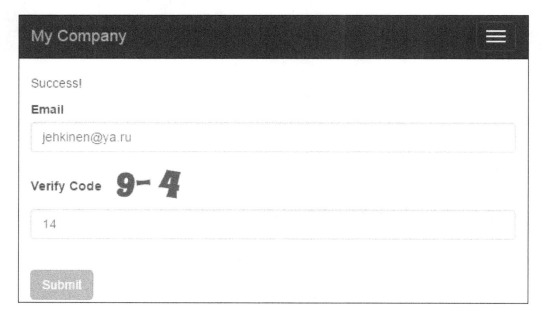

We override two `CaptchaAction` methods. In `generateVerifyCode()`, we generate a random number instead of text. Then, as we need to render an expression instead of just showing text, we override `renderImage`. The expression itself is generated in our custom `getText()` method.

The `$minLength` and `$maxLenght` properties are already defined in `CaptchaAction`, so we don't have to add them to our `MathCaptchaAction` class.

For further information, refer to the following:

- `http://www.yiiframework.com/doc-2.0/yii-captcha-captcha.html`
- `http://www.yiiframework.com/doc-2.0/yii-captcha-captchaaction.html`
- The *Using standalone actions* recipe in *Chapter 2, Routing, Controllers, and Views*

Creating a custom input widget

Yii has a very good set of form widgets, but as with every framework out there, Yii does not have them all. In this recipe, we will learn how to create your own input widget. For our example, we will create a range input widget.

Getting ready

Create a new application by using the Composer package manager, as described in the official guide at `http://www.yiiframework.com/doc-2.0/guide-start-installation.html`.

How to do it...

1. Create a widget file, `@app/components/RangeInputWidget.php`, as follows:

```php
<?php
namespace app\components;
use yii\base\Exception;
use yii\base\Model;
use yii\base\Widget;
use yii\helpers\Html;
class RangeInputWidget extends Widget
{
    public $model;
    public $attributeFrom;
    public $attributeTo;
    public $htmlOptions = [];
    protected function hasModel()
    {
```

```
        return $this->model instanceof Model
        && $this->attributeFrom !== null
        && $this->attributeTo !== null;
    }
    public function run()
    {
        if (!$this->hasModel()) {
            throw new Exception('Model must be set');
        }
        return Html::activeTextInput($this->model, $this->attributeFrom, $this->htmlOptions)
            .' &rarr; '
            .Html::activeTextInput($this->model, $this->attributeTo, $this->htmlOptions);
    }
}
```

2. Create a controller file, @app/controllers/RangeController.php, as follows:

```php
<?php
namespace app\controllers;
use Yii;
use yii\web\Controller;
use app\models\RangeForm;
class RangeController extends Controller
{
    public function actionIndex()
    {
        $model = new RangeForm();
        if ($model->load(Yii::$app->request->post()) &&
        $model->validate()) {
            Yii::$app->session->setFlash('rangeFormSubmitted',
                'The form was successfully processed!'
            );
        }
        return $this->render('index', array(
            'model' => $model,
        ));
    }
}
```

3. Create a form file, @app/models/RangeForm.php, as follows:

```php
<?php
namespace app\models;
use yii\base\Model;
class RangeForm extends Model
{
    public $from;
    public $to;
    public function rules()
    {
        return [
            [['from', 'to'], 'number', 'integerOnly' =>
            true],
            ['from', 'compare', 'compareAttribute' => 'to',
            'operator' => '<='],
        ];
    }
}
```

4. Create a view file, @app/views/range/index.php, as follows:

```php
<?php
use yii\helpers\Html;
use yii\bootstrap\ActiveForm;
use app\components\RangeInputWidget;
?>
<h1>Range form</h1>
<?php if (Yii::$app->session-
    >hasFlash('rangeFormSubmitted')): ?>
    <div class="alert alert-success">
        <?= Yii::$app->session-
        >getFlash('rangeFormSubmitted'); ?>
    </div>
<?php endif?>
<?= Html::errorSummary($model, ['class'=>'alert alert-danger'])?>
<?php $form = ActiveForm::begin([
    'options' => [
        'class' => 'form-inline'
    ]
]); ?>
    <div class="form-group">
        <?= RangeInputWidget::widget([
            'model' => $model,
```

```
                    'attributeFrom' => 'from',
                    'attributeTo' => 'to',
                    'htmlOptions' => [
                        'class' =>'form-control'
                    ]
            ]) ?>
        </div>
        <?= Html::submitButton('Submit', ['class' => 'btn btn-
        primary', 'name' => 'contact-button']) ?>
    <?php ActiveForm::end(); ?>
```

5. Run a `range` controller by opening `index.php?r=range` and you'll get the following:

6. Enter `300` in the first text input field and `200` in the second, and you'll get the following:

7. The widget outputs an error if the first value is bigger than the second; that is it. Try to input correct values, 100 and 200, for the first and second inputs, respectively:

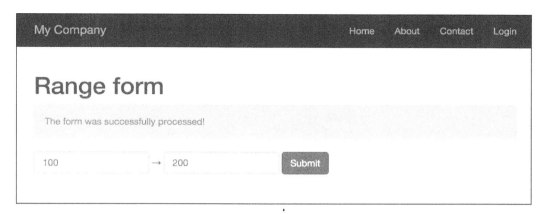

How it works...

We write the range input widget, which requires four parameters:

- ▸ model: If it is not set, an exception will be thrown
- ▸ attributeFrom: This is used to set minimum range value
- ▸ attributeTo: This is used to set maximum range value
- ▸ htmlOptions: It is passed to each input

This widget is used in form validation, and is set to check that the first value is less than or equal to the second value.

There's more...

The Yii2 framework has an official Twitter Bootstrap extension that provides you with a pack of PHP wrappers over Twitter Bootstrap widgets. Before you write your own widget, check whether a Bootstrap widget exists at http://www.yiiframework.com/doc-2.0/ext-bootstrap-index.html.

See also

In order to learn more about widgets, you can use the following resources:

▸ `http://www.yiiframework.com/doc-2.0/yii-base-widget.html`

▸ `https://github.com/yiisoft/yii2-bootstrap/blob/master/docs/guide/usage-widgets.md`

Tabular input

In this section, we will show you how to use a model to save and validate related models. Sometimes you will need to handle multiple models of the same kind in a single form.

For instance, we have contests and prizes for contests. Any contest might contain an unlimited number of prizes. So, we need the ability to create a contest with prizes, validate them, display all errors, and save the primary model (contest model) and all related models (prize models) to the database.

Getting ready

1. Create a new application by using the Composer package manager, as described in the official guide at `http://www.yiiframework.com/doc-2.0/guide-start-installation.html`.

2. Create migrations for contest and prize tables with the following commands:

```
./yii migrate/create create_table_contest_and_prize_table
Update just created migration's methods up() and down() by
following code
public function up()
{
    $tableOptions = null;
    if ($this->db->driverName === 'mysql') {
        $tableOptions = 'CHARACTER SET utf8 COLLATE
        utf8_general_ci ENGINE=InnoDB';
    }
    $this->createTable('{{%contest}}', [
        'id' => Schema::TYPE_PK,
        'name' => Schema::TYPE_STRING . ' NOT NULL',
    ], $tableOptions);
    $this->createTable('{{%prize}}', [
        'id' => Schema::TYPE_PK,
```

```
          'name' => Schema::TYPE_STRING,
          'amount' => Schema::TYPE_INTEGER,
    ], $tableOptions);
    $this->createTable('{{%contest_prize_assn}}', [
        'contest_id' => Schema::TYPE_INTEGER,
        'prize_id' => Schema::TYPE_INTEGER,
    ], $tableOptions);
    $this-addForeignKey('fk_contest_prize_assn_contest_id',
    '{{%contest_prize_assn}}', 'contest_id', {{%contest}}',
    'id');
    $this->addForeignKey('fk_contest_prize_assn_prize_id',
    '{{%contest_prize_assn}}', 'prize_id', '{{%prize}}',
    'id');
}
public function down()
{
    $this-dropForeignKey(
        'fk_contest_prize_assn_contest_id',
    '{{%contest_prize_assn}}');
    $this->dropForeignKey('fk_contest_prize_assn_prize_id',
    '{{%contest_prize_assn}}');
    $this->dropTable('{{%contest_prize_assn}}');
    $this->dropTable('{{%prize}}');
    $this->dropTable('{{%contest}}');
}
```

3. Then, install migration with the following command:

   ```
   ./yii migrate/up
   ```

4. With Gii, generate contest, prize, and ContestPrizeAssn models.

How to do it...

1. Let's create @app/controllers/ContestController.php with the following code:

   ```php
   <?php
   namespace app\controllers;
   use app\models\Contest;
   use app\models\ContestPrizeAssn;
   use app\models\Prize;
   use Yii;
   use yii\base\Model;
   ```

```
use yii\helpers\VarDumper;
use yii\web\Controller;
class ContestController extends Controller
{
    public function actionCreate()
    {
        $contestName = 'Happy New Year';
        $firstPrize = new Prize();
        $firstPrize->name = 'Iphone 6s';
        $firstPrize->amount = 4;
        $secondPrize = new Prize();
        $secondPrize->name = 'Sony Playstation 4';
        $secondPrize->amount = 2;
        $contest = new Contest();
        $contest->name = $contestName;
        $prizes = [$firstPrize, $secondPrize];
        if ($contest->validate() &&
        Model::validateMultiple($prizes)) {
            $contest->save(false);
            foreach ($prizes as $prize) {
                $prize->save(false);
                $contestPrizeAssn = new ContestPrizeAssn();
                $contestPrizeAssn->prize_id = $prize->id;
                $contestPrizeAssn->contest_id =
                $contest>id;
                $contestPrizeAssn->save(false);
            }
            return $this->renderContent(
                'All prizes have been successfully saved!'
            );
        } else {
            return $this->renderContent(
                VarDumper::dumpAsString($contest-
                >getErrors())
            );
        }
    }
    public function actionUpdate()
    {
        $prizes = Prize::find()->all();
```

```
        if (Model::loadMultiple($prizes, Yii::$app-
        >request->post()) &&
        Model::validateMultiple($prizes)) {
            foreach ($prizes as $prize) {
                $prize->save(false);
            }
            return $this->renderContent(
                'All prizes have been successfully saved!'
            );
        }
        return $this->render('update', ['prizes' =>
        $prizes]);
    }
}
```

2. Create @app/views/contest/update.php and place the following code inside it:

```php
<?php
use yii\helpers\Html;
use yii\widgets\ActiveForm;
$form = ActiveForm::begin();
foreach ($prizes as $i => $prize) {
    echo $form->field($prize, "[$i]amount")->label($prize-
    >name);
}
echo Html::submitButton('submit' , ['class' => 'btn btn-
success']);
ActiveForm::end();
```

How it works...

The following information shows how to implement tabular input with Yii.

In the contest/update action, we will be able to display all prizes with their amounts and edit them all at once. We've used two special Yii methods:

▶ Model::loadMultiple(): This method populates a set of models with data from the end user

▶ Model::validateMultiple(): This methods takes a set of models and validates them all at once

Because we've validated our models before with validateMultiple(), we're passing false as a parameter to save() to avoid running validation twice.

First, visit `/index.php?r=contest/create` page. After visiting, you will see the page that will validate and create `'Happy New Year'` with two prizes, and will pass the prizes to the current contest model. You should note that we will only save the contest model and prizes to the database if they are valid:

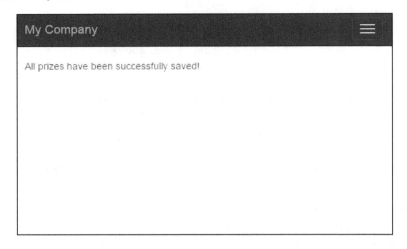

It is provided by following condition:

```
if ($contest->validate() && Model::validateMultiple($prizes)) { ...}
```

Go to the `/index.php?r=contest/update` page and you will see this form:

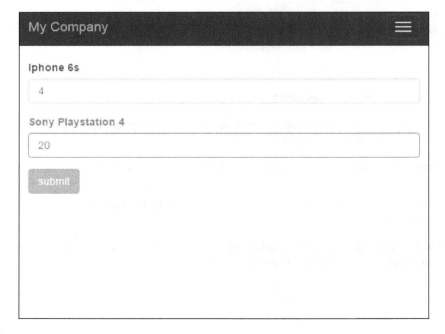

In the `@app/views/contest/update.php` for each prize, we render a name and an input with an amount. We must add an index to each input name so that `Model::loadMultiple()` may identify which model to fill with which values.

In conclusion, this approach is used for collecting tabular input data when you process all your attributes from a view form and populate parent and related models from the form.

See also

For further information, refer to the following URL:

`http://www.yiiframework.com/doc-2.0/guide-input-tabular-input.html#collecting-tabular-input`

Conditional validation

There are cases when it is necessary to enable or disable specific validation rules in the model. Yii2 provides a mechanism to do that.

Getting ready

Create a new application by using the Composer package manager, as described in the official guide at `http://www.yiiframework.com/doc-2.0/guide-start-installation.html`.

How to do it...

1. Create a form file, `@app/models/DeliveryForm.php`, as follows:

```php
<?php
namespace app\models;
use app\components\WordsValidator;
use yii\base\Model;
class DeliveryForm extends Model
{
    const TYPE_PICKUP = 1;
    const TYPE_COURIER = 2;
    public $type;
    public $address;
    public function rules()
    {
```

```
                return [
                    ['type', 'required'],
                    ['type', 'in', 'range'=>[self::TYPE_PICKUP,
self::TYPE_COURIER]],
                    ['address', 'required', 'when' => function ($model) {
                        return $model->type == self::TYPE_COURIER;
                    }, 'whenClient' => "function (attribute, value) {
                        return $('#deliveryform-type').val() ==
'".self::TYPE_COURIER."';
                    }"]
                ];
        }
        public function typeList()
        {
            return [
                self::TYPE_PICKUP => 'Pickup',
                self::TYPE_COURIER => 'Courier delivery',
            ];
        }
    }
```

2. Create a controller file, @app/controllers/ValidationController.php, as follows:

```php
<?php
namespace app\controllers;
use Yii;
use yii\web\Controller;
use app\models\DeliveryForm;
class ValidationController extends Controller
{
    public function actionIndex()
    {
        $model = new DeliveryForm();
        if ($model->load(Yii::$app->request->post()) &&
        $model->validate()) {
            Yii::$app->session->setFlash('success',
                'The form was successfully processed!'
            );
        }
        return $this->render('index', array(
            'model' => $model,
        ));
    }
}
```

3. Create a view file, `@app/views/validation/index.php`, as follows:

```php
<?php
use yii\bootstrap\ActiveForm;
use yii\helpers\Html;
?>
    <h1>Delivery form</h1>
    <?php if (Yii::$app->session->hasFlash('success')): ?>
    <div class="alert alert-success"><?= Yii::$app-
    >session->getFlash('success'); ?></div>
    <?php endif; ?>
    <?php $form = ActiveForm::begin(); ?>
    <?= $form->field($model, 'type')->dropDownList($model-
    >typeList(), [
        'prompt'=>'Select delivery type']
    ) ?>
    <?= $form->field($model, 'address') ?>
    <div class="form-group">
        <?= Html::submitButton('Submit', ['class' => 'btn
        btn-primary']) ?>
    </div>
<?php ActiveForm::end(); ?>
```

4. Run the `validation` controller by opening the `index.php?r=validation` URL, and choose the `courier delivery` value for type input; then you'll get the following:

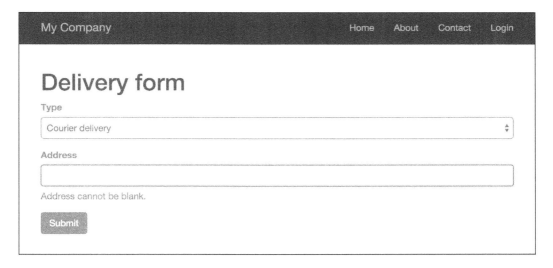

How it works...

The `DeliveryForm address` attribute is required when the `type` attribute is set to `DeliveryForm::TYPE_COURIER`; otherwise, we choose the `Courier delivery` option in `type` select.

Also, to support client-side conditional validation, we configure the `whenClient` property, which takes a string representing a JavaScript function whose return value determines whether to apply the rule or not.

See also

For further information, refer to `http://www.yiiframework.com/doc-2.0/guide-input-validation.html#conditional-validation`

Complex forms with multiple models

When dealing with some complex data, it is possible that you may need to use multiple different models to collect the user input. For example, you have an order form with user information such as first name, last name, and phone number; you also have a delivery address and some kind of product.

You would like to save all this data in one form. With Yii models and support forms, you can easily do this. Assuming that the user info will be stored in the user table and in the order form, we will save product information and the `user_id` of the user who has ordered a product. We also have a product table with some information in it.

Getting ready

1. Create a new application by using the Composer package manger, as described in the official guide at `http://www.yiiframework.com/doc-2.0/guide-start-installation.html`.

2. Create migrations for contest and prize tables with the following commands:

   ```
   ./yii migrate/create create_order_tables
   ```

3. Update the newly-created migration's `up()` and `down()` methods with the following code:

   ```php
   <?php
   use yii\db\Schema;
   use yii\db\Migration;
   ```

```php
use app\models\Product;
class m150813_161817_create_order_form_tables extends Migration
{
    public function up()
    {
        $tableOptions = null;
        if ($this->db->driverName === 'mysql') {
            $tableOptions = 'CHARACTER SET utf8 COLLATE
            utf8_general_ci ENGINE=InnoDB';
        }
        $this->createTable('user', [
            'id' => Schema::TYPE_PK,
            'first_name' => Schema::TYPE_STRING . ' NOT
            NULL',
            'last_name' => Schema::TYPE_STRING . ' NOT
            NULL',
            'phone' => Schema::TYPE_STRING . ' NOT NULL',
        ], $tableOptions);
        $this->createTable('product', [
            'id' => Schema::TYPE_PK,
            'title' => Schema::TYPE_STRING . ' NOT NULL',
            'price' => Schema::TYPE_FLOAT . '(6,2) ',
        ], $tableOptions);
        $this->createTable('order', [
            'id' => Schema::TYPE_PK,
            'user_id' => Schema::TYPE_INTEGER . ' NULL',
            'address' => Schema::TYPE_STRING . ' NOT NULL',
            'product_id' => Schema::TYPE_INTEGER . ' NOT
            NULL',
        ], $tableOptions);
        $product1 = new Product();
        $product1->title = 'Iphone 6';
        $product1->price = 400.5;
        $product1->save();
        $product3 = new Product();
        $product3->title = 'Samsung Galaxy Note 5';
        $product3->price = 900;
        $product3->save();
        $this->addForeignKey('fk_order_product_id',
        'order', 'product_id', 'product', 'id');
    }
}
```

```
        public function down()
        {
            $this->dropTable('order');
            $this->dropTable('user');
            $this->dropTable('product');
        }
    }
```

4. Then, install migration with the following command:

   ```
   ./yii migrate/up
   ```

5. With Gii, generate user, order, and product models.

How to do it...

1. Create @app/controllers/TestController with the following code:

```php
<?php
namespace app\controllers;
use app\models\Order;
use app\models\User;
use Yii;
use yii\web\Controller;
class TestController extends Controller
{
    public function actionOrder()
    {
        $user = new User();
        $order = new Order();
        if ($user->load(Yii::$app->request->post()) &&
        $order->load(Yii::$app->request->post())) {
        if ($user->validate() && $order->validate()) {
            $user->save(false);
            $order->user_id = $user->id;
            $order->save(false);
            $this->redirect(['/test/result', 'id' =>
            $order->id]);
            }
        }
        return $this->render('order', ['user' => $user,
        'order' => $order]);
    }
```

```php
        public function actionResult($id)
        {
            $order = Order::find($id)->with('product', 'user')-
            >one();
            return $this->renderContent(
                'Product: ' . $order->product->
                title . '</br>' .
                'Price: ' . $order->product->price . '</br>' .
                'Customer: ' . $order->user->first_name . ' ' .
                $order->user->last_name . '</br>' .
                'Address: ' . $order->address
            );
        }
    }
```

2. Then create a view file, `@app/views/test/order.php`, and add the following code:

```php
<?php
use yii\helpers\Html;
use yii\widgets\ActiveForm;
use app\models\Product;
use yii\helpers\ArrayHelper;
/**
 * @var $user \app\models\User
 * @var $order \app\models\Order
 */
$form = ActiveForm::begin([
    'id' => 'order-form',
    'options' => ['class' => 'form-horizontal'],
]) ?>
<?= $form->field($user, 'first_name')->textInput(); ?>
<?= $form->field($user, 'last_name')->textInput(); ?>
<?= $form->field($user, 'phone')->textInput(); ?>
<?= $form->field($order, 'product_id')->dropDownList(ArrayHelper::
map(Product::find()->all(),
'id', 'title')); ?>
<?= $form->field($order, 'address')->textInput(); ?>
<?= Html::submitButton('Save', ['class' => 'btn btn-primary']) ?>
<?php ActiveForm::end() ?>
```

How it works...

You can see the form at `http://yii-book.app/index.php?r=test/order`. Our form collects information from the user and order models.

Let's fill out our form:

After saving, you will see the following result:

In the controller, we validate and store it. Of course, this example is very simple. In real projects, you may have more than one model and you will be able to use this approach for them. This approach is very useful when you want to create or update more than one instance in the same form.

See also

See also

For further information, refer to `http://www.yiiframework.com/doc-2.0/guide-input-multiple-models.html`

AJAX-dependent drop-down list

Often, you'll need a form with two dropdowns, and one dropdown's values will be dependent on the value of the other dropdown. Using Yii's built-in AJAX functionality, you can create such a dropdown.

Getting ready

1. Create a new application by using composer, as described in the official guide at `http://www.yiiframework.com/doc-2.0/guide-start-installation.html`.

2. Create an `@app/model/Product.php` model as follows:

```php
<?php
namespace app\models;
use yii\db\ActiveRecord;
class Product extends ActiveRecord
{
    public function rules()
    {
        return [
            ['title', 'string'],
            [['title', 'category_id', 'sub_category_id'],
            'required'],
            ['category_id', 'exist', 'targetAttribute' =>
            'id', 'targetClass' => 'app\models\Category'],
            ['sub_category_id', 'exist', 'targetAttribute'
            => 'id', 'targetClass' =>
            'app\models\Category'],
        ];
    }
    public function attributeLabels()
    {
        return [
```

```
                'category_id' => 'Category',
                'sub_category_id' => 'Sub category',
            ];
        }
    }
```

3. Create an `@app/models/Category.php` model as follows:

```php
<?php
namespace app\models;
use yii\db\ActiveRecord;
class Category extends ActiveRecord
{
    public function rules()
    {
        return [
            ['title', 'string'],
        ];
    }
    /**
     * @return array
     */
    public static function getSubCategories($categoryId)
    {
        $subCategories = [];
        if ($categoryId) {
            $subCategories = self::find()
                ->where(['category_id' => $categoryId])
                ->asArray()
                ->all();
        }
        return $subCategories;
    }
}
```

4. Create a `create_category_and_product_tables` migration with the following command:

```
./yii migrate/create create_category_and_product_tables
```

5. Update the just-created migration's methods and list of imported classes as follows:

```php
<?php
use yii\db\Schema;
```

```php
use yii\db\Migration;
class m150813_005030_create_categories extends Migration
{
    public function up()
    {
        $tableOptions = null;
        $this->createTable('{{%product}}', [
            'id' => Schema::TYPE_PK,
            'category_id' => Schema::TYPE_INTEGER . ' NOT
            NULL',
            'sub_category_id' => Schema::TYPE_INTEGER . '
            NOT NULL',
            'title' => Schema::TYPE_STRING . ' NOT NULL',
        ], $tableOptions);
        $this->createTable('{{%category}}', [
            'id' => Schema::TYPE_PK,
            'category_id' => Schema::TYPE_INTEGER,
            'title' => Schema::TYPE_STRING . ' NOT NULL',
        ], $tableOptions);
        $this->addForeignKey('fk_product_category_id',
        '{{%product}}', 'category_id', '{{%category}}',
        'id');
        $this->addForeignKey('fk_product_sub_category_id',
        '{{%product}}', 'category_id', '{{%category}}',
        'id');
        $this->batchInsert('{{%category}}', ['id',
        'title'], [
            [1, 'TV, Audio/Video'],
            [2, 'Photo'],
            [3, 'Video']
        ]);
        $this->batchInsert('{{%category}}', ['category_id',
        'title'], [
            [1, 'TV'],
            [1, 'Acoustic System'],
            [2, 'Cameras'],
            [2, 'Flashes and Lenses '],
            [3, 'Video Cams'],
            [3, 'Action Cams'],
            [3, 'Accessories']
        ]);
    }
```

```php
    public function down()
    {
        $this->dropTable('{{%product}}');
        $this->dropTable('{{%category}}');
    }
}
```

How to do it...

1. Create a controller file, `@app/controllers/DropdownController.php`, as follows:

```php
<?php
namespace app\controllers;
use app\models\Product;
use app\models\Category;
use app\models\SubCategory;
use Yii;
use yii\helpers\ArrayHelper;
use yii\helpers\Json;
use yii\web\Controller;
use yii\web\HttpException;
class DropdownController extends Controller
{
    public function actionGetSubCategories($id)
    {
        if (!Yii::$app->request->isAjax) {
            throw new HttpException(400, 'Only ajax request
            is allowed.');
        }
        return
        Json::encode(Category::getSubCategories($id));
    }
    public function actionIndex()
    {
        $model = new Product();
        if ($model->load(Yii::$app->request->post()) &&
        $model->validate()) {
            Yii::$app->session->setFlash('success',
            'Model was successfully saved'
            );
        }
```

```
            return $this->render('index', [
                'model' => $model,
            ]);
        }
    }
```

2. Create a view file, @app/views/dropdown/index.php, as follows:

```php
<?php
use yii\bootstrap\ActiveForm;
use yii\helpers\Html;
use yii\helpers\Url;
use app\models\Category;
use yii\helpers\ArrayHelper;
use yii\web\View;
$url = Url::toRoute(['dropdown/get-sub-categories']);
$this->registerJs("
(function(){
    var select = $('#product-sub_category_id');
    var buildOptions = function(options) {
        if (typeof options === 'object') {
            select.children('option').remove();
            $('<option />')
                .appendTo(select)
                .html('Select a sub category')
            $.each(options, function(index, option) {
                $('<option />', {value:option.id})
                .appendTo(select)
                .html(option.title);
            });
        }
    };
    var categoryOnChange = function(category_id){
        $.ajax({
            dataType: 'json',
            url: '" . $url . "&id=' + category_id ,
            success: buildOptions
        });
    };
    window.buildOptions = buildOptions;
```

```
        window.categoryOnChange = categoryOnChange;
})();
", View::POS_READY);
?>
<h1>Product</h1>
<?php if (Yii::$app->session->hasFlash('success')): ?>
    <div class="alert alert-success"><?= Yii::$app-
    >session->getFlash('success'); ?></div>
<?php endif; ?>
<?php $form = ActiveForm::begin(); ?>
    <?= $form->field($model, 'title')->textInput() ?>
    <?= $form->field($model, 'category_id')->dropDownList(
    ArrayHelper::map(
        Category::find()->where('category_id IS NULL')-
        >asArray()->all(),'id', 'title'), [
        'prompt' => 'Select a category',
        'onChange' => 'categoryOnChange($(this).val());',
    ]) ?>
    <?= $form->field($model, 'sub_category_id')-
    >dropDownList(
        ArrayHelper::map(Category::getSubCategories($model-
        >sub_category_id), 'id' ,'title'), [
        'prompt' => 'Select a sub category',
    ]) ?>
    <div class="form-group">
        <?= Html::submitButton('Submit', ['class' => 'btn
        btn-primary']) ?>
    </div>
<?php ActiveForm::end(); ?>
```

3. Run the `dropdown` controller by opening `index.php?r=dropdown`, then add a new product with the value `Canon - EOS Rebel T6i DSLR` for the title field:

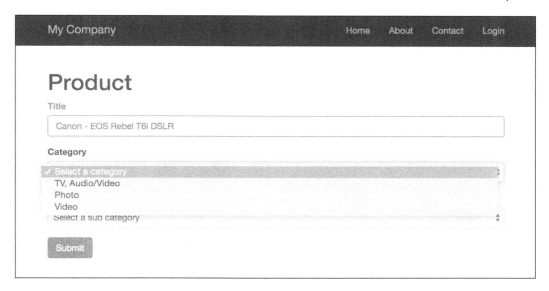

4. As you can see, the `Category` input has three options. Let's select the **Photo** option and after that, the second input selection will have two further options:

5. That is it. If you select another category, you will get sub-categories of this category.

How it works...

In this example, we have two dependent lists with categories and sub-categories, and one model, `Category`. The main idea is simple: we just bound the JQuery `onChange` event to the `category_id` field in our form. Every time a user changes this field, our app sends an AJAX request to the `get-sub-categories` action. This action returns a JSON-formatted list of sub-categories, and then, on the client-side, we build a list of options for our sub-categories list.

AJAX validation

Some validations can only be done on the server-side, because only the server has the necessary information. For example, to validate that a company name or user e-mail is unique, we have to check the corresponding tables on the server side. In this case, you should use built-in AJAX validation. Yii2 supports AJAX form validation, which essentially sends the form values to the server, validates them, and sends back the validation errors, all without leaving the page. It does this every time you tab out of a (changed) field.

Getting ready

Create a new application by using the Composer package manager, as described in the official guide at `http://www.yiiframework.com/doc-2.0/guide-start-installation.html`.

How to do it...

1. In the basic app template, we have a simple contact form. You can see this page at `http://yii-book.app/index.php?r=site/contact`. Open and modify the related view form, `@app/views/site/contact.php`. To enable AJAX validation for the whole form, set up the `enableAjaxValidation` option as `true` in the `form` config:

```
$form = ActiveForm::begin([
    'id' => 'contact-form',
    'enableAjaxValidation' => true,
]);
```

2. Also, you should add handling for the AJAX validation on the server-side. This code snippet just checks whether the current request is AJAX and if it's a POST request. If it is, we will receive errors in JSON format:

```
if (Yii::$app->request->isAjax && $model->load(Yii::$app->request->post())) {
    Yii::$app->response->format = Response::FORMAT_JSON;
    return ActiveForm::validate($model);
}
```

3. Let's modify our `actionContact()` in the `SiteController` with the following code:

```
public function actionContact()
{
    $model = new ContactForm();
    if (Yii::$app->request->isAjax && $model->load(Yii::$app->request->post())) {
        Yii::$app->response->format = Response::FORMAT_JSON;
        return ActiveForm::validate($model);
    }
    if ($model->load(Yii::$app->request->post()) && $model->contact(Yii::$app->params['adminEmail'])) {
        Yii::$app->session->setFlash('contactFormSubmitted');
        return $this->refresh();
    } else {
        return $this->render('contact', [
            'model' => $model,
        ]);
    }
}
```

How it works...

The previous code will check whether the current request is AJAX. If it is, it will respond to this request by running the validation and returning the errors in JSON format.

You can check the response from the server in the debug panel in the browser. Try to submit an empty form and you will see the response.

For example, in the Google Chrome browser, press *F12* and select the **Network** tab in the development toolbar. You will see the JSON array with errors and messages:

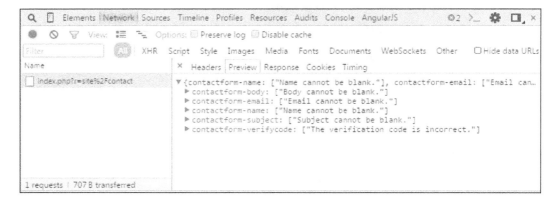

See also

```
http://www.yiiframework.com/doc-2.0/guide-input-validation.html#ajax-
validation
```

Creating a custom client-side validation

In the *Writing your own validators* recipe, we created a standalone validator. In this recipe, we will modify a validator to create extra client-side validation, which also checks the number of words.

Getting ready

Create a new application by using the Composer package manger, as described in the official guide at `http://www.yiiframework.com/doc-2.0/guide-start-installation.html`.

How to do it...

1. Create @app/components/WordsValidator.php as follows:

```php
<?php
namespace app\components;
use yii\validators\Validator;
class WordsValidator extends Validator
{
```

```php
    public $size = 50;
    public $message = 'The number of words must be less
    than {size}';
    public function validateValue($value)
    {
        preg_match_all('/(\w+)/i', $value, $matches);
        if (count($matches[0]) > $this->size) {
            return [$this->message, ['size' => $this-
                >size]];
        }
    }
    public function clientValidateAttribute($model,
    $attribute, $view)
    {
        $message = strtr($this->message, ['{size}' =>
        $this->size]);
        return <<<JS
        if (value.split(/\w+/gi).length > $this->size ) {
            messages.push("$message");
        }
JS;
    }
}
```

2. Create @app/models/Article.php as follows:

```php
<?php
namespace app\models;
use app\components\WordsValidator;
use yii\base\Model;
class Article extends Model
{
    public $title;
    public function rules()
    {
        return [
            ['title', 'string'],
            ['title', WordsValidator::className(), 'size'
                => 10],
        ];
    }
}
```

3. Create @app/controllers/ValidationController.php as follows:

```php
<?php
namespace app\controllers;
use app\models\Article;
use Yii;
use yii\web\Controller;
class ValidationController extends Controller
{
    public function actionIndex()
    {
        $model = new Article();
        if ($model->load(Yii::$app->request->post()) &&
        $model->validate()) {
            Yii::$app->session->setFlash('success', 'Model
            is valid');
        }
        return $this->render('index', [
            'model' => $model,
        ]);
    }
}
```

4. Create @app/views/validation/index.php as follows:

```php
<?php
use yii\bootstrap\ActiveForm;
use yii\helpers\Html;
?>
<h1>Article form</h1>
<?php if (Yii::$app->session->hasFlash('success')): ?>
    <div class="alert alert-success"><?= Yii::$app-
    >session->getFlash('success'); ?></div>
<?php endif; ?>
<?php $form = ActiveForm::begin(); ?>
    <?= $form->field($model, 'title') ?>
    <div class="form-group">
        <?= Html::submitButton('Submit', ['class' => 'btn
        btn-primary']) ?>
    </div>
<?php ActiveForm::end(); ?>
```

How it works...

Run the validation controller by opening `index.php?r=validation`. You will see an example of an incorrect value if you enter more than ten words:

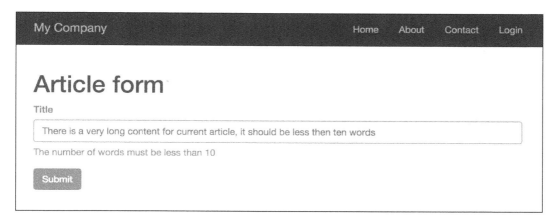

If you enter fewer than ten words, client-side validation will be successful:

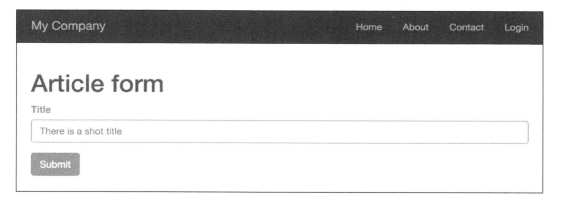

First, we created `@app/components/WordsValidator.php`, which extends the `@yii\validators\Validator` class, and added the newly-created validator class to the title attribute of the `Article` model:

```
..
['title', WordsValidator::className(), 'size' => 10],
..
```

Inside our validator, we've defined two special methods: `validateValue()` and `clientValidateAttribute()`.

Our validator class implements the `validateValue()` method to support data validation out of the context of a data model. The second method just returns the JavaScript needed for performing client-side validation.

There's more...

If we would like to hide validator realization, or want to control all validation processes only on the server-side, we can create a `Deferred` object.

First, modify the `WordsValidator` validator as follows:

```php
<?php
namespace app\components;
use yii\validators\Validator;
use yii\helpers\Url;
class WordsValidator extends Validator
{
    public $size = 50;
    public $message = 'The number of words must be less
    than {size}';
    public function validateValue($value)
    {
        if (str_word_count($value) > $this->size) {
            return ['The number of words must be less
            than {size}', ['size' => $this->size]];
        }
        return false;
    }
    public function clientValidateAttribute($model,
    $attribute, $view)
    {
        $url = Url::toRoute(['validation/check-words']);
        return <<<JS
        deferred.push($.get("$url", {
        words: value}).done(function(data) {
            if (!data.result) {
                messages.push(data.error);
            }
        }));
        JS;
    }
}
```

In the preceding code, the deferred variable is provided by Yii, which is an array of `Deferred` objects. The `$.get()` jQuery method creates a `Deferred` object, which is pushed to the `deferred` array.

Second, add this `checkWords` action to the `validation` controller:

```
public function actionCheckWords()
{
    \Yii::$app->response->
    format = \yii\web\Response::FORMAT_JSON;
    $value = Yii::$app->getRequest()->get('words');
    $validator = new WordsValidator([
    'size' => 10,
    ]);
    $result = $validator->validate($value, $error);
    return [
    'result' => $result,
    'error' => $error
    ];
}
```

See also

For further information, refer to the following URLs:

▸ http://www.yiiframework.com/doc-2.0/guide-input-validation.
html#implementing-client-side-validation

▸ http://www.yiiframework.com/doc-2.0/guide-input-validation.
html#deferred-validation

5
Security

In this chapter, we will cover the following topics:

- ▶ Authentication
- ▶ Using controller filters
- ▶ Preventing XSS
- ▶ Preventing SQL injections
- ▶ Preventing CSRF
- ▶ Using RBAC
- ▶ Encrypting/Decrypting data

Introduction

Security is a crucial part of any web application.

In this chapter, you will learn how to keep your application secure according to the general web application security principle "filter input, escape output". We will cover topics such as creating your own controller filters, preventing XSS, CSRF, and SQL injections, escaping output, and using role-based access control. To know security best practices refer to `http://www.yiiframework.com/doc-2.0/guide-security-best-practices.html#avoiding-debug-info-and-tools-at-production`.

Authentication

Most web applications provide a way for users to log in or reset their forgotten passwords. In Yii2, we don't have this opportunity by default. For a `basic` application template, Yii provides only two test users by default, which are statically described in the `User` model. So, we have to implement special code to be able to enable user login from the database.

Getting ready

1. Create a new application by using the Composer package manager, as described in the official guide at `http://www.yiiframework.com/doc-2.0/guide-start-installation.html`.

2. In the component section of your config, add:

```
'user' => [
    'identityClass' => 'app\models\User',
    'enableAutoLogin' => true,
],
```

3. Create a `User` table. Create a migration by entering the following command:

`./yii migrate/create create_user_table`

4. Update the just created migration with the following code:

```php
<?php

use yii\db\Schema;
use yii\db\Migration;

class m150626_112049_create_user_table extends Migration
{
  public function up()
  {
      $tableOptions = null;
      if ($this->db->driverName === 'mysql') {
          $tableOptions = 'CHARACTER SET utf8 COLLATE
          utf8_general_ci ENGINE=InnoDB';
      }

      $this->createTable('{{%user}}', [
          'id' => Schema::TYPE_PK,
          'username' => Schema::TYPE_STRING . ' NOT NULL',
          'auth_key' => Schema::TYPE_STRING . '(32) NOT
          NULL',
```

```
            'password_hash' => Schema::TYPE_STRING . ' NOT
            NULL',
            'password_reset_token' => Schema::TYPE_STRING,
        ], $tableOptions);
    }

    public function down()
    {
        $this->dropTable('{{%user}}');
    }
}
```

5. Update the existing `models/User` model with the following code:

```php
<?php

namespace app\models;
use yii\db\ActiveRecord;
use yii\web\IdentityInterface;
use yii\base\NotSupportedException;
use Yii;

class User extends ActiveRecord implements IdentityInterface
{
  /**
   * @inheritdoc
   */
  public function rules()
  {
      return [

          ['username', 'required'],
          ['username', 'unique'],
          ['username', 'string', 'min' => 3],
          ['username', 'match', 'pattern' => '~^[A-Za-z][A-
          Za-z0-9]+$~', 'message' => 'Username can contain
          only alphanumeric characters.'],

          [['username', 'password_hash',
          'password_reset_token'],
              'string', 'max' => 255
          ],
          ['auth_key', 'string', 'max' => 32],
      ];
  }
```

```php
/**
 * @inheritdoc
 */
public static function findIdentity($id)
{
    return static::findOne($id);
}

public static function findIdentityByAccessToken($token,
$type = null)
{
    throw new NotSupportedException
    ('"findIdentityByAccessToken" is not implemented.');
}

/**
 * Finds user by username
 *
 * @param   string      $username
 * @return User
 */
public static function findByUsername($username)
{
    return static::findOne(['username' => $username]);
}
/**
 * @inheritdoc
 */
public function getId()
{
    return $this->getPrimaryKey();
}

/**
 * @inheritdoc
 */
public function getAuthKey()
{
    return $this->auth_key;
}

/**
 * @inheritdoc
 */
```

```php
public function validateAuthKey($authKey)
{
    return $this->getAuthKey() === $authKey;
}

/**
 * Validates password
 *
 * @param  string  $password password to validate
 * @return boolean if password provided is valid for
 current user
 */
public function validatePassword($password)
{
    return Yii::$app->getSecurity()-
    >validatePassword($password, $this->password_hash);
}

/**
 * Generates password hash from password and sets it to
 the model
 *
 * @param string $password
 */
public function setPassword($password)
{
    $this->password_hash = Yii::$app->getSecurity()-
    >generatePasswordHash($password);
}

/**
 * Generates "remember me" authentication key
 */
public function generateAuthKey()
{
    $this->auth_key = Yii::$app->getSecurity()-
    >generateRandomString();
}

/**
 * Generates new password reset token
 */
public function generatePasswordResetToken()
{
```

```php
        $this->password_reset_token = Yii::$app-
        >getSecurity()->generateRandomString() .
        '_' . time();
    }

    /**
     * Finds user by password reset token
     *
     * @param  string        $token password reset token
     * @return static|null
     */

    public static function findByPasswordResetToken($token)
    {
        $expire = Yii::$app-
        >params['user.passwordResetTokenExpire'];
        $parts = explode('_', $token);
        $timestamp = (int) end($parts);
        if ($timestamp + $expire < time()) {
            return null;
        }
        return static::findOne([
            'password_reset_token' => $token
        ]);
    }
}
```

6. Create a migration, which will add a test user. Use the following command:

   `./yii migrate/create create_test_user`

7. Update the just created migration with the following code:

```php
<?php

use yii\db\Migration;
use app\models\User;

class m150626_120355_create_test_user extends Migration
{
  public function up()
  {
        $testUser = new User();
        $testUser->username = 'admin';
        $testUser->setPassword('admin');
        $testUser->generateAuthKey();
```

```
    $testUser->save();

    }

    public function down()
    {
        User::findByUsername('turbulence')->delete();
        return false;
    }
}
```

8. Install all migrations with the following command:

    ./yii migrate up

How to do it...

1. Now, follow the URL `site/login` action and enter `admin/admin` as your credentials:

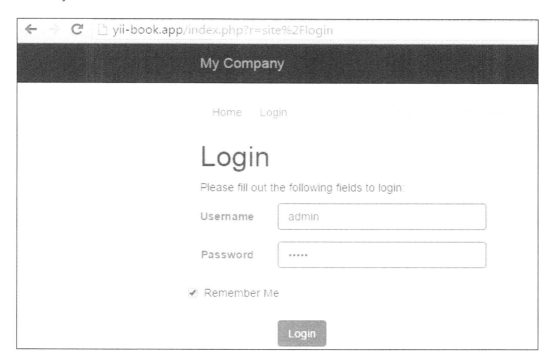

2. Congratulations! If you have completed these steps, you should able to log in.

How it works...

1. First, we created a migration for the user table. Apart from our ID and username, our table contains special fields such as `auth_key` (the main use of this is to authenticate the user by cookie), `password_hash` (for security reasons we won't store the password as it is and will store only the password hash), and `password_ reset_token` (used when we need to reset the user's password).

2. The result after installation and `create_test_user` migration should look like the following screenshot:

id	username	auth_key	password_hash	password_reset_token
1	admin	01rtC0h3jOC5ziMxAk92CpYZJ1cMSGMM	$2y$13$KJ8RjbY3DCgdFxQOvW82N.m2Zrh6F6pPjde2FNg3gH8...	NULL

We've also added special methods to the `User` model and changed the inheritance to `class User extends ActiveRecord implements IdentityInterface` because we need to be able to find users in the database.

You also can copy the `User` model from an advanced app at `https://github.com/ yiisoft/yii2-app-advanced/blob/master/common/models/User.php`.

See also

For further information, refer to `http://www.yiiframework.com/doc-2.0/guide- security-authentication.html`

Using controller filters

In many cases, we need to filter the incoming data or perform some actions based on the data. For example, with custom filters, we can filter visitors by IP, force users to use HTTPS, or redirect the user to an installation page prior to using the application.

In Yii2, filters are essentially a special kind of behavior, so using filters is the same as using behaviors.

Yii has a lot of built-in usable filters, which include:

► Core
► Custom
► Authentication
► Content Negotiator
► HttpCache

- ▶ PageCache
- ▶ RateLimiter
- ▶ Verb
- ▶ Cors

In this recipe, we will implement the following:

- ▶ Limiting access to the controller action to authorized users only
- ▶ Limiting access to the controller action to specified IPs
- ▶ Limiting access to specific user roles

Getting ready

1. Create a new application by using the Composer package manager, as described in the official guide at `http://www.yiiframework.com/doc-2.0/guide-start-installation.html`.

2. Create `app/components/AccessRule.php`:

```php
<?php

namespace app\components;

use app\models\User;
class AccessRule extends \yii\filters\AccessRule {

  /**
   * @inheritdoc
   */
  protected function matchRole($user)
  {
      if (empty($this->roles)) {
          return true;
      }
      $isGuest = $user->getIsGuest();
      foreach ($this->roles as $role) {
          switch($role) {
              case '?':
                  return ($isGuest) ? true : false;
              case User::ROLE_USER:
                  return (!$isGuest) ? true : false;
              case $user->identity->role: // Check if the
              user is logged in, and the roles match
```

```
                            return (!$isGuest) ? true : false;
                    default:
                            return false;
                }
            }
            return false;
        }
    }
```

3. Create app/controllers/AccessController.php as follows:

```php
<?php

namespace app\controllers;
use app\models\User;
use Yii;
use yii\filters\AccessControl;
use app\components\AccessRule;
use yii\web\Controller;

class AccessController extends Controller
{
    public function behaviors()
    {
        return [
            'access' => [
                'class' => AccessControl::className(),
                // We will override the default rule config
                with the new AccessRule class
                'ruleConfig' => [
                    'class' => AccessRule::className(),
                ],
                'rules' => [
                    [
                        'allow' => true,
                        'actions' => ['auth-only'],
                        'roles' => [User::ROLE_USER]
                    ],
                    [
                        'allow' => true,
                        'actions' => ['ip'],
                        'ips' => ['127.0.0.1'],
                    ],
                    [
                        'allow' => true,
```

```php
                        'actions' => ['user'],
                        'roles' => [ User::ROLE_ADMIN],
                    ],
                    [
                        'allow' => false,
                    ]
                ],
            ]
        ];
    }

    public function actionAuthOnly()
    {
        echo "Looks like you are authorized to run me.";
    }
    public function actionIp()
    {
        echo "Your IP is in our list. Lucky you!";
    }
    public function actionUser()
    {
        echo "You're the right man. Welcome!";
    }
}
```

4. Modify the User class as follows:

```php
<?php

namespace app\models;

class User extends \yii\base\Object implements \yii\web\
IdentityInterface
{
 // add roles contstants
  CONST ROLE_USER  = 200;
  CONST ROLE_ADMIN  = 100;

  public $id;
  public $username;
  public $password;
  public $authKey;
  public $accessToken;
  public $role;
```

```
private static $users = [
    '100' => [
        'id' => '100',
        'username' => 'admin',
        'password' => 'admin',
        'authKey' => 'test100key',
        'accessToken' => '100-token',
        'role' => USER::ROLE_ADMIN // add admin role for
         admin user
    ],
    '101' => [
        'id' => '101',
        'username' => 'demo',
        'password' => 'demo',
        'authKey' => 'test101key',
        'accessToken' => '101-token',
        'role' => USER::ROLE_USER // add user role for
        admin user
    ],
];
...
}
```

How to do it...

1. To use `AccessControl`, declare it in the `behaviors()` method of your controller class. We do this as follows:

```
public function behaviors()
{
    return [
        'access' => [
            'class' => AccessControl::className(),
            'rules' => [
                [
                    'allow' => true,
                    'actions' => ['auth-only'],
                    'roles' => ['@'],
                ],
                [
                    'allow' => true,
                    'actions' => ['ip'],
                    'ips' => ['127.0.0.1'],
                ],
                [
```

```
                  'allow' => true,
                  'actions' => ['user'],
                    'roles' => ['admin'],
             ],
             [
                'allow' => true,
                'actions' => ['user'],
                'matchCallback' => function
                ($rule, $action) {
                  return preg_match('/MSIE
                  9/',$_SERVER['HTTP_USER_AGENT']) !==
                  false;
                }
             ],

             ['allow' => false]
          ],
       ]
    ];
  }
```

2. Now try to run controller actions using Internet Explorer and other browsers by using both the `admin` and `demo` usernames.

How it works...

We will start with limiting access to the controller action to authorized users only. See the following code in the `rules` array:

```
[
   'allow' => true,
   'actions' => ['auth-only'],
   'roles' => [User::ROLE_USER]
],
```

Each array here is an access rule. You can either use `allow=true` or `allow=false` for a deny rule. For each rule, there are several parameters.

By default, Yii does not deny everything, so consider adding `['allow' => false]` to the end of your rules list if you need maximum security.

In our rule, we use two parameters. The first is the actions parameter, which takes an array of actions to which the rule will be applied. The second is the roles parameter, which takes an array of user roles to determine the users this rule applies to.

Yii2's built in Access Control supports only two roles by default: guest (not logged in), represented by ?, and authenticated, represented by @.

With simple access controls, we can just limit access to specific pages or controller actions based on the login state. If users are not logged in when they visit these pages, Yii will redirect them to the login page.

Rules are executed one by one, starting from the top, until one matches. If nothing matches, then the action is treated as allowed.

The next task is to limit access to specific IPs. In this case, the following two access rules are involved:

```
[
    'allow' => true,
    'actions' => ['ip'],
    'ips' => ['127.0.0.1'],
],
```

The first rule allows access to the IP action from a list of IPs specified. In our case, we are using a loopback address, which always points to our own computer. Try changing it to 127.0.0.2, for example, to see how it works when the address does not match. The second rule denies everything, including all other IPs.

Next, we limit access to one specific user role, as follows:

```
[
   'allow' => true,
   'actions' => ['user'],
   'roles' => [ User::ROLE_ADMIN],
],
```

The preceding rule allows a user with a role equal to admin to run the user action. Therefore, if you log in as admin, it will let you in, but if you log in as demo, it will not.

We have overridden the standard `AccessRule` class on our own, which is located in the `components/AccessRule.php` file. Inside our `AccessRule` class, we have overridden the `matchRole` method on our own, where we get and check the current user role and match it with roles from our rules.

Finally, we need to deny access to a specific browser. For this recipe, we are denying only Internet Explorer 9. The rule itself is put on top, so it executes first, as follows:

```
[
    'allow' => true,
    'actions' => ['user'],
    'matchCallback' => function ($rule, $action) {
        return preg_match('/MSIE 9/',$_SERVER['HTTP_USER_AGENT'])
        !== false;
    }
],
```

The detection technique that we are using is not very reliable, as MSIE is contained in many other user agent strings. For a list of possible user agent strings, you can refer to `http://www.useragentstring.com/`.

In the preceding code, we used another filter rule property named `'matchCallback'`. This property will apply only when functions which are described in this property return `true`.

Our function checks if the user agent string contains MSIE 9.0 sting. Depending on your requirements, you can specify any PHP code.

In order to learn more about access control and filters, refer to the following:

- ▸ `http://www.yiiframework.com/doc-2.0/guide-structure-filters.html`
- ▸ `http://www.yiiframework.com/doc-2.0/yii-filters-accesscontrol.html`
- ▸ `http://www.yiiframework.com/doc-2.0/yii-filters-accessrule.html`
- ▸ `https://github.com/yiisoft/yii2/blob/master/docs/guide/structure-filters.md`
- ▸ `http://www.yiiframework.com/doc-2.0/guide-security-authorization.html#access-control-filter`
- ▸ The *Using RBAC* recipe

Preventing XSS

XSS stands for cross-site scripting and is a type of vulnerability that allows one to inject a client-side script (typically JavaScript) in a page viewed by other users. Considering the power of client-side scripting, this can lead to very serious consequences such as bypassing security checks, getting other user's credentials, or data leaks.

In this recipe, we will see how to prevent XSS by escaping the output with both `\yii\helpers\Html` and `\yii\helpers\HtmlPurifier`.

Getting ready

1. Create a new application by using the Composer package manager, as described in the official guide at `http://www.yiiframework.com/doc-2.0/guide-start-installation.html`.

2. Create `controllers/XssController.php`:

```php
<?php

namespace app\controllers;

use Yii;
use yii\helpers\Html;
use yii\web\Controller;

/**
* Class SiteController.
```

```
 * @package app\controllers
 */
class XssController extends Controller
{
    /**
     * @return string
     */
    public function actionIndex()
    {
        $username = Yii::$app->request->get('username',
        'nobody');

        return $this->renderContent(Html::tag('h1',
            'Hello, ' . $username . '!'
        ));
    }
}
```

3. Normally, it will be used as `/xss/simple?username=Administrator`. However, as the main security principle *filter input, escape output* was not taken into account, malicious users will be able to use it in the following way:

    ```
    /xss/simple?username=<script>alert('XSS');</script>
    ```

4. The previous code will result in a script execution, as shown in the following screenshot:

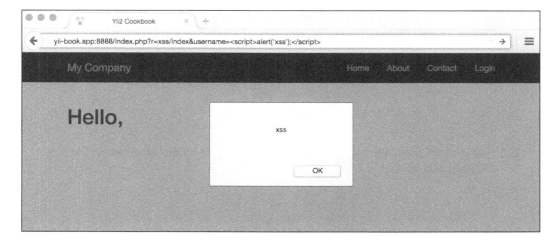

How to do it...

Carry out the following steps:

1. In order to prevent the XSS alert shown in the previous screenshot, we need to escape the data before passing it to the browser. We do this as follows:

```php
<?php

namespace app\controllers;

use Yii;
use yii\helpers\Html;
use yii\web\Controller;

/**
 * Class SiteController.
 * @package app\controllers
 */
class XssController extends Controller
{
    /**
     * @return string
     */
    public function actionIndex()
    {
        $username = Yii::$app->request->get('username',
        'nobody');

        return $this->renderContent(Html::tag('h1',
            Html::encode('Hello, ' . $username . '!')
        ));
    }
}
```

2. Now instead of an alert, we will get properly escaped HTML, as shown in the following screenshot:

3. Therefore, the basic rule is to always escape all dynamic data. For example, we should do the same for a link name:

```
use \yii\helpers\Html;

echo Html::a(Html::encode($_GET['username']), array());
```

That's it. You have a page that is free from XSS. Now, what if we want to allow some HTML to pass? We cannot use \yii\helpers\Html::encode anymore because it will render HTML as just a code and we need the actual representation. Fortunately, there is a tool bundled with Yii that allows you to filter the malicious HTML. It is named HTML Purifier and can be used in the following way:

```php
<?php

namespace app\controllers;

use Yii;
use yii\helpers\Html;
use yii\helpers\HtmlPurifier;
use yii\web\Controller;

/**
 * Class SiteController.
 * @package app\controllers
 */
class XssController extends Controller
{
    /**
     * @return string
     */
```

```
public function actionIndex()
{
    $username = Yii::$app->request->get('username', 'nobody');

    $content = Html::tag('h1', 'Hello, ' . $username . '!');

    return $this->renderContent(
        HtmlPurifier::process($content)
    );
}
}
```

Now if we access the HTML action using a URL such as /xss/
index?username=<i>username</i>!<script>alert('XSS')</script>, HTML
Purifier will remove the malicious part and we will get the following result:

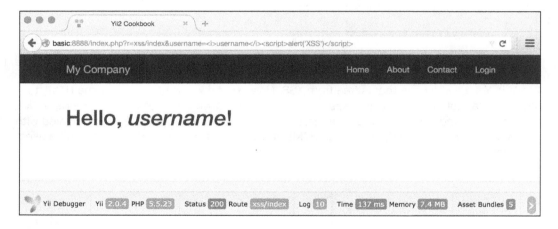

How it works...

1. Internally, \yii\helpers\Html::encode looks like the following:

```
public static function encode($content, $doubleEncode = true)
{
    return htmlspecialchars($content, ENT_QUOTES | ENT_SUBSTITUTE,
Yii::$app ? Yii::$app->charset : 'UTF-8', $doubleEncode);
}
```

2. So basically, we use PHP's internal htmlspecialchars function, which is pretty
secure if one does not forget to pass the correct charset in the third argument.

`\yii\helpers\HtmlPurifier` uses the HTML Purifier library, which is the most advanced solution out there to prevent XSS inside of HTML. We have used its default configuration, which is okay for most user-entered content.

There's more...

There are more things to know about XSS and HTML Purifier; they are discussed in the following section.

XSS types

There are two main types of XSS injections, which are as follows:

- Non-persistent
- Persistent

The first type is the one we have used in the recipe and is the most common XSS type; it can be found in most insecure web applications. Data passed by the user or through a URL is not stored anywhere, so the injected script will be executed only once and only for the user who entered it. Still, it is not as secure as it looks. Malicious users can include XSS in a link to another website and their core will be executed when another user follows the link.

The second type is much more serious, as the data entered by a malicious user is stored in the database and is shown to many, if not all, website users. Using this type of XSS, malicious users can literally destroy your website by commanding all users to delete all data to which they have access.

See also

In order to learn more about XSS and how to deal with it, refer to the following resources:

- `http://htmlpurifier.org/docs`
- `http://ha.ckers.org/xss.html`
- `http://shiflett.org/blog/2007/may/character-encoding-and-xss`

Preventing SQL injections

SQL injection is a type of code injection that uses vulnerability at the database level and allows you to execute arbitrary SQL, allowing malicious users to carry out actions such as deleting data or raising their privileges.

In this recipe, we will see examples of vulnerable code and fix them.

Getting ready

1. Create a new application by using the Composer package manager, as described in the official guide at `http://www.yiiframework.com/doc-2.0/guide-start-installation.html`.

2. Execute the following SQL:
```
DROP TABLE IF EXISTS `user`;
CREATE TABLE `user` (
    `id` int(11) unsigned NOT NULL AUTO_INCREMENT,
    `username` varchar(100) NOT NULL,
    `password` varchar(32) NOT NULL,
    PRIMARY KEY (`id`)
);

INSERT INTO `user`(`id`,`username`,`password`) VALUES (
'1','Alex','202cb962ac59075b964b07152d234b70');

INSERT INTO `user`(`id`,`username`,`password`) VALUES (
'2','Qiang','202cb962ac59075b964b07152d234b70');
```

3. Generate a `User` model using Gii.

How to do it...

1. First, we will implement a simple action that checks whether the username and password that came from a URL are correct. Create `app/controllers/SqlController.php`:
```php
<?php

namespace app\controllers;

use app\models\User;
use Yii;
use yii\base\Controller;
use yii\base\Exception;
use yii\helpers\ArrayHelper;
use yii\helpers\Html;

/**
 * Class SqlController.
 * @package app\controllers
 */
```

```
class SqlController extends Controller
{
    protected function renderContentByResult($result)
    {
        if ($result) {
            $content = "Success";
        } else {
            $content = "Failure";
        }

        return $this->renderContent($content);
    }

    public function actionSimple()
    {
        $userName = Yii::$app->request->get('username');
        $password = Yii::$app->request->get('password');

        $passwordHash = md5($password);

        $sql = "SELECT * FROM `user`"
                ." WHERE `username` = '".$userName."'"
                ." AND password = '".$passwordHash."' LIMIT |
                1";

        $result = Yii::$app->db->createCommand($sql)-
        >queryOne();

        return $this->renderContentByResult($result);
    }

}
```

2. Let's try to access it using the /sql/simple?username=test&password=test
    URL. As we are unaware of both the username and password, it will, as expected,
    print **Failure**.

3. Now try /sql/simple?username=%27+or+%271%27%3D%271%27%3B+--
    &password=whatever. This time, it lets us in, even though we still don't know
    anything about the actual credentials. The decoded part of usernamevalue looks
    like the following:

    ```
    ' or '1'='1'; --
    ```

4. Close the quote so that the syntax stays correct. Add OR `'1'='1'`, which makes the condition always true. Use `;  --` to end the query and comment the rest.

5. As no escaping was done, the whole query executed was:

```
SELECT * FROM user WHERE username = '' or '1'='1'; --' AND
password = '008c5926ca861023c1d2a36653fd88e2' LIMIT 1;
```

6. The best way to fix this is to use a prepared statement, as follows:

```
public function actionPrepared()
{
    $userName = Yii::$app->request->get('username');
    $password = Yii::$app->request->get('password');

    $passwordHash = md5($password);

    $sql = "SELECT * FROM `user`"
            ." WHERE `username` = :username"
            ." AND password = :password LIMIT 1";

    $command = Yii::$app->db->createCommand($sql);
    $command->bindValue(':username', $userName);
    $command->bindValue(':password', $passwordHash);
    $result = $command->queryOne();

    return $this->renderContentByResult($result);
}
```

7. Now check `/sql/prepared` with the same malicious parameters. This time everything was fine and we received the **Failure** message. The same principle applies to ActiveRecord. The only difference here is that AR uses other syntax:

```
public function actionAr()
{
    $userName = Yii::$app->request->get('username');
    $password = Yii::$app->request->get('password');

    $passwordHash = md5($password);

    $result = User::findOne([
        'username' => $userName,
        'password' => $passwordHash
    ]);

    return $this->renderContentByResult($result);
}
```

8. In the previous code, we used the `username` and `password` parameters like an array key with a value style. If we had written the previous code by using only the first argument, it would be vulnerable:

```
public function actionWrongAr()
{
    $userName = Yii::$app->request->get('username');
    $password = Yii::$app->request->get('password');

    $passwordHash = md5($password);

    $condition = "`username` = '".$userName."' AND `password` =
'".$passwordHash."'";

    $result = User::find()->where($condition)->one();

    return $this->renderContentByResult($result);
}
```

9. If used properly, prepared statements can save you from all types of SQL injections. Still, there are some common problems:

   ❏ You can only bind one value to a single parameter, so if you want to query `WHERE IN(1, 2, 3, 4)`, you will have to create and bind four parameters.

   ❏ Prepared statements cannot be used for table names, column names, and other keywords.

10. When using `ActiveRecord`, the first problem can be solved by adding `where`, as follows:

```
public function actionIn()
{
    $names  = ['Alex', 'Qiang'];
    $users = User::find()->where(['username' => $names])-
>all();

    return $this->renderContent(Html::ul(
        ArrayHelper::getColumn($users, 'username')
    ));
}
```

11. The second problem can be solved in multiple ways. The first way is to rely on active record and PDO quoting:

```
public function actionColumn()
{
    $attr = Yii::$app->request->get('attr');
```

```php
    $value = Yii::$app->request->get('value');

    $users = User::find()->where([$attr => $value])->all();

    return $this->renderContent(Html::ul(
        ArrayHelper::getColumn($users, 'username')
    ));
}
```

12. But the most secure way is to use the whitelist approach, as follows:

```php
public function actionWhiteList()
{
    $attr = Yii::$app->request->get('attr');
    $value = Yii::$app->request->get('value');

    $allowedAttr = ['username', 'id'];

    if (!in_array($attr, $allowedAttr)) {
        throw new Exception("Attribute specified is not
        allowed.");
    }

    $users = User::find()->where([$attr => $value])->all();

    return $this->renderContent(Html::ul(
        ArrayHelper::getColumn($users, 'username')
    ));
}
```

How it works...

The main goal when preventing SQL injection is to properly filter the input. In all cases except table names, we have used prepared statements—a feature supported by most relational database servers. They allows you to build statements once and then use them multiple times, and they provide a safe way of binding parameter values.

In Yii, you can use prepared statements for both Active Record and DAO. When using DAO, it can be achieved by using either `bindValue` or `bindParam`. The latter is useful when we want to execute multiple queries of the same type while varying parameter values:

```php
public function actionBind()
{
    $userName = 'Alex';
    $passwordHash = md5('password1');
```

```
$sql = "INSERT INTO `user` (`username`, `password`) VALUES
(:username, :password);";

// insert first user
$command = Yii::$app->db->createCommand($sql);
$command->bindParam('username', $userName);
$command->bindParam('password', $passwordHash);
$command->execute();

// insert second user
$userName = 'Qiang';
$passwordHash = md5('password2');
$command->execute();

return $this->renderContent(Html::ul(
    ArrayHelper::getColumn(User::find()->all(), 'username')
));
}
```

Most Active Record methods accept parameters. To be safe, you should use these instead of just passing the raw data in.

As for quoting table names, columns, and other keywords, you can either rely on Active Record or use the whitelist approach.

See also

In order to learn more about SQL injections and working with databases through Yii, refer to the following:

- ▶ http://www.slideshare.net/billkarwin/sql-injection-myths-and-fallacies
- ▶ http://www.yiiframework.com/doc-2.0/yii-db-connection.html
- ▶ http://www.yiiframework.com/doc-2.0/yii-db-command.html
- ▶ http://www.yiiframework.com/doc-2.0/guide-security-best-practices.html#avoiding-sql-injections
- ▶ The *Getting data from a database* recipe in *Chapter 3, ActiveRecord, Model, and Database*

Preventing CSRF

CSRF is an abbreviation for cross-site request forgery, where a malicious user tricks the user's browser into silently performing an HTTP request to the website when the user is logged in.

An example of such an attack is inserting an invisible image tag with `src` pointing to `http://example.com/site/logout`. Even if the `image` tag is inserted in another website, you will be immediately logged out from `example.com`. The consequences of CSRF can be very serious: destroying website data, preventing all website users from logging in, exposing private data, and so on.

Some facts about CSRF:

▶ As CSRF should be performed by the victim user's browser, the attacker cannot normally change the HTTP headers sent. However, there are both browser and Flash plugin vulnerabilities that exist which allow users to spoof headers, so we should not rely on these.

▶ The attacker should pass the same parameters and values as the user would normally.

Considering these, a good method of dealing with CSRF is by passing and checking a unique token during form submissions and, additionally, using GET according to the HTTP specification.

Yii includes built-in token generation and token checking. Additionally, it can automate inserting a token into the HTML forms.

In order to avoid CSRF, you should always:

▶ Follow, HTTP specification, that is, `GET` should not change its application state

▶ Keep Yii CSRF protection enabled

In this recipe, we will see how to make sure our application is CSRF-resistant.

Getting ready

Create a new application by using the Composer package manager, as described in the official guide at `http://www.yiiframework.com/doc-2.0/guide-start-installation.html`.

How to do it...

1. In order to turn ON the anti-CSRF protection, we should add `config/main.php` as follows:

```
'components' => [
    ..
    request => [
        ..
        'enableCsrfValidation => true,
        ..
    ],
    ..
],
```

2. The option `enableCsrfValidation` defaults to `true`. When CSRF validation is enabled, forms submitted to a Yii web application must originate from the same application. If not, a `400 HTTP exception` will be raised.

   Note that this feature requires that the user client accepts cookies.

3. After configuring the application, you should use `ActiveForm::begin()` and `ActiveForm::end()` instead of HTML form tags in view with ActiveForm:

```
<?php $form = ActiveForm::begin(['id' => 'login-form']); ?>
    <input type='text' name='name'
    .........
<?php ActiveForm::end(); ?>
```

4. OR manually:

```
<form action='#' method='POST'>
    <input type="hidden" name="<?= Yii::$app->request-
    >csrfParam ?>" value="<?=Yii::$app->request-
    >getCsrfToken()?>" />
    ....
</form>
```

5. In the first case, Yii automatically adds a hidden token field, as follows:

```
        <form action="/csrf/create" method="post">
        <div style="display:none"><input type="hidden"
        value="e4d1021e79ac
        269e8d6289043a7a8bc154d7115a" name="YII_CSRF_TOKEN"
        />
```

6. If you save this form as HTML and try submitting it, you will get a message like the one shown in the following screenshot instead of regular data processing:

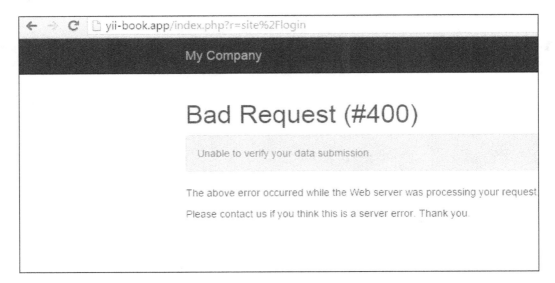

How it works...

Internally, during form rendering, we have code like this:

```
if ($request->enableCsrfValidation && !strcasecmp($method, 'post')) {
    $hiddenInputs[] = static::hiddenInput($request->csrfParam,
    $request->getCsrfToken());
}

if (!empty($hiddenInputs)) {
    $form .= "\n" . implode("\n", $hiddenInputs);
}
```

In the previous code, `getCsrfToken()` generates a unique token value and writes it to a cookie. Then, on subsequent requests, both the cookie and POST values are compared. If they don't match, an error message is shown instead of usual data processing.

If you need to perform a POST request but don't want to build a form using CHtml, then you can pass a parameter with a name from `Yii::app()->request->csrfParam` and a value from `Yii::$app->request->getCsrfToken()`.

There's more...

Lets have a look at some more features.

Disabling CSRF-tokens for all actions

1. If you have a problem with `enableCsrfValidation` you can switch it off.
2. To disable CSRF, add this code to your controller:

```
public function beforeAction($action) {
    $this->enableCsrfValidation = false;
    return parent::beforeAction($action);
}
```

Disabling CSRF-tokens for a specific action

```
public function beforeAction($action) {
    $this->enableCsrfValidation =  ($action->id !== "actionId");
    return parent::beforeAction($action);
}
```

CSRF validation for Ajax-calls

When the `enableCsrfValidation` option is enabled in the main layout,
add `csrfMetaTags`:

```
<head>
  .......
  <?= Html::csrfMetaTags() ?>
</head>

Now you will be able to simply add it to ajax-call
var csrfToken = $('meta[name="csrf-token"]').attr("content");
$.ajax({
        url: 'request'
        type: 'post',
        dataType: 'json',
        data: {param1: param1, _csrf : csrfToken},
});
```

Additionally [rename]

If your application requires a very high security level, such as a bank account management
system, extra measures can be taken.

First, you can turn off the remember me feature using `config/main.php`, as follows:

```
'components' => [
    ..
    'user' => [
        ..
        'enableAutoLogin' => false,
        ..
    ],
    ..
],
```

Note that this will not work if the `enabledSession` option is `true`.

Then, you can lower the session timeout, as follows:

```
'components' => [
    ..
    'session' => [
        ..
        'timeout' => 200,
        ..
    ],
    ..
],
```

This sets the number of seconds after which data will be seen as *garbage* and cleaned up.

Of course, these measures will make the user experience worse, but they will add an additional level of security.

Using GET and POST properly

HTTP insists on not using `GET` operations that change data or state. Sticking to this rule is good practice. It will not prevent all types of CSRF, but it will at least implement some injections, such as `<img src=, pointless>`.

See also

In order to learn more about SQL injections and working with databases through Yii, refer to the following URLs:

► `http://en.wikipedia.org/wiki/Cross-site_request_forgery`
► `http://www.yiiframework.com/doc-2.0/guide-security-best-practices.html#avoiding-csrf`

▸ http://www.yiiframework.com/doc-2.0/yii-web-request.
  html#$enableCsrfValidation-detail

▸ The *Preventing XSS* recipe.

Using RBAC

Role-Based Access Control (**RBAC**) provides simple yet powerful centralized access control. It is the most powerful access control method available in Yii. It is described in the guide, but since it is rather complex and powerful, it is not as easy to understand without getting under the hood a little.

In this recipe, we will take the roles hierarchy from the definitive guide, import it, and explain what is happening internally.

Getting ready

1. Create a new application by using the Composer package manager, as described in the official guide at http://www.yiiframework.com/doc-2.0/guide-start-installation.html.

2. Create a MySQL database and configure it.

3. Configure the `authManager` component in your `config/main.php` and `config/console.php` as follows:

```
return [
    // ...
    'components' => [
        'authManager' => [
            'class' => 'yii\rbac\DbManager',
        ],
        // ...
    ],
];
```

4. Run the migration:

```
yii migrate --migrationPath=@yii/rbac/migrations
```

How to do it...

Carry out the following steps:

1. Create the access rule `rbac/AuthorRule.php`:

```php
<?php

namespace app\rbac;

use yii\rbac\Rule;

/**
 * Class AuthorRule.
 * @package app\rbac
 */
class AuthorRule extends Rule
{
    public $name = 'isAuthor';

    /**
     * @param int|string $user
     * @param \yii\rbac\Item $item
     * @param array $params
     *
     * @return bool
     */
    public function execute($user, $item, $params)
    {
        return isset($params['post']) ? $params['post']-
>createdBy == $user : false;
    }
}
```

2. Create a console command, `command/RbacController.php`, to init the RBAC rules command:

```php
<?php

namespace app\commands;

use app\models\User;
use Yii;
use yii\console\Controller;

/**
```

```php
* Class RbacController.
* @package app\commands
*/
class RbacController extends Controller
{
    public function actionInit()
    {
        $auth = Yii::$app->authManager;

        $createPost = $auth->createPermission('createPost');
        $createPost->description = 'Create a post';

        $updatePost = $auth->createPermission('updatePost');
        $updatePost->description = 'Update a post';

        $updatePost = $auth->createPermission('updatePost');
        $updatePost->description = 'Update a post';

        $deletePost = $auth->createPermission('deletePost');
        $deletePost->description = 'Delete a post';

        $readPost = $auth->createPermission('readPost');
        $readPost->description = 'Read a post';

        $authorRule = new \app\rbac\AuthorRule();

        // add permissions
        $auth->add($createPost);
        $auth->add($updatePost);
        $auth->add($deletePost);
        $auth->add($readPost);
        $auth->add($authorRule);

        // add the "updateOwnPost" permission and associate
        the rule with it.
        $updateOwnPost = $auth-
        >createPermission('updateOwnPost');
        $updateOwnPost->description = 'Update own post';
        $updateOwnPost->ruleName = $authorRule->name;

        $auth->add($updateOwnPost);
        $auth->addChild($updateOwnPost, $updatePost);
```

```
        // create Author role
        $author = $auth->createRole('author');
        $auth->add($author);
        $auth->addChild($author, $createPost);
        $auth->addChild($author, $updateOwnPost);
        $auth->addChild($author, $readPost);

        // create Admin role
        $admin = $auth->createRole('admin');
        $auth->add($admin);
        $auth->addChild($admin, $updatePost);
        $auth->addChild($admin, $deletePost);
        $auth->addChild($admin, $author);

        // assign roles
        $auth->assign($admin, User::findByUsername('admin')-
>id);
        $auth->assign($author, User::findByUsername('demo')-
>id);

        echo "Done!\n";
    }
}
```

3. That's it. Run it in the console:

   yii rbac/init

4. Create `controllers/RbacController.php` as follows:

```php
<?php

namespace app\controllers;

use app\models\User;
use stdClass;
use Yii;
use yii\filters\AccessControl;
use yii\helpers\Html;
use yii\web\Controller;

/**
 * Class RbacController.
 */
class RbacController extends Controller
{
```

```php
public function behaviors()
{
    return [
        'access' => [
            'class' => AccessControl::className(),
            'rules' => [
                [
                    'allow' => true,
                    'actions' => ['delete'],
                    'roles' => ['deletePost'],
                ],
                [
                    'allow' => true,
                    'actions' => ['test'],
                ],
            ],
        ],
    ];
}

public function actionDelete()
{
    return $this->renderContent(
        Html::tag('h1', 'Post deleted.')
    );
}

/**
 * @param $description
 * @param $rule
 * @param array $params
 *
 * @return string
 */
protected function renderAccess($description, $rule,
$params = [])
{
    $access = Yii::$app->user->can($rule, $params);

    return $description.': '.($access ? 'yes' : 'no');
}

public function actionTest()
{
```

```
                    $post = new stdClass();
                    $post->createdBy = User::findByUsername('demo')->id;

                    return $this->renderContent(
                        Html::tag('h1', 'Current permissions').
                        Html::ul([
                            $this->renderAccess('Use can create post',
                            'createPost'),
                            $this->renderAccess('Use can read post',
                            'readPost'),
                            $this->renderAccess('Use can update post',
                            'updatePost'),
                            $this->renderAccess('Use can own update
                            post', 'updateOwnPost', [
                                'post' => $post,
                            ]),
                            $this->renderAccess('Use can delete post',
                            'deletePost'),
                        ])
                    );
                }
            }
```

5. Now run `rbac/test` once to check access to all the created permissions of the RBAC hierarchy:

6. Then, try to log in as `demo` (the password is `demo`) and run `rbac/test` again:

7. Then, try to log in as `admin` (the password is `admin`) and run `rbac/test` again:

8. Log in as `demo` user and run `rbac/delete`:

9. Log in as `admin` and run `rbac/delete`:

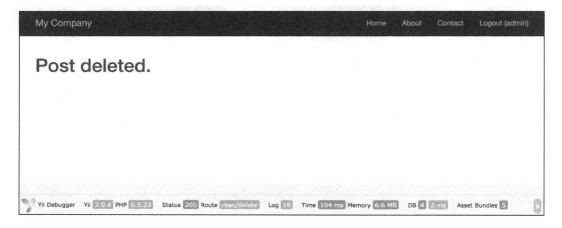

How it works...

Yii implements a general hierarchical RBAC following the `NIST RBAC` model. It provides RBAC functionality through the `authManagerapplication` component.

The RBAC hierarchy is a directed acyclic graph, that is, a set of nodes and their directed connections or edges. There are three types of node available: roles, permissions, and rules.

A role represents a collection of permissions (for example creating posts and updating posts). A role may be assigned to one or multiple users. To check if a user has a specified permission, we may check whether the user is assigned with a role that contains that permission.

Both roles and permissions can be organized in a hierarchy. In particular, a role may consist of other roles or permissions, and a permission may consist of other permissions. Yii implements a partial-order hierarchy, which includes the more special `tree` hierarchy. While a role can contain a permission, it is not true vice versa.

For testing permissions, we have created two actions. The first action, `test`, contains checkers for created permissions and roles. The second action is `delete`, which is limited through the access filter. The rule for the access filter contains the following code:

```
[
    'allow' => true,
    'actions' => ['delete'],
    'roles' => ['deletePost'],
],
```

This means that we are allowing all users who have the `deletePost` permission to run the `deletePost` action. Yii starts checking with the `deletePost` permission. Besides the fact that the access rule element is named as `roles`, you can specify an RBAC hierarchy node be it a role, rule, or permission. Checking for `updatePost` is complex:

```
Yii::$app->user->can('updatePost', ['post' => $post]);
```

We use a second parameter to pass a post (in our case, we have simulated it with `stdClass`). If a user is logged in as `demo`, then to get access we need to go from `updatePost` to author. If you're lucky, you only have to go through `updatePost`, `updateOwnPost`, and author.

As `updateOwnPost` has a rule defined, it will be run with a parameter passed to `checkAccess`. If the result is true, then access will be granted. As Yii does not know what the shortest way is, it tries to check all possibilities until it is successful, or no alternatives are left.

There's more...

There are some useful tricks that will help you to use RBAC efficiently, which are discussed in the following subsections.

Keeping hierarchy simple and efficient

Follow these recommendations where possible to maximize the performance and reduce hierarchy complexity:

- Avoid attaching multiple roles to a single user
- Don't connect nodes of the same type; so, for example, avoid connecting one task to another

Naming RBAC nodes

A complex hierarchy becomes difficult to understand without using some kind of naming convention. One possible convention that helps to limit confusion is as follows:

```
[group_][own_]entity_action
```

Where `own` is used when the rule determines an ability to modify an element only if the current user is the owner of the element and the `group` is just a namespace. The `entity` is the name of the entity we are working with and `action` is the action that we are performing.

For example, if we need to create a rule that determines whether the user can delete a blog post, we will name it `blog_post_delete`. If the rule determines whether a user can edit his or her own blog comment, the name will be `blog_own_comment_edit`.

See also

In order to learn more about SQL injections and working with databases through Yii, refer to the following:

▶ `http://csrc.nist.gov/rbac/sandhu-ferraiolo-kuhn-00.pdf`

▶ `http://en.wikipedia.org/wiki/Role-based_access_control`

▶ `http://en.wikipedia.org/wiki/Directed_acyclic_graph`

▶ `http://www.yiiframework.com/doc-2.0/guide-security-authorization.html#role-based-access-control-rbac`

▶ The *Using controller filters* recipe

Encrypting/Decrypting data

The Yii2 framework contains a special security component that provides a set of methods for handling common security-related tasks. The `\yii\base\Security` class requires the `OpenSSL` PHP extension instead of `mcrypt`.

Getting ready

1. Create a new application by using the Composer package manager, as described in the official guide at `http://www.yiiframework.com/doc-2.0/guide-start-installation.html`.

2. Set up the database connection and create a table named `order`, as follows:

```
DROP TABLE IF EXISTS `order`;
CREATE TABLE IF NOT EXISTS `order` (
`id` INT(10) UNSIGNED NOT NULL AUTO_INCREMENT,
`client` VARCHAR(255) NOT NULL,
```

```
`total` FLOAT NOT NULL,
`encrypted_field` BLOB NOT NULL,
PRIMARY KEY (`id`)
);
```

3. Generate an `Order` model using Gii.

How to do it...

1. Add an additional key parameter to `config/params.php`, as follows:

```php
<?php

return [
    'adminEmail' => 'admin@example.com',
    'key' => 'mysecretkey'
];
```

2. Add the `behaviors` and `helper` properties to the `Order` model as follows:

```php
public $encrypted_field_temp;

public function behaviors()
{
    return [
        [
            'class' => AttributeBehavior::className(),
            'attributes' => [
                ActiveRecord::EVENT_BEFORE_INSERT =>
                'encrypted_field',
                ActiveRecord::EVENT_BEFORE_UPDATE =>
                'encrypted_field',
            ],
            'value' => function ($event) {
                $event->sender->encrypted_field_temp =
                $event->sender->encrypted_field;
                return Yii::$app->security->encryptByKey(
                    $event->sender->encrypted_field,
                    Yii::$app->params['key']
                );
            },
        ],
        [
            'class' => AttributeBehavior::className(),
            'attributes' => [
```

```php
                    ActiveRecord::EVENT_AFTER_INSERT =>
                    'encrypted_field',
                    ActiveRecord::EVENT_AFTER_UPDATE =>
                    'encrypted_field',
                ],
                'value' => function ($event) {
                    return $event->sender->encrypted_field_temp;
                },
            ],
            [
                'class' => AttributeBehavior::className(),
                'attributes' => [
                    ActiveRecord::EVENT_AFTER_FIND =>
                    'encrypted_field',
                ],
                'value' => function ($event) {
                    return Yii::$app->security->decryptByKey(
                        $event->sender->encrypted_field,
                        Yii::$app->params['key']
                    );
                },
            ],
        ];
    }
```

3. Add `controllers/CryptoController.php`:

```php
<?php

namespace app\controllers;

use app\models\Order;
use Yii;
use yii\db\Query;
use yii\helpers\ArrayHelper;
use yii\helpers\Html;
use yii\helpers\VarDumper;
use yii\web\Controller;
```

```php
/**
* Class CryptoController.
* @package app\controllers
*/
class CryptoController extends Controller
{
    public function actionTest()
    {
        $newOrder = new Order();
        $newOrder->client = "Alex";
        $newOrder->total = 100;
        $newOrder->encrypted_field = 'very-secret-info';
        $newOrder->save();

        $findOrder = Order::findOne($newOrder->id);

        return $this->renderContent(Html::ul([
            'New model: ' .
            VarDumper::dumpAsString($newOrder->attributes),
            'Find model: ' .
            VarDumper::dumpAsString($findOrder->attributes)
        ]));

    }


    public function actionRaw()
    {
        $row = (new Query())->from('order')
            ->where(['client' => 'Alex'])
            ->one();

        return $this->renderContent(Html::ul(
            $row
        ));
    }
}
```

4. Run `crypto/test` and you will get the following:

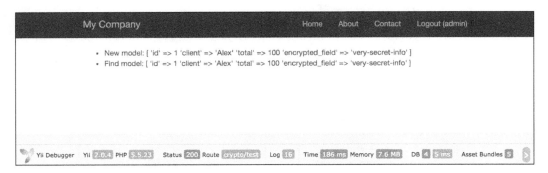

5. To view raw data, run `crypto/raw`:

How it works...

Firstly, we have added the `AttributeBehavior`, which automatically processes our data when certain events happen. Our certain events are `ActiveRecord::EVENT_AFTER_INSERT`, `ActiveRecord::EVENT_AFTER_UPDATE` and `ActiveRecord::EVENT_AFTER_FIND`.

During insert and update events, we decrypt our data with a special method: `Yii::$app->security->encryptByKey();`. This method uses HKDF and a random salt to decrypt our data before saving it to the database. After getting data from the database, we can also use the `ActiveRecord::EVENT_AFTER_FIND` method to decrypt our data. In this case, we also use the special Yii2 method `Yii::$app->security->encryptByKey();`. This method accepts two params: encrypted data and key.

There's more...

Besides data encryption and data decryption, a secure component also provides key derivation using standard algorithms, data tampering prevention, and password validation.

Working with passwords

Verifying a password:

```
if (Yii::$app->getSecurity()->validatePassword($password, $hash)) {
 // all good, logging user in
} else {
 // wrong password
}
```

See also

In order to learn more about SQL injections and working with databases through Yii, refer to http://www.yiiframework.com/doc-2.0/guide-security-passwords.html

RESTful Web Services

6

In this chapter, we will cover the following topics:

- ▶ Creating a REST server
- ▶ Authentication
- ▶ Rate limiting
- ▶ Versioning
- ▶ Error handling

Introduction

This chapter will help you to learn some handy things about the Yii URL router, controllers, and views. You will be able to make your controllers and views more flexible.

Creating a REST server

In the following recipe, we use an example that illustrates how you can build and set up RESTful APIs with minimal coding effort. This recipe will be reused in other recipes in this chapter.

Getting ready

1. Create a new application by using the Composer package manager, as described in the official guide at `http://www.yiiframework.com/doc-2.0/guide-start-installation.html`.

2. Create a migration for creating an article table with the following command:

```
./yii migrate/create create_film_table
```

3. Then, update the just-created migration method, `up`, with the following code:

```
public function up()
    {
        $tableOptions = null;
        if ($this->db->driverName === 'mysql') {
            $tableOptions = 'CHARACTER SET utf8 COLLATE
                utf8_general_ci ENGINE=InnoDB';
        }
        $this->createTable('{{%film}}', [
            'id' => $this->primaryKey(),
            'title' => $this->string(64)->notNull(),
            'release_year' => $this->integer(4)->notNull(),
        ], $tableOptions);

        $this->batchInsert('{{%film}}', ['id',
            'title','release_year'], [
            [1, 'Interstellar', 2014],
            [2, "Harry Potter and the Philosopher's Stone",
            2001],
            [3, 'Back to the Future', 1985],
            [4, 'Blade Runner', 1982],
            [5, 'Dallas Buyers Club', 2013],
        ]);
    }
```

Update the `down` method with the following code:

```
public function down()
{
    $this->dropTable('film');
}
```

4. Run the created `create_film_table` migration.

5. Generate the `Film` model with the Gii module.

6. Configure your application server to use clean URLs. If you are using Apache with `mod_rewrite` and `AllowOverride` turned on, then you should add the following lines to the `.htaccess` file under your `@web` directory:

```
Options +FollowSymLinks
IndexIgnore */*
RewriteEngine on
# if a directory or a file exists, use it directly
```

```
RewriteCond %{REQUEST_FILENAME} !-f
RewriteCond %{REQUEST_FILENAME} !-d
# otherwise forward it to index.php
RewriteRule . index.php
```

How to do it...

1. Create a controller, `@app/controller/FilmController.php`, with the following code:

```php
<?php
    namespace app\controllers;

    use yii\rest\ActiveController;

    class FilmController extends ActiveController
    {
        public $modelClass = app\models\Film';
    }
```

Update the `@app/config/web.php` configuration file. Add the following config of the `urlManager` component:

```php
'urlManager' => [
    'enablePrettyUrl' => true,
    'enableStrictParsing' => true,
    'showScriptName' => false,
    'rules' => [
        ['class' => 'yii\rest\UrlRule', 'controller' => 'films'],
    ],
],
```

2. Reconfigure the request component in `@app/config/web.php`:

```php
'request' => [
    'cookieValidationKey' => 'mySecretKey',
    'parsers' => [
        'application/json' => 'yii\web\JsonParser',
    ],
]
```

How it works...

We extend `\yii\rest\ActiveController` to create our own controller, then for the created controller, the `modelClass` property was set. The `\yii\rest\ActiveController` class implements a common set of actions for supporting RESTful access to ActiveRecord.

With the above minimal amount of effort, you have already finished creating RESTful APIs for accessing film data.

The APIs you have created include:

- ▶ `GET /films`: This lists all films page by page
- ▶ `HEAD /films`: This shows the overview information of a film listing
- ▶ `POST /films`: This creates a new film
- ▶ `GET /films/5`: This returns the details of film 5
- ▶ `HEAD /films/5`: This shows the overview information of film 5
- ▶ `PATCH /films/5 and PUT /films/5`: This updates film 5
- ▶ `DELETE /films/5`: This deletes film 5
- ▶ `OPTIONS /films`: This shows the supported verbs regarding the `/films` endpoint
- ▶ `OPTIONS /films/5`: This shows the supported verbs regarding the `/films/5` endpoint

It works like this because `\yii\rest\ActiveController` supports the following actions:

- ▶ `index`: This lists the models
- ▶ `view`: This returns the details of a model
- ▶ `create`: This creates a new model
- ▶ `update`: This updates an existing model
- ▶ `delete`: This deletes an existing model
- ▶ `options`: This returns the allowed HTTP methods

And there's also a `verbs()` method that defines the allowed request methods for each action.

To check that our RESTful API is working correctly, let's send several requests.

Let's begin with the `GET` request. Run this in the console:

```
curl -i -H "Accept:application/json" "http://yii-book.app/films"
```

You will get the following output:

```
HTTP/1.1 200 OK
Date: Wed, 23 Sep 2015 17:46:35 GMT
Server: Apache
X-Powered-By: PHP/5.5.23
X-Pagination-Total-Count: 5
X-Pagination-Page-Count: 1
X-Pagination-Current-Page: 1
X-Pagination-Per-Page: 20
Link: <http://yii-book.app/films?page=1>; rel=self
Content-Length: 301
Content-Type: application/json; charset=UTF-8

[{"id":1,"title":"Interstellar","release_year":2014},{"id":2,"title":
"Harry Potter and the Philosopher's Stone","release_year":2001},{"id
":3,"title":"Back to the Future","release_year":1985},{"id":4,"title
":"Blade Runner","release_year":1982},{"id":5,"title":"Dallas Buyers
Club","release_year":2013}]
```

Let's send a POST request. Run this in the console:

**curl -i -H "Accept:application/json" -X POST -d title="New film" -d
release_year=2015 "http://yii-book.app/films"**

You will get the following output:

```
HTTP/1.1 201 Created
Date: Wed, 23 Sep 2015 17:48:06 GMT
Server: Apache
X-Powered-By: PHP/5.5.23
Location: http://yii-book.app/films/6
Content-Length: 49
Content-Type: application/json; charset=UTF-8

{"title":"New film","release_year":"2015","id":6}
```

Let's get the created film. Run in this the console:

curl -i -H "Accept:application/json" "http://yii-book.app/films/6"

You will get the following output:

```
HTTP/1.1 200 OK
Date: Wed, 23 Sep 2015 17:48:36 GMT
Server: Apache
```

```
X-Powered-By: PHP/5.5.23
Content-Length: 47
Content-Type: application/json; charset=UTF-8

{"id":6,"title":"New film","release_year":2015}
```

Let's send a DELETE request. Run this in the console:

```
curl -i -H "Accept:application/json" -X DELETE "http://yii-book.app/
films/6"
```

And you will get the following output:

```
HTTP/1.1 204 No Content
Date: Wed, 23 Sep 2015 17:48:55 GMT
Server: Apache
X-Powered-By: PHP/5.5.23
Content-Length: 0
Content-Type: application/json; charset=UTF-8
```

There's more...

We will now look at content negotiation and customizing the Rest URL rule:

Content negotiation

You can also easily format your response with content negotiation behavior.

For example, you can put this code to your controller and all data will be returned in an XML format.

You should have a look at the full list of formats in the documentation.

```
use yii\web\Response;
public function behaviors()
{
    $behaviors = parent::behaviors();
    $behaviors['contentNegotiator']['formats']['application/xml']
        = Response::FORMAT_XML;
    return $behaviors;
}
```

Run this in the console:

```
curl -i -H "Accept:application/xml" "http://yii-book.app/films"
```

You will get the following output:

```
HTTP/1.1 200 OK
Date: Wed, 23 Sep 2015 18:02:47 GMT
Server: Apache
X-Powered-By: PHP/5.5.23
X-Pagination-Total-Count: 5
X-Pagination-Page-Count: 1
X-Pagination-Current-Page: 1
X-Pagination-Per-Page: 20
Link: <http://yii-book.app/films?page=1>; rel=self
Content-Length: 516
Content-Type: application/xml; charset=UTF-8

<?xml version="1.0" encoding="UTF-8"?>
<response>
    <item>
        <id>1</id>
        <title>Interstellar</title>
        <release_year>2014
        </release_year>
    </item>
    <item>
        <id>2</id>


<title>Harry Potter and the Philosopher's Stone</title>
        <release_year>2001
        </release_year>
    </item>
    <item>
        <id>3</id>
        <title>Back to the Future</title>
        <release_year>1985
        </release_year>
    </item>
    <item>
        <id>4</id>
        <title>Blade Runner</title>
        <release_year>1982
        </release_year>
```

```
        </item>
        <item>
            <id>5</id>
            <title>Dallas Buyers Club</title>
            <release_year>2013
            </release_year>
        </item>
    </response>
```

Customizing the Rest URL rule

You have to remember a controller ID, by default, is defined in plural form. This is because `yii\rest\UrlRule` automatically pluralizes controller IDs. You can simply disable this by setting `yii\rest\UrlRule::$pluralize` to false:

```
'urlManager' => [
    //..
    'rules' => [
        [
            'class' => 'yii\rest\UrlRule',
            'controller' => 'film'
            'pluralize' => false
        ],
    ],
    //..
]
```

If you would also like to specify how a controller ID should appear in the patterns, you are able to add a custom name to an array as a key value pair, where the array key is the controller ID and the array value is the actual controller ID. For example:

```
'urlManager' => [
    //..
    'rules' => [
        [
            'class' => 'yii\rest\UrlRule',
            'controller' => ['super-films' => 'film']
        ],
    ],
    //..
]
```

For further information, refer to the following URL:

- ▸ http://www.yiiframework.com/doc-2.0/guide-rest-quick-start.html
- ▸ http://www.yiiframework.com/doc-2.0/yii-rest-urlrule.html
- ▸ http://www.yiiframework.com/doc-2.0/guide-rest-response-formatting.html
- ▸ http://budiirawan.com/setup-restful-api-yii2/

Authentication

In this recipe will have the authentication model set up.

Getting ready

Repeat all steps from the *Creating a REST server* recipe in *Getting ready* and *How to do it* sections.

How to do it...

1. Modify @app/controllers/FilmController to the following:

```php
<?php

namespace app\controllers;

use app\models\User;
use Yii;
use yii\helpers\ArrayHelper;
use yii\rest\ActiveController;
use yii\filters\auth\HttpBasicAuth;

class FilmController extends ActiveController
{
    public $modelClass = 'app\models\Film';

    public function behaviors()
    {
        return ArrayHelper::merge(parent::behaviors(),
        [
            'authenticator' => [
            'authMethods' => [
                'basicAuth' => [
```

```
                                'class' =>
                                HttpBasicAuth::className(),
                                'auth' => function ($username,
                                $password) {
                                    $user =
                                    User::findByUsername($username);

                                    if ($user !== null && $user-
        >validatePassword($password)){
                                            return $user;
                                    }

                                    return null;
                                },
                            ]
                        ]
                    ]

                ]);
            }
        }
```

Open `http://yii-book.app/films` in a browser and make sure that we configure HTTP Basic Authentication:

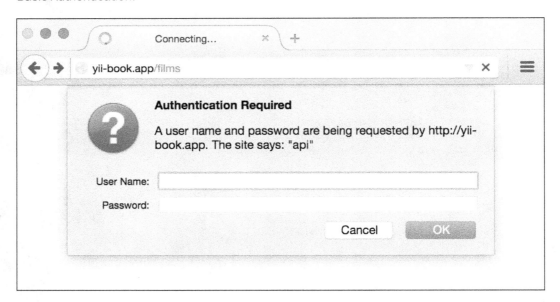

Let's try to authenticate. Run this in the console:

```
curl -i -H "Accept:application/json" "http://yii-book.app/films"
```

And you will get the following:

```
HTTP/1.1 401 Unauthorized
Date: Thu, 24 Sep 2015 01:01:24 GMT
Server: Apache
X-Powered-By: PHP/5.5.23
Www-Authenticate: Basic realm="api"
Content-Length: 149
Content-Type: application/json; charset=UTF-8

{"name":"Unauthorized","message":"You are requesting with an
invalid credential.","code":0,"status":401,"type":"yii\\web\\
UnauthorizedHttpException"}
```

1. And now try `auth` with cURL:

    ```
    curl -i -H "Accept:application/json" -u admin:admin "http://yii-
    book.app/films"
    ```

2. You should then get a response that looks like this:

    ```
    HTTP/1.1 200 OK
    Date: Thu, 24 Sep 2015 01:01:40 GMT
    Server: Apache
    X-Powered-By: PHP/5.5.23
    Set-Cookie: PHPSESSID=8b3726040bf8850ebd07209090333103; path=/;
    HttpOnly
    Expires: Thu, 19 Nov 1981 08:52:00 GMT
    Cache-Control: no-store, no-cache, must-revalidate, post-check=0,
    pre-check=0
    Pragma: no-cache
    X-Pagination-Total-Count: 5
    X-Pagination-Page-Count: 1
    X-Pagination-Current-Page: 1
    X-Pagination-Per-Page: 20
    Link: <http://yii-book.app/films?page=1>; rel=self
    Content-Length: 301
    Content-Type: application/json; charset=UTF-8
    [{"id":1,"title":"Interstellar","release_year":2014},{"id":2,"titl
    e":"Harry Potter and the Philosopher's Stone","release_year":2001}
    ,{"id":3,"title":"Back to the Future","release_year":1985},{"id":4
    ,"title":"Blade Runner","release_year":1982},{"id":5,"title":"Dall
    as Buyers Club","release_year":2013}]
    ```

How it works...

We've also added the `authenticator` behavior to the `HttpBasicAuth` class, so we will be able to authenticate with just a login and password. You might implement any authentication method that is described in the official guide in the RESTful web services section.

There's more...

There are different ways to send an access token:

▶ HTTP Basic Auth

▶ Query parameter

▶ OAuth

Yii supports all of these authentication methods.

See also

For further information, refer to `http://www.yiiframework.com/doc-2.0/guide-rest-rate-limiting.html`.

Rate limiting

To prevent abuse, you should consider adding rate limiting to your APIs. For example, you may want to limit the API usage of each user to be, at most, five API calls within a period of one minute. If too many requests are received from a user within the stated period of time, a response with the status code 429 (*Too Many Requests*) should be returned.

Getting ready

Repeat all the steps from the *Creating a REST server* recipe's *Getting ready* and *How to do it...* sections.

1. Create a migration for creating a user allowance table with the following command:

   ```
   ./yii migrate/create create_user_allowance_table
   ```

2. Then, update the just-created migration method, up, with the following code:

   ```
   public function up()
       {
           $tableOptions = null;
           if ($this->db->driverName === 'mysql') {
   ```

```
        $tableOptions = 'CHARACTER SET utf8 COLLATE
        utf8_general_ci ENGINE=InnoDB';
    }
    $this->createTable('{{%user_allowance}}', [
        'user_id' => $this->primaryKey(),
        'allowed_number_requests' => $this->integer(10)
        ->notNull(),
        'last_check_time' => $this->integer(10)
        ->notNull()
    ], $tableOptions);
}
```

3. Update the `down` methodwith the following code:

```
public function down()
    {
        $this->dropTable('{{%user_allowance}}');
    }
```

4. Run the created `create_film_table` migration.

5. Generate the `UserAllowance` model with the Gii module.

How to do it...

First, you have to update `@app/controllers/FilmController.php` with the following code:

```
<?php

namespace app\controllers;

use yii\rest\ActiveController;
use yii\filters\RateLimiter;
use yii\filters\auth\QueryParamAuth;

class FilmController extends ActiveController
{
    public $modelClass = 'app\models\Film';

    public function behaviors()
    {
        $behaviors = parent::behaviors();
```

```
                    $behaviors['authenticator'] = [
                    'class' => QueryParamAuth::className(),
                    ];

                    $behaviors['rateLimiter'] = [
                    'class' => RateLimiter::className(),
                    'enableRateLimitHeaders' => true
                    ];


                return $behaviors;
            }
        }
```

To enable rate limiting, the User model class should implement yii\filters\
RateLimitInterface and requires the implementation of three methods:
getRateLimit(), loadAllowance(), and saveAllowance(). You have to
add them with RATE_LIMIT_NUMBER and RATE_LIMIT_RESET constants:

```php
<?php

    namespace app\models;

    class User extends \yii\base\Object implements
    \yii\web\IdentityInterface,
    \yii\filters\RateLimitInterface
    {
        public $id;
        public $username;
        public $password;
        public $authKey;
        public $accessToken;

        const RATE_LIMIT_NUMBER = 5;
        const RATE_LIMIT_RESET = 60;

    // it means that user allowed only 5 requests per one minute
        public function getRateLimit($request, $action)
        {
            return [self::RATE_LIMIT_NUMBER,
            self::RATE_LIMIT_RESET];
        }

        public function loadAllowance($request, $action)
        {
```

```
                $userAllowance = UserAllowance::
                findOne($this->id);

                return $userAllowance ?
                [$userAllowance->allowed_number_requests,
                $userAllowance->last_check_time] :
                 $this->getRateLimit($request, $action);
            }

        public function saveAllowance($request, $action,
         $allowance, $timestamp)
        {
            $userAllowance = ($allowanceModel =
            UserAllowance::findOne($this->id)) ?
            $allowanceModel : new UserAllowance();
            $userAllowance->user_id = $this->id;
            $userAllowance->last_check_time = $timestamp;
            $userAllowance->allowed_number_requests =
            $allowance;
            $userAllowance->save();
        }

        // other User model methods
    }
```

How it works...

Once the identity class implements the required interface, Yii will automatically use [[yii\
filters\RateLimiter]] configured as an action filter for [[yii\rest\Controller]]
to perform a rate limiting check. We've also added the 'authenticator' behavior with
the QueryParamAuth class. So, we are now able to authenticate with just an access token
passed through a query parameter. You can add any authentication method that is described
in the official guide in the RESTful web services section.

Let's explain our methods. They are pretty easy to understand.

getRateLimit(): This returns the maximum number of allowed requests and the
time period (example, [100, 600] means there can be at most 100 API calls within
600 seconds)

loadAllowance(): This returns the number of remaining requests allowed and the
corresponding UNIX timestamp when the rate limit was last checked

saveAllowance(): This saves both the number of remaining requests allowed and the
current UNIX timestamp

We store our data in the MySQL database. For performance, you might use a NoSQL database or another storage system with a higher time to get and load data.

Now let's try to check the rate limit feature. Run this in the console:

```
curl -i "http://yii-book.app/films?access-token=100-token"
```

You will get the following output:

```
HTTP/1.1 200 OK
Date: Thu, 24 Sep 2015 01:35:51 GMT
Server: Apache
X-Powered-By: PHP/5.5.23
Set-Cookie: PHPSESSID=495a928978cc732bee853b83f521eba2; path=/;
HttpOnly
Expires: Thu, 19 Nov 1981 08:52:00 GMT
Cache-Control: no-store, no-cache, must-revalidate, post-check=0, pre-
check=0
Pragma: no-cache
X-Rate-Limit-Limit: 5
X-Rate-Limit-Remaining: 4
X-Rate-Limit-Reset: 0
X-Pagination-Total-Count: 5
X-Pagination-Page-Count: 1
X-Pagination-Current-Page: 1
X-Pagination-Per-Page: 20
Link: <http://yii-book.app/films?access-token=100-token&page=1>;
rel=self
Content-Length: 301
Content-Type: application/json; charset=UTF-8

[{"id":1,"title":"Interstellar","release_year":2014},{"id":2,"title":
"Harry Potter and the Philosopher's Stone","release_year":2001},{"id
":3,"title":"Back to the Future","release_year":1985},{"id":4,"title
":"Blade Runner","release_year":1982},{"id":5,"title":"Dallas Buyers
Club","release_year":2013}]
```

Let's learn about returned headers. When rate limiting is enabled, by default every response will be sent with the following HTTP headers containing the current rate limiting information:

X-Rate-Limit-Limit: This is the maximum number of requests allowed within a time period

X-Rate-Limit-Remaining: This is the number of remaining requests in the current time period

X-Rate-Limit-Reset: This is the number of seconds to wait in order to get the maximum number of allowed requests

So, now try to exceed the limit, request the following URL more than five times per minute and you will see `TooManyRequestsHttpExeption`:

```
HTTP/1.1 429 Too Many Requests
Date: Thu, 24 Sep 2015 01:37:24 GMT
Server: Apache
X-Powered-By: PHP/5.5.23
Set-Cookie: PHPSESSID=bb630ca8a641ef92bd210c0a936e3149; path=/;
HttpOnly
Expires: Thu, 19 Nov 1981 08:52:00 GMT
Cache-Control: no-store, no-cache, must-revalidate, post-check=0, pre-
check=0
Pragma: no-cache
X-Rate-Limit-Limit: 5
X-Rate-Limit-Remaining: 0
X-Rate-Limit-Reset: 60
Content-Length: 131
Content-Type: application/json; charset=UTF-8
{"name":"Too Many Requests","message":"Rate limit exceeded.","code":0,
"status":429,"type":"yii\\web\\TooManyRequestsHttpException"}
```

See also

For further information, refer to the following URLs:

- https://en.wikipedia.org/wiki/Leaky_bucket
- http://www.yiiframework.com/doc-2.0/guide-rest-rate-limiting. html
- http://www.yiiframework.com/doc-2.0/yii-filters-ratelimiter. html

Versioning

If you build your API unversioned, it's terrifying. Let's imagine you're pushing out a breaking change – basically any change that runs counter to what client developers have planned for, such as renaming or deleting a parameter or changing the format of the response – you run the risk of bringing down many, if not all, of your customers' systems, leading to angry support calls or, worse, massive churn. That's why you have to keep your API versioned. In Yii2, versioning can be easily done through modules, so versions will be represented as isolated block of code.

Getting ready

Repeat all steps from the *Creating a REST server* recipe's *Getting ready* and *How to do it...* sections.

How to do it...

1. Create the following structure in your app folder. In total, you have to create the @ app/`modules` folder with the `v1` and `v2` folders inside it. In each module's folder, you must create controllers and models folders:

```
app/
    modules/
        v1/
            controllers/
                FilmController.php
            Module.php
        v2/
            controllers/
                FilmController.php
            Module.php
```

2. Add the import modules to @app/`config/web.php`:

```
'modules' => [
    'v1' => [
        'class' => 'app\modules\v1\Module',
    ],
     'v2' => [
        'class' => 'app\modules\v2\Module'
    ]
],
```

3. Create @app/`modules/v1/controllers/FilmController.php` and @app/`modules/v2/controllers/FilmController.php` with the following code:

```php
<?php

namespace app\modules\v2\controllers;

use yii\rest\ActiveController;


class FilmController extends ActiveController
{
```

```
        public $modelClass = 'app\models\Film';
    }

<?php

    namespace app\modules\v1\controllers;

    use yii\rest\ActiveController;


    class FilmController extends ActiveController
    {
        public $modelClass = 'app\models\Film';
    }
```

Create @app/modules/v1/Module.php and @app/modules/v2/Module.php with the following code:

```
<?php
    namespace app\modules\v1;

    class Module extends  \yii\base\Module
    {
        public function init()
        {
            parent::init();
        }
    }

<?php
    namespace app\modules\v2;

    class Module extends  \yii\base\Module
    {
        public function init()
        {
            parent::init();
        }
    }
```

How it works...

Each module represents an independent version of our API.

Now you will be able to specify the API's version in two ways:

1. By the API's URL. You can specify either v1 or v2 versions. The result is that `http://yii-book.app/v1/film` will return a list of films for version 1 and `http://yii-book.app/v2/film` will do so for version 2.

2. You can also put a version number through HTTP request headers. As usual, it can be done through the `Accept` header:

```
// as a vendor content type
Accept: application/vnd.company.myproject-v1+json
// via a parameter
Accept: application/json; version=v1
```

So, we now have two versions of our API, and we can easily modify the v2 version without any headaches. Our old customers continue to work with the v1 version, and new customers or those who would like to upgrade will use the v2 version.

There's more...

Fur further information, refer to:

▶ `http://www.yiiframework.com/doc-2.0/guide-rest-versioning.html`

▶ `http://budiirawan.com/setup-restful-api-yii2/`

Error handling

Sometimes you may want to customize the default error response format. For example, we need to know the response timestamp and whether the response is successful. Frameworks provide an easy way to do this.

Getting ready

Repeat all the steps from the *Creating a REST server* recipe's in the *Getting ready* and *How to do it...* sections.

How to do it...

To achieve this goal, you can respond to the `beforeSend` event of the response component in `@app/config/web.php`, as follows:

```php
'response' => [
    'class' => 'yii\web\Response',
    'on beforeSend' => function ($event) {
        $response = $event->sender;
        if ($response->data !== null) {
            $response->data = [
            'success' => $response->isSuccessful,
            'timestamp' => time(),
            'path' => Yii::$app->request->getPathInfo(),
            'data' => $response->data,
            ];
        }
    },
],
```

How it works...

To learn what happens in this code, let's play a bit with it. First, run this in console:

```
curl -i "http://yii-book.app/films/1"
```

You will get the following output:

```
HTTP/1.1 200 OK
Date: Thu, 24 Sep 2015 04:24:52 GMT
Server: Apache
X-Powered-By: PHP/5.5.23
Content-Length: 115
Content-Type: application/json; charset=UTF-8

{"success":true,"timestamp":1443068692,"path":"films/1","data":{"id":1
,"title":"Interstellar","release_year":2014}}
```

Secondly, run this in your console:

```
curl -i "http://yii-book.app/films/1000"
```

And you will get the following:

```
HTTP/1.1 404 Not Found
Date: Thu, 24 Sep 2015 04:24:26 GMT
Server: Apache
X-Powered-By: PHP/5.5.23
Content-Length: 186
Content-Type: application/json; charset=UTF-8

{"success":false,"timestamp":1443068666,"path":"films/1000","data":{"n
ame":"Not Found","message":"Object not found: 1000","code":0,"status":
404,"type":"yii\\web\\NotFoundHttpException"}}
```

We've changed the response content before sending. That way, it is easy to define whether the response is successful or not.

See also

For further information, refer to `http://www.yiiframework.com/doc-2.0/guide-rest-error-handling.html`.

7
Official Extensions

In this chapter, we will cover the following topics:

- ▶ Authentication client
- ▶ SwiftMailer e-mail library
- ▶ Faker fixture data generator
- ▶ Imagine library
- ▶ MongoDB driver
- ▶ ElasticSearch engine adapter
- ▶ Gii code generator
- ▶ Pjax jQuery plugin
- ▶ Redis database driver

Introduction

Yii2's official repository provides adapters for some popular libraries, databases, and search engines. In this chapter, we will show you how to install and use official extensions in your project. You will also learn how to write your own extension and share it with other developers.

Authentication client

This extension adds OpenID, OAuth, and OAuth2 consumers for the Yii 2.0 framework.

Getting ready

1. Create a new application by using composer, as described in the official guide at `http://www.yiiframework.com/doc-2.0/guide-start-installation.html`.

2. Install the extension with the following command:

```
composer require yiisoft/yii2-authclient
```

How to do it...

1. Open your GitHub applications page `https://github.com/settings/applications` and add your own new application:

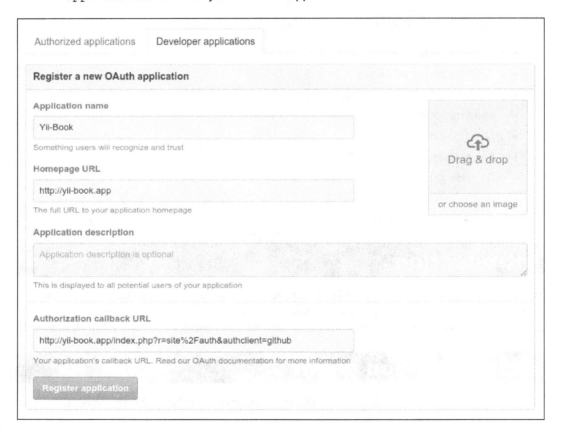

2. Get the **Client ID** and **Client Secret**:

3. Configure your web configuration and set the corresponding options for your `authClientCollection` component:

```
'components' => [
    // ...
    'authClientCollection' => [
        'class' => 'yii\authclient\Collection',
        'clients' => [
            'google' => [
                'class' =>
                'yii\authclient\clients\GoogleOpenId'
            ],
            'github' => [
                'class' => 'yii\authclient\clients\GitHub',
                'clientId' => '87f0784aae2ac48f78a',
                'clientSecret' =>
                'fb5953a54dea4640f3a70d8abd96fbd25592ff18',
            ],
                // etc.
        ],
    ],
],
```

4. Open your `SiteController` and add the `auth` standalone action and success callback method:

```php
use yii\authclient\ClientInterface;

public function actions()
{
    return [
        // ...
        'auth' => [
            'class' => 'yii\authclient\AuthAction',
            'successCallback' => [$this, 'onAuthSuccess'],
        ],
    ];
}

public function onAuthSuccess(ClientInterface $client)
{
    $attributes = $client->getUserAttributes();
    \yii\helpers\VarDumper::dump($attributes, 10, true);
    exit;
}
```

5. Open the `views/site/login.php` file and insert the `AuthChoice` widget:

```php
<div class="site-login">
    <h1><?= Html::encode($this->title) ?></h1>

    <div class="panel panel-default">
        <div class="panel-body">
            <?= yii\authclient\widgets\AuthChoice::widget([
            'baseAuthUrl' => ['site/auth'],
            'popupMode' => false,
            ]) ?>
        </div>
    </div>

    <p>Please fill out the following fields to login:</p>
    ...
</div>
```

6. You will see icons for the providers you've configured:

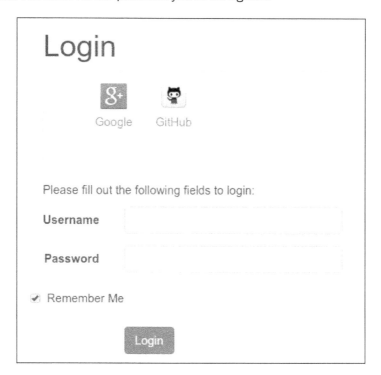

7. Try to authorize with the GitHub provider:

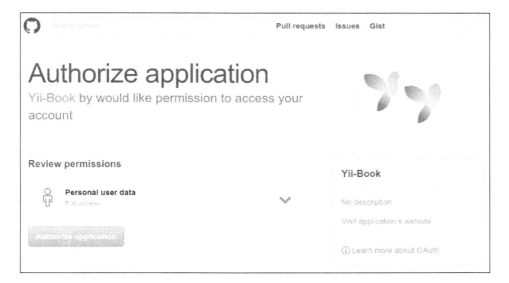

8. If successful, your callback will show authorized user attributes:

```
[
    'login' => 'Name'
    'id' => 0000000
    'avatar_url' =>
    'https://avatars.githubusercontent.com/u/0000000?v=3'
    'gravatar_id' => ''
    'url' => 'https://api.github.com/users/Name'
    'html_url' => 'https://github.com/Name'
    ...
    'name' => 'YourName'
    'blog' =>site.com'
    'email => mail@site.com'
    ...
]
```

9. Create your own authorization code in the `onAuthSuccess` method, like the example at `https://github.com/yiisoft/yii2-authclient/blob/master/docs/guide/quick-start.md`.

How it works...

The extension provides OpenID, OAuth, and OAuth2 auth clients for your application.

The `AuthChoice` widget opens an authenticate page on a selected service's site, storing the `auth` action URL. After authentication, the current service redirects users back while sending authentication data via a POST-request. `AuthAction` receives the request and calls the corresponding callback.

You can use any existing client or create your own one.

See also

► To get more information about extension usage, refer to:

  ❏ `https://github.com/yiisoft/yii2-authclient/tree/master/docs/guide`

  ❏ `http://www.yiiframework.com/doc-2.0/ext-authclient-index.html`

► To learn more about OpenID, OAuth, and OAuth2 authentication technologies, refer to:

  ❏ `http://openid.net`

  ❏ `http://oauth.net`

SwiftMailer e-mail library

Many web applications need to send notifications and confirm client actions by e-mail for security reasons. The Yii2 framework provides a wrapper, `yiisoft/yii2-swiftmailer`, for the established library `SwiftMailer`.

Getting ready

Create a new application by using composer, as described in the official guide at `http://www.yiiframework.com/doc-2.0/guide-start-installation.html`.

Both basic and advanced applications contain this extension out of the box.

How to do it...

Now we will try to send any kind of e-mails from our own application.

Sending plain text e-mails

1. Set the mailer configuration into the `config/console.php` file:

```
'components' => [
    // ...
    'mailer' => [
        'class' => 'yii\swiftmailer\Mailer',
        'useFileTransport' => true,
    ],
    // ...
],
```

2. Create a test console controller, `MailController`, with the following code:

```php
<?php

namespace app\commands;

use yii\console\Controller;
use Yii;

class MailController extends Controller
{
    public function actionSend()
    {
        Yii::$app->mailer->compose()
        ->setTo('to@yii-book.app')
```

```
->setFrom(['from@yii-book.app' => Yii::$app
->name])
->setSubject('My Test Message')
->setTextBody('My Text Body')
->send();
    }
}
```

3. Run the following console command:

   php yii mail/send

4. Examine your `runtime/mail` directory. It should contain files with your mails.

 Note: Mail files contain messages in the special e-mail source format, compatible with any mailing software. You can open this field as a plain text too.

5. Set the `useFileTransport` parameter as false or remove this string from the configuration:

```
'mailer' => [
    'class' => 'yii\swiftmailer\Mailer',
],
```

Then put your real e-mail ID into the `setTo()` method:

```
->setTo('my@real-email.com')
```

6. Run the console command again:

   php yii mail/send

7. Check your `inbox` directory.

 Note: SwiftMailer uses a standard PHP function, `mail()`, for sending mails by default. Please check that your server is correctly configured for sending mails via the `mail()` function.

Many mail systems reject mails without DKIM and SPF signatures (sent by the `mail()` function as example) or put them into a `Spam` folder.

Sending HTML content

1. Check that your application contains the `mail/layouts/html.php` file and add the `mail/layouts/text.php` file with the following content:

```php
<?php
/* @var $this \yii\web\View */
/* @var $message \yii\mail\MessageInterface */
/* @var $content string */
?>
<?php $this->beginPage() ?>
<?php $this->beginBody() ?>
<?= $content ?>
<?php $this->endBody() ?>
<?php $this->endPage() ?>
```

2. Create your own view in the `mail/message-html.php` file:

```php
<?php
use yii\helpers\Html;

/* @var $this yii\web\View */
/* @var $name string */
?>

<p>Hello, <?= Html::encode($name) ?>!</p>
```

Create a `mail/message-text.php` file with the same content, but without HTML tags:

```php
<?php
    use yii\helpers\Html;

/* @var $this yii\web\View */
/* @var $name string */
?>

    Hello, <?= Html::encode($name) ?>!
```

3. Create a console controller, `MailController`, with the following code:

```php
<?php

namespace app\commands;

use yii\console\Controller;
use Yii;

class MailController extends Controller
{
    public function actionSendHtml()
    {
        $name = 'John';

        Yii::$app->mailer->compose('message-html',
        ['name' => $name])
        ->setTo('to@yii-book.app')
        ->setFrom(['from@yii-book.app'
            => Yii::$app->name])
        ->setSubject('My Test Message')
        ->send();
    }

    public function actionSendCombine()
    {
        $name = 'John';

        Yii::$app->mailer->compose(['html' =>
        'message-html', 'text' => 'message-text'], [
        'name' => $name,
        ])
        ->setTo('to@yii-book.app')
        ->setFrom(['from@yii-book.app'
            => Yii::$app->name])
        ->setSubject('My Test Message')
        ->send();
    }
}
```

4. Run the following console commands:

```
php yii mail/send-html
php yii mail/send-combine
```

Working with SMTP transport

1. Set the `transport` parameter for the `mailer` component like this:

```
'mailer' => [
    'class' => 'yii\swiftmailer\Mailer',
    'transport' => [
        'class' => 'Swift_SmtpTransport',
        'host' => 'smtp.gmail.com',
        'username' => 'username@gmail.com',
        'password' => 'password',
        'port' => '587',
        'encryption' => 'tls',
    ],
],
```

2. Write and run the following code:

```
Yii::$app->mailer->compose()
    ->setTo('to@yii-book.app')
    ->setFrom('username@gmail.com')
    ->setSubject('My Test Message')
    ->setTextBody('My Text Body')
    ->send();
```

3. Check your Gmail inbox.

> **Note**: Gmail automatically rewrites the `From` field to your default profile e-mail ID, but other e-mail systems do not do the same. Always use an identical e-mail ID in the transport configuration and in the `setFrom()` method for passing antispam policies for other e-mail systems.

Attaching file and embedding images

Add the corresponding method to attach any file to your mail:

```
class MailController extends Controller
{
    public function actionSendAttach()
    {
        Yii::$app->mailer->compose()
            ->setTo('to@yii-book.app')
            ->setFrom(['from@yii-book.app' => Yii::$app->name])
            ->setSubject('My Test Message')
            ->setTextBody('My Text Body')
```

```
            ->attach(Yii::getAlias('@app/README.md'))
            ->send();
    }
}
```

Or use the `embed()` method in your e-mail view file to paste an image in your e-mail content:

```
<img src="<?= $message->embed($imageFile); ?>">
```

It automatically attaches an image file and inserts its unique identifier.

How it works...

The wrapper implements the base `\yii\mail\MailerInterface`. Its `compose()` method returns a message object (an implementation of `\yii\mail\MessageInterface`).

You can manually set plain text and HTML contents with the help of methods `setTextBody()` and `setHtmlBody()`, or you can pass your view and view parameters into the `compose()` method. In this case, the mailer calls the `\yii\web\View::render()` method for rendering corresponding content.

The `useFileTransport` parameter stores mails in files instead of real sending. It is helpful for local development and application testing.

See also

▶ For more information about the `yii2-swiftmailer` extension, visit the following guides:

   ❏ `http://www.yiiframework.com/doc-2.0/guide-tutorial-mailing.html`

   ❏ `http://www.yiiframework.com/doc-2.0/ext-swiftmailer-index.html`

▶ In order to learn more about the original `SwiftMailer` library, refer to the following URLs:

   ❏ `http://swiftmailer.org/docs/introduction.html`

   ❏ `https://github.com/swiftmailer/swiftmailer`

Faker fixture data generator

The `fzaninotto/faker` is a PHP library that generates fake data of many kinds: names, phones, addresses, random strings and numbers, and so on. It can help you to generate many randomized records for performance and logic testing. You can extend your supported types collection by writing your own formatters and generators.

In the Yii2 application skeletons, the `yiisoft/yii2-faker` wrapper is included in the `require-dev` section of the `composer.json` file and is used for testing code (*Chapter 11, Testing*). This wrapper provides the `FixtureController` console for use in your console application and test environment.

Getting ready

Create a new application by using composer as described in the official guide at `http://www.yiiframework.com/doc-2.0/guide-start-installation.html`.

How to do it...

1. Open the directory `tests/codeception/templates` and add the fixture template file, `users.txt`:

```php
<?php
/**
 * @var $faker \Faker\Generator
 * @var $index integer
 */
    return [
        'name' => $faker->firstName,
        'phone' => $faker->phoneNumber,
        'city' => $faker->city,
        'about' => $faker->sentence(7, true),
        'password' => Yii::$app->getSecurity()
        ->generatePasswordHash('password_' . $index),
        'auth_key' => Yii::$app->getSecurity()
        ->generateRandomString(),
    ];
```

2. Run the test console `yii` command:

```
php tests/codeception/bin/yii fixture/generate users --count=2
```

3. Confirm migration generation.

4. Check that the `tests/codeception/fixtures` directory contains the new `users.php` file, with autogenerated data like this:

```php
return [
    [
        'name' => 'Isadore',
        'phone' => '952.877.8545x190',
        'city' => 'New Marvinburgh',
        'about' => 'Ut quidem voluptatem itaque veniam
            voluptas dolores.',
        'password' => '$2y$13$Fi3LOl/sKlomUH.DLgqBkOB
            /uCLmgCoPPL1KXiW0hffnkrdkjCzAC',
        'auth_key' => '1m05hlgaAG8zfm0cyDyoRGMkbQ9W6hj1',
    ],
    [

        'name' => 'Raleigh',
        'phone' => '1-655-488-3585x699',
        'city' => 'Reedstad',
        'about' => 'Dolorem quae impedit tempore libero
            doloribus nobis dicta tempora facere.',
        'password' => '$2y$13$U7Qte5Y1jVLrx
            /pnhwdwt.1uXDegGXuNVzEQyUsb65WkBtjyjUuYm',
        'auth_key' => 'uWWJDgy5jNRk6KjqpxS5JuPv0OHearqE',
    ],
],
```

Working with your own data types

1. Create your own provider with your custom value generating logic:

```php
<?php
namespace tests\codeception\faker\providers;

use Faker\Provider\Base;

class UserStatus extends Base
{
    public function userStatus()
    {
        return $this->randomElement([0, 10, 20, 30]);
    }
}
```

2. Add the provider into the providers list in the `/tests/codeception/config/config.php` file:

```
return [
    'controllerMap' => [
        'fixture' => [
            'class' => 'yii\faker\FixtureController',
            'fixtureDataPath' => '@tests/codeception/fixtures',
            'templatePath' => '@tests/codeception/templates',
            'namespace' => 'tests\codeception\fixtures',
            'providers' => [
                'tests\codeception\faker\providers\UserStatus',
            ],
        ],
    ],
    // ...
];
```

3. Add the `status` field into your fixture template file:

```php
<?php
/**
 * @var $faker \Faker\Generator
 * @var $index integer
 */
    return [
        'name' => $faker->firstName,
        'status' => $faker->userStatus,
    ];
```

4. Regenerate fixtures with the console command:

php tests/codeception/bin/yii fixture/generate users --count=2

5. Check that the generated code in the `fixtures/users.php` file contains your custom values:

```
return [
    [
        'name' => 'Christelle',
        'status' => 30,
    ],
    [
        'name' => 'Theo',
        'status' => 10,
    ],
];
```

How it works...

The `yii2-faker` extension contains a console generator (which uses your templates for generating fixture data files) and gives you a prepared instance of the original `Faker` object. You can generate all or specific fixtures and can pass custom counts or language in console arguments.

 Note: Be careful with the existing test files if your tests use these fixtures, because autogenerating totally rewrites old data.

See also

▸ For the source code and more information about the extension, see:

❏ https://github.com/yiisoft/yii2-faker/tree/master/docs/guide

❏ http://www.yiiframework.com/doc-2.0/ext-faker-index.html

▸ And to learn more about the original library, refer to:

❏ https://github.com/fzaninotto/Faker

❏ *Chapter 11, Testing*

Imagine library

Imagine is an OOP library for image manipulation. It allows you to crop, resize, and perform other manipulations with different images with the help of GD, Imagic, and Gmagic PHP extensions. Yii2-Imagine is a lightweight static wrapper for the library.

Getting ready

1. Create a new application by using composer, as described in the official guide at http://www.yiiframework.com/doc-2.0/guide-start-installation.html.

2. Install the extension with the following command:

```
composer require yiisoft/yii2-imagine
```

How to do it...

In your projects, you can use the extension in two ways:

- ► Using it as a factory
- ► Using inner methods

Using it as a factory

You can use an instance of the original `Imagine` library class:

```
$imagine = new Imagine\Gd\Imagine();
// or
$imagine = new Imagine\Imagick\Imagine();
// or
$imagine = new Imagine\Gmagick\Imagine();
```

However, this depends on the existing corresponding PHP extensions in your system. You can use the `getImagine()` method:

```
$imagine = \yii\imagine\Image::getImagine();
```

Using inner methods

You can use the `crop()`, `thumbnail()`, `watermark()`, `text()`, and `frame()` methods for common high-level manipulations like this:

```php
<?php
    use yii\imagine\Image;
    Image::crop('path/to/image.jpg', 100, 100,
        ManipulatorInterface::THUMBNAIL_OUTBOUND)
    ->save('path/to/destination/image.jpg', ['quality' => 90]);
```

See the signatures of all supported methods in the source code of the `\yii\imagine\` `BaseImage` class for more details.

How it works...

The extension prepares user data, creates an original Imagine object, and calls the corresponding method on it. All methods return this original image object. You can continue to manipulate the image or save the result to your disk.

▶ For more information about the extension, refer to the following URLs:

  ❑ `http://www.yiiframework.com/doc-2.0/ext-imagine-index.html`

  ❑ `https://github.com/yiisoft/yii2-imagine`

▶ For information about the original library, refer to `http://imagine.readthedocs.org/en/latest/`

MongoDB driver

This extension provides the MongoDB integration for the Yii2 framework and allows you to work with MongoDB collection's records via the `ActiveRecord-style` model.

Getting ready

1. Create a new application by using composer, as described in the official guide at `http://www.yiiframework.com/doc-2.0/guide-start-installation.html`.

2. Install MongoDB using the correct installation process from `https://docs.mongodb.org/manual/installation/` for your system.

3. Install the `php5-mongo` PHP extension.

4. Install the component with the following command:

```
composer require yiisoft/yii2-mongodb
```

How to do it...

1. First of all, create the new MongoDB database. Run it in the `mongo-client` shell and type the database name:

```
mongo

> use mydatabase
```

2. Add this connection information to your `components` config section:

```
return [
    // ...
    'components' => [
        // ...
        'mongodb' => [
            'class' => '\yii\mongodb\Connection',
```

```
                'dsn' =>
                    'mongodb://localhost:27017/mydatabase',
            ],
        ],
    ];
```

3. Add the new console controller to your console configuration file:

```
return [
    // ...
    'controllerMap' => [
        'mongodb-migrate' =>
        'yii\mongodb\console\controllers\MigrateController'
    ],
];
```

4. Create the new migration with the shell command:

   php yii mongodb-migrate/create create_customer_collection

5. Type the following code into the up() and down() methods:

```
<?php

use yii\mongodb\Migration;

class m160201_102003_create_customer_collection
    extends Migration
{
    public function up()
    {
        $this->createCollection('customer');
    }

    public function down()
    {
        $this->dropCollection('customer');
    }
}
```

6. Apply the migration:

   php yii mongodb-migrate/up

7. Put the MongoDB debug panel and models generator into your configuration:

```
if (YII_ENV_DEV) {
    // configuration adjustments for 'dev' environment
    $config['bootstrap'][] = 'debug';
    $config['modules']['debug'] = [
```

```
            'class' => 'yii\debug\Module',
            'panels' => [
                'mongodb' => [
                    'class' =>
                        'yii\mongodb\debug\MongoDbPanel',
                ],
            ],
        ];

        $config['bootstrap'][] = 'gii';
        $config['modules']['gii'] = [
            'class' => 'yii\gii\Module',
            'generators' => [
                'mongoDbModel' => [
                    'class' =>
                        'yii\mongodb\gii\model\Generator'
                ]
            ],
        ];
    }
```

8. Run the Gii generator:

9. Start the new `MongoDB Model Generator` to generate the new model for your own collection:

10. Click the **Preview** and **Generate** buttons.

11. Check that you have the new model, `app\models\Customer`:

```php
<?php

namespace app\models;

use Yii;
use yii\mongodb\ActiveRecord;

/**
 * This is the model class for collection "customer".
 *
```

```
 * @property \MongoId|string $_id
 * @property mixed $name
 * @property mixed $email
 * @property mixed $address
 * @property mixed $status
 */
    class Customer extends ActiveRecord
    {
        public static function collectionName()
        {
            return 'customer';
        }

        public function attributes()
        {
            return [
                '_id',
                'name',
                'email',
                'address',
                'status',
            ];
        }

        public function rules()
        {
            return [
            [['name', 'email', 'address', 'status'],
                'safe']
            ];
        }

        public function attributeLabels()
        {
            return [
                '_id' => 'ID',
                'name' => 'Name',
                'email' => 'Email',
                'address' => 'Address',
                'status' => 'Status',
            ];
        }
    }
```

12. Run Gii again and generate the CRUD:

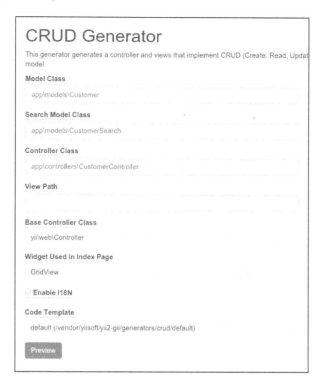

13. Check that you have generated the `CustomerController` class and run the new customer manager page:

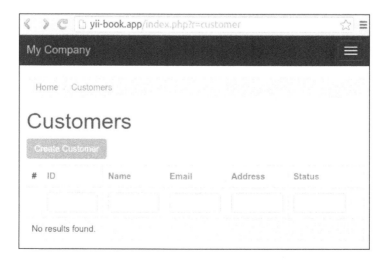

14. You may create, update, and delete your customers' data right now.

15. Look for the **Debug** panel in the page footer:

16. You can see the total MongoDB query count and total execution time. Click on the count badge and inspect the queries:

Basic usage

You may access databases and collections via the \yii\mongodb\Collection instance:

```
$collection = Yii::$app->mongodb->getCollection('customer');
$collection->insert(['name' => 'John Smith', 'status' => 1]);
```

To perform the find queries, you should use \yii\mongodb\Query:

```
use yii\mongodb\Query;
$query = new Query;
// compose the query
$query->select(['name', 'status'])
    ->from('customer')
    ->limit(10);
// execute the query
$rows = $query->all();
```

Note: The MongoDB document id ("_id" field) is not scalar, but an instance of the \MongoId class.

You must not care about the conversion from integer or string $id values to \MongoId, because query builder converts it automatically:

```
$query = new \yii\mongodb\Query;
$row = $query->from('item')
    ->where(['_id' => $id]) // implicit typecast to \MongoId
    ->one();
```

To get the actual Mongo ID string, you should typecast the \MongoId instance to a string:

$query = new Query;

```
$row = $query->from('customer')->one();
var_dump($row['_id']); // outputs: "object(MongoId)"
var_dump((string)$row['_id']);
```

How it works...

The Query, ActiveQuery, and ActiveRecord classes of this extension extends yii\db\QueryInterface and yii\db\BaseActiveRecord, and therefore they are compatible with the built-in framework Query, ActiveQuery, and ActiveRecord classes.

You can use the yii\mongodb\ActiveRecord class for your models and the yii\mongodb\ActiveQuery builder to retrieve your models and use them in your data provider:

```
use yii\data\ActiveDataProvider;
use app\models\Customer;
$provider = new ActiveDataProvider([
    'query' => Customer::find(),
    'pagination' => [
        'pageSize' => 10,
    ]
]);
```

For general information on how to use Yii's ActiveRecord, please refer to the *Chapter 3, ActiveRecord, Model, and Database*.

See also

▶ For more information about the extension, refer to the following URLs:

    ❏ `https://github.com/yiisoft/yii2-mongodb/blob/master/docs/guide/README.md`

    ❏ `http://www.yiiframework.com/doc-2.0/ext-mongodb-index.html`

▶ And for information about the original library, refer to:

    ❏ `https://docs.mongodb.org/manual/`

▶ For ActiveRecord usage refer to the *Chapter 3, ActiveRecord, Model, and Database*

ElasticSearch engine adapter

This extension is an ActiveRecord-like wrapper for ElasticSearch full text search engine integration into the Yii2 framework. It allows you to work with any model data and use the ActiveRecord pattern to retrieve and store records in ElasticSearch collections.

Getting ready

1. Create a new application by using composer, as described in the official guide at `http://www.yiiframework.com/doc-2.0/guide-start-installation.html`.

2. Install the `ElasticSearch` service found at `https://www.elastic.co/downloads/elasticsearch`.

3. Install the extension with the following command:

```
composer require yiisoft/yii2-elasticsearch
```

How to do it...

Set the new `ElasticSearch` connection in your application configuration:

```
return [
    //....
    'components' => [
        'elasticsearch' => [
            'class' => 'yii\elasticsearch\Connection',
            'nodes' => [
                ['http_address' => '127.0.0.1:9200'],
```

```
                // configure more hosts if you have a cluster
            ],
        ],
    ]
];
```

Using the Query class

You can use the `Query` class for the low-level querying of records from any collection:

```
use  \yii\elasticsearch\Query;

$query = new Query;
$query->fields('id, name')
    ->from('myindex', 'users')
    ->limit(10);

$query->search();
```

You can also create a command and run it directly:

```
$command = $query->createCommand();
$rows = $command->search();
```

Using ActiveRecord

Using `ActiveRecord` is a common way to access your records. Just extend the `yii\elasticsearch\ActiveRecord` class and implement the `attributes()` method to define the attributes of your documents.

For example, you can write the `Customer` model:

```
class Buyer extends \yii\elasticsearch\ActiveRecord
{
    public function attributes()
    {
        return ['id', 'name', 'address', 'registration_date'];
    }
    public function getOrders()
    {
        return $this->hasMany(Order::className(),
            ['buyer_id' => 'id'])->orderBy('id');
    }
}
```

Then write the `Order` model:

```
class Order extends \yii\elasticsearch\ActiveRecord
{
    public function attributes()
    {
        return ['id', 'user_id', 'date'];
    }

    public function getBuyer()
    {
        return $this->hasOne(Customer::className(),
            ['id' => 'buyer_id']);
    }
}
```

You may override `index()` and `type()` to define the index and type this record represents.

The following is a usage example:

```
$buyer = new Buyer();
$buyer->primaryKey = 1; // it equivalent to $buyer->id = 1;
$buyer>name = 'test';
$buyer>save();

$buyer = Buyer::get(1);

$buyer = Buyer::mget([1,2,3]);

$buyer = Buyer::find()->where(['name' => 'test'])->one();
```

You can use Query DSL for specific queries:

```
$result = Article::find()->query(["match" =>
    ["title" => "yii"]])->all();
        $query = Article::find()->query([
        "fuzzy_like_this" => [
            "fields" => ["title", "description"],
            "like_text" => "Some search text",
            "max_query_terms" => 12
        ]
]);
$query->all();
```

You can add facets to your search:

```
$query->addStatisticalFacet('click_stats',
    ['field' => 'visit_count']);
$query->search();
```

Using the ElasticSearch DebugPanel

This extension contains a special panel for the `yii2-debug` module. It allows you to view all executed queries. You can include this panel in your configuration file:

```
if (YII_ENV_DEV) {
    // configuration adjustments for 'dev' environment
    $config['bootstrap'][] = 'debug';
    $config['modules']['debug'] =  [
        'class' => 'yii\debug\Module',
        'panels' => [
            'elasticsearch' => [
                'class' => 'yii\elasticsearch\DebugPanel',
            ],
        ],
    ];

    $config['bootstrap'][] = 'gii';
    $config['modules']['gii'] = 'yii\gii\Module';
}
```

How it works...

The extension provides a low-level command builder and high-level `ActiveRecord` implementation for querying records from the `ElasticSearch` index.

The extension's ActiveRecord usage is very similar to the database `ActiveRecord` as described in *Chapter 3, ActiveRecord, Model, and Database*, besides the `join()`, `groupBy()`, `having()`, and `union()` ActiveQuery operators.

 Note: `ElasticSearch` limits the number of returned records to ten items by default. Take care with limits if you use relations with the `via()` option.

See also

▶ For more information about the extension, see:

  ❑ `https://github.com/yiisoft/yii2-elasticsearch/blob/master/docs/guide/README.md`

  ❑ `http://www.yiiframework.com/doc-2.0/ext-elasticsearch-index.html`

▶ You can also visit the official extension site at `https://www.elastic.co/products/elasticsearch`.

▶ For more information about Query DSL, you can visit:

  ❑ `http://www.elastic.co/guide/en/elasticsearch/reference/current/query-dsl-match-query.html`

  ❑ `http://www.elastic.co/guide/en/elasticsearch/reference/current/query-dsl-flt-query.html`

▶ For ActiveRecord usage refer to the *Chapter 3, ActiveRecord, Model, and Database*

Gii code generator

This extension provides a web-based code generator called Gii for Yii 2 applications. You can use Gii to quickly generate models, forms, modules, CRUD, and many more.

Getting ready

1. Create a new application by using composer, as described in the official guide at `http://www.yiiframework.com/doc-2.0/guide-start-installation.html`.

2. Create a new migration with the shell command:

   php yii migrate/create create_customer_table

3. Put the following code into the `up()` and `down()` methods:

```
use yii\db\Schema;
use yii\db\Migration;

class m160201_154207_create_customer_table extends Migration
{
    public function up()
    {
        $tableOptions = null;
        if ($this->db->driverName === 'mysql') {
```

```
            $tableOptions =
                'CHARACTER SET utf8 COLLATE
                    utf8_unicode_ci ENGINE=InnoDB';
        }
        $this->createTable('{{%customer}}', [
            'id' => Schema::TYPE_PK,
            'name' => Schema::TYPE_STRING . ' NOT NULL',
            'email' => Schema::TYPE_STRING . ' NOT NULL',
            'address' => Schema::TYPE_STRING,
        ], $tableOptions);
    }

    public function down()
    {
        $this->dropTable('{{%customer}}');
    }
}
```

4. Apply the migration:

```
php yii migrate/up
```

How to do it...

In your projects, you can use this extension in two ways:

▸ Working with GUI

▸ Working with CLI

Working with GUI

1. Check that your web configuration file contains the following code:

```
if (YII_ENV_DEV) {
    $config['bootstrap'][] = 'gii';
    $config['modules']['gii'] = [
        'class' => 'yii\gii\Module',
    ];
}
```

2. Your web/index.php file will define the development environment:

```
defined('YII_ENV') or define('YII_ENV', 'dev');
```

The previous configuration states that when in a development environment, the application should include a module named gii, which is of the class yii\gii\Module.

By default, the module allows access from the IP address, `127.0.0.1`. If you work from another location, add your address in the `allowedIPs` property:

```
$config['modules']['gii'] = [
    'class' => 'yii\gii\Module',
    allowedIPs = ['127.0.0.1', '::1', '192.168.0.*'],
];
```

3. Go to the `gii` route of your application: `http://localhost/index.php?r=gii`.

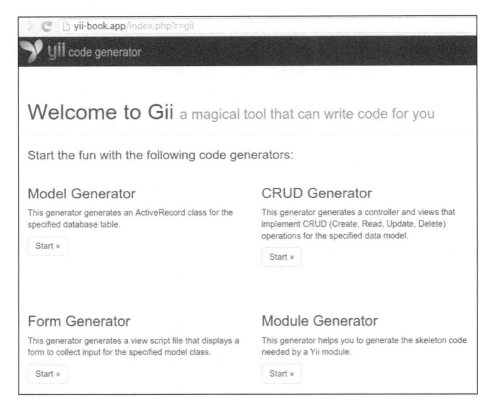

4. Click on the **Model Generator** button and type your table name and model name in the form:

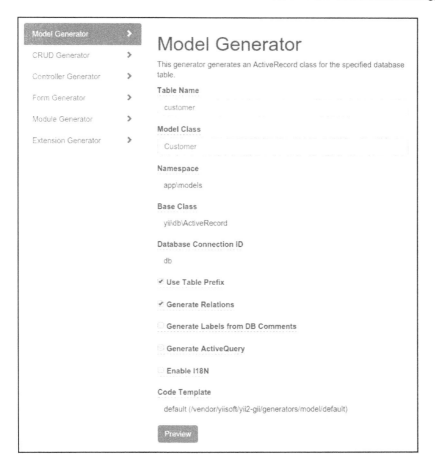

5. Click the **Preview** button. You must view the featured files list:

6. If you want to regenerate existing files, Gii will mark those in yellow:

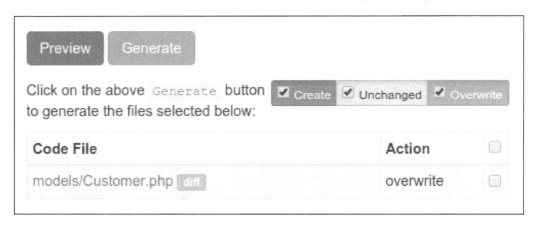

7. In this case, you can view the difference between existing and new files and overwrite the target if needed.

8. After all that, click the **Generate** button:

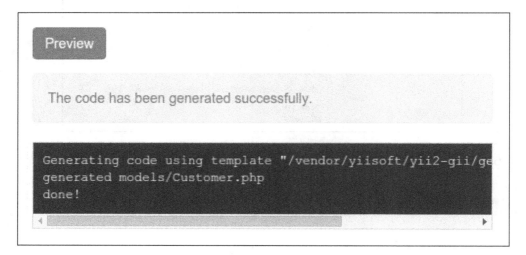

9. Check that the new class, `\app\models\Customer`, exists.

10. CRUD is an abbreviation for the four common tasks using data on most websites: Create, Read, Update, and Delete. To create CRUD using Gii, select the **CRUD Generator** section. Specify your model class and type the other fields:

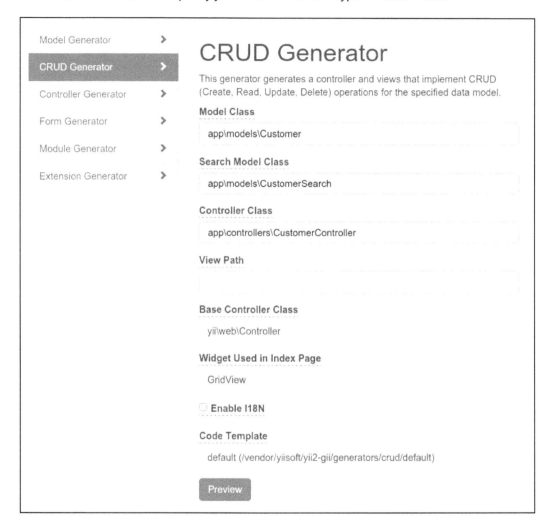

11. Generate the new items:

12. After that, try to open the new controller:

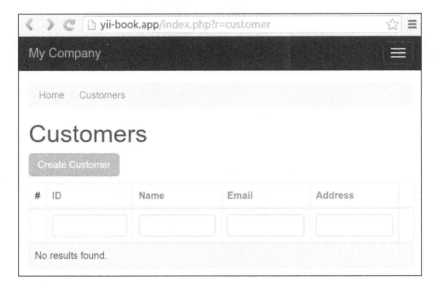

You will see a data grid showing the customers in the database table. Try to create a new item. You may sort the grid or filter it by entering filter conditions in the column headers.

Working with CLI

Gii also provides a console controller for code generation.

1. Check that your console configuration contains the Gii module settings:

```
return [
    // ...
    'modules' => [
        'gii' => 'yii\gii\Module',
    ],
    // ...
];
```

2. Run any shell command for help:

```
php yii help gii
php yii help gii/model
```

3. Type the following command to start the model generation process:

```
php yii gii/model --tableName=customer --modelClass=Customer --useTablePrefix=1
```

4. Check that the new class, `\app\models\Customer`, exists.

5. Generate CRUD for your model:

```
php yii gii/crud --modelClass=app\\models\\Customer \
    --searchModelClass=app\\models\\CustomerSearch \
    --controllerClass=app\\controllers\\CustomerController
```

How it works...

Gii allows you to generate some standard code elements instead of manually typing. It provides web-based and console interfaces to work with every generator.

See also

▸ For more information about the extension's usage, see:

- ❑ http://www.yiiframework.com/doc-2.0/guide-start-gii.html
- ❑ http://www.yiiframework.com/doc-2.0/ext-gii-index.html
- ❑ https://github.com/yiisoft/yii2-gii/tree/master/docs/guide

> ▶ For MongoDB integration refer to the *Creating a widget* recipe in *Chapter 8, Extending Yii*

Pjax jQuery plugin

Pjax is a widget that integrates the **pjax jQuery** plugin. All content that is wrapped by this widget will be reloaded by AJAX without refreshing the current page. The widget also uses the HTML5 History API to change the current URL in your browser's address line.

Getting ready

Create a new application by using composer, as described in the official guide at http://www.yiiframework.com/doc-2.0/guide-start-installation.html.

How to do it...

In the following example, you can see how you use Pjax with the yii\grid\GridView widget:

```php
<?php
    use yii\widgets\Pjax;
?>
<?php Pjax::begin(); ?>
    <?= GridView::widget([...]); ?>
<?php Pjax::end(); ?>
```

Just wrap any code fragment in the Pjax::begin() and Pjax::end() calls.

This will render the following HTML code:

```html
<div id="w1">
    <div id="w2" class="grid-view">...</div>
</div>

<script type="text/javascript">jQuery(document).ready(function () {
    jQuery(document).pjax("#w1 a", "#w1", {...});
});</script>
```

All the wrapped content with pagination and sorting links will be reloaded by AJAX.

Specifying a custom ID

Pjax gets page content from AJAX requests and then extracts its own DOM element with the same ID. You can optimize page rendering performance by rendering content without layout, especially for Pjax requests:

```php
public function actionIndex()
{
    $dataProvider = …;

    if (Yii::$app->request->isPjax) {
        return $this->renderPartial('_items', [
            'dataProvider' => $dataProvider,
        ]);
    } else {
        return $this->render('index', [
            'dataProvider' => $dataProvider,
        ]);
    }
}
```

By default, the `yii\base\Widget::getId` method increments identifiers, and therefore widgets, on any page that has incremented attributes:

```html
<nav id="w0">...</nav> // Main navigation
<ul id="w1">...</ul> // Breadcrumbs widget
<div id="w2">...</div> // Pjax widget
```

To render using the `renderPartial()` or `renderAjax()` methods, without rendering the layout, your own page will have only one widget with the number `0`:

```html
<div id="w0">...</div> // Pjax widget
```

In the result, your own widget will not have found its own block with the `w2` selector at the next request.

However, Pjax will find the same block with the `w2` selector in the Ajax response. In the result, your own widget will not have found the block with the `w2` selector at the next request.

Therefore, you must manually specify a unique identifier for all your Pjax widgets to avoid different conflicts:

```php
<?php Pjax::begin(['id' => 'countries']) ?>
    <?= GridView::widget([...]); ?>
<?php Pjax::end() ?>
```

Using ActiveForm

By default, Pjax works only with links in the wrapped block. If you want to use it with the `ActiveForm` widget, you must use the `data-pjax` option of the form:

```php
<?php
use \yii\widgets\Pjax
use \yii\widgets\ActiveForm;

<?php yii\widgets\Pjax::begin(['id' => 'my-block']) ?>
    <?php $form = ActiveForm::begin(['options' => [
        'data-pjax' => true,
    ]]); ?>
        <?= $form->field($model, 'name') ?>
    <?php ActiveForm::end(); ?>
<?php Pjax::end(); ?>
```

It adds corresponding listeners on the form submitting event.

You can also use the `$formSelector` option of the Pjax widget to specify which form submission may trigger `pjax`.

Working with the client-side script

You can subscribe to container events:

```php
<?php $this->registerJs('
    $("#my-block").on("pjax:complete", function() {
        alert('Pjax is completed');
    });
'); ?>
```

Or, you can reload the container manually by using its selector:

```php
<?php $this->registerJs('
    $("#my-button").on("click", function() {
        $.pjax.reload({container:"#my-block"});
    });
'); ?>
```

How it works...

Pjax is a simple wrapper for any code fragment. It subscribes to click events of all links in the fragment and replaces the whole page, reloading it into Ajax calls. We can use the `data-pjax` attribute for wrapped forms, and any form submissions will trigger an Ajax request.

The widget will load and update on-the-fly widget body content without, loading the layout resources (JS, CSS).

You may configure the `$linkSelector` of the widget to specify which links should trigger Pjax, and configure `$formSelector` to specify which form submission may trigger Pjax.

You may disable Pjax for a specific link inside the container by adding the `data-pjax="0"` attribute to this link.

See also

▶ For more information about the extension's usage, see:

  ❑ `http://www.yiiframework.com/doc-2.0/yii-widgets-pjax.html`

  ❑ `https://github.com/yiisoft/jquery-pjax`

▶ For more information about client-side options and methods, refer to `https://github.com/yiisoft/jquery-pjax#usage`

Redis database driver

This extension allows you to use Redis key-value storage in any project on the Yii2 framework. It contains the `Cache` and `Session` storage handlers, as well as the extension, which implements the ActiveRecord pattern for access to the Redis database records.

Getting ready

1. Create a new application by using composer, as described in the official guide at `http://www.yiiframework.com/doc-2.0/guide-start-installation.html`.

2. Install the storage: `http://redis.io`.

3. Install all migrations with the following command:

```
composer require yiisoft/yii2-redis
```

How to do it...

First of all, configure the `Connection` class in your configuration file:

```
return [
    //....
    'components' => [
        'redis' => [
```

```
            'class' => 'yii\redis\Connection',
            'hostname' => 'localhost',
            'port' => 6379,
            'database' => 0,
        ],
    ]
];
```

Direct usage

For low-level working with Redis commands, you can use the `executeCommand` method of the connection component:

```
Yii::$app->redis->executeCommand('hmset', ['test_collection', 'key1',
'val1', 'key2', 'val2']);
```

You can also use simplified shortcuts instead of `executeCommand` calls:

```
Yii::$app->redis->hmset('test_collection', 'key1', 'val1', 'key2',
'val2')
```

Using ActiveRecord

For access to Redis records via the `ActiveRecord` pattern, your record class needs to extend from the `yii\redis\ActiveRecord` base class and implement the `attributes()` method:

```
class Customer extends \yii\redis\ActiveRecord
{
    public function attributes()
    {
        return ['id', 'name', 'address', 'registration_date'];
    }
    public function getOrders()
    {
        return $this->hasMany(Order::className(),
            ['customer_id' => 'id']);
    }
}
```

A primary key of any model can be defined via the `primaryKey()` method, which defaults to `id` if not specified. The primary key needs to be placed in the attribute list if you do not manually specify it in the `primaryKey()` method.

The following is a usage example:

```
$customer = new Customer();
$customer->name = 'test';
$customer->save();
echo $customer->id; // id will automatically be incremented if not set
explicitly
// find by query
$customer = Customer::find()->where(['name' => 'test'])->one();
```

How it works...

The extension provides a `Connection` component for low-level access to Redis storage records.

You can also use an ActiveRecord-like model with a limited set of methods (`where()`, `limit()`, `offset()`, and `indexBy()`). Other methods do not exist because Redis does not support SQL queries.

There are no tables in Redis, so you cannot define via relations via a junction table name. You can only define many-to-many relations via other `hasMany` relations.

For general information on how to use Yii's ActiveRecord, please refer to *Chapter 3, ActiveRecord, Model, and Database.*

See also

▶ For more information about the extension's usage, see:

❑ https://github.com/yiisoft/yii2-redis/blob/master/docs/guide/README.md

❑ http://www.yiiframework.com/doc-2.0/ext-redis-index.html

▶ For information about Redis key-value storage, refer: http://redis.io/documentation

▶ *Chapter 3, ActiveRecord, Model, and Database* for ActiveRecord usage

8
Extending Yii

In this chapter, we will cover the following topics:

- ▸ Creating helpers
- ▸ Creating model behaviors
- ▸ Creating components
- ▸ Creating reusable controller actions
- ▸ Creating reusable controllers
- ▸ Creating a widget
- ▸ Creating CLI commands
- ▸ Creating filters
- ▸ Creating modules
- ▸ Creating a custom view renderer
- ▸ Creating a multilanguage application
- ▸ Making extensions distribution-ready

Introduction

In this chapter, we will show you not only how to implement your own Yii extension, but also how to make your extension reusable and useful for the community. In addition, we will focus on many things you should do in order to make your extension as efficient as possible.

Creating helpers

There are a lot of built-in framework helpers such as StringHelper in the yii\helpers namespace. These contain sets of helpful static methods for manipulating strings, files, arrays, and other subjects.

In many cases, for additional behavior you can create a own helper and put any static function into one. For example, we implement the number helper in this recipe.

Getting ready

Create a new yii2-app-basic application using the composer package manager as described in the official guide at http://www.yiiframework.com/doc-2.0/guide-start-installation.html.

How to do it...

1. Create the helpers directory in your project and write the NumberHelper class:

```php
<?php
namespace app\helpers;

class NumberHelper
{
    public static function format($value, $decimal = 2)
    {
        return number_format($value, $decimal, '.', ',');
    }
}
```

2. Add the actionNumbers method to SiteController:

```php
<?php
...
class SiteController extends Controller
{
    ...

    public function actionNumbers()
    {
        return $this->render('numbers', ['value' =>
        18878334526.3]);
    }
}
```

3. Add the `views/site/numbers.php` view:

```php
<?php
use app\helpers\NumberHelper;
use yii\helpers\Html;

/* @var $this yii\web\View */
/* @var $value float */

$this->title = 'Numbers';
$this->params['breadcrumbs'][] = $this->title;
?>
<div class="site-numbers">
    <h1><?= Html::encode($this->title) ?></h1>

    <p>
        Raw number:<br />
        <b><?= $value ?></b>
    </p>
    <p>
        Formatted number:<br />
        <b><?= NumberHelper::format($value) ?></b>
    </p>
</div>
```

4. Open the action. You should see the following result:

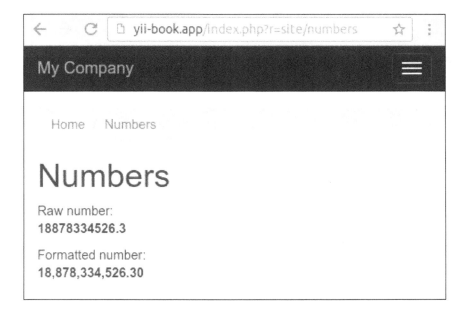

In other cases, you can specify another count of decimal numbers. Observe the following example:

```
NumberHelper::format($value, 3)
```

How it works...

Any helper in Yii2 is just a set of functions, implemented as static methods in the corresponding classes.

You can use a helper for implementing any different formats of output, for manipulations with values of any variables, and for other cases.

 Usually, static helpers are lightweight clean functions with a small count of arguments. Avoid putting your business logic and other complicated manipulations into helpers. Use widgets or other components instead of helpers in other cases.

See also

For more information about helpers, refer to:

`http://www.yiiframework.com/doc-2.0/guide-helper-overview.html`.

For examples of built-in helpers, refer to sources in the `helpers` directory of framework. For the framework, refer to:

`https://github.com/yiisoft/yii2/tree/master/framework/helpers`.

Creating model behaviors

There are many similar solutions in today's web applications. Leading products such as Google's Gmail are defining nice UI patterns. One of these is soft delete. Instead of a permanent deletion with tons of confirmations, Gmail allows us to immediately mark messages as deleted and then easily undo it. The same behavior can be applied to any object such as blog posts, comments, and so on.

Let's create a behavior that will allow marking models as deleted, restoring models, selecting not yet deleted models, deleted models, and all models. In this recipe, we'll follow a test-driven development approach to plan the behavior and test if the implementation is correct.

Getting ready

1. Create a new `yii2-app-basic` application using the composer as described in the official guide at `http://www.yiiframework.com/doc-2.0/guide-start-installation.html`.

2. Create two databases for working and for tests.

3. Configure Yii to use the first database in your primary application in `config/db.php`. Make sure the test application uses the second database in `tests/codeception/config/config.php`.

4. Create a new migration:

```php
<?php
use yii\db\Migration;

class m160427_103115_create_post_table extends Migration
{
    public function up()
    {
        $this->createTable('{{%post}}', [
            'id' => $this->primaryKey(),
            'title' => $this->string()->notNull(),
            'content_markdown' => $this->text(),
            'content_html' => $this->text(),
        ]);
    }

    public function down()
    {
        $this->dropTable('{{%post}}');
    }
}
```

5. Apply the migration to both the working and test databases:

```
./yii migrate
tests/codeception/bin/yii migrate
```

6. Create the `Post` model:

```php
<?php
namespace app\models;
```

```php
use app\behaviors\MarkdownBehavior;
use yii\db\ActiveRecord;

/**
 * @property integer $id
 * @property string $title
 * @property string $content_markdown
 * @property string $content_html
 */
class Post extends ActiveRecord
{
    public static function tableName()
    {
        return '{{%post}}';
    }

    public function rules()
    {
        return [
            [['title'], 'required'],
            [['content_markdown'], 'string'],
            [['title'], 'string', 'max' => 255],
        ];
    }
}
```

How to do it...

Let's prepare a test environment first starting with defining fixtures for the `Post` model. Create the `tests/codeception/unit/fixtures/PostFixture.php` file:

```php
<?php
namespace app\tests\codeception\unit\fixtures;

use yii\test\ActiveFixture;

class PostFixture extends ActiveFixture
{
    public $modelClass = 'app\models\Post';
    public $dataFile =
        '@tests/codeception/unit/fixtures/data/post.php';
}
```

1. Add a fixture data file to `tests/codeception/unit/fixtures/data/post.php`:

```php
<?php
return [
    [
        'id' => 1,
        'title' => 'Post 1',
        'content_markdown' => 'Stored *markdown* text 1',
        'content_html' => "<p>Stored <em>markdown</em>
            text 1</p>\n",
    ],
];
```

2. Then, we need to create a test case, `tests/codeception/unit/MarkdownBehaviorTest.php`:

```php
<?php
namespace app\tests\codeception\unit;

use app\models\Post;
use app\tests\codeception\unit\fixtures\PostFixture;
use yii\codeception\DbTestCase;

class MarkdownBehaviorTest extends DbTestCase
{
    public function testNewModelSave()
    {
        $post = new Post();
        $post->title = 'Title';
        $post->content_markdown = 'New *markdown* text';

        $this->assertTrue($post->save());
        $this->assertEquals("<p>New <em>markdown</em>
            text</p>\n", $post->content_html);
    }

    public function testExistingModelSave()
    {
        $post = Post::findOne(1);

        $post->content_markdown = 'Other *markdown* text';
        $this->assertTrue($post->save());

        $this->assertEquals("<p>Other <em>markdown</em>
            text</p>\n", $post->content_html);
```

```
        }

        public function fixtures()
        {
            return [
                'posts' => [
                    'class' => PostFixture::className(),
                ]
            ];
        }
    }
```

3. Run the unit tests:

   codecept run unit MarkdownBehaviorTest

   Ensure that tests has not passed:

   Codeception PHP Testing Framework v2.0.9

   Powered by PHPUnit 4.8.27 by Sebastian Bergmann and contributors.

   **Unit Tests (2) ---
   -----------------------**

   **Trying to test ... MarkdownBehaviorTest::testNewModelSave
   Error**

   **Trying to test ... MarkdownBehaviorTest::testExistingModelSave
   Error**

   **---
   ----------**

   Time: 289 ms, Memory: 16.75MB

4. Now we need to implement behavior, attach it to the model, and make sure the test passes. Create a new directory, `behaviors`. Under this directory, create a `MarkdownBehavior` class:

   ```php
   <?php
   namespace app\behaviors;

   use yii\base\Behavior;
   use yii\base\Event;
   use yii\base\InvalidConfigException;
   use yii\db\ActiveRecord;
   use yii\helpers\Markdown;
   ```

```
class MarkdownBehavior extends Behavior
{
    public $sourceAttribute;
    public $targetAttribute;

    public function init()
    {
        if (empty($this->sourceAttribute) ||
            empty($this->targetAttribute)) {
            throw new InvalidConfigException
                ('Source and target must be set.');
        }
        parent::init();
    }

    public function events()
    {
        return [
            ActiveRecord::EVENT_BEFORE_INSERT
                => 'onBeforeSave',
            ActiveRecord::EVENT_BEFORE_UPDATE
                => 'onBeforeSave',
        ];
    }

    public function onBeforeSave(Event $event)
    {
        if ($this->owner->isAttributeChanged
            ($this->sourceAttribute)) {
            $this->processContent();
        }
    }

    private function processContent()
    {
        $model = $this->owner;
        $source = $model->{$this->sourceAttribute};
        $model->{$this->targetAttribute}
            = Markdown::process($source);
    }
}
```

5. Let's attach the behavior to the Post model:

```
class Post extends ActiveRecord
{
```

```
. . .

public function behaviors()
{
    return [
        'markdown' => [
            'class' => MarkdownBehavior::className(),
            'sourceAttribute' => 'content_markdown',
            'targetAttribute' => 'content_html',
        ],
    ];
}
}
```

6. Run the test and make sure it passes:

```
Codeception PHP Testing Framework v2.0.9
Powered by PHPUnit 4.8.27 by Sebastian Bergmann and contributors.


Unit Tests (2) -----------------------------------------------------
-----------------------
Trying to test ... MarkdownBehaviorTest::testNewModelSave
Ok
Trying to test ... MarkdownBehaviorTest::testExistingModelSave
Ok
------------------------------------------------------------------
---------


Time: 329 ms, Memory: 17.00MB
```

7. That's it. We've created a reusable behavior and can use it for all future projects by just connecting it to a model.

How it works...

Let's start with the test case. Since we want to use a set of models, we are defining fixtures. A fixture set is put into the "database" each time the test method is executed.

We prepare unit tests for specifying how the behavior must work:

▶ First, we are testing a processing of a new model content. The behavior must convert the Markdown text from the source attribute to HTML and store the second one to the target attribute.

▶ Second, we are testing to update the content of the existing model. After changing the Markdown content and saving the model, we must get the updated HTML content.

Now let's move to the interesting implementation details. In behavior, we can add our own methods, which will be mixed into the model that the behavior is attached to. Also, we can subscribe to the owner component events. We are using it to add an own listener:

```
public function events()
{
    return [
        ActiveRecord::EVENT_BEFORE_INSERT => 'onBeforeSave',
        ActiveRecord::EVENT_BEFORE_UPDATE => 'onBeforeSave',
    ];
}
```

Now we can implement this listener:

```
public function onBeforeSave(Event $event)
{
    if ($this->owner->isAttributeChanged($this->sourceAttribute))
    {
        $this->processContent();
    }
}
```

In all the methods, we can use the `owner` property to get the object the behavior is attached to. In general, we can attach any behavior to our models, controllers, applications, and other components that extend the `yii\base\Component` class. Also, we can attach one behavior repeatedly to the model for processing different attributes:

```
class Post extends ActiveRecord
{
    ...

    public function behaviors()
    {
        return [
            [
                'class' => MarkdownBehavior::className(),
                'sourceAttribute' => 'description_markdown',
                'targetAttribute' => 'description_html',
            ],
            [
                'class' => MarkdownBehavior::className(),
                'sourceAttribute' => 'content_markdown',
```

```
                    'targetAttribute' => 'content_html',
            ],
        ];
    }
}
```

Besides, we can extend the `yii\base\AttributeBehavior` class like `yii\behaviors\TimestampBehavior` for updating specified attributes for any events.

See also

To learn more about behaviors and events, refer to the following pages:

- ▸ http://www.yiiframework.com/doc-2.0/guide-concept-behaviors.html
- ▸ http://www.yiiframework.com/doc-2.0/guide-concept-events.html

For more information about the Markdown syntax, refer to http://daringfireball.net/projects/markdown/.

Also, refer to the *Making extensions distribution-ready* recipe of this chapter.

Creating components

If you have some code that looks like it can be reused but you don't know if it's a behavior, widget, or something else, most probably it's a component. A component should be inherited from the `yii\base\Component` class. Later on, the component can be attached to the application and configured using the `components` section of the configuration file. That's the main advantage compared with using just a plain PHP class. Additionally, we are getting behavior, event, getter, and setter support.

For our example, we'll implement a simple Exchange application component that will be able to get currency rates from the `http://fixer.io` site, attach it to the application, and use it.

Getting ready

Create a new `yii2-app-basic` application using the composer, as described in the official guide at http://www.yiiframework.com/doc-2.0/guide-start-installation.html.

How to do it...

For getting the currency rates, our component should send a HTTP GET query to a service URL such as http://api.fixer.io/2016-05-14?base=USD.

The service must return all supported rates on the nearest working day:

```
{
    "base":"USD",
    "date":"2016-05-13",
    "rates": {
        "AUD":1.3728,
        "BGN":1.7235,
        ...
        "ZAR":15.168,
        "EUR":0.88121
    }
}
```

The component should extract needle currency from the response in JSON format and return a target rate:

1. Create the `components` directory in your application structure.

2. Create the component class example with the following interface:

```php
<?php
namespace app\components;

use yii\base\Component;

class Exchange extends Component
{
    public function getRate($source, $destination,
        $date = null)
    {

    }
}
```

3. Implement the `component` functional:

```php
<?php
namespace app\components;

use yii\base\Component;
use yii\base\InvalidConfigException;
use yii\base\InvalidParamException;
use yii\caching\Cache;
use yii\di\Instance;
use yii\helpers\Json;
```

```php
class Exchange extends Component
{
    /**
    * @var string remote host
    */
    public $host = 'http://api.fixer.io';
    /**
    * @var bool cache results or not
    */
    public $enableCaching = false;
    /**
    * @var string|Cache component ID
    */
    public $cache = 'cache';

    public function init()
    {
        if (empty($this->host)) {
            throw new InvalidConfigException
                ('Host must be set.');
        }
        if ($this->enableCaching) {
            $this->cache = Instance::ensure
                ($this->cache, Cache::className());
        }
        parent::init();
    }

    public function getRate($source, $destination,
        $date = null)
    {
        $this->validateCurrency($source);
        $this->validateCurrency($destination);
        $date = $this->validateDate($date);
        $cacheKey = $this->generateCacheKey
            ($source, $destination, $date);
        if (!$this->enableCaching || ($result =
            $this->cache->get($cacheKey)) === false) {
            $result = $this->getRemoteRate($source,
                $destination, $date);
            if ($this->enableCaching) {
                $this->cache->set($cacheKey, $result);
            }
        }
        return $result;
```

```
        }

        private function getRemoteRate($source, $destination,
            $date)
        {
            $url = $this->host . '/' . $date . '?base=' .
                $source;
            $response = Json::decode(file_get_contents($url));
            if (!isset($response['rates'][$destination])) {
                throw new \RuntimeException('Rate not found.');
            }
            return $response['rates'][$destination];
        }

        private function validateCurrency($source)
        {
            if (!preg_match('#^[A-Z]{3}$#s', $source)) {
                throw new InvalidParamException
                    ('Invalid currency format.');
            }
        }

        private function validateDate($date)
        {
            if (!empty($date) && !preg_match
                ('#\d{4}\-\d{2}-\d{2}#s', $date)) {
                throw new InvalidParamException('Invalid date
                    format.');
            }
            if (empty($date)) {
                $date = date('Y-m-d');
            }
            return $date;
        }

        private function generateCacheKey($source,
            $destination, $date)
        {
            return [__CLASS__, $source, $destination, $date];
        }
    }
```

4. Attach the component to your `config/console.php` or `config/web.php` configuration files:

```
'components' => [
```

```
        'cache' => [
            'class' => 'yii\caching\FileCache',
        ],
        'exchange' => [
            'class' => 'app\components\Exchange',
            'enableCaching' => true,
        ],
        // ...
        db' => $db,
    ],
```

5. Right now, we can use a new component directly or via the `get` method:

```
echo \Yii::$app->exchange->getRate('USD', 'EUR');
echo \Yii::$app->get('exchange')->getRate('USD', 'EUR',
    '2014-04-12');
```

6. Create a demonstration console controller:

```php
<?php
namespace app\commands;

use yii\console\Controller;

class ExchangeController extends Controller
{
    public function actionTest($currency, $date = null)
    {
        echo \Yii::$app->exchange->getRate('USD',
            $currency, $date) . PHP_EOL;
    }
}
```

7. Now try to run any command:

```
$ ./yii exchange/test EUR
> 0.90196

$ ./yii exchange/test EUR 2015-11-24
> 0.93888



$ ./yii exchange/test OTHER
> Exception 'yii\base\InvalidParamException' with message 'Invalid
currency format.'
```

```
$ ./yii exchange/test EUR 2015/24/11
Exception 'yii\base\InvalidParamException' with message 'Invalid
date format.'

$ ./yii exchange/test ASD
> Exception 'RuntimeException' with message 'Rate not found.'
```

As a result, you must see the rate values in the success cases or specific exceptions in the error ones. Besides creating your own components, you can do more.

Overriding existing application components

Most of the time, there will be no need to create your own application components since other types of extension such as widgets or behaviors, cover almost all types of reusable codes. However, overriding core framework components is a common practice and can be used to customize the framework's behavior for your specific needs without hacking into the core.

For example, to be able to format numbers using the `Yii::app()->formatter->asNumber($value)` method instead of our `NumberHelper::format` method from the *Creating helpers* recipe, you can follow the next steps:

1. Extend the `yii\i18n\Formatter` component as follows:

    ```php
    <?php
    namespace app\components;

    class Formatter extends \yii\i18n\Formatter
    {
        public function asNumber($value, $decimal = 2)
        {
            return number_format($value, $decimal, '.', ',');
        }
    }
    ```

2. Override the class of the built-in `formatter` component:

    ```php
    'components' => [
        // ...
        formatter => [
            'class' => 'app\components\Formatter,
        ],
        // ...
    ],
    ```

3. Right now, we can use this method directly:

    ```php
    echo Yii::app()->formatter->asNumber(1534635.2, 3);
    ```

Alternatively, it can be used as a new format for the `GridView` and `DetailView` widgets:

```
<?= \yii\grid\GridView::widget([
    'dataProvider' => $dataProvider,
    'columns' => [
        'id',
        'created_at:datetime',
        'title',
        'value:number',
    ],
]) ?>
```

4. Also, you can extend every existing component without overwriting its source code.

How it works...

To be able to attach a component to an application, it can be extended from the `yii\base\Component` class. Attaching is as simple as adding a new array to the components section of configuration. There, a class value specifies the component's class, and all other values are set to a component through the corresponding component's public properties and setter methods.

Implementation itself is very straightforward; we are wrapping the `http://api.fixer.io` calls into a comfortable API with validators and caching. We can access our class by its component name using `Yii::$app`. In our case, it will be `Yii::$app->exchange`.

See also

For official information about components, refer to `http://www.yiiframework.com/doc-2.0/guide-concept-components.html`.

For the `NumberHelper` class sources, refer to the *Creating helpers* recipe.

Creating reusable controller actions

Common actions such as deleting the AR model by the primary key or getting data for AJAX autocomplete could be moved into reusable controller actions and later attached to controllers as needed.

In this recipe, we will create a reusable delete action that will delete the specified AR model by its primary key.

Getting ready

1. Create a new `yii2-app-basic` application using the composer as described in the official guide at `http://www.yiiframework.com/doc-2.0/guide-start-installation.html`.

2. Create a new database and configure it.

3. Create and apply the following migration:

```php
<?php
use yii\db\Migration;

class m160308_093233_create_post_table extends Migration
{
    public function up()
    {
        $this->createTable('{{%post}}', [
            'id' => $this->primaryKey(),
            'title' => $this->string()->notNull(),
            'text' => $this->text()->notNull(),
        ]);
    }

    public function down()
    {
        $this->dropTable('{{%post}}');
    }
}
```

4. Generate models for posts and comments using Gii.

5. Generate the standard CRUD controller `app\controllers\PostController` in Gii.

6. Ensure that CRUD properly works:

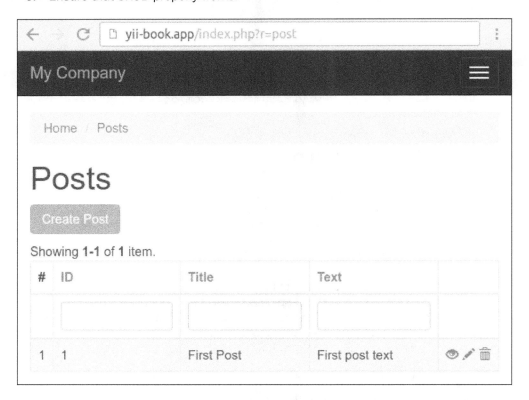

7. In a success case, add a set of example posts.

How to do it...

Carry out the following steps:

1. Create the actions directory and add the `DeleteAction` standalone action:

```php
<?php
namespace app\actions;

use yii\base\Action;
use yii\base\InvalidConfigException;
use yii\web\MethodNotAllowedHttpException;
use yii\web\NotFoundHttpException;

class DeleteAction extends Action
{
```

```php
    public $modelClass;
    public $redirectTo = ['index'];

    public function init()
    {
        if (empty($this->modelClass)) {
            throw new InvalidConfigException('Empty model
                class.');
        }
        parent::init();
    }

    public function run($id)
    {
        if (!\Yii::$app->getRequest()->getIsPost()) {
            throw new MethodNotAllowedHttpException
                ('Method not allowed.');
        }
        $model = $this->findModel($id);
        $model->delete();
        return $this->controller->redirect($this
            ->redirectTo);
    }

    /**
     * @param $id
     * @return \yii\db\ActiveRecord
     * @throws NotFoundHttpException
     */
    private function findModel($id)
    {
        $class = $this->modelClass;
        if (($model = $class::findOne($id)) !== null) {
            return $model;
        } else {
            throw new NotFoundHttpException('Page does not
                exist.');
        }
    }
}
```

2. Now we need to attach it to the `controllers/PostController.php` controller. Remove the controller's `actionDelete` and `behaviors` methods and attach your own action in the `action` method:

```php
<?php
namespace app\controllers;

use app\actions\DeleteAction;
use Yii;
use app\models\Post;
use app\models\PostSearch;
use yii\web\Controller;
use yii\web\NotFoundHttpException;

class PostController extends Controller
{
    public function actions()
    {
        return [
            'delete' => [
                'class' => DeleteAction::className(),
                'modelClass' => Post::className(),
            ],
        ];
    }

    public function actionIndex()  {  ...  }

    public function actionView($id)  {  ...  }

    public function actionCreate()  {  ...  }

    public function actionUpdate($id)  {  ...  }

    protected function findModel($id)
    {
        if (($model = Post::findOne($id)) !== null) {
            return $model;
        } else {
            throw new NotFoundHttpException('The requested page
does not exist.');
        }
    }
}
```

3. That is it. Ensure that the delete operation still works correctly, and after the deletion, you will be redirected to a corresponding index action.

How it works...

To create an external controller action, you need to extend your class from `yii\base\Action`. The only mandatory method to implement is `run`. In our case, it accepts the parameter named `$id` from `$_GET` using the automatic parameter binding feature of Yii and tries to delete a corresponding model.

To make it customizable, we've created two public properties configurable from the controller. These are `modelName`, which holds the name of the model we are working with, and `redirectTo` that specifies a route the user will be redirected to.

The configuration itself is done by implementing the actions method in your controller. There, you can attach the action once or multiple times and configure its public properties.

You can access the original controller object via the controller property if you need it to redirect to another action or render a specific view.

See also

▶ To learn more about controllers and actions refer, to `http://www.yiiframework.com/doc-2.0/guide-structure-controllers.html`

▶ The *Creating reusable controllers* recipe in this chapter

Creating reusable controllers

In Yii, you can create reusable controllers. If you are creating a lot of applications or controllers that are of the same type, moving all common code into a reusable controller will save you a lot of time.

In this recipe, we try to create a common `CleanController`, which will clear temporary directories and flush cached data.

Getting ready

Create a new `yii2-app-basic` application using the composer as described in the official guide at `http://www.yiiframework.com/doc-2.0/guide-start-installation.html`.

How to do it...

Carry out the following steps to create reusable controllers:

1. Create the `cleaner` directory and add the standalone `CleanController` controller:

```php
<?php
namespace app\cleaner;

use Yii;
use yii\filters\VerbFilter;
use yii\helpers\FileHelper;
use yii\web\Controller;

class CleanController extends Controller
{
    public $assetPaths = ['@app/web/assets'];
    public $runtimePaths = ['@runtime'];
    public $caches = ['cache'];

    public function behaviors()
    {
        return [
            'verbs' => [
                'class' => VerbFilter::className(),
                'actions' => [
                    'assets' => ['post'],
                    'runtime' => ['post'],
                    'cache' => ['post'],
                ],
            ],
        ];
    }

    public function actionIndex()
    {
        return $this->render('@app/cleaner/views/index');
    }

    public function actionAssets()
    {
        foreach ((array)$this->assetPaths as $path) {
            $this->cleanDir($path);
            Yii::$app->session->addFlash(
                'cleaner',
                'Assets path "' . $path . '" is cleaned.'
            );
        }
```

```php
            return $this->redirect(['index']);
    }

    public function actionRuntime()
    {
        foreach ((array)$this->runtimePaths as $path) {
            $this->cleanDir($path);
            Yii::$app->session->addFlash(
                'cleaner',
                'Runtime path "' . $path . '" is cleaned.'
            );
        }
        return $this->redirect(['index']);
    }

    public function actionCache()
    {
        foreach ((array)$this->caches as $cache) {
            Yii::$app->get($cache)->flush();
            Yii::$app->session->addFlash(
                'cleaner',
                'Cache "' . $cache . '" is cleaned.'
            );
        }
        return $this->redirect(['index']);
    }

    private function cleanDir($dir)
    {
        $iterator = new
            \DirectoryIterator(Yii::getAlias($dir));
        foreach($iterator as $sub) {
            if (!$sub->isDot() && $sub->isDir()) {
                FileHelper::removeDirectory($sub
                    ->getPathname());
            }
        }
    }
}
```

2. Create the `cleaner/views/index.php` view file for the `actionIndex` method:

```php
<?php
use yii\helpers\Html;
/* @var $this yii\web\View */
```

```php
$this->title = 'Cleaner';
$this->params['breadcrumbs'][] = $this->title;
?>
<div class="clean-index">
    <h1><?= Html::encode($this->title) ?></h1>

    <?php if (Yii::$app->session->hasFlash('cleaner')): ?>
    <?php foreach ((array)Yii::$app->session
            ->getFlash('cleaner', []) as $message): ?>
    <div class="alert alert-success">
        <?= $message ?>
    </div>
    <?php endforeach; ?>
    <?php endif; ?>


    <p>
        <?= Html::a('Clear Caches', ['cache'], [
            'class' => 'btn btn-primary',
            'data' => [
                'confirm' => 'Are you sure you want to
                    clear all cache data?',
                'method' => 'post',
            ],
        ]) ?>
        <?= Html::a('Clear Assets', ['assets'],
            ['class' => 'btn btn-primary',
                'data' => [
                    'confirm' => 'Are you sure you want to
                        clear all temporary assets?',
                    'method' => 'post',
                ],
        ]) ?>
        <?= Html::a('Clear Runtime', ['runtime'],
            ['class' => 'btn btn-primary',
                'data' => [
                    'confirm' => 'Are you sure you want to
                        clear all runtime files?',
                        'method' => 'post',
                ],
        ]) ?>
    </p>
</div>
```

3. Attach the controller to application via the `controllerMap` section of the `config/web.php` configuration file:

```
$config = [
    'id' => 'basic',
    'basePath' => dirname(__DIR__),
    'bootstrap' => ['log'],
    'controllerMap' => [
        'clean' => 'app\cleaner\CleanController',
    ],
    'components' => [
        ...
    ]
    ...
];
```

4. Add a new item to the main menu:

```
echo Nav::widget([
    'options' => ['class' => 'navbar-nav navbar-right'],
    'items' => [
        ['label' => 'Home', 'url' => ['/site/index']],
        ['label' => 'Cleaner', 'url' => ['/clean/index']],
        ['label' => 'About', 'url' => ['/site/about']],
        ...
    ],
]);
```

5. Open the controller and clear the assets:

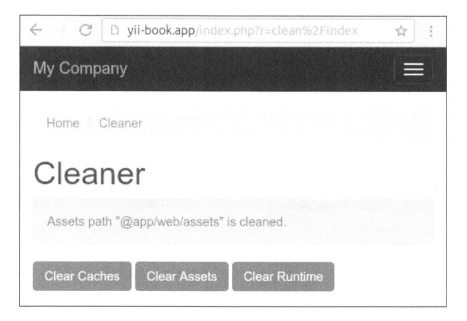

6. In case you use the yii2-app-advanced application template, just specify the correct paths in the configuration:

```
'controllerMap' => [
    'clean' => 'app\cleaner\CleanController',
    'assetPaths' => [
        '@backend/web/assets',
        '@frontend/web/assets',
    ],
    'runtimePaths' => [
        '@backend/runtime',
        '@frontend/runtime',
        '@console/runtime',
    ],
],
```

Now we can attach the controller to any application.

How it works...

When you are running an application and passing a route such as `clean/index`, prior to executing `CleanController::actionIndex`, Yii checks if there is `controllerMap` defined. Since we have a clean controller defined there, Yii executes it instead of going the usual way.

In the controller itself we defined the `assetPaths`, `runtimePaths`, and `caches` properties to be able to connect the controller to applications with different directory and cache structures. We are setting it when attaching the controller.

See also

▶ In order to learn more about controllers and about the controllers map, refer to `http://www.yiiframework.com/doc-2.0/guide-structure-controllers.html`

▶ The *Creating reusable controllers* recipe in this chapter

Creating a widget

A widget is a reusable part of a view that not only renders some data but also does it according to some logic. It can even get data from models and use its own views, so it is like a reduced reusable version of a module.

Let's create a widget that will draw a pie chart using Google APIs.

Getting ready

Create a new `yii2-app-basic` application using the composer as described in the official guide at `http://www.yiiframework.com/doc-2.0/guide-start-installation.html`.

How to do it...

1. Create the `widgets` directory and add the `ChartWidget` class:

```php
<?php
namespace app\widgets;

use yii\base\Widget;

class ChartWidget extends Widget
{
    public $title;
    public $width = 300;
    public $height = 200;
    public $data = [];
    public $labels = [];

    public function run()
    {
        $path = 'http://chart.apis.google.com/chart';

        $query = http_build_query([
            'chtt' => $this->title,
            'cht' => 'pc',
            'chs' => $this->width . 'x' . $this->height,
            'chd' => 't:' . implode(',', $this->data),
            'chds' => 'a',
            'chl' => implode('|', $this->labels),
            'chxt' => 'y',
            'chxl' => '0:|0|' . max($this->data)
        ]);

        $url = $path  . '?' . $query;

        return $this->render('chart', [
            'url' => $url,
        ]);
    }
}
```

2. Create the `widgets/views/chart.php` view:

```php
<?php
use yii\helpers\Html;

/* @var $this yii\web\View */
/* @var $url string */
?>

<div class="chart">
    <?= Html::img($url) ?>
</div>
```

3. Now create a `ChartController` controller:

```php
<?php
namespace app\controllers;

use yii\base\Controller;

class ChartController extends Controller
{
    public function actionIndex()
    {
        return $this->render('index');
    }
}
```

4. Add the `views/chart/index.php` view:

```php
<?php
use app\widgets\ChartWidget;
use yii\helpers\Html;

/* @var $this yii\web\View */

$this->title = 'Chart';
$this->params['breadcrumbs'][] =
    $this->title;
?>
<div class="site-about">
    <h1><?= Html::encode($this->title) ?></h1>

    <?= ChartWidget::widget([
        'title' => 'My Chart Diagram',
        'data' => [
            100 - 32,
```

```
                32,
            ],
            'labels' => [
                'Big',
                'Small',
            ],
        ]) ?>
    </div>
```

5. Now try to run the index action of the controller. You should see a pie chart like the following:

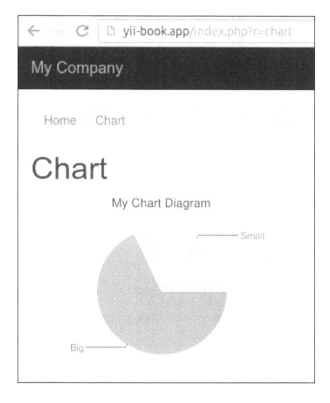

6. You can show any chart with different sizes and data sets.

How it works...

As in every other type of extension, we are creating some public properties we can configure when calling a widget using its `widget` method. In this case, we are configuring the title, data set, and data labels.

The main method of a widget is `run()`. In our widget, we are generating a URL and rendering the widget view, which uses the Google charting API for printing the `<img>` tag.

See also

▶ To learn more about widgets, refer to `http://www.yiiframework.com/doc-2.0/guide-structure-widgets.html`

▶ The *Making extensions distribution-ready* recipe in this chapter

Creating CLI commands

Yii has good command-line support and allows creating reusable console commands. Console commands are faster to create than web GUIs. If you need to create some kind of utility for your application that will be used by developers or administrators, console commands are the right tool.

To show how to create a console command, we'll create a simple command that will clean up various things, such as assets and temp directories.

Getting ready

Create a new `yii2-app-basic` application using the composer, as described in the official guide at `http://www.yiiframework.com/doc-2.0/guide-start-installation.html`.

How to do it...

Carry out the following steps to create CLI commands:

1. Create the `commands/CleanController.php` file with the following code:

```php
<?php
namespace app\commands;

use yii\console\Controller;
use yii\helpers\FileHelper;

/**
 * Removes content of assets and runtime directories.
 */
class CleanController extends Controller
{
    public $assetPaths = ['@app/web/assets'];
    public $runtimePaths = ['@runtime'];
```

```php
/**
 * Removes temporary assets.
 */
public function actionAssets()
{
    foreach ((array)$this->assetPaths as $path) {
        $this->cleanDir($path);
    }

    $this->stdout('Done' . PHP_EOL);
}

/**
 * Removes runtime content.
 */
public function actionRuntime()
{
    foreach ((array)$this->runtimePaths as $path) {
        $this->cleanDir($path);
    }

    $this->stdout('Done' . PHP_EOL);
}

private function cleanDir($dir)
{
    $iterator = new
        \DirectoryIterator(\Yii::getAlias($dir));
    foreach($iterator as $sub) {
        if(!$sub->isDot() && $sub->isDir()) {
            $this->stdout('Removed ' . $sub
                ->getPathname() . PHP_EOL);
            FileHelper::removeDirectory($sub
                ->getPathname());
        }
    }
}
```

2. Now we can use our own console controller with default settings. Just run the `yii` shell script:

   ./yii

3. Look for own `clean` commands:

```
This is Yii version 2.0.7.

The following commands are available:

- asset                    Allows you to combine...
    asset/compress         Combines and compresses the asset...
    asset/template         Creates template of configuration
file...


   ...


- clean                    Removes content of assets and runtime
directories.
    clean/assets           Removes temporary assets.
    clean/runtime          Removes runtime content.


- fixture                  Manages fixture data loading and
unloading.
    fixture/load (default) Loads the specified fixture data.
    fixture/unload         Unloads the specified fixtures.


   ...
```

4. Right now run asset cleaning:

```
.yii clean/assets
```

5. See the process report:

```
Removed /yii-book.app/web/assets/25f82b8a
Removed /yii-book.app/web/assets/9b3b2888
Removed /yii-book.app/web/assets/f4307424
Done
```

6. If you want to use this controller in the `yii2-app-advanced` application, just specify the custom working paths:

```
return [
    'id' => 'app-console',
    'basePath' => dirname(__DIR__),
    'bootstrap' => ['log'],
```

```
            'controllerNamespace' => 'console\controllers',
            'controllerMap' => [
                'clean' => [
                    'class' =>
                        'console\controllers\CleanController',
                    'assetPaths' => [
                        '@backend/web/assets',
                        '@frontend/web/assets',
                    ],
                    'runtimePaths' => [
                        '@backend/runtime',
                        '@frontend/runtime',
                        '@console/runtime',
                    ],
                ],
            ],
            // ...
        ];
```

How it works...

All console commands should be extended from the `yii\console\Controller` class. Since all console commands are run in `yii\console\Application` instead of `yii\web\Application`, we don't have a way to determine the value of the `@webroot` alias. Also, in the `yii2-app-advanced` template we have backend, frontend, and console subdirectories by default. For this purpose, we are creating configurable public properties called `assetPaths` and `runtimePaths`.

The console command structure itself is like a typical controller. We are defining several actions we can run via `yii <console command>/<command action>`.

As you can see, there are no views used, so we can focus on programming tasks instead of design, markup, and so on. Still, you need to provide some useful output so that users will know what is going on. This is done through simple PHP echo statements.

If your command is relatively complex such as message or migrate bundled with Yii, it's a good decision to provide some extra description of the available options and actions. It can be done by overriding the `getHelp` method:

```php
public function getHelp()
{
    $out = "Clean command allows you to clean up various temporary
data Yii and an application are generating.\n\n";
    return $out . parent::getHelp();
}
```

Run the following command:

```
./yii help clean
```

You can see the full output as follows:

```
DESCRIPTION
Clean command allows you to clean up various temporary data Yii and an
application are generating.
Removes content of assets and runtime directories.
SUB-COMMANDS
- clean/assets    Removes temporary assets.
- clean/runtime   Removes runtime content.
```

By default, when we run the shell command:

```
./yii
```

We have seen simplified description of all commands in the output list:

```
- clean                    Removes content of assets and runtime
directories.
    clean/assets           Removes temporary assets.
    clean/runtime          Removes runtime content.
```

This description will be taken from comments before class and actions:

```
/**
 * Removes content of assets and runtime directories.
 */
class CleanController extends Controller
{
    /**
     * Removes temporary assets.
     */
    public function actionAssets() { … }


     * Removes runtime content.
     */
    public function actionRuntime() { … }
}
```

It is optional to add descriptions for your classes. You must not do it for your own CLI commands.

- ▸ The *Creating reusable controllers* recipe in this chapter
- ▸ The *Making extensions distribution-ready* recipe in this chapter

Creating filters

A filter is a class that can run before/after an action is executed. It can be used to modify execution context or decorate output. In our example, we'll implement a simple access filter that will allow the user to see private content only after accepting the **User agreement**.

Getting ready

Create a new `yii2-app-basic` application using the composer, as described in the official guide at `http://www.yiiframework.com/doc-2.0/guide-start-installation.html`.

How to do it...

1. Create the agreement form model:

```php
<?php
namespace app\models;

use yii\base\Model;

class AgreementForm extends Model
{
    public $accept;

    public function rules()
    {
        return [
            ['accept', 'required'],
            ['accept', 'compare', 'compareValue' => 1,
                'message' => 'You must agree the rules.'],
        ];
    }

    public function attributeLabels()
    {
```

```php
        return [
            'accept' => 'I completely accept the rules.'
        ];
    }
}
```

2. Create the agreement checker service:

```php
<?php

namespace app\services;

use Yii;
use yii\web\Cookie;

class AgreementChecker
{
    public function isAllowed()
    {
        return Yii::$app->request->cookies->has('agree');
    }

    public function allowAccess()
    {
        Yii::$app->response->cookies->add(new Cookie([
            'name' => 'agree',
            'value' => 'on',
            'expire' => time() + 3600 * 24 * 90, // 90 days
        ]));
    }
}
```

   1. It encapsulates work with the agreement cookies.

3. Create the filter class:

```php
<?php

namespace app\filters;

use app\services\AgreementChecker;
use Yii;
use yii\base\ActionFilter;

class AgreementFilter extends ActionFilter
{
    public function beforeAction($action)
    {
        $checker = new AgreementChecker();
```

```php
        if (!$checker->isAllowed()) {
            Yii::$app->response
                ->redirect(['/content/agreement'])->send();
            return false;
        }
        return true;
    }
}
```

4. Create the content controller and attach the filter to its behaviors:

```php
<?php
namespace app\controllers;

use app\filters\AgreementFilter;
use app\models\AgreementForm;
use app\services\AgreementChecker;
use Yii;
use yii\web\Controller;

class ContentController extends Controller
{
    public function behaviors()
    {
        return [
            [
                'class' => AgreementFilter::className(),
                'only' => ['index'],
            ],
        ];
    }

    public function actionIndex()
    {
        return $this->render('index');
    }

    public function actionAgreement()
    {
        $model = new AgreementForm();
        if ($model->load(Yii::$app->request->post())
            && $model->validate()) {
            $checker = new AgreementChecker();
            $checker->allowAccess();
            return $this->redirect(['index']);
```

```
            } else {
                return $this->render('agreement', [
                    'model' => $model,
                ]);
            }
        }
    }
}
```

5. Add the `views/content/index.php` view with private content:

```php
<?php
use yii\helpers\Html;

/* @var $this yii\web\View */
$this->title = 'Content';
$this->params['breadcrumbs'][] = $this->title;
?>
<div class="site-about">
    <h1><?= Html::encode($this->title) ?></h1>

    <div class="well">
        This is our private page.
    </div>
</div>
```

6. Add the `views/content/agreement.php` view with the form:

```php
<?php
use yii\helpers\Html;
use yii\bootstrap\ActiveForm;

/* @var $this yii\web\View */
/* @var $form yii\bootstrap\ActiveForm */
/* @var $model app\models\AgreementForm */

$this->title = 'User agreement';
$this->params['breadcrumbs'][] = $this->title;
?>
<div class="site-login">
    <h1><?= Html::encode($this->title) ?></h1>

    <p>Please agree with our rules:</p>

    <?php $form = ActiveForm::begin(); ?>

        <?= $form->field($model, 'accept')->checkbox() ?>
```

```
    <div class="form-group">
        <?= Html::submitButton('Accept', ['class' =>
            'btn btn-success']) ?>
        <?= Html::a('Cancel', ['/site/index'], ['class'
            => 'btn btn-danger']) ?>
    </div>

    <?php ActiveForm::end(); ?>
</div>
```

7. Add the main menu item to the `views/layouts/main.php` file:

```
echo Nav::widget([
    'options' => ['class' => 'navbar-nav navbar-right'],
    'items' => [
        ['label' => 'Home', 'url' => ['/site/index']],
        ['label' => 'Content', 'url' =>
            ['/content/index']],
        ['label' => 'About', 'url' => ['/site/about']],
        ...
    ],
]);
```

8. Try to open the content page. The filter must redirect you to the agreement page:

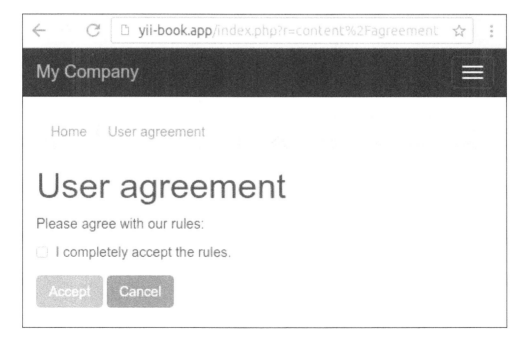

9. Only after accepting the rules can you see the private content:

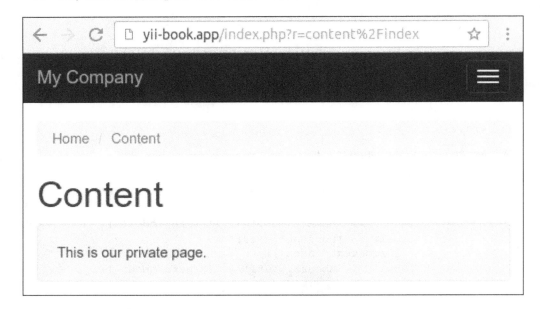

10. Also, you can attach the filter to other controllers or modules.

How it works...

A filter should extend the `yii\base\ActionFilter` class, which extends `yii\base\Behavior`. We can override the `beforeAction` or `afterAction` method if we want to do post- and pre-filtering.

For example, we can check user access and throw corresponding HTTP-exceptions in a fail case. In this recipe, we redirect the user to the agreement page if the specific cookie value does not exist:

```
class AgreementFilter extends ActionFilter
{
    public function beforeAction($action)
    {
        $checker = new AgreementChecker();
        if (!$checker->isAllowed()) {
            Yii::$app->response->redirect(['/content/agreement'])
                ->send();
            return false;
        }
        return true;
    }
}
```

You can attach filters to any controller or module. To specify the list of necessary routes, just use the `only` or `except` options. For example, we apply our filter only for the index action of the controller:

```
public function behaviors()
{
    return [
        [
            'class' => AgreementFilter::className(),
            'only' => ['index'],
        ],
    ];
}
```

> Do not forget to return a `true` value in the success case from the `beforeAction` method. Otherwise, the controller action will not be executed.

See also

For more information about filters, refer to `http://www.yiiframework.com/doc-2.0/guide-structure-filters.html`.

For build-in cache and access control filters, refer to:

- `http://www.yiiframework.com/doc-2.0/guide-caching-http.html`
- `http://www.yiiframework.com/doc-2.0/guide-security-authorization.html`
- The *Creating model behaviors* recipe

Creating modules

If you have created a complex application part and want to use it with some degree of customization in your next project, most probably you need to create a module. In this recipe, we will see how to create an application log view module.

Getting ready

Create a new `yii2-app-basic` application using the composer, as described in the official guide at `http://www.yiiframework.com/doc-2.0/guide-start-installation.html`.

How to do it...

Let's do some planning first.

In `yii2-app-basic` with default configuration, all log entries are stored in the `runtime/logs/app.log` file. We can extract all messages from this file with help of regular expressions and display them on the **GridView** widget. Besides, we must allow the user to configure the path to the custom log file.

Carry out the following steps:

1. Create the `modules/log` directory and create the `Module` class with the new file option:

```php
<?php
namespace app\modules\log;

class Module extends \yii\base\Module
{
    public $file = '@runtime/logs/app.log';
}
```

2. Create a simple model for transferring rows from the log file:

```php
<?php
namespace app\modules\log\models;

use yii\base\Object;

class LogRow extends Object
{
    public $time;
    public $ip;
    public $userId;
    public $sessionId;
    public $level;
    public $category;
    public $text;
}
```

3. Write a log file reader class that will parse file rows, reverse its order, and return array of instances of the `LogRow` models:

```php
<?php
namespace app\modules\log\services;

use app\modules\log\models\LogRow;
```

```php
class LogReader
{
    public function getRows($file)
    {
        $result = [];
        $handle = @fopen($file, "r");
        if ($handle) {
            while (($row = fgets($handle)) !== false) {
                $pattern =
                    '#^' .
                    '(?P<time>\d{4}\-\d{2}\-\d{2}
                    \d{2}:\d{2}:\d{2}) ' .
                    '\[(?P<ip>[^\]]+)\]' .
                    '\[(?P<userId>[^\]]+)\]' .
                    '\[(?P<sessionId>[^\]]+)\]' .
                    '\[(?P<level>[^\]]+)\]' .
                    '\[(?P<category>[^\]]+)\]' .
                    ' (?P<text>.*?)' .
                    '(\$\_(GET|POST|REQUEST|COOKIE|SERVER)
                        = \[)?' .
                    '$#i';
                if (preg_match($pattern, $row, $matches)) {
                    if ($matches['text']) {
                        $result[] = new LogRow([
                            'time' => $matches['time'],
                            'ip' => $matches['ip'],
                            'userId' => $matches['userId'],
                            'sessionId' =>
                                $matches['sessionId'],
                            'level' => $matches['level'],
                            'category' =>
                                $matches['category'],
                            'text' => $matches['text'],
                        ]);
                    }
                }
            }
            fclose($handle);
        }
        return array_reverse($result);
    }
}
```

4. Add a helper for displaying pretty HTML-badges for the log levels:

```php
<?php
namespace app\modules\log\helpers;

use yii\helpers\ArrayHelper;
use yii\helpers\Html;

class LogHelper
{
    public static function levelLabel($level)
    {
        $classes = [
            'error' => 'danger',
            'warning' => 'warning',
            'info' => 'primary',
            'trace' => 'default',
            'profile' => 'success',
            'profile begin' => 'info',
            'profile end' => 'info',
        ];

        $class = ArrayHelper::getValue($classes, $level,
            'default');
        return Html::tag('span', Html::encode($level),
            ['class' => 'label-' . $class]);
    }
}
```

5. Create a module controller that will get an array of rows from the reader and pass them into `ArrayDataProvider`:

```php
<?php
namespace app\modules\log\controllers;

use app\modules\log\services\LogReader;
use yii\data\ArrayDataProvider;
use yii\web\Controller;

class DefaultController extends Controller
{
    public function actionIndex()
    {
        $reader = new LogReader();
        $dataProvider = new ArrayDataProvider([
            'allModels' => $reader->getRows($this
```

```
                    ->getFile()),
        ]);
        return $this->render('index', [
            'dataProvider' => $dataProvider,
        ]);
    }

    private function getFile()
    {
        return \Yii::getAlias($this->module->file);
    }
}
```

6. Now, create the `modules/log/default/index.php` view file:

```php
<?php
use app\modules\log\helpers\LogHelper;
use app\modules\log\models\LogRow;
use yii\grid\GridView;
use yii\helpers\Html;

/* @var $this yii\web\View */
/* @var $dataProvider yii\data\ArrayDataProvider */

$this->title = 'Application log';
$this->params['breadcrumbs'][] = $this->title;
?>
<div class="log-index">
    <h1><?= Html::encode($this->title) ?></h1>

    <?= GridView::widget([
        'dataProvider' => $dataProvider,
        'columns' => [
            [


                'attribute' => 'time',
                    'format' => 'datetime',
                    'contentOptions' => [
                        'style' => 'white-space: nowrap',
                    ],
            ],
            'ip:text:IP',
            'userId:text:User',
            [
                'attribute' => 'level',
                'value' => function (LogRow $row) {
```

```
                            return LogHelper::levelLabel
                                ($row->level);
                        },
                        'format' => 'raw',
                    ],
                    'category',
                    'text',
                ],
            ]) ?>
    </div>
```

7. Attach the module to your application in the `config/web.php` file:

```
$config = [
    'id' => 'basic',
    'basePath' => dirname(__DIR__),
    'bootstrap' => ['log'],
    'modules' => [
        'log' => 'app\modules\log\Module',
    ],
    'components' => [

    ],
    ...
];
```

8. Add a link to the controller in the `views/layouts/main.php` file:

```
echo Nav::widget([
    'options' => ['class' => 'navbar-nav navbar-right'],
    'items' => [
        ['label' => 'Home', 'url' => ['/site/index']],
        ['label' => 'Log', 'url' =>
            ['/log/default/index']],
        ['label' => 'About', 'url' => ['/site/about']],
        ['label' => 'Contact', 'url' => ['/site/contact']],
        ...
    ],
]);
NavBar::end();
```

9. Go to url `/index.php?r=log` and ensure that the module works:

Home   Application log

Application log

Showing **1-20** of **47** items.

Time	IP	User	Level	Category	Text
Jul 30, 2016, 12:53:26 PM	127.0.0.1	-	error	yii\web\HttpException:404	exception 'yii\base\InvalidRouteExcepti in vendor/yiisoft/yii2/base/Module.php:4
Jul 30, 2016, 12:26:46 PM	127.0.0.1	-	error	yii\base\ErrorException:2	exception 'yii\base\ErrorException' with at offset 211' in /log/LogReader.php:24
Jul 28, 2016, 4:33:33 PM	-	-	error	yii\console\Exception	exception 'yii\base\InvalidRouteExcepti hello/test' in /yiisoft/yii2/base/Controller.
Jul 27, 2016, 10:35:49 AM	-	-	error	yii\db\Exception	exception 'PDOException' with messag book-tests' in /vendor/yiisoft/yii2/db/Cor
Jul 27, 2016, 10:35:29 AM	-	-	error	yii\db\Exception	exception 'PDOException' with messag 'yii2_basic_tests' in /vendor/yiisoft/yii2/d
Jul 11, 2016, 5:14:06 PM	-	-	error	yii\db\Exception	exception 'PDOException' with messag column list: 1136 Column count doesn't /vendor/yiisoft/yii2/db/Command.php:78

« **1** 2 3 »

How it works...

You can group your controllers, models, views, and other components by separated modules and attach them into your application. You can generate a module template with the help of Gii or make it manually.

Each module contains a main module class where we can define configurable properties, define change paths, attach controllers, and so on. By default, a module generated with Gii runs the `index` action of the default controller.

See also

- For more information about modules and about best practices, refer to `http://www.yiiframework.com/doc-2.0/guide-structure-modules.html`
- The _Making extensions distribution-ready_ recipe

Creating a custom view renderer

There are many PHP template engines out there. Yii2 only offers native PHP templates. If you want to use one of the existing template engines or create your own one, you have to implement it—of course, if it's not yet implemented by the Yii community.

In this recipe we'll re-implement the Smarty templates support.

Getting ready

1. Create a new `yii2-app-basic` application using the composer, as described in the official guide at `http://www.yiiframework.com/doc-2.0/guide-start-installation.html`.

2. Install the Smarty library:

   ```
   composer require smarty/smarty
   ```

How to do it...

Carry out the following steps for creating a custom view renderer:

1. Create the `smarty/ViewRenderer.php` file:

   ```php
   <?php
   namespace app\smarty;

   use Smarty;
   use Yii;

   class ViewRenderer extends \yii\base\ViewRenderer
   {
       public $cachePath = '@runtime/smarty/cache';
       public $compilePath = '@runtime/smarty/compile';

       /**
        * @var Smarty
        */
       private $smarty;

       public function init()
       {
           $this->smarty = new Smarty();
           $this->smarty->setCompileDir(Yii::getAlias($this
               ->compilePath));
   ```

```
            $this->smarty->setCacheDir(Yii::getAlias($this
                ->cachePath));
            $this->smarty->setTemplateDir([
                dirname(Yii::$app->getView()->getViewFile()),
                Yii::$app->getViewPath(),
            ]);
        }

        public function render($view, $file, $params)
        {
            $templateParams = empty($params) ? null : $params;
            $template = $this->smarty->createTemplate($file,
                null, null, $templateParams, false);
            $template->assign('app', \Yii::$app);
            $template->assign('this', $view);
            return $template->fetch();
        }
    }
```

2. Now we need to connect the view renderer to the application. In `config/web php`, we need to add renderers of the view component:

```
'components' => [
    ....
    'view' => [
        'renderers' => [
            'tpl' => [
                'class' => 'app\smarty\ViewRenderer',
            ],
        ],
    ],
    ...
];
```

3. Now let's test it. Create a new `SmartyController`:

```
<?php
namespace app\controllers;

use yii\web\Controller;

class SmartyController extends Controller
{
    public function actionIndex()
    {
        return $this->render('index.tpl', [
            'name' => 'Bond',
```

```
        ]);
    }
}
```

4. Next, we need to create the `views/smarty/index.tpl` view:

```
<div class="smarty-index">
    <h1>Smarty Example</h1>
    <p>Hello, {$name}!</p>
</div>
```

5. Now try running the controller. In a success case, you should get the following as output:

How it works...

A view renderer is a child of the `yii\base\ViewRenderer` abstract class that implements only one method, called `render`:

```php
<?php
namespace yii\base;

abstract class ViewRenderer extends Component
{
    /**
     * Renders a view file.
     *
     * This method is invoked by [[View]] whenever it tries to
     * render a view.
     * Child classes must implement this method to render the given
     * view file.
```

```
         *
         * @param View $view the view object used for rendering the
         file.
         * @param string $file the view file.
         * @param array $params the parameters to be passed to the view
         file.
         * @return string the rendering result
         */
        abstract public function render($view, $file, $params);
    }
```

Therefore, we are getting a view component, file path, and render variables. We need to process the file and return the rendered result. In our case, processing itself is done by the Smarty template engine, so we need to properly initialize it and call its processing methods:

```
class ViewRenderer extends \yii\base\ViewRenderer
{
    public $cachePath = '@runtime/smarty/cache';
    public $compilePath = '@runtime/smarty/compile';
    private $smarty;

    public function init()
    {
        $this->smarty = new Smarty();
        $this->smarty->setCompileDir(Yii::getAlias($this-
        >compilePath));
        $this->smarty->setCacheDir(Yii::getAlias($this-
        >cachePath));
        $this->smarty->setTemplateDir([
            dirname(Yii::$app->getView()->getViewFile()),
            Yii::$app->getViewPath(),
        ]);
    }
    ...
}
```

It is a good practice to store Yii temporary files in the application runtime directory. That is why we are setting the compile directory, where Smarty stores its templates compiled into PHP, to runtime/smarty/compile.

Rendering itself is a bit simpler:

```
public function render($view, $file, $params)
{
    $templateParams = empty($params) ? null : $params;
    $template = $this->smarty->createTemplate($file, null, null,
        $templateParams, false);
```

```
$template->assign('app', \Yii::$app);
$template->assign('this', $view);
return $template->fetch();
}
```

All data set via `$this->render` is passed to the Smarty template as it is. Also, we are creating special Smarty template variables named `app` and `this` that point to `Yii::$app` and `Yii::$app->view` and allow us to get application properties inside a template.

Then, we are rendering the templates.

See also

You can get ready to use Smarty view renderer with plugins and configuration support at `https://github.com/yiisoft/yii2-smarty`.

To learn more about Smarty and view renderers in general, refer to the following URLs:

- `http://www.smarty.net`
- `http://www.yiiframework.com/doc-2.0/guide-tutorial-template-engines.html`
- `http://www.yiiframework.com/doc-2.0/guide-structure-views.html`

Creating a multilanguage application

Every day, we meet more and more international companies, software products, and information resources that publish content on multiple languages. Yii2 provides built-in i18n support for making multilanguage applications.

In this recipe, we are translating the application interface to different languages.

Getting ready

Create a new `yii2-app-basic` application using the composer, as described in the official guide at `http://www.yiiframework.com/doc-2.0/guide-start-installation.html`.

How to do it...

1. Change the main menu labels in the `views/layouts/main.php` file to use the `Yii::t('app/nav', '...')` method:

```
echo Nav::widget([
    'options' => ['class' => 'navbar-nav navbar-right'],
```

```
            'items' => [
                ['label' => Yii::t('app/nav', 'Home'), 'url' =>
                    ['/site/index']],
                ['label' => Yii::t('app/nav', 'About'), 'url' =>
                    ['/site/about']],
                ['label' => Yii::t('app/nav', 'Contact'), 'url' =>
                    ['/site/contact']],
                ...
            ],
        ]);
```

2. Change all your titles and breadcrumbs to use the common `Yii::t('app, '...')` method:

```
$this->title = Yii::t('app', 'Contact');
$this->params['breadcrumbs'][] = $this->title;
```

3. Also, change all the labels of your buttons:

```
<div class="form-group">
    <?= Html::submitButton(Yii::t('app', 'Submit'),
        ['class' => 'btn btn-primary'']) ?>
</div>
```

Change other hard-coded messages as well:

```
<p>
    <?= Yii::t('app', 'The above error occurred while the
        Web server was processing your request.') ?>
</p>
```

4. Change the attribute labels of your `ContactForm` model:

```
class LoginForm extends Model
{
    ...

    public function attributeLabels()
    {
        return [
            'username' => Yii::t('app/user', 'Username'),
            'password' => Yii::t('app/user', 'Password'),
            'rememberMe' => Yii::t('app/user', 'Remember
                Me'),
        ];
    }
}
```

Also, change the attribute labels of the `LoginForm` model:

```
class ContactForm extends Model
{
    ...

    public function attributeLabels()
    {
        return [
            'name' => Yii::t('app/contact', 'Name'),
            'email' => Yii::t('app/contact', 'Email'),
            'subject' => Yii::t('app/contact', 'Subject'),
            'body' => Yii::t('app/contact', 'Body'),
            'verifyCode' => Yii::t('app', 'Verification
                Code'),
        ];
    }
}
```

It will output translated labels for the current language instead of originals.

5. To prepare translations, create the `messages` directory. Right now, we can create translation files for all needed languages. We can do it manually, but there is a helpful crawler that can scan all project files and extract all messages from `Yii::t()` constructions. Let's use it.

6. Generate the configuration file for the message scanner:

    ./yii message/config-template config/messages.php

7. Open the configuration file and set the following values:

    ```php
    <?php

    return [
        'sourcePath' => '@app',
        'languages' => ['de', 'fr'],
        'translator' => 'Yii::t',
        'sort' => false,
        'removeUnused' => false,
        'markUnused' => true,
        'only' => ['*.php'],
        'except' => [
            '.svn',
            '.git',
            '.gitignore',
            '.gitkeep',
            '.hgignore',
    ```

```
            '.hgkeep',
            '/messages',
            '/vendor',
        ],

        'format' => 'php',
        'messagePath' => '@app/messages',
        'overwrite' => true,

        'ignoreCategories' => [
            'yii',
        ],
    ];
```

8. Run crawler while passing this configuration file to it:

    ./yii message config/messages.php

9. After the process, we must get the following directory structure:

```
messages
├── de
│   ├── app
│   │   ├── contact.php
│   │   ├── nav.php
│   │   └── user.php
│   └── app.php
└── fr
    ├── app
    │   ├── contact.php
    │   ├── nav.php
    │   └── user.php
    └── app.php
```

10. For example, the `messages/de/app/contact` file contains the following content:

```
<?php
...
return [
    'Body' => '',
    'Email' => '',
    'Name' => '',
    'Subject' => '',
];
```

11. It is a plain PHP array with original sentences in keys and translated messages in values.

12. Just put in the values needed to translate messages from Deutsch:

```php
<?php
...
return [
    'Password' => 'Passwort',
    'Remember Me' => 'Erinnere dich an mich',
    'Username' => 'Benutzername',
];
```

13. Attach these translations to the `i18n` component of application in the `config/web.php` file:

```php
$config = [
    'id' => 'basic',
    'basePath' => dirname(__DIR__),
    'bootstrap' => ['log'],
    'components' => [
        ...
        'i18n' => [
            'translations' => [
                'app*' => [
                    'class' => 'yii\i18n\PhpMessageSource',
                    'sourceLanguage' => 'en-US',
                ],
            ],
        ],
        'db' => require(__DIR__ . '/db.php'),
    ],
    'params' => $params,
];
```

14. Open the login page with the default language:

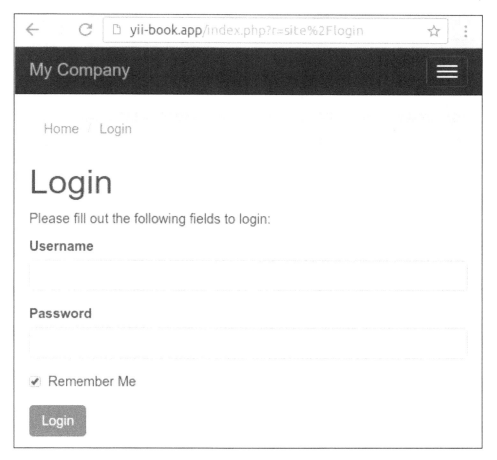

15. Switch the application language to `de`:

```
$config = [
    'id' => 'basic',
    'language' => 'de',
    'basePath' => dirname(__DIR__),
    'bootstrap' => ['log'],
    ...
];
```

Then refresh the login page:

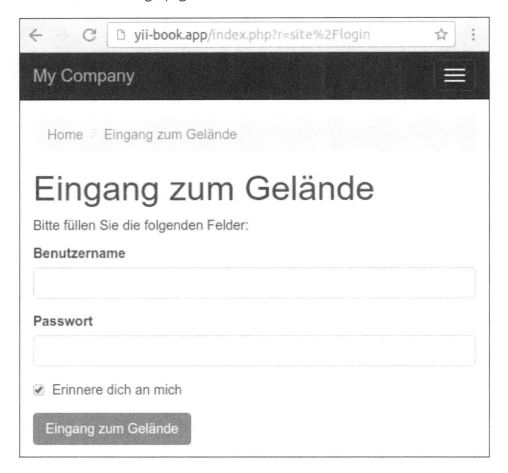

16. The built-in frameworks messages and default validation errors will be translated automatically.

How it works...

Yii2 provides the `Yii::t()` method for translating interface messages via the `i18n` component, which supports different types of sources. In this recipe, we use `yii\i18n\hpMessageSource`, which stores translated messages in plain PHP files.

The framework does not have artificial intelligence and does not translate messages by itself. You must put prepared translations in files or in the database and framework to get the needed message from this message source.

You can set the current language manually:

```
$config = [
    'id' => 'basic',
    'language' => 'de',
    ...
];
```

Instead of setting the language in the configuration file, you can switch the application language in runtime:

```
Yii::$app->language = 'fr';
```

For example, if you store the user language in the lang field of the User model, you can create the language loader:

```
<?php
namespace app\bootstrap;

use yii\base\BootstrapInterface;

class LanguageBootstrap implements BootstrapInterface
{
    public function bootstrap($app)
    {
        if (!$app->user->isGuest) {
            $app->language = $app->user->identity->lang;
        }
    }
}
```

Register this class in the bootstrapping list:

```
$config = [
    'id' => 'basic',
    'basePath' => dirname(__DIR__),
    'bootstrap' => ['log', 'app'bootstrap\LanguageBoostrap'],
    ...
];
```

Now, every authenticated user will see the interface in their own language.

Also, you can override the yii\web\UrlManager class for passing the current language as a GET parameter or as a prefix of a URL. Also, as an alternative you can store selected languages in browser cookies.

When you generate models and another code with Gii, you can check the following option:

All labels in the generated code will be embraced into the `Yii::t()` calls.

 We did not cover the translating of model content in this recipe. However, for example, you can store translated texts in separate tables (such as the `post_lang` table for post model table) in a database and use the value of the `Yii::$app->language` property to get the current language and extract needed content for your models by the value.

See also

For more information about internationalization in Yii2, refer to `http://www.yiiframework.com/doc-2.0/guide-tutorial-i18n.html`.

Making extensions distribution-ready

In this chapter, you learned how to create various types of Yii extensions. Now we'll talk about how to share your results with people and why it's important.

Getting ready

Let's form a checklist for a good extension first. A good programming product should follow these points:

- Good coding style
- People should be able to find it
- A consistent, easy to read, and easy to use API
- Good documentation
- Extension should apply to the most common use cases
- Should be maintained
- Well-tested code, ideally with unit tests
- You need to provide support for it

Of course, having all these requires a lot of work, but these are necessary to create a good product.

How to do it...

1. Every modern PHP product must follow the PSR4 standards of autoloading and the PSR1 and PSR2 standards of the coding style from the `http://www.php-fig.org/psr/` guide.

2. Let's review our list in more detail, starting with the API. The API should be consistent, easy to read, and easy to use. Consistent means that the overall style should not change, so no different variable naming, no inconsistent names such as `isFlag1()` and `isNotFlag2()`, and so on. Everything should obey the rules you've defined for your code. This allows less checking of documentation and allows you to focus on coding.

3. A code without any documentation is almost useless. An exception is a relatively simple code, but even if it's only a few lines, it doesn't feel right if there is not a single word about how to install and use it. What makes good documentation? The purpose of the code and its pros should be as visible as possible and should be written loud and clear.

4. A code is useless if developers don't know where to put it and what should be in the application configuration. Don't expect that people know how to do framework-specific things. The installation guide should be verbose. A step-by-step form is preferred by a majority of developers. If the code needs SQL schema to work, provide it.

5. Even if your API methods and properties are named properly, you still need to document them with PHPDoc comments specifying argument types and return types, providing a brief description for each method. Don't forget protected and private methods and properties since sometimes it's necessary to read these to understand the details of how code works. Also, consider listing public methods and properties in documentation so it can be used as a reference.

6. Provide use case examples with well-commented code. Try to cover the most common ways of extension usage.

7. In an example, don't try to solve multiple problems at a time since it can be confusing.

8. It's important to make your code flexible so it will apply to many use cases. However, since it's not possible to create code for every possible use case, try to cover the most common ones.

9. It's important to make people feel comfortable. Providing a good documentation is a first step. The second is providing a proof that your code works as expected and will work with further updates. The best way to do it is a set of unit tests.

10. Extension should be maintained, at least until it's stable and there are no more feature requests and bug reports. So expect questions and reports, and reserve some time to work on the code further. If you can't devote more time to maintain extensions, but it's very innovative and no one did it before, it's still worth sharing. If the community likes it, someone will definitely offer his or her help.

11. Finally, you need to make extensions available. Create the Composer package from your extension, push it on GitHub or other shared repository storage, and publish it on the `https://packagist.org` site.

12. Each extension should have a version number and a change log. It will allow the community to check if they have the latest version and check what is changed before upgrading. We recommend to follow the **Semantic Versioning** rules from the `http://semver.org` site.

13. Even if your extension is relatively simple and documentation is good, there could be questions, and for the first time, the only person who can answer them is you. Typically, questions are asked at official forums, so it is better to create a topic where people can discuss your code and provide a link at the extension page.

How it works...

If you want to share an extension with the community and be sure it will be useful and popular, you need to do more than just write code. Making extensions distribution-ready is much more work to do. It can be even more than creating an extension itself. So, why is it good to share extensions with the community in the first place?

Making the code you use in your own projects open source has its pros. You are getting people, a lot more people than you can get to test your closed source project. People who are using your extension are testing it, giving valuable feedback, and reporting bugs. If your code is popular, there will be passionate developers who will try to improve your code, to make it more extensive, more stable, and reusable. Moreover, it just feels good because you are doing a good thing.

We have covered the most important things. Still, there are more things to check out. Try existing extensions before writing your own. If an extension almost fits, try contacting the extension author and contributing ideas you have. Reviewing existing code helps you find out useful tricks, dos, and don'ts. Also, check wiki articles and the official forum from time to time; there is a lot of useful information about creating extensions and developing using Yii in general.

See also

▸ For modern information about PHP coding standards, refer to `http://www.php-fig.org/psr/`

▸ To learn more about semantic versioning, refer to `http://semver.org`

9

Performance Tuning

In this chapter, we will cover the following topics:

- ▶ Following best practices
- ▶ Speeding up session handling
- ▶ Using cache dependencies and chains
- ▶ Profiling an application with Yii
- ▶ Leveraging HTTP caching
- ▶ Combining and minimizing assets
- ▶ Running Yii2 on HHVM

Yii is one of the fastest frameworks available. Nevertheless, when developing and deploying an application, it is good to have some extra performance for free, and to follow the best practices for the application itself. In this chapter, you will see how to configure Yii to gain extra performance. In addition, you will learn some best practices for developing an application that will run smoothly until you have very high loads.

Following best practices

In this recipe, you will see how to configure Yii2 for the best performance and some additional principles of building responsive applications. These principles are both general and Yii-related. Therefore, we will be able to apply some of these even without using Yii2.

Getting ready

Create a new `yii2-app-basic` application using the Composer package manager, as described in the official guide at `http://www.yiiframework.com/doc-2.0/guide-start-installation.html`.

How to do it...

1. Update your PHP to the latest stable version. Major releases of PHP may bring significant performance improvements. Turn off the debug mode and set the `prod` environment. This can be done by editing `web/index.php` as follows:

```
defined('YII_DEBUG') or define('YII_DEBUG', false);
defined('YII_ENV') or define('YII_ENV', 'prod');
```

> **Note**: In the `yii2-app-advanced` application skeleton, you can use the shell command `php init` and opt production environment for loading optimized `index.php` and configuration files.

2. Enable the `cache` component:

```
'components' => [
    'cache' => [
        'class' => 'yii\caching\FileCache',
    ],
],
```

You can use any cache storage instead of `FileCache`. Also, you can register multiple cache application components and use `Yii::$app->cache` and `Yii::$app->cache2` for different data types:

```
'components' => [
    'cache' => [
        'class' => 'yii\caching\MemCache',
        'useMemcached' => true,
    ],
    'cache2' => [
        'class' => 'yii\caching\FileCache',
    ],
],
```

The framework uses the `cache` component by default in its own classes.

3. Enable table schema caching for the `db` component as follows:

```
return [
    // ...
    'components' => [
```

```
        // ...
        'cache' => [
            'class' => 'yii\caching\FileCache',
        ],
        'db' => [
            'class' => 'yii\db\Connection',
            'dsn' =>
            'mysql:host=localhost;dbname=mydatabase',
            'username' => 'root',
            'password' => '',
            'enableSchemaCache' => true,

            // Optional. Default value is 3600 seconds
            schemaCacheDuration' => 3600,

            // Optional. Default value is 'cache'
            'schemaCache' => 'cache',
        ],
    ],
];
```

4. Use plain arrays instead of Active Record objects for listing sets of elements:

```
$categoriesArray = Categories::find()->asArray()->all();
```

5. Use `each()` instead of `all()` in `foreach` for a large count of results:

```
foreach (Post::find()->each() as $post) {
    // ...
}
```

6. Because Composer's autoloader is used to include most third-party class files, you should consider optimizing it by executing the following command:

```
composer dump-autoload -o
```

How it works...

When `YII_DEBUG` is set to `false`, Yii turns OFF all the trace level logging and uses less error handling code. Also, when you set `YII_ENV` to `prod` your application does not load Yii and Debug panel modules.

Setting `schemaCachingDuration` to a number of seconds allows caching the database schema used by Yii's Active Record. This is highly recommended for production servers and it significantly improves the Active Record performance. In order for it to work, you need to properly configure the `cache` component as follows:

```
'cache' => [
    'class' => 'yii\cache\FileCache',
],
```

Enabling the cache also has a positive effect on other Yii components. For example, Yii router or urlManager starts to cache routes.

Of course, you can get into a situation where the preceding settings will not help to achieve a sufficient performance level. In most cases, it means that either the application itself is a bottleneck or you need more hardware.

- **Server-side performance is just a part of the big picture**: Server-side performance is only one of the things that affect the overall performance. By optimizing the client side such as serving CSS, images, and JavaScript files, proper caching and minimizing the amount of HTTP-requests can give a good visual performance gain even without optimizing the PHP code.

- **Things to be done without using Yii**: Some things are best done without Yii. For example, image resizing on-the-fly is better in a separate PHP script in order to avoid the extra overhead.

- **Active Record versus Query Builder and SQL**: Use Query Builder or SQL in performance-critical application parts. Generally, AR is most useful when adding and editing records, as it adds a convenient validation layer, and is less useful when selecting records.

- **Always check for slow queries first**: Database can become a bottleneck in a second if a developer accidentally forgets to add an index to a table that is being read often or vice versa, or adds too many indexes to a table we are writing to very often. The same goes for selecting unnecessary data and unneeded JOINs.

- **Cache or save results of heavy processes**: If you can avoid running a heavy process in every page load, it is better to do so. For example, it is a good practice to save or cache results of parsing the markdown text, purify it (this is a very resource-intensive process) once, and then to use the ready-to-display HTML.

- **Handling too much processing**: Sometimes there is too much processing to be handled immediately. It can be building complex reports or simply sending e-mails (if your project is heavily loaded). In this case, it is better to put it into a queue and process it later using cron or other specialized tools.

See also

For more information about performance tuning and caching refer to the following URLs:

- `http://www.yiiframework.com/doc-2.0/guide-tutorial-performance-tuning.html`

- `http://www.yiiframework.com/doc-2.0/guide-caching-overview.html`

Speeding up session handling

Native session handling in PHP is fine in most cases. There are at least two possible reasons why you will want to change the way sessions are handled:

- ▸ When using multiple servers, you need to have common session storage for both servers.

- ▸ Default PHP sessions use files, so the maximum performance possible is limited by disk I/O.

- ▸ Default PHP sessions are blocking concurrent session storages. In this recipe, we will see how to use efficient storage for Yii sessions.

Getting ready

Create a new `yii2-app-basic` application using the Composer package manager, as described in the official guide at `http://www.yiiframework.com/doc-2.0/guide-start-installation.html`, and install the Memcache server and the `memcache` PHP extension.

How to do it...

We will stress-test the website using the Apache `ab` tool. It is distributed with Apache binaries, so if you are using Apache, you will find it inside the `bin` directory.

1. Run the following command replacing your website with the actual hostname you are using:

```
ab -n 1000 -c 5 http://yii-book.app/index.php?r=site/contact
```

This will send 1,000 requests, five at a time, and will output stats as follows:

```
This is ApacheBench, Version 2.3 <$Revision: 1528965 $>
Copyright 1996 Adam Twiss, Zeus Technology Ltd, http://www.
zeustech.net/
Licensed to The Apache Software Foundation, http://www.apache.org/
...
Server Software:        nginx
Server Hostname:        yii-book.app
Server Port:            80

Document Path:          /index.php?r=site/contact
Document Length:        14866 bytes
Concurrency Level:      5
```

Time taken for tests:	10.961 seconds
Complete requests:	1000
Failed requests:	0
Total transferred:	15442000 bytes
HTML transferred:	14866000 bytes
Requests per second:	91.24 [#/sec] (mean)
Time per request:	54.803 [ms] (mean)
Time per request:	10.961 [ms] (mean, across all concurrent requests)
Transfer rate:	1375.84 [Kbytes/sec] received

Connection Times (ms)

	min	mean[+/-sd]	median	max
Connect:	0	0 0.0	0	0
Processing:	18	55 324.9	29	4702
Waiting:	15	41 255.1	24	4695
Total:	18	55 324.9	29	4702

We are interested in the requests-per-second metric. The number means that the website can process 91.24 requests per second if there are five requests at a time.

> Note that debuging is not turned off since we are interested in changes to the session handling speed.

2. Now add the following to the `/config/web.php` components section:

```
'session' => array(
    'class' => 'yii\web\CacheSession',
    'cache' => 'sessionCache',
),
'sessionCache' => array(
    'class' => 'yii\caching\MemCache',
),
```

3. Run ab again with the same settings. This time, you should get better results. In my case, it was 139.07 requests per second. This means Memcache, as a session handler, performed 52% better than the default file-based session handler.

Don't rely on the exact results provided here. It all depends on software versions, settings, and hardware used. Always try to run all tests yourself in an environment where you are going to deploy your application.

4. You can get a significant performance gain by choosing the right session handling backend. Yii supports more caching backends out-of-the-box, including WinCache, XCache, and Zend data cache, which comes with the Zend Server. Moreover, you can implement your own cache backend to use fast noSQL storage, such as Redis.

How it works...

By default, Yii uses native PHP sessions; this means that the filesystem is used in most cases. A filesystem cannot deal with high concurrency efficiently.

Memcache or other platforms perform fine in the following situation:

```
'session' => array(
    'class' => 'yii\web\CacheSession',
    'cache' => 'sessionCache',
),
'sessionCache' => array(
    'class' => 'yii\caching\MemCache',
),
```

In the preceding config section, we instruct Yii to use `CacheSession` as a session handler. With this component, we can delegate session handling to the cache component specified in `cache`. This time we are using `MemCache`.

When using a memcached backend, you should take into account the fact that when using these solutions the application user can possibly lose the session if the maximum cache capacity is reached.

Note that, when using a cache backend for a session, you cannot rely on a session as a temporary data storage, since then there will be no memory to store more data in memcached. In such a case, this will just purge all data or delete some of it.

If you are using multiple servers, you cannot use file storage. There is no way to share the session data between servers. In the case of memcached, it is easy because it can be easily accessed from as many servers as you want.

Also, for sharing the session data you can use `DbSession`:

```
return [
    // ...
    'components' => [
        'session' => [
            'class' => 'yii\web\DbSession',
        ],
    ],
];
```

Now, create a new table in your database:

```
CREATE TABLE session (
    id CHAR(40) NOT NULL PRIMARY KEY,
    expire INTEGER,
    data BLOB
)
```

There's more...

It is a good idea to close the session as soon as possible. If you're not going to store anything in the session during the current request, you can even close it at the very beginning of your controller action. This way, even when using files as storage your application should be fine.

Use the following command:

```
Yii:$app->session->close();
```

See also

For more information about performance and caching refer to the following URLs:

▶ http://www.yiiframework.com/doc-2.0/guide-tutorial-performance-tuning.html

▶ http://www.yiiframework.com/doc-2.0/guide-caching-overview.html

Using cache dependencies and chains

Yii supports many cache backends, but what really makes the Yii cache flexible is the dependency and dependency chaining support. There are situations when you cannot simply cache data for an hour because the information cached can be changed at any time.

In this recipe, we will see how to cache a whole page and still always get fresh data when it is updated. The page will be of the dashboard-type and will show the five latest articles added and a total calculated for an account.

 Note that an operation cannot be edited as it is added, but an article can be.

Getting ready

Create a new `yii2-app-basic` application using the Composer package manager, as described in the official guide at `http://www.yiiframework.com/doc-2.0/guide-start-installation.html`.

1. Activate the caching component in `config/web.php` as follows:

```
return [
    // ...
    'components' => [
        cache => [
            'class' => 'yii\caching\FileCache,
        ],
    ],
];
```

2. Set up a fresh database and configure it into `config/db.php`.

3. Run the following migration:

```php
<?php

use yii\db\Schema;
use yii\db\Migration;

class m160308_093233_create_example_tables extends Migration
{
    public function up()
    {
        $tableOptions = null;
        if ($this->db->driverName === 'mysql') {
            $tableOptions = 'CHARACTER SET utf8 COLLATE
            utf8_general_ci ENGINE=InnoDB';
        }

        $this->createTable('{{%account}}', [
            'id' => Schema::TYPE_PK,
```

```
            'amount' => Schema::TYPE_DECIMAL . '(10,2) NOT
            NULL',
        ], $tableOptions);

        $this->createTable('{{%article}}', [
            'id' => Schema::TYPE_PK,
            'title' => Schema::TYPE_STRING . ' NOT NULL',
            'text' => Schema::TYPE_TEXT . ' NOT NULL',
        ], $tableOptions);
    }

    public function down()
    {
        $this->dropTable('{{%article}}');
        $this->dropTable('{{%account}}');
    }
}
```

4. Generate models for the account and article tables using Yii.

5. Create `protected/controllers/DashboardController.php` as follows:

```php
<?php

namespace app\controllers;

use app\models\Account;
use app\models\Article;
use yii\web\Controller;

class DashboardController extends Controller
{
    public function actionIndex()
    {
        $total = Account::find()->sum('amount');
        $articles = Article::find()->orderBy('id DESC')-
        >limit(5)->all();

        return $this->render('index', array(
            'total' => $total,
```

```
                'articles' => $articles,
        ));
    }

    public function actionRandomOperation()
    {
        $rec = new Account();
        $rec->amount = rand(-1000, 1000);
        $rec->save();

        echo 'OK';
    }

    public function actionRandomArticle()
    {
        $n = rand(0, 1000);

        $article = new Article();
        $article->title = "Title #".$n;
        $article->text = "Text #".$n;
        $article->save();

        echo 'OK';
    }
}
```

6. Create `views/dashboard/index.php` as follows:

```php
<?php
use yii\helpers\Html;
/* @var $this yii\web\View */
/* @var $total int */
/* @var $articles app\models\Article[] */
?>

<h1>Total: <?= $total ?></h1>
<h2>5 latest articles:</h2>
<?php foreach($articles as $article): ?>
    <h3><?= Html::encode($article->title) ?></h3>
    <div><?= Html::encode($article->text) ?></div>
<?php endforeach ?>
```

7. Run `dashboard/random-operation` and `dashboard/random-article` several times. Then, run `dashboard/index` and you should see a screen similar to the one shown in the following screenshot:

8. Click on the number of database queries in the debug panel at the bottom of the page:

See a query list:

Database Queries

Total **4** items.

#	Time	Duration ↓?	Type	Query
		▼		
1	12:56:34.390	0.5 ms	SHOW	SHOW FULL COLUMNS FROM `article` /work/Dropbox/SERVER/home/yii-book.app/www/controllers/DashboardController.php (34)
2	12:56:34.387	0.3 ms	SELECT	SELECT SUM(amount) FROM `account` /work/Dropbox/SERVER/home/yii-book.app/www/controllers/DashboardController.php (33)
3	12:56:34.389	0.3 ms	SELECT	SELECT * FROM `article` ORDER BY `id` DESC LIMIT 5 /work/Dropbox/SERVER/home/yii-book.app/www/controllers/DashboardController.php (34)
4	12:56:34.391	0.2 ms	SHOW	SHOW CREATE TABLE `article` /work/Dropbox/SERVER/home/yii-book.app/www/controllers/DashboardController.php (34)

How to do it...

Carry out the following steps:

1. We need to modify the controller code as follows:

```php
<?php

namespace app\controllers;

use app\models\Account;
use app\models\Article;
use yii\caching\DbDependency;
use yii\caching\TagDependency;
use yii\web\Controller;
```

```php
class DashboardController extends Controller
{
    public function behaviors()
    {
        return [
            'pageCache' => [
                'class' => 'yii\filters\PageCache',
                'only' => ['index'],
                'duration' => 24 * 3600 * 365, // 1 year
                'dependency' => [
                    'class' =>
                    'yii\caching\ChainedDependency',
                    'dependencies' => [
                        new TagDependency(['tags' =>
                        ['articles']]),
                        new DbDependency(['sql' => 'SELECT
                        MAX(id) FROM ' .
                        Account::tableName()])
                    ]
                ],
            ],
        ];
    }

    public function actionIndex()
    {
        $total = Account::find()->sum('amount');
        $articles = Article::find()->orderBy('id DESC')-
        >limit(5)->all();

        return $this->render('index', array(
            'total' => $total,
            'articles' => $articles,
        ));
    }

    public function actionRandomOperation()
    {
```

```
        $rec = new Account();
        $rec->amount = rand(-1000, 1000);
        $rec->save();

        echo 'OK';
    }

    public function actionRandomArticle()
    {
        $n = rand(0, 1000);

        $article = new Article();
        $article->title = "Title #".$n;
        $article->text = "Text #".$n;
        $article->save();

        TagDependency::invalidate(\Yii::$app->cache,
        'articles');

        echo 'OK';
    }
}
```

2. That is it. Now, after loading `dashboard/index` several times, you will get only one simple query in the latest snapshot, as shown in the following screenshot:

Also, try to run either `dashboard/random-operation` or `dashboard/random-article` and refresh `dashboard/index` after that. The data should change as follows:

Database Queries

Total **5** items.

#	Time	Duration ↓↑	Type	Query
			▼	
1	12:49:37.380	0.4 ms	SHOW	SHOW FULL COLUMNS FROM `article` /work/Dropbox/SERVER/home/yii-book.app/www/controllers/DashboardController.php (34)
2	12:49:37.402	0.3 ms	SELECT	SELECT MAX(id) FROM account
3	12:49:37.378	0.3 ms	SELECT	SELECT SUM(amount) FROM `account` /work/Dropbox/SERVER/home/yii-book.app/www/controllers/DashboardController.php (33)
4	12:49:37.379	0.2 ms	SELECT	SELECT * FROM `article` ORDER BY `id` DESC LIMIT 5 /work/Dropbox/SERVER/home/yii-book.app/www/controllers/DashboardController.php (34)
5	12:49:37.382	0.2 ms	SHOW	SHOW CREATE TABLE `article` /work/Dropbox/SERVER/home/yii-book.app/www/controllers/DashboardController.php (34)

How it works...

In order to achieve maximum performance while doing minimal code modification, we use a full-page cache using a filter as follows:

```
public function behaviors()
{
    return [
        'pageCache' => [
            'class' => 'yii\filters\PageCache',
            'only' => ['index'],
            'duration' => 24 * 3600 * 365, // 1 year
            'dependency' => [
                'class' => 'yii\caching\ChainedDependency',
                'dependencies' => [
```

```
                    new TagDependency(['tags' => ['articles']]),
                    new DbDependency(['sql' => 'SELECT MAX(id)
                    FROM account'])
                ]
            ],
        ],
    ];
}
```

The preceding code means that we apply a full-page cache to the `index` action. The page will be cached for a year and the cache will refresh if one of the dependency data changes. Therefore, in general, the dependency works as follows:

▶ The first run gets the fresh data as described in the dependency, saves it for future reference, and updates the cache

▶ It gets the fresh data as described in dependency, gets the saved data, and then compares the two

▶ If they are equal, it uses the cached data

▶ If not, it updates the cache, uses the fresh data, and saves the fresh dependency data for future reference

In our case, two dependency types are used—tag and DB. A tag dependency marks data with the custom string tag and checks it to decide if we need to invalidate the cache, while a DB dependency uses the SQL query result for the same purpose.

The question that you have now is probably, "Why have we used DB for one case and tags for another?" That is a good question!

The goal of using the DB dependency is to replace heavy calculations and select a light query that gets as little data as possible. The best thing about this type of dependency is that we don't need to embed any additional logic in the existing code. In our case, we can use this type of dependency for account operations, but cannot use it for articles as the article content can be changed. Therefore, for articles, we set a global tag named article which basically means that we can manually call the following when we want to invalidate total the article cache:

```
TagDependency::invalidate(\Yii::$app->cache, 'articles');
```

See also

In order to learn more about caching and using cache dependencies, refer to `http://www.yiiframework.com/doc-2.0/guide-caching-overview.html`

Profiling an application with Yii

If all of the best practices for deploying a Yii application are applied and you still do not have the performance you want, then most probably there are some bottlenecks with the application itself. The main principle while dealing with these bottlenecks is that you should never assume anything and always test and profile the code before trying to optimize it.

In this recipe, we will try to find bottlenecks in the Yii2 mini application.

Getting ready

Create a new `yii2-app-basic` application using the Composer package manager, as described in the official guide at `http://www.yiiframework.com/doc-2.0/guide-start-installation.html`.

1. Set up your database connection and apply the following migration:

```php
<?php
use yii\db\Migration;

class m160308_093233_create_example_tables extends Migration
{
    public function up()
    {
        $tableOptions = null;
        if ($this->db->driverName === 'mysql') {
            $tableOptions = 'CHARACTER SET utf8 COLLATE
            utf8_general_ci ENGINE=InnoDB';
        }

        $this->createTable('{{%category}}', [
            'id' => $this->primaryKey(),
            'name' => $this->string()->notNull(),
        ], $tableOptions);

        $this->createTable('{{%article}}', [
            'id' => $this->primaryKey(),
            'category_id' => $this->integer()->notNull(),
            'title' => $this->string()->notNull(),
            'text' => $this->text()->notNull(),
        ], $tableOptions);

        $this->createIndex('idx-article-category_id',
        '{{%article}}', 'category_id');
```

```php
$this->addForeignKey('fk-article-category_id',
'{{%article}}', 'category_id', '{{%category}}',
'id');
    }

    public function down()
    {
        $this->dropTable('{{%article}}');
        $this->dropTable('{{%category}}');
    }
}
```

2. Generate models for each table in Yii.

3. Write the following console command:

```php
<?php
namespace app\commands;

use app\models\Article;
use app\models\Category;
use Faker\Factory;
use yii\console\Controller;

class DataController extends Controller
{
    public function actionInit()
    {
        $db = \Yii::$app->db;
        $faker = Factory::create();

        $transaction = $db->beginTransaction();
        try {
            $categories = [];
            for ($id = 1; $id <= 100; $id++) {
                $categories[] = [
                    'id' => $id,
                    'name' => $faker->name,
                ];
            }

            $db->createCommand()
            ->batchInsert(Category::tableName(), ['id',
            'name'], $categories)
            ->execute();
```

```php
                    $articles = [];
                    for ($id = 1; $id <= 100; $id++) {
                        $articles[] = [
                            'id' => $id,
                            'category_id' => $faker
                            ->numberBetween(1, 100),
                            'title' => $faker->text($maxNbChars =
                             100),
                            'text' => $faker->text($maxNbChars =
                             200),
                        ];
                    }

                    $db->createCommand()
                    ->batchInsert(Article::tableName(), ['id',
                    'category_id', 'title', 'text'], $articles)
                    ->execute();

                    $transaction->commit();
                } catch (\Exception $e) {
                    $transaction->rollBack();
                    throw $e;
                }
            }
        }
```

And execute it:

./yii data/init

4. Add the `ArticleController` class as follows:

```php
<?php
namespace app\controllers;

use Yii;
use app\models\Article;
use yii\data\ActiveDataProvider;
use yii\web\Controller;

class ArticleController extends Controller
{
    public function actionIndex()
    {
        $query = Article::find();
        $dataProvider = new ActiveDataProvider([
```

```
                'query' => $query,
        ]);

        return $this->render('index', [
            'dataProvider' => $dataProvider,
        ]);
    }
}
```

5. Add the `views/article/index.php` view as follows:

```php
<?php
use yii\helpers\Html;
use yii\widgets\ListView;

/* @var $this yii\web\View */
/* @var $dataProvider yii\data\ActiveDataProvider */

$this->title = 'Articles';
$this->params['breadcrumbs'][] = $this->title;
?>
<div class="article-index">
    <h1><?= Html::encode($this->title) ?></h1>
    <?= ListView::widget([
        'dataProvider' => $dataProvider,
        'itemOptions' => ['class' => 'item'],
        'itemView' => '_item',
    ]) ?>
/div>
```

Then add `views/article/_item.php`:

```php
<?php
use yii\helpers\Html;

/* @var $this yii\web\View */
/* @var $model app\models\Article */
?>

<div class="panel panel-default">
    <div class="panel-heading"><?= Html::encode($model
    ->title); ?></div>
    <div class="panel-body">
        Category: <?= Html::encode($model->category->name) ?>
    </div>
</div>
```

How to do it...

Follow these steps to profile an application with Yii:

1. Open the articles page:

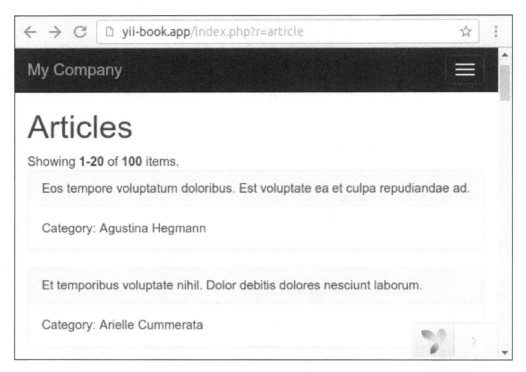

2. Open the `views/article/index.php` file and add profiler calls before and after the `ListView` widget:

```php
<div class="article-index">
    <h1><?= Html::encode($this->title) ?></h1>

    <?php Yii::beginProfile('articles') ?>

    <?= ListView::widget([
        'dataProvider' => $dataProvider,
        'itemOptions' => ['class' => 'item'],
        'itemView' => '_item',
    ]) ?>

    <?php Yii::endProfile('articles') ?>
```

```
</div>
```

Now refresh the page.

3. Expand the debug panel at the bottom of page and click on the timing badge (**73 ms in our case**):

Now examine the **Profiling** report:

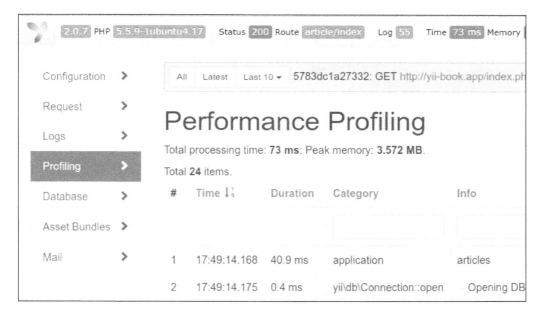

We can see that our articles block has taken close to 40 milliseconds.

4. Open our controller and add eager loading for article's `category` relation as follows:

```
class ArticleController extends Controller
{
    public function actionIndex()
    {
        $query = Article::find()->with('category');

        $dataProvider = new ActiveDataProvider([
            'query' => $query,
        ]);
```

```
        return $this->render('index', [
            'dataProvider' => $dataProvider,
        ]);
    }
}
```

5. Go back to the site, refresh the page, and open the **Profiling** report again:

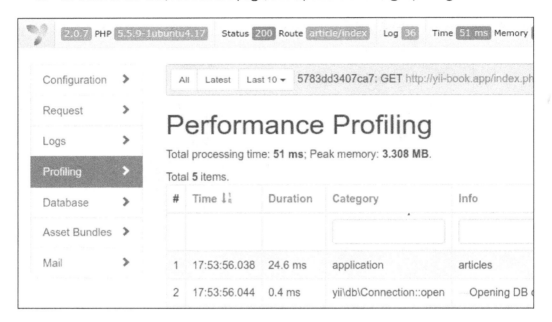

Right now the articles listing has taken close to 25 milliseconds because the application makes fewer SQL queries with eager loading of related models.

How it works...

You can enclose any fragment of source code with `Yii::beginProfile` and `Yii::endProfile` calls:

```
Yii::beginProfile('articles');
// ...
Yii::endProfile('articles');
```

After executing the page, you can see the report with all timings on the **Profiling** page of the debug module.

Also, you can use nested profiling calls as follows:

```
Yii::beginProfile('outer');
```

```
Yii::beginProfile('inner');
    // ...
Yii::endProfile('inner');
Yii::endProfile('outer');
```

 Note: Take care with correct opening and closing calls in this case and correct block naming. If you the miss `Yii::endProfile` call or switch the order of `Yii::endProfile('inner')` and `Yii::endProfile('outer')`, performance profiling will not work.

See also

▶ For more information about logging refer to the following URL: `http://www.yiiframework.com/doc-2.0/guide-runtime-logging.html#performance-profiling`

▶ About tuning of the application performance refer to the following URL: `http://www.yiiframework.com/doc-2.0/guide-tutorial-performance-tuning.html`

Leveraging HTTP caching

Instead of only server-side caching implementation you can use client-side caching via specific HTTP-headers.

In this recipe, we will cover full-page caching on the basis of the `Last-Modified` and `ETag` headers.

Getting ready

Create a new `yii2-app-basic` application using the Composer package manager, as described in the official guide at `http://www.yiiframework.com/doc-2.0/guide-start-installation.html`.

1. Create and run migration as follows:

```php
<?php
use yii\db\Migration;

class m160308_093233_create_example_tables extends Migration
{
    public function up()
    {
        $this->createTable('{{%article}}', [
```

```
            'id' => $this->primaryKey(),
            'created_at' => $this->integer()->unsigned()-
            >notNull(),
            'updated_at' => $this->integer()->unsigned()-
            >notNull(),
            'title' => $this->string()->notNull(),
            'text' => $this->text()->notNull(),
        ]);
    }

    public function down()
    {
        $this->dropTable('{{%article}}');
    }
}
```

2. Create an `Article` model as follows:

```php
<?php
namespace app\models;

use Yii;
use yii\behaviors\TimestampBehavior;
use yii\db\ActiveRecord;

class Article extends ActiveRecord
{
    public static function tableName()
    {
        return '{{%article}}';
    }

    public function behaviors()
    {
        return [
            TimestampBehavior::className(),
        ];
    }
}
```

3. Create a blog controller with the following actions:

```php
<?php
namespace app\controllers;

use app\models\Article;
```

```
use yii\web\Controller;
use yii\web\NotFoundHttpException;

class BlogController extends Controller
{
    public function actionIndex()
    {
        $articles = Article::find()->orderBy(['id' => SORT_DESC])-
        >all();
        return $this->render('index', array(
            'articles' => $articles,
        ));
    }

    public function actionView($id)
    {
        $article = $this->findModel($id);
        return $this->render('view', array(
            'article' => $article,
        ));
    }

    public function actionCreate()
    {
        $n = rand(0, 1000);
        $article = new Article();
        $article->title = 'Title #' . $n;
        $article->text = 'Text #' . $n;
        $article->save();
        echo 'OK';
    }

    public function actionUpdate($id)
    {
        $article = $this->findModel($id);
        $n = rand(0, 1000);
        $article->title = 'Title #' . $n;
        $article->text = 'Text #' . $n;
        $article->save();
        echo 'OK';
    }
    private function findModel($id)
    {
        if (($model = Article::findOne($id)) !== null) {
```

```
                return $model;
        } else {
            throw new NotFoundHttpException('The requested
            page does not exist.');
        }
    }
}
```

4. Add the `views/blog/index.php` view:

```php
<?php
use yii\helpers\Html;

$this->title = 'Articles';;
$this->params['breadcrumbs'][] = $this->title;
?>

<?php foreach($articles as $article): ?>
    <h3><?= Html::a(Html::encode($article->title), ['view',
    'id' => $article->id]) ?></h3>
    <div>Created <?= Yii::$app->formatter-
    >asDatetime($article->created_at) ?></div>
    <div>Updated <?= Yii::$app->formatter-
    >asDatetime($article->updated_at) ?></div>
<?php endforeach ?>
```

5. Add the `views/blog/view.php` view file:

```php
<?php
use yii\helpers\Html;

$this->title = $article->title;
$this->params['breadcrumbs'][] = ['label' => 'Articles', 'url' =>
['index']];
$this->params['breadcrumbs'][] = $this->title;
?>

<h1><?= Html::encode($article->title) ?></h1>
<div>Created <?= Yii::$app->formatter->asDatetime($article-
>created_at) ?></div>
<div>Updated <?= Yii::$app->formatter->asDatetime($article-
>updated_at) ?></div>
<hr />
<p><?= Yii::$app->formatter->asNtext($article->text) ?></p>
```

How to do it...

Follow these steps to leverage HTTP caching:

1. Access this URL `http://yii-book.app/index.php?r=blog/create` three times to generate three articles.

2. Open the following blog page:

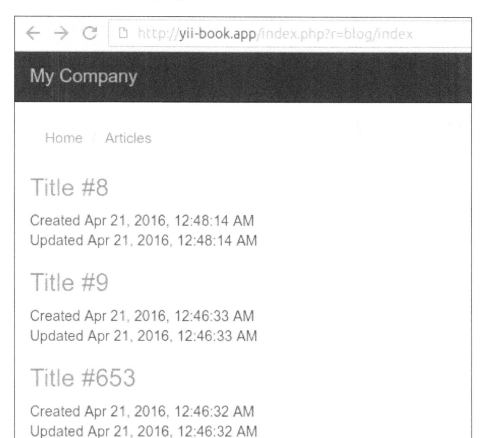

3. Open the developer console in your browser and see the 200 OK response status for each reloading of the blog page:

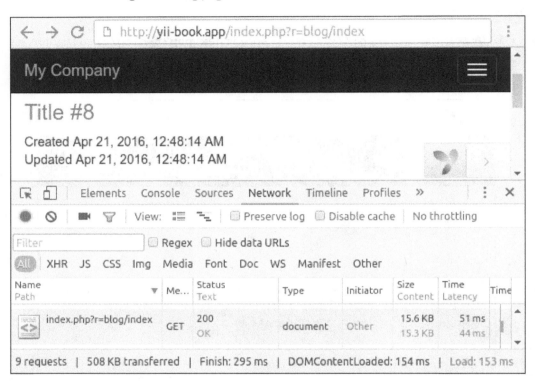

4. Open BlogController and attach the following behaviors:

```php
class BlogController extends Controller
{
    public function behaviors()
    {
        return [
            [
                'class' => 'yii\filters\HttpCache',
                'only' => ['index'],
                'lastModified' => function ($action,
                $params) {
                    return Article::find()-
                    >max('updated_at');
                },
            ],
            [
                'class' => 'yii\filters\HttpCache',
```

```
                    'only' => ['view'],
                    'etagSeed' => function ($action, $params) {
                        $article = $this
                        ->findModel(\Yii::$app->request
                        ->get('id'));
                        return serialize([$article->title,
                        $article->text]);
                    },
                ],
            ];
        }

        // ...
    }
```

5. Next, reload the page a few times and check that the server returns the `304 Not Modified` status instead of `200 OK`:

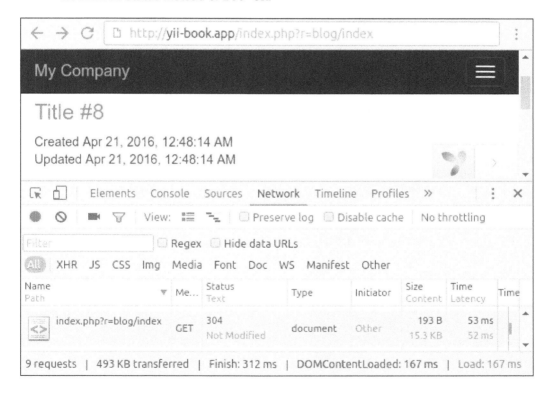

6. Open the relevant page using the following URL to update random articles: `http://yii-book.app/index.php?r=blog/update`.

7. After updating the blog page, check that the server returns `200 OK` the first time and `304 Not Modified` thereafter, and verify that you see the new updated time on the page:

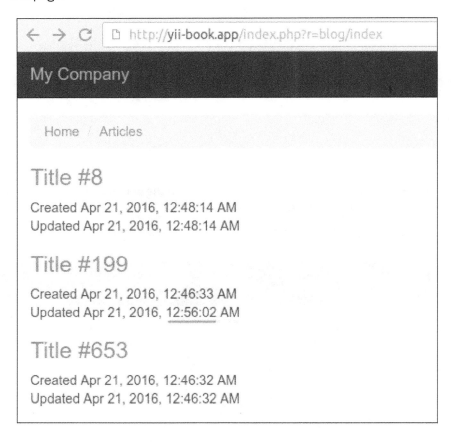

8. Open any page from our article, as follows:

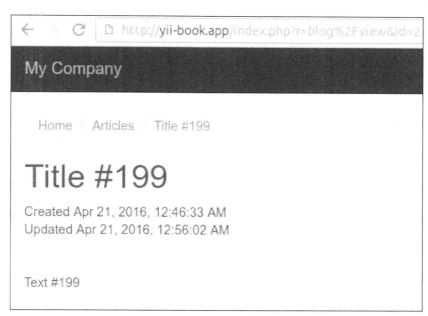

Verify that the server returns `200 OK` the first time and `304 Not Modified` on subsequent requests.

How it works...

There are time-based and content-based approaches to check the availability of the cached response content for your browser with the help of HTTP-headers.

Last-Modified

This approach suggests that the server must return the last modification date of every document. After storing the date, our browser can attach it in the `If-Modified-Since` header for every subsequent request.

We must attach the `action` filter to our controller and specify the `lastModified` callback as follows:

```
class BlogController extends Controller
{
    public function behaviors()
```

```
        {
            return [
                [
                    'class' => 'yii\filters\HttpCache',
                    'only' => ['index'],
                    'lastModified' => function ($action, $params) {
                        return Article::find()->max('updated_at');
                    },
                ],
                // ...
            ];
        }

        // ...
    }
```

The `\yii\filters\HttpCache` class calls the callback and compares the returned value with the `$_SERVER['HTTP_IF_MODIFIED_SINCE']` system variable. If the document has still not changed, `HttpCache` will send a lightweight `304` response header without running the action.

However, if the document has been updated, the cache will be ignored and the server will return a full response.

Request	Response
First request with full response	

`GET /index.php?r=blog HTTP 1.1`	`HTTP/1.1 200 OK`
	`Cache-Control: public, max-age=3600`
	`Last-Modified: Thu, 21 Apr 2016 00:56:02 GMT`
	
	`<!DOCTYPE html>`
	`<html lang="en-US">`
	`...`

Second request with `If-Modified-Since` with blank response	

`GET /index.php?r=blog HTTP 1.1`
 	
`If-Modified-Since: Thu, 21 Apr 2016 00:56:02 GMT`
	`HTTP/1.1 304 Not Modified`
	`Cache-Control: public, max-age=3600`

Request	Response
Third request after updating the posts with a full response	
| ```
GET /index.php?r=blog HTTP
1.1

If-Modified-Since: Thu, 21
Apr 2016 00:56:02 GMT
``` | ```
HTTP/1.1 200 OK
Cache-Control: public, max-age=3600
Last-Modified: Thu, 21 Apr 2016
01:12:02 GMT


<!DOCTYPE html>
<html lang="en-US">
...
``` |

As an alternative or an addition to the `Last-Modified` header variable, you can use `ETag`.

Entity Tag

In cases when we do not store the last modified date in our documents or pages, we can use custom hashes, which can be generated at the base of the document content.

For example, we can use a content title for our document to hash a specific tag:

```
class BlogController extends Controller
{
    public function behaviors()
    {
        return [
            [
                'class' => 'yii\filters\HttpCache',
                'only' => ['view'],
                'etagSeed' => function ($action, $params) {
                    $article = $this->findModel(\Yii::$app
                    ->request->get('id'));
                    return serialize([$article->title,
                    $article->text]);
                },
            ],
        ];
    }
    // ...
}
```

The `HttpCache` filter will attach this tag to the server response as an `ETag` header variable.

After storing `ETag`, our browser can attach it in the `If-None-Match` header for every subsequent request.

If the document still has not changed, `HttpCache` will send a lightweight `304` response header without running the action.

Request	Response
First request with full response	

`GET index.php?r=blog/`
`view&id=3 HTTP 1.1`
	`HTTP/1.1 200 OK`
	`Cache-Control: public, max-age=3600`
	`Etag: "VYkwdOXBzV23KhnzTTJXU"`
	
	`<!DOCTYPE html>`
	`<html lang="en-US">`
	`...`

Second request with `If-None-Match` and blank response	

`GET index.php?r=blog/`
`view&id=3 HTTP 1.1`
`If-None-Match:`
`"VYkwdOXBzV23KhnzTTJXU"`
	`HTTP/1.1 304 Not Modified`
	`Cache-Control: public, max-age=3600`
	`Etag: "VYkwdOXBzV23KhnzTTJXU"`

Third request after updating the post with a full response	

`GET index.php?r=blog/`
`view&id=3 HTTP 1.1`
`If-None-Match:`
`"VYkwdOXBzV23KhnzTTJXU"`
	`HTTP/1.1 200 OK`
	`Cache-Control: public,`
	`max-age=3600Etag:`
	`"Ur4Ghd6hdYthrn82Ph44dhF"`
	
	`<!DOCTYPE html>`
	`<html lang="en-US">`
	`...`

When the cache is valid, our application will send the `304 Not Modified` response HTTP-headers instead of the page content and will not run controllers and actions repeatedly.

See also

► For more information about HTTP caching refer to `https://developers.google.com/web/fundamentals/performance/optimizing-content-efficiency/http-caching`

► For HTTP-caching in Yii2 refer to `http://www.yiiframework.com/doc-2.0/guide-caching-http.html`

Combining and minimizing assets

If your web page includes many CSS and/or JavaScript files, the page will open very slowly because the browser sends a large number of HTTP requests to download each file in separated threads. To reduce the number of requests and connections, we can combine and compress multiple CSS/JavaScript files into one or very few files in production mode, and then include these compressed files on the page instead of the original ones.

Getting ready

- ▶ Create a new `yii2-app-basic` application using the Composer package manager, as described in the official guide at `http://www.yiiframework.com/doc-2.0/guide-start-installation.html`

- ▶ Download the `compiler.jar` file from `https://developers.google.com/closure/compiler/`

- ▶ Download the `yuicompressor.jar` file from `https://github.com/yui/yuicompressor/releases`

- ▶ Download and install the **Java Runtime Environment** (**JRE**) from `http://www.java.com`

How to do it...

Follow these steps to combine and minimize assets:

1. Open the source HTML code of the `index` page of your application. Check whether it is similar to the following structure:

```html
<!DOCTYPE html>
<html lang="en-US">
<head>
    ...
    <title>My Yii Application</title>
    <link href="/assets/9b3b2888/css/bootstrap.css"
    rel="stylesheet">
    <link href="/css/site.css" rel="stylesheet">
</head>
<body>
    ...
    <script src="/assets/25f82b8a/jquery.js"></script>
    <script src="/assets/f4307424/yii.js"></script>
    <script
    src="/assets/9b3b2888/js/bootstrap.js"></script>
```

```
</body>
</html>
```

The page includes three JavaScript files.

2. Open the `config/console.php` file and add the `@webroot` and `@web` alias definitions:

```php
<?php
Yii::setAlias('@webroot', __DIR__ . '/../web');
Yii::setAlias('@web', '/');
```

3. Open a console and run the following command:

`yii asset/template assets.php`

4. Open the generated `assets.php` file and configure it as follows:

```php
<?php
return [
    'jsCompressor' => 'java -jar compiler.jar --js {from}
    --js_output_file {to}',
    'cssCompressor' => 'java -jar yuicompressor.jar --type
    css {from} -o {to}',
    'bundles' => [
        'app\assets\AppAsset',
        'yii\bootstrap\BootstrapPluginAsset',
    ],
    'targets' => [
        'all' => [
            'class' => 'yii\web\AssetBundle',
            'basePath' => '@webroot/assets',
            'baseUrl' => '@web/assets',
            'js' => 'all-{hash}.js',
            'css' => 'all-{hash}.css',
        ],
    ],
    'assetManager' => [
        'basePath' => '@webroot/assets',
        'baseUrl' => '@web/assets',
    ],
];
```

5. Run the combining command `yii asset assets.php config/assets-prod.php`. If this is successful you must get the `config/assets-prod.php` file with the following configuration:

```php
<?php
return [
```

```
'all' => [
    'class' => 'yii\\web\\AssetBundle',
    'basePath' => '@webroot/assets',
    'baseUrl' => '@web/assets',
    'js' => [
        'all-fe792d4766bead53e7a9d851adfc6ec2.js',
    ],
    'css' => [
        'all-37cfb42649f74eb0a4bfe0d0e715c420.css',
    ],
],
'yii\\web\\JqueryAsset' => [
    'sourcePath' => null,
    'js' => [],
    'css' => [],
    'depends' => [
        'all',
    ],
],
'yii\\web\\YiiAsset' => [
    'sourcePath' => null,
    'js' => [],
    'css' => [],
    'depends' => [
        'yii\\web\\JqueryAsset',
        'all',
    ],
],
'yii\\bootstrap\\BootstrapAsset' => [
    'sourcePath' => null,
    'js' => [],
    'css' => [],
    'depends' => [
        'all',
    ],
],
'app\\assets\\AppAsset' => [
    'sourcePath' => null,
    'js' => [],
    'css' => [],
    'depends' => [
        'yii\\web\\YiiAsset',
        'yii\\bootstrap\\BootstrapAsset',
        'all',
```

```
                ],
        ],
        'yii\\bootstrap\\BootstrapPluginAsset' => [
            'sourcePath' => null,
            'js' => [],
            'css' => [],
            'depends' => [
                'yii\\web\\JqueryAsset',
                'yii\\bootstrap\\BootstrapAsset',
                'all',
            ],
        ],
    ];
```

6. Add the configuration for the `assetManager` component into the `config/web.php` file:

```
'components' => [
    // ...
    'assetManager' => [
        'bundles' => YII_ENV_PROD ? require(__DIR__ . '/assets-
prod.php') : [],
    ],
],
```

7. Turn on production mode in `web/index.php`:

```
defined('YII_ENV') or define('YII_ENV', 'prod');
```

8. Reload the page in your browser and see the HTML code again. Now it must contain single lines to include our compressed files:

```
<!DOCTYPE html>
<html lang="en-US">
    <head>
        ...
        <title>My Yii Application</title>
        <link href="/assets/all-
37cfb42649f74eb0a4bfe0d0e715c420.css"
        rel="stylesheet">
    </head>
    <body>
        ...
        <script src="/assets/all-
fe792d4766bead53e7a9d851adfc6ec2.js"></script>
    </body>
</html>
```

How it works...

First of all, our page had a set of included files:

```
<link href="/assets/9b3b2888/css/bootstrap.css" rel="stylesheet">
<link href="/css/site.css" rel="stylesheet">
...
<script src="/assets/25f82b8a/jquery.js"></script>
<script src="/assets/f4307424/yii.js"></script>
<script src="/assets/9b3b2888/js/bootstrap.js"></script>
```

Next, we generated the `assets.php` configuration file and specified bundles for compressing:

```
'bundles' => [
    'app\assets\AppAsset',
    'yii\bootstrap\BootstrapPluginAsset',
],
```

> **Note**: We could specify all intermediate asset bundles such as `yii\web\JqueryAsset` and `yii\web\YiiAsset`, but these assets are already specified as dependencies of `AppAsset` and `BootstrapPluginAsset`, and the compressing command automatically resolves all these dependencies.

The AssetManager publishes all assets into the classic subdirectories in `web/assets` and after publishing it runs compressors to combine all CSS and JS files into `all-{hash}.js` and `all-{hash}.css`.

Check whether the CSS file includes other resources by relative paths such as the `bootstrap.css` file:

```
@font-face {
    font-family: 'Glyphicons Halflings';
    src: url('../fonts/glyphicons-halflings-regular.eot');
}
```

If it is so, then in the combined file, our compressor changes all relative paths for storing all relationships as follows:

```
@font-face{
    font-family: 'Glyphicons Halflings';
    src: url('9b3b2888/fonts/glyphicons-halflings-regular.eot');
}
```

After processing, we get the `assets-prod.php` file with the bundles configuration of the `assetManager` component. It defines the new virtual asset as a dependency of clean copies of the original bundles:

```php
return [
    'all' => [
        'class' => 'yii\\web\\AssetBundle',
        'basePath' => '@webroot/assets',
        'baseUrl' => '@web/assets',
        'js' => [
            'all-fe792d4766bead53e7a9d851adfc6ec2.js',
        ],
        'css' => [
            'all-37cfb42649f74eb0a4bfe0d0e715c420.css',
        ],
    ],
    'yii\\web\\JqueryAsset' => [
        'sourcePath' => null,
        'js' => [],
        'css' => [],
        'depends' => [
            'all',
        ],
    ],
    // ...
]
```

Now we can require this configuration into the `config/web.php` file:

```php
'components' => [
    // ...
    'assetManager' => [
        'bundles' => require(__DIR__ . '/assets-prod.php'),
    ],
],
```

Alternatively, we can require the file for the production environment only:

```php
'components' => [
    // ...
    'assetManager' => [
        'bundles' => YII_ENV_PROD ? require(__DIR__ . '/assets-
        prod.php') : [],
    ],
],
```

Note: Do not forget to regenerate all compressed and combining files after any updates of the original resources.

See also

 ▶ For more information about assets refer to the following URL: `http://www.yiiframework.com/doc-2.0/guide-structure-assets.html`

 ▶ For Closure Compiler refer to the following URL: `https://developers.google.com/closure/compiler/`

 ▶ For YUI Compressor refer to the following URL: `https://github.com/yui/yuicompressor/`

Running Yii2 on HHVM

HipHop Virtual Machine (**HHVM**) is a process virtual machine from Facebook based on just-in-time (JIT) compilation. HHVM transforms PHP code into intermediate **HipHop bytecode** (**HHBC**) and dynamically translates PHP code into machine code, which will be optimized and natively executed.

Getting ready

Create a new `yii2-app-basic` application using the Composer package manager, as described in the official guide at `http://www.yiiframework.com/doc-2.0/guide-start-installation.html`.

How to do it...

Follow these steps to run Yii on HHVM:

1. Install the Apache2 or Nginx web server.
2. Follow the guide for installing HHVM on Linux or Mac available at `https://docs.hhvm.com/hhvm/installation/introduction`. For example, on Ubuntu you must run the following commands:

```
sudo apt-get install software-properties-common

sudo apt-key adv --recv-keys --keyserver hkp://keyserver.ubuntu.com:80 0x5a16e7281be7a449

sudo add-apt-repository "deb http://dl.hhvm.com/ubuntu $(lsb_release -sc) main"

sudo apt-get update
```

```
sudo apt-get install hhvm
```

After installing, you will see the following tips in your terminal:

```
********************************************************************
**
* HHVM is installed.
*
* Running PHP web scripts with HHVM is done by having your
* webserver talk to HHVM over FastCGI. Install nginx or Apache,
* and then:
* $ sudo /usr/share/hhvm/install_fastcgi.sh
* $ sudo /etc/init.d/hhvm restart
* (if using nginx)  $ sudo /etc/init.d/nginx restart
* (if using apache) $ sudo /etc/init.d/apache restart
*
* Detailed FastCGI directions are online at:
* https://github.com/facebook/hhvm/wiki/FastCGI
*
* If you're using HHVM to run web scripts, you probably want it
* to start at boot:
* $ sudo update-rc.d hhvm defaults
*
* Running command-line scripts with HHVM requires no special
setup:
* $ hhvm whatever.php
*
* You can use HHVM for /usr/bin/php even if you have php-cli
* installed:
* $ sudo /usr/bin/update-alternatives \
*     --install /usr/bin/php php /usr/bin/hhvm 60
********************************************************************
**
```

3. Try to start the built-in server manually for your site:

```
cd web
hhvm -m server -p 8080
```

Open the `localhost:8080` host in your browser:

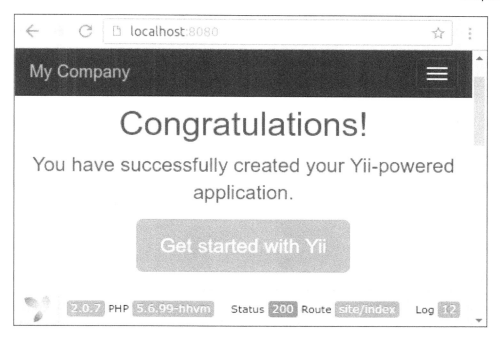

Right now you can use HHVM to develop your project.

4. If you use the Nginx or Apache2 server, then HHVM automatically creates its own configuration files in the /etc/nginx and /etc/apache2 directories. In the case of Nginx, it creates the /etc/nginx/hhvm.conf template to include configuration file to your projects. For example, let's create a new virtual host called yii-book-hhvm. app:

```
server {
    listen 127.0.0.1:80;
    server_name .yii-book-hhvm.app;
    root /var/www/yii-book-hhvm.app/web;
    charset utf-8;
    index index.php index.html index.htm;
    include /etc/nginx/hhvm.conf;
}
```

Add the hostname into your /etc/hosts:

127.0.0.1   yii-book-hhvm.app

Now restart the Nginx server:

sudo service nginx restart

Finally, open the new host in your browser.

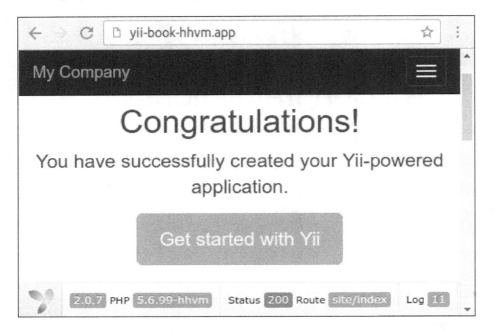

Your server is successfully set up.

How it works...

You can use HHVM as an alternative PHP process in the `fastcgi` mode. By default, it listens to the `9000` port. You can change the default port of the `fastcgi` process in the `/etc/hhvm/server.ini` file:

```
hhvm.server.port = 9000
```

Configure the specific PHP options in the `/etc/hhvm/php.ini` file.

See also

For more information about installing HHVM, refer to the following URLs:

▶   `https://docs.hhvm.com/hhvm/installation/linux`
▶   `https://docs.hhvm.com/hhvm/installation/mac`

In order to learn more information about HHVM usage refer to `https://docs.hhvm.com/hhvm/`.

10
Deployment

In this chapter, we will cover the following recipes:

- ► Changing the Yii directory layout
- ► Moving an application webroot
- ► Changing an advanced application template
- ► Moving configuration parts into separate files
- ► Using multiple configurations to simplify the deployment
- ► Implementing and executing cron jobs
- ► Maintenance mode
- ► Deployment tools

Introduction

In this chapter, we will cover various tips that are especially useful during application deployment; these tips will also come in handy when developing an application in a team or when you just want to make your development environment more comfortable.

Changing the Yii directory layout

By default, we have the Basic and Advanced Yii2 application skeletons with different directory structures. But these structures are not dogmatic, and we can customize them if required.

For example, we can move the runtime directory out of the project.

Getting ready

Create a new `yii2-app-basic` application by using the Composer the package manager, as described in the official guide at `http://www.yiiframework.com/doc-2.0/guide-start-installation.html`.

How to do it...

Changing the location of the runtime directory

Open `config/web.php` and `config/console.php` and define the `runtimePath` parameter:

```
$config = [
    'id' => 'basic',
    'basePath' => dirname(__DIR__),
    'bootstrap' => ['log'],
    'runtimePath' => '/tmp/runtime',
    'components' => [
        // ...
    ],
]
```

Move the runtime directory to the new location.

Changing the location of the vendor directory

1. Open `config/web.php` and `config/console.php` and define the `vendorPath` parameter:

```
$config = [
    'id' => 'basic',
    'basePath' => dirname(__DIR__),
    'bootstrap' => ['log'],
    'vendorPath' => dirname(__DIR__), '/../vendor,
    'components' => [
        // ...
    ],
]
```

2. Move the `vendor` directory with the `composer.json` and `composer.lock` files to the new location.

3. Open the `web/index.php` and `yii` files and find these rows:

```
require(__DIR__ . '/../vendor/autoload.php');
require(__DIR__ . '/../vendor/yiisoft/yii2/Yii.php');
```

4. Change the including paths.

Changing the location of the controllers

1. Rename the `commands` directory to `console`.

2. Change the namespace of `app\commands\HelloController` to `app\console\HelloController`.

3. Open `config/console.php` and redefine the `controllerNamespace` parameter:

```
$config = [
    'id' => 'basic-console',
    'basePath' => dirname(__DIR__),
    'bootstrap' => ['log'],
    'controllerNamespace' => 'app\console,
    'components' => [
        // ...
    ],
]
```

Changing the locations of the views directory

1. Open `config/web.php` and define `viewPath` parameter:

```
$config = [
    'id' => 'basic',
    'basePath' => dirname(__DIR__),
    'bootstrap' => ['log'],
    'viewPath' => '@app/myviews',
    'components' => [
        // ...
    ],
]
```

2. Rename your `views` directory.

How it works...

In the `yii\base\Application::preInit` method our application defines `basePath`, `runtimePath`, and `vendorPath` parameters.

By default, these values lead to the root application directory, `runtime` and `vendor` path in the root respectively.

For example, you can redefine `vendorPath` if you want to share the vendor directory with some instances of the same projects. But take care of the package's versions compatibility.

The yii\base\Application class extends yii\base\Module, which contains the controllerNamespace and viewPath parameters. The first one allows you to change the base namespace of the application and modules. It is helpful if you want to provide frontend and backend controllers in the same module directory. Just change the controllers directory to frontend and backend or create subdirectories and configure your frontend and backend applications:

```
return [
    'id' => 'app-frontend',
    'basePath' => dirname(__DIR__),
    'controllerNamespace' => frontend\controllers',
    'bootstrap' => ['log'],
    'modules' => [
        'user' => [
            'my\user\Module',
            'controllerNamespace' =>
            'my\user\controllers\frontend',
        ]
    ],
    // ...
]
return [
    'id' => 'app-backend',
    'basePath' => dirname(__DIR__),
    'controllerNamespace' => 'backend\controllers',
    'bootstrap' => ['log'],
    'modules' => [
        'user' => [
            'my\user\Module',
            'controllerNamespace' =>
            'my\user\controllers\backend',
        ]
    ],
    // ...
]
```

See also

In order to learn more about application structures, refer to http://www.yiiframework.com/doc-2.0/guide-structure-applications.html.

Moving an application webroot

By default, Yii2 applications work from the `web` directory for your site's entry script. But shared hosting environments are often quite limited when it comes to the configuration and directory structure. You cannot change the working directory for your site. Most servers provide only the `public_html` directory for your site entry scripts.

Getting ready

Create a new `yii2-app-basic` application by using the Composer package manager, as described in the official guide at `http://www.yiiframework.com/doc-2.0/guide-start-installation.html`.

How to do it...

Let's discuss the ways to move an application webroot.

Placing files in the root

1. Upload the application files into your hosting.
2. Rename the `web` directory to `public_html`.
3. Check that the site works correctly.

Placing files in a subdirectory

A hosting user directory may contain other files and folders. Here's how you can move files to a subdirectory:

1. Create the `application` and `public_html` directories.
2. Move the application files to the `application` directory.
3. Move the content of the `application/web` directory to `public_html`.
4. Open the `public_html/index.php` file and change the include paths:

    ```
    require(__DIR__ .
    '/../application/vendor/autoload.php');
    require(__DIR__ .
    '/../application/vendor/yiisoft/yii2/Yii.php');
    ```

How it works...

The Yii2 application automatically sets the `@web` and `@webroot` alias paths on the base of the entry script location. Therefore we can easily move or rename a `web` directory without changing the application configurations.

For `yii2-app-advanced`, you can move the `web` directory content from `backend` to a subdirectory, such as `admin`:

```
public_html
    index.php
    ...
    admin
        index.php
        ...
backend
common
console
frontend
...
```

See also

To get more information on installing Yii on a shared hosting environment, refer to `http://www.yiiframework.com/doc-2.0/guide-tutorial-shared-hosting.html`.

Changing an advanced application template

By default, Yii2's Advanced template has `console`, `frontend`, and `backend` applications. However, in your specific case, you can rename the existing ones and create your own applications. For example you can add the `api` application if you develop an API for your site.

Getting ready

Create a new `yii2-app-advanced` project by using the Composer package manager, as described in the official guide at `https://github.com/yiisoft/yii2-app-advanced/blob/master/docs/guide/start-installation.md`.

How to do it...

1. Copy the `backend` directory content to a new `api` directory in the root of your application.

2. Open the `api/config/main.php` file and change the `controllerNamespace` option value:

    ```
    return [
        'id' => 'app-manager',
        'basePath' => dirname(__DIR__),
        'controllerNamespace' =>
    ```

```
        'api\controllers',
        // ....
    ]
```

3. Open `api/assets/AppAsset.php` and `api/controllers/SiteController.php` and change the namespaces from `backend` to `api` like this:

```
namespaces api\assets;
namespaces api\controllers;
```

4. Open the `api/views/layouts/main.php` file and find the following row:

```
use backend\assets\AppAsset;
```

Change it to this:

```
use api\assets\AppAsset;
```

5. Open `common/config/bootstrap.php` and add the `@api` alias for the new application:

```
<?php
Yii::setAlias('@common', dirname(__DIR__));
Yii::setAlias('@frontend', dirname(dirname(__DIR__)) . '/
frontend');
Yii::setAlias('@backend', dirname(dirname(__DIR__)) . '/backend');
Yii::setAlias('@console', dirname(dirname(__DIR__)) . '/console');
Yii::setAlias('@api', dirname(dirname(__DIR__)) . '/api);
```

6. Open the `environments` directory, and in the `dev` and `prod` subdirectories make the `api` directories copies of `backend`.

7. Open the `environments/index.php` file and add rows for the `api` application:

```
return [
    'Development' => [
        'path' => 'dev',
        'setWritable' => [
            'backend/runtime',
            'backend/web/assets',
            'frontend/runtime',
            'frontend/web/assets',
            'api/runtime',
            'api/web/assets',
        ],
        'setExecutable' => [
            'yii',
            'tests/codeception/
            bin/yii',
        ],
```

```
            'setCookieValidationKey'
            => [
                'backend/config/main-
                local.php',
                'frontend/config/main-
                local.php',
                'api/config/main-
                local.php',
            ],
        ],
        'Production' => [
            'path' => 'prod',
            'setWritable' => [
                'backend/runtime',
                'backend/web/assets',
                'frontend/runtime',
                'frontend/web/assets',
                'api/runtime',
                'api/web/assets',
            ],
            'setExecutable' => [
                'yii',
            ],
            'setCookieValidationKey'
            => [
                'backend/config/main-
                local.php',
                'frontend/config/main-
                local.php',
                'api/config/main-
                local.php',
            ],
        ],
    ],
];
```

Now you have the `console`, `frontend`, `backend`, and `api` applications.

How it works...

The Advanced application template is a set of applications with custom aliases, such as `@frontend`, `@backend`, `@common`, and `@console` and corresponding namespaces instead of the simple `@app` alias for the `Basic` template.

You can easily add, remove, or rename this applications (with their aliases and namespaces) if needed.

See also

For getting more information about the usage of application directory structures refer to `https://github.com/yiisoft/yii2-app-advanced/tree/master/docs/guide`.

Moving configuration parts into separate files

In the basic application template we have separated web and console configuration files. And usually we set some application components in the both the configuration files.

Moreover, when we develop a big application, we may face some inconvenience. For example, if we need to adjust some settings, we would most probably end up repeating the changes in both the web application config and console application config.

Getting ready

Create a new `yii2-app-basic` application by using the Composer package manager, as described in the official guide at `http://www.yiiframework.com/doc-2.0/guide-start-installation.html`.

How to do it...

1. Open the `config/web.php` file and add the `urlManager` section to the components configuration:

```
'components' => [
    // ...
    'db' => require(__DIR__ .
    '/db.php'),
    'urlManager' => [
        'class' =>
        'yii\web\UrlManager',
        'enablePrettyUrl' => true,
        'showScriptName' => false,
        'rules' => [
            '' => 'site/index',
            '<_c:[\w\-
            ]+>/<id:\d+>' =>
            '<_c>/view',
            '<_c:[\w\-]+/<_a:[\w\-
            ]+>>/<id:\d+>' =>
            '<_c>/<_a>',
            '<_c:[\w\-]+>' =>
```

```
            '<_c>/index',
        ],
    ],
],
```

2. Create the `config/urlRules.php` file and move rules array into it:

```php
<?php
return [
    '' => 'site/index',
    '<_c:[\w\-]+>/<id:\d+>' =>
    '<_c>/view',
    '<_c:[\w\-]+/<_a:[\w\
    -]+>>/<id:\d+>' =>
    '<_c>/<_a>',
    '<_c:[\w\-]+>' =>
    '<_c>/index',
];
```

3. Replace the rule array with the file that requires this:

```php
'urlManager' => [
    'class' =>
    'yii\web\UrlManager',
    'enablePrettyUrl' => true,
    'showScriptName' => false,
    'rules' => require(__DIR__ .
    '/urlRules.php'),
],
```

How it works...

The preceding technique relies on the fact that Yii configuration files are native PHP files with arrays:

```php
<?php
return [...];
```

Let's look at the `require` construct:

```php
'rules' => require(__DIR__ . '/urlRules.php'),
```

When we use this, it reads the file specified, and, if there is a `return` statement inside this file, it returns a value.

Therefore, moving a part out of the main configuration file into a separate file requires creating a separate file, moving the configuration part into it right after the `return` statement, and using `require` in the main configuration file.

If separate applications (in our example, these are web applications and console applications) require some common configuration parts, then we can use `require` to move them into a separate file.

See also

In order to learn more about PHP `require` and `include` statements, refer to the following URLs:

- `http://php.net/manual/en/function.require.php`
- `http://php.net/manual/en/function.include.php`

Using multiple configurations to simplify the deployment

The Advanced application template uses different configuration files for each of its applications:

```
common
    config
        main.php
        main-local.php
        params.php
        params-local.php
console
    config
        main.php
        main-local.php
        params.php
        params-local.php
backend
    config
        main.php
        main-local.php
        params.php
        params-local.php
frontend
    config
        main.php
        main-local.php
        params.php
        params-local.php
```

Each entry `web/index.php` script merges own set of configuration files:

```
$config = yii\helpers\ArrayHelper::merge(
    require(__DIR__ .
    '/../../common/config/main.php'),
    require(__DIR__ .
    '/../../common/config/main-local.php'),
    require(__DIR__ . '/../config/main.php'),
    require(__DIR__ . '/../config/main-
    local.php')
);
$application = new yii\web\Application($config);
$application->run();
```

Each `config/main.php` file merges parameters:

```
<?php
$params = array_merge(
    require(__DIR__ .
    '/../../common/config/params.php'),
    require(__DIR__ .
    '/../../common/config/params-local.php'),
    require(__DIR__ . '/params.php'),
    require(__DIR__ . '/params-local.php')
);
return [
    // ...
    'params' => $params,
];
```

This system allows you to configure both common and specific application properties and components of our applications. And we can store default configuration files on the version control system and ignore all the `*-local.php` files.

All local files templates are prepared in the `environments` directory. When you run `php init` in your console and choose a needle environment, this initialization script makes copies of the corresponded files and places them into target folders.

But the Basic application template does not contain an agile configuration system and provides only the following files:

```
config
    console.php
    web.php
    db.php
    params.php
```

Let's try to add an advanced configuration system to the `yii2-app-basic` application template.

Create a new `yii2-app-basic` application by using the Composer package manager, as described in the official guide at `http://www.yiiframework.com/doc-2.0/guide-start-installation.html`.

How to do it...

1. Create the `config/common.php` file:

```php
<?php
$params = array_merge(
    require(__DIR__ . '/params.php'),
    require(__DIR__ . '/params-local.php')
);
return [
    'basePath' => dirname(__DIR__),
    'components' => [
        'cache' => [
            'class' =>
            'yii\caching\FileCache',
        ],
        'mailer' => [
            'class' =>
            'yii\swiftmailer\Mailer',
        ],
        'db' => [],
    ],
    'params' => $params,
];
```

2. Create the `config/common-local` file:

```php
<?php
return [
    'components' => [
        'db' => [
            'class' =>
            'yii\db\Connection',
            'dsn' =>
            'mysql:host=localhost;
            dbname=yii2basic',
```

```php
                'username' => 'root',
                'password' => '',
                'charset' => 'utf8',
            ],
            'mailer' => [
                'useFileTransport' => true,
            ],
        ],
    ];
```

3. Remove the `config/db.php` file.

4. Remove repetitive code from `config/console.php`:

```php
<?php
Yii::setAlias('@tests', dirname(__DIR__)
. '/tests');
return [
    'id' => 'basic-console',
    'bootstrap' => ['log', 'gii'],
    'controllerNamespace' =>
    'app\commands',
    'modules' => [
        'gii' => 'yii\gii\Module',
    ],
    'components' => [
        'log' => [
            'targets' => [
                [
                    'class' =>
                    'yii\log\
                    FileTarget',
                    'levels' =>
                    ['error',
                    'warning'],
                ],
            ],
        ],
    ],
];
```

5. Create the `config/console-local.php` file with an empty array:

```php
<?php
return [
];
```

6. Change the `config/web.php` file:

```
$config = [
    'id' => 'basic',
    'bootstrap' => ['log'],
    'components' => [
        'user' => [
            'identityClass' =>
            'app\models\User',
            'enableAutoLogin' => true,
        ],
        'errorHandler' => [
            'errorAction' =>
            'site/error',
        ],
        'log' => [
            'traceLevel' => YII_DEBUG ?
            3 : 0,
            'targets' => [
                [
                    'class' =>
                    'yii\log\
                    FileTarget',
                    'levels' =>
                    ['error',
                    'warning'],
                ],
            ],
        ],
    ],
];
if (YII_ENV_DEV) {
    // configuration adjustments for
    'dev' environment
    $config['bootstrap'][] = 'debug';
    $config['modules']['debug'] =
    'yii\debug\Module';

    $config['bootstrap'][] = 'gii';
    $config['modules']['gii'] =
    'yii\gii\Module';
}
return $config;
```

7. Move the `request` configuration into `config/web-local.php`:

```
<?php
```

```php
    return [
        'components' => [
            'request' => [
                'cookieValidationKey' =>
        'TRk9G1La5kvLFwqMEQTp6PmC1NHdjtkq',
            ],
        ],
    ];
```

8. Remove the e-mail ID from `config/params.php`:

```php
<?php
return [
    'adminEmail' => '',
];
```

9. Paste the ID into `config/params-local.php`:

```php
<?php
return [
    'adminEmail' =>
    'admin@example.com',
];
```

10. Remove the `dsn` string from `tests/codeception/config/config.php`:

```php
<?php
/**
 * Application configuration shared by all test types
 */
return [
    'controllerMap' => [
        // ...
    ],
    'components' => [
        'db' => [
            'dsn' => '',
        ],
        'mailer' => [
            'useFileTransport' =>
            true,
        ],
        'urlManager' => [
            'showScriptName' => true,
        ],
    ],
];
```

11. Put the string into a new `tests/codeception/config/config-local.php` file:

```php
<?php
return [
    'components' => [
        'db' => [
            'dsn' =>
            'mysql:host=localhost;
            dbname=yii2_basic_tests',
        ],
    ],
];
```

12. Add configuration merging to the `web/index.php` file:

```php
$config =
yii\helpers\ArrayHelper::merge(
    require(__DIR__ .
    '/../config/common.php'),
    require(__DIR__ .
    '/../config/common-local.php'),
    require(__DIR__ .
    '/../config/web.php'),
    require(__DIR__ .
    '/../config/web-local.php')
);
```

13. Add configuration merging to the console entry script, `yii`:

```php
$config =
yii\helpers\ArrayHelper::merge(
    require(__DIR__ .
    '/config/common.php'),
    require(__DIR__ .
    '/config/common-local.php'),
    require(__DIR__ .
    '/config/console.php'),
    require(__DIR__ .
    '/config/console-local.php')
);
```

14. Add configuration merging to the testing configurations of the unit, functional, and acceptance tests from `tests/codeception/config`:

```php
return yii\helpers\ArrayHelper::merge(
    require(__DIR__ .
    '/../../../config/common.php'),
    require(__DIR__ .
    '/../../../config/common-
    local.php'),
```

```
require(__DIR__ .
'/../../../config/web.php'),
require(__DIR__ .
'/../../../config/web-
local.php'),
require(__DIR__ . '/config.php'),
require(__DIR__ . '/config-
local.php'),
[
    // ...
]
);
```

15. Add configuration merging to the testing environment console's entry script,
    `tests/codeception/bin/yii`:

```
$config =
yii\helpers\ArrayHelper::merge(
    require(YII_APP_BASE_PATH .
    '/config/common.php'),
    require(YII_APP_BASE_PATH .
    '/config/common-local.php'),
    require(YII_APP_BASE_PATH .
    '/config/console.php'),
    require(YII_APP_BASE_PATH .
    '/config/console-local.php'),
    require(__DIR__ .
    '/../config/config.php'),
    require(__DIR__ .
    '/../config/config-local.php')
);
```

16. As a result, you must get the following content in your configuration directory:

```
config
    common.php
    common-local.php
    console.php
    console-local.php
    web.php
    web-local.php
    params.php
    params-local.php
```

17. After all, you can add a new `.gitignore` file with this content into your `config` and
    `tests/codeception/config` directories so you can ignore local configuration files
    by the Git version control system:

```
/*-local.php
```

How it works...

You can store common application components configuration in the `config/common.php` file and also set specific configurations for web and console applications. You can put your temporary and secure configuration data into the `*-local.php` files.

Also, you can copy the initialization shell script from `yii2-app-advanced`.

1. Create a new `environments` directory and copy your templates into it:

```
environments
    dev
        config
            common-local.php
            console-local.php
            web-local.php
            params-local.php
        web
            index.php
            index-test.php
        tests
            codeception
                config
                    config.php
                    config-local.php
        yii
    prod
        config
            common-local.php
            console-local.php
            web-local.php
            params-local.php
        web
            index.php
        yii
```

2. Create the `environments/index.php` file with this code:

```php
<?php
return [
    'Development' => [
        'path' => 'dev',
        'setWritable' => [
            'runtime',
            'web/assets',
        ],
```

```
            'setExecutable' => [
                'yii',
                'tests/codeception/
                bin/yii',
            ],
            'setCookieValidationKey' => [
                'config/web-local.php',
            ],
        ],
        'Production' => [
            'path' => 'prod',
            'setWritable' => [
                'runtime',
                'web/assets',
            ],
            'setExecutable' => [
                'yii',
            ],
            'setCookieValidationKey' => [
                'config/web-local.php',
            ],
        ],
    ];
```

3. Remove the default `Installer::postCreateProject` configuration from your `composer.json`:

```json
"extra": {
    "asset-installer-paths": {
        "npm-asset-library":
        "vendor/npm",
        "bower-asset-library":
        "vendor/bower"
    }
}
```

4. Copy the `init` and `init.bat` scripts from the Advanced template, `https://github.com/yiisoft/yii2-app-advanced` and you can run the initialization process using the command `php init` after the cloning of the project from the repository.

See also

For more information about application configurations refer to `http://www.yiiframework.com/doc-2.0/guide-concept-configurations.html`.

Implementing and executing cron jobs

Sometimes, an application requires some background tasks, such as regenerating a site map or refreshing statistics. A common way to implement this is by using cron jobs. When using Yii, there is a way to use a command to run as a job.

In this recipe, we will see how to implement both. For our recipe, we will implement writing the current timestamp into a `timestamp.txt` file under the protected directory.

Getting ready

Create a new `yii2-app-basic` application by using the Composer, as described in the official guide at `http://www.yiiframework.com/doc-2.0/guide-start-installation.html`.

How to do it...

Running the Hello command

Let us try to run `app\commands\HelloController::actionIndex` as a shell command:

```php
<?php
namespace app\commands;
use yii\console\Controller;

/**
 * This command echoes the first argument that you have entered.
 */
class HelloController extends Controller
{
    /**
     * This command echoes what you have entered as the message.
     * @param string $message the message to be echoed.
     */
    public function actionIndex($message =
    'hello world')
    {
        echo $message . "\n";
    }
}
```

1. Open the shell in your application directory and execute this command:

    php yii

Alternatively, you also can call the following and ensure that the shell works:

```
./yii
```

2. Type the following command for the display `hello`:

```
./yii help hello
```

3. The framework must display some information:

```
DESCRIPTION

This command echoes what you have entered as the message.


USAGE

yii hello [message] [...options...]
- message: string (defaults to 'hello world')
  the message to be echoed.
```

4. Run the default command action:

```
./yii hello
```

Alternatively, run the concrete `index` action:

```
./yii hello/index
```

5. You must now see the default phrase:

```
Hello world
```

6. Run the command with any parameter and see the response:

```
./yii hello 'Bond, James Bond'
```

Creating your own command

You also can create your own console controllers. For example, create a `commands/CronController.php` file with the sample code:

```php
<?php
namespace app\commands;

use yii\console\Controller;
use yii\helpers\Console;
use Yii;

/**
 * Console crontab actions
 */
class CronController extends Controller
```

```
{
    /**
     * Regenerates timestamp
     */
    public function actionTimestamp()
    {
        file_put_contents(Yii::getAlias(
        '@app/timestamp.txt'),
        time());
        $this->stdout('Done!',
        Console::FG_GREEN, Console::BOLD);
        $this->stdout(PHP_EOL);
    }
}
```

After all is done, run the command in a shell:

./yii cron/timestamp

Then, check the response text and the existence of a new file, namely timestamp.txt.

Setting the cron schedule

Create /etc/cron.d/myapp on your Linux server and add the following row to run our command at every midnight:

0 0 * * * www-data /path/to/yii cron/timestamp >/dev/null

How it works...

A console command is defined as a controller class that extends from yii\console\ Controller. In the controller class, you define one or more actions that correspond to the subcommands of the controller. Within each action, you write code that implements the appropriate tasks for that particular sub-command.

When running a command, you need to specify the route to the controller action. For example, the route migrate/create invokes the sub-command that corresponds to the MigrateCo ntroller::actionCreate() action method. If a route offered during the execution does not contain an action ID, the default action will be executed (as with a web controller).

Take care that your console controllers are placed in the directory defined in the controllerNamespace option in your web/console.php config.

See also

▶ For getting more information about Yii2 console commands, refer to http://www. yiiframework.com/doc-2.0/guide-tutorial-console.html

> ▶ In order to learn more about the Cron daemon, refer to `https://en.wikipedia.org/wiki/Cron`

> ▶ The *Changing the Yii directory layout* recipe for `controllerNamespace`

Maintenance mode

Sometimes, there is a need to fine tune some application settings or restore a database from a backup. When working on tasks such as these, it is not desirable to allow everyone to use the application because it can lead to losing the recent user messages or showing the application implementation details.

In this recipe, we will see how to show everyone except the developer a maintenance message.

Getting ready

Create a new `yii2-app-basic` application by using the Composer package manager, as described in the official guide at `http://www.yiiframework.com/doc-2.0/guide-start-installation.html`.

How to do it...

Carry out the following steps:

1. First, we need to create `protected/controllers/MaintenanceController.php`. We do this as follows:

```php
class MaintenanceController extends Controller
{
    public function actionIndex()
    {
        $this-
        >renderPartial("index");
    }
}
```

2. Then we create a view named `views/maintenance/index.php`, as follows:

```php
<?php
use yii\helpers\Html;
?>
<!doctype html>
<head>
    <meta charset="utf-8" />
    <title><?php echo
```

```
    Html::encode(Yii::$app->name)?>
    is under maintenance</title>
</head>
<body>
    <h1><?php echo
    Html::encode(Yii::$app->name)?>
    is under maintenance</h1>
    <p>We'll be back soon. If we
    aren't back for too long,
    please drop a message to <?php
    echo Yii::$app->params
    ['adminEmail']?>.</p>
    <p>Meanwhile, it's a good time to
    get a cup of coffee,
    to read a book or to check
    email.</p>
</body>
```

3. Now we need to add a single line of code to `config/web.php`, as follows:

```
$config = [
    'catchAll' =>
    file_exists(dirname(__DIR__) .
    '/.maintenance')
    && !(isset($_COOKIE['secret']) &&
    $_COOKIE['secret']=="password") ?
    ['maintenance/index'] : null,
    // …
]
```

4. Now in order to go into the maintenance mode, you need to create a file named `.maintenance` in your site directory. After you do this, you should see this page.

In order to get it back to normal, you just need to delete it. To view the website in the maintenance mode, you can create a cookie named `secret` with its value equal to `password`.

How it works...

A Yii web application offers a way to intercept all the possible requests and route these to a single controller action. You can do this by setting `yii\web\Application::catchAll` to an array containing the application route as follows:

`'catchAll' => ['maintenance/index'],`

The maintenance controller itself is nothing special; it just renders a view with some text.

We need an easy way to turn the maintenance mode on and off. As the application config is a regular PHP file, we can achieve it with a simple check to confirm the file exists, as follows:

```
file_exists(dirname(__DIR__) .
'/.maintenance')
```

In addition, we check for the cookie value to be able to override the maintenance mode. We do this as follows:

```
!(isset($_COOKIE['secret']) &&
$_COOKIE['secret']=="password")
```

See also

In order to learn more about how to catch all the requests in a Yii application and check the production ready solution for maintenance, refer to `http://www.yiiframework.com/doc-2.0/yii-web-application.html#$catchAll-detail`.

Deployment tools

If you are using a version control system such as Git, for your project's code and pushing releases into remote repository, you can use Git to deploy code to your production server via the `git pull` shell command instead of uploading files manually. Also, you can write your own shell script to pull new repository commits, update vendors, apply migrations, and do more things.

However, there are many tools available for automating the deployment process. In this recipe, we consider the tool named Deployer.

Getting ready

Create a new `yii2-app-basic` application by using the Composer package manager, as described in the official guide at `http://www.yiiframework.com/doc-2.0/guide-start-installation.html`.

How to do it...

If you have a shared remote repository, you can use it for deployment source.

Step 1 - Preparing the remote host

1. Go to your remote host and install Composer and `asset-plugin` too:

```
global require 'fxp/composer-asset-plugin:~1.1.1'
```

2. Generate the SSH key via `ssh-keygen`.

3. Add the `~/.ssh/id_rsa.pub` file content into deployment the SSH keys page of your repository settings on GitHub, Bitbucket, or other repositories storage.

4. Try to clone your repository manually:

   git clone git@github.com:user/repo.git

5. Add the Github address and the list of known hosts if the system asks you to do it.

Step 2 - Preparing the localhost

1. Install `deployer.phar` globally on your local host:

```
sudo wget http://deployer.org/deployer.phar
sudo mv deployer.phar /usr/local/bin/dep
sudo chmod +x /usr/local/bin/dep
```

2. Add the `deploy.php` file with the deployment configuration:

```php
<?php
require 'recipe/yii2-app-basic.php';

set('shared_files', [
    'config/db.php',
    'config/params.php',
    'web/index.php',
    'yii',
]);

server('prod', 'site.com', 22) // SSH access to remote server
    ->user('user')
    // ->password(password) // uncomment for authentication by
password
    // ->identityFile()               // uncomment for
authentication by SSH key
    ->stage('production')
    ->env('deploy_path', '/var/www/project');

set('repository', 'git@github.com:user/repo.git');
```

3. Try to prepare remote project directories structure:

   dep deploy:prepare prod

Step 3 - Adding remote configuration

1. Open the server's `/var/www/project` directory. It has two subdirectories after the initialization:

    ```
    project
    ├── releases
    └── shared
    ```

2. Create original files with private configurations in a `shared` directory like this:

    ```
    project
    ├── releases
    └── shared
                ├── config
                │       ├── db.php
                │       └── params.php
                ├── web
                │       └── index.php
                └── yii
    ```

The Deployer tool will include these files in every release subdirectory via symbolic links.

Specify your private configuration in `share/config/db.php`:

```php
<?php
return [
    'class' => 'yii\db\Connection',
    dsn' => 'mysql:host=localhost;dbname=catalog',
    'username' => 'root',
    'password' => 'root',
    'charset' => 'utf8',
];
```

Also, specify it in `share/config/params.php`:

```php
<?php
return [
    'adminEmail' => 'admin@example.com',
];
```

Set the content of `share/web/index.php`:

```php
<?php
defined('YII_DEBUG') or define('YII_DEBUG',
false);
defined('YII_ENV') or define('YII_ENV',
'prod');
```

```php
$dir = dirname($_SERVER['SCRIPT_FILENAME']);

require($dir . '/../vendor/autoload.php');
require($dir .
'/../vendor/yiisoft/yii2/Yii.php');

$config = require($dir .
'/../config/web.php');

(new yii\web\Application($config))->run();
```

Also, set the content of the `share/yii` file:

```php
#!/usr/bin/env php
<?php
defined('YII_DEBUG') or define('YII_DEBUG',
false);
defined('YII_ENV') or define('YII_ENV',
'prod');

$dir =
dirname($_SERVER['SCRIPT_FILENAME']);

require($dir . '/vendor/autoload.php');
require($dir .
'/vendor/yiisoft/yii2/Yii.php');

$config = require($dir.
'/config/console.php');

$application = new
yii\console\Application($config);
$exitCode = $application->run();
exit($exitCode);
```

Note: We deliberately use the `dirname($_SERVER['SCRIPT_FILENAME'])` code instead of the original `__DIR__` constant because `__DIR__` will return incorrect value when the file is included via symbolic link.

Note: If you use the `yii2-app-advanced` template you can redeclare only the `config/main-local.php` and `config/params-local.php` files of every (backend, frontend, console, and common) because `web/index.php` and `yii` files will be created automatically by the `init` command.

Step 4 - Trying to deploy

1. Come back to the localhost with the `deploy.php` file and run the deploy command:

    dep deploy prod

2. If successful, you will see the deployment report:

```
✓ Executing task deploy:prepare

✓ Executing task deploy:release

✓ Executing task deploy:update_code

✓ Executing task deploy:shared

✓ Executing task deploy:vendors

✓ Executing task deploy:run_migrations

✓ Executing task deploy:symlink

✓ Executing task cleanup

➤ Executing task success
Successfully deployed!

✓ Ok
```

3. Deployer created a new release subdirectory on your remote server and added symlinks from your project to the shared items and from the `current` directory to the current release:

```
project
├── current -> releases/20160412140556
├── releases
│    └── 20160412140556
│            ├── ...
│            ├── runtime -> /../../shared/runtime
│            ├── web
│            ├── vendor
│            ├── ...
│            └── yii -> /../../shared/yii
└── shared
     ├── config
     │    ├── db.php
     │    └── params.php
     ├── runtime
```

```
├── web
│   └── index.php
└── yii
```

4. After all is done, you must set up the `DocumentRoot` of your server in `project/current/web` directory.

5. If something goes wrong during the deployment process you can roll back to the previous working release:

dep rollback prod

The `current` directory will lead to your previous release files.

How it works...

Most of the deployment tools do the same tasks:

▶ Create a new release subdirectory

▶ Clone repository files

▶ Make symlinks from the project to shared directories and to local configuration files

▶ Install Composer packages

▶ Apply project migrations

▶ Switch the symlink from the server's `DocumentRoot` path to the current release directory

The Deployer tool has predefined recipes for popular frameworks. You can extend any existing recipe or write a new one for your specific case.

See also

▶ For more information about Deployer, refer to `http://deployer.org/docs`

▶ And about creating SSH keys refer to `https://git-scm.com/book/en/v2/Git-on-the-Server-Generating-Your-SSH-Public-Key`

11
Testing

In this chapter, we will cover the following topics:

- ▶ Testing application with Codeception
- ▶ Unit testing with PHPUnit
- ▶ Unit testing with Atoum
- ▶ Unit testing with Behat

Introduction

In this chapter, you will learn how to use the best technologies for testing, such as Codeception, PhpUnit, Atoum, and Behat. You will be introduced to how to write simple tests and how to avoid regression errors in your application.

Testing application with Codeception

By default, the basic and advanced Yii2 application skeletons use **Codeception** as a testing framework. Codeception supports writing of unit, functional, and acceptance tests out of the box. For unit tests, it uses the PHPUnit test framework, which will be covered in the next recipe.

Getting ready

1. Create a new `yii2-app-basic` application using the Composer package manager, as described in the official guide at `http://www.yiiframework.com/doc-2.0/guide-start-installation.html`.

 Note: If your use version 2.0.9 (or earlier) of the basic application just upgrade manually `tests` directory, and also add `config/test.php`, `config/test_db.php` and `web/index-test.php` files. Besides you must copy `require` and `require-dev` sections of `composer.json` file and run `composer update`.

2. Create and apply the following migration:

```php
<?php
use yii\db\Migration;

class m160309_070856_create_post extends Migration
{
    public function up()
    {
        $this->createTable('{{%post}}', [
            'id' => $this->primaryKey(),
            'title' => $this->string()->notNull(),
            'text' => $this->text()->notNull(),
            'status' => $this->smallInteger()->notNull()-
            >defaultValue(0),
        ]);
    }

    public function down()
    {
        $this->dropTable('{{%post}}');
    }
}
```

3. Create the `Post` model:

```php
namespace app\models;

use Yii;
```

```
use yii\db\ActiveRecord;

/**
 * @property integer $id
 * @property string $title
 * @property string $text
 * @property integer $status
 * @property integer $created_at
 * @property integer $updated_at
 */
class Post extends ActiveRecord
{
    const STATUS_DRAFT = 0;
    const STATUS_ACTIVE = 1;

    public static function tableName()
    {
        return '{{%post}}';
    }

    public function rules()
    {
        return [
            [['title', 'text'], 'required'],
            [['text'], 'string'],
            ['status', 'in', 'range' => [self::STATUS_DRAFT,
            self::STATUS_ACTIVE]],
            ['status', 'default', 'value' => self::STATUS_DRAFT],
            [['title'], 'string', 'max' => 255],
        ];
    }

    public function behaviors()
    {
        return [
            TimestampBehavior::className(),
        ];
    }

    public static function getStatusList()
    {
        return [
            self::STATUS_DRAFT => 'Draft',
            self::STATUS_ACTIVE => 'Active',
        ];
    }
```

```
    public function publish()
    {
        if ($this->status == self::STATUS_ACTIVE) {
            throw new \DomainException('Post is already
            published.');
        }
        $this->status = self::STATUS_ACTIVE;
    }

    public function draft()
    {
        if ($this->status == self::STATUS_DRAFT) {
            throw new \DomainException('Post is already
            drafted.');
        }
        $this->status = self::STATUS_DRAFT;
    }
}
```

4. Generate CRUD:

CRUD Generator

This generator generates a controller and views that implement CRUD (Create, Read, Upda
model.

Model Class

app\models\Post

Search Model Class

app\models\PostSearch

Controller Class

app\controllers\admin\PostsController

View Path

@app/views/admin/posts

Base Controller Class

yii\web\Controller

Widget Used in Index Page

GridView

5. Also, add the status drop-down list for the `status` field and name for the submit button in `views/admin/posts/_form.php`:

```php
<div class="post-form">

    <?php $form = ActiveForm::begin(); ?>

    <?= $form->field($model, 'title')->textInput(['maxlength' =>
    true]) ?>

    <?= $form->field($model, 'text')->textarea(['rows' => 6]) ?>

    <?= $form->field($model, 'status')-
    >dropDownList(Post::getStatusList()) ?>

    <div class="form-group">
        <?= Html::submitButton($model->isNewRecord ? 'Create' :
        'Update', [
            'class' => $model->isNewRecord ? 'btn btn-success' :
            'btn btn-primary',
            'name' => 'submit-button',
        ]) ?>
    </div>

    <?php ActiveForm::end(); ?>

</div>
```

6. Now check that the controller works:

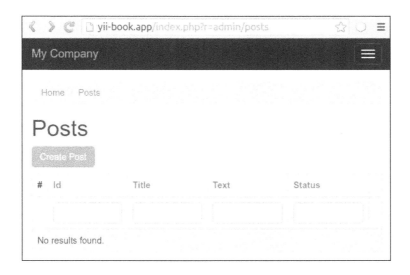

Create any demo posts.

How to do it...

Preparing for the tests

Follow these steps to prepare for the tests:

1. Create `yii2_basic_tests` or other test database and update it by applying migrations:

   `tests/bin/yii migrate`

   You can specify your test database options in configuration file `/config/test_db.php`.

2. Codeception uses autogenerated Actor classes for own test suites. Build them with this command:

   `composer exec codecept build`

Running unit and functional tests

We can run any types of the application's tests right now:

```
# run all available tests
composer exec codecept run


# run functional tests
composer exec codecept run functional


# run unit tests
composer exec codecept run unit
```

As a result, you can view, testing report like this:

```
Codeception PHP Testing Framework v2.2.5
Powered by PHPUnit 4.8.27 by Sebastian Bergmann and contributors.

Unit Tests (15) -----------------------------------
✓ ContactFormTest: Email is sent on contact (0.09s)

✓ LoginFormTest: Login no user (0.01s)

✓ LoginFormTest: Login wrong password (0.00s)

✓ LoginFormTest: Login correct (0.00s)

✓ PostTest: Validate empty (0.06s)

✓ PostTest: Validate correct (0.03s)

✓ PostTest: Save (0.03s)

✓ PostTest: Publish (0.03s)

✓ PostTest: Already published (0.03s)

✓ PostTest: Draft (0.03s)

✓ PostTest: Already drafted (0.04s)

✓ UserTest: Find user by id (0.00s)

✓ UserTest: Find user by access token (0.00s)

✓ UserTest: Find user by username (0.00s)

✓ UserTest: Validate user (0.00s)
---------------------------------------------------

Time: 1.65 seconds, Memory: 29.00MB|

OK (15 tests, 45 assertions)
```

Getting coverage reports

You can get code coverage reports for your code. By default, code coverage is disabled in the `codeception.yml` configuration file; you should uncomment the necessary rows to be able to collect code coverage:

```
coverage:
    enabled: true
    whitelist:
        include:
            - models/*
            - controllers/*
```

```
            - commands/*
            - mail/*
    blacklist:
        include:
            - assets/*
            - config/*
            - runtime/*
            - vendor/*
            - views/*
            - web/*
            - tests/*
```

You must install the XDebug PHP extension from `https://xdebug.org`. For example, on Ubuntu or Debian you can type the following in your terminal:

`sudo apt-get install php5-xdebug`

On Windows, you must open the `php.ini` file and add the custom code with the path to your PHP installation directory:

```
[xdebug]
zend_extension_ts=C:/php/ext/php_xdebug.dll
```

Alternatively, if you use the non-thread safe edition, type the following:

```
[xdebug]
zend_extension=C:/php/ext/php_xdebug.dll
```

Finally, you can run tests and collect the coverage report with the following command:

```
#collect coverage for all tests
composer exec codecept run --coverage-html


#collect coverage only for unit tests
composer exec codecept run unit --coverage-html


#collect coverage for unit and functional tests
composer exec codecept run functional,unit --coverage-html
```

You can see the text code coverage output in the terminal:

```
Code Coverage Report:
  2016-03-31 08:13:05

 Summary:
  Classes: 20.00% (1/5)
  Methods: 40.91% (9/22)
  Lines:   30.65% (38/124)


\app\models::ContactForm
  Methods:  33.33% ( 1/ 3)    Lines:  80.00% ( 12/ 15)
\app\models::LoginForm
  Methods: 100.00% ( 4/ 4)    Lines: 100.00% ( 18/ 18)
\app\models::User
  Methods:  57.14% ( 4/ 7)    Lines:  53.33% (  8/ 15)
Remote CodeCoverage reports are not printed to console


HTML report generated in coverage
```

Also, you can see HTML-report under the `tests/_output/coverage` directory:

	Lines		Functions and Methods		Classes and Traits	
			Code Coverage			
Total	30.65%	38 / 124	40.91%	9 / 22	20.00%	1 / 5
commands	0.00%	0 / 3	0.00%	0 / 1	0.00%	0 / 1
controllers	0.00%	0 / 66	0.00%	0 / 7	0.00%	0 / 1
mail	0.00%	0 / 7	100.00%	0 / 0		0 / 0
models	79.17%	38 / 48	64.29%	9 / 14	33.33%	1 / 3

You can click on any class and analyze which lines of code have not been executed during the testing process.

Running acceptance tests

In acceptance tests you can use PhpBrowser for requesting server via Curl. It helps to check your site controllers and to parse HTTP and HTML response codes. But if you want to test your CSS or JavaScript behavior, you must use real browser.

Selenium Server is an interactive tool, which integrates into Firefox and other browsers and allows to open site pages and emulate human actions.

For working with real browser we must install Selenium Server:

1. Require full Codeception package instead of basic:

    ```
    composer require --dev codeception/codeception
    composer remove --dev codeception/base
    ```

2. Download the following software:

    ❑   Install Mozilla Firefox browser from https://www.mozilla.org

    ❑   Install Java Runtime Environment from https://www.java.com/en/download/

    ❑   Download Selenium Standalone Server from http://www.seleniumhq.org/download/

    ❑   Download Geckodriver from https://github.com/mozilla/geckodriver/releases

3. Launch server with the driver in new terminal window:

    ```
    java -jar -Dwebdriver.gecko.driver=~/geckodriver ~/selenium-
    server-standalone-x.xx.x.jar
    ```

4. Copy `tests/acceptance.suite.yml.example` to `tests/acceptance.suite.yml` file and configure one like this:

    ```
    class_name: AcceptanceTester
    modules:
        enabled:
            - WebDriver:
                url: http://127.0.0.1:8080/
                browser: firefox
            - Yii2:
                part: orm
                entryScript: index-test.php
                cleanup: false
    ```

5. Open new terminal frame and start web server:

```
tests/bin/yii serve
```

6. Run acceptance tests:

```
composer exec codecept run acceptance
```

And you should see how Selenium starts the browser and check all site pages.

Creating database fixtures

Before running own tests, we must clear the own test database and load specific test data into it. The `yii2-codeception` extension provides the `ActiveFixture` base class for creating test data sets for own models. Follow these steps to create database fixtures:

1. Create the fixture class for the `Post` model:

```php
<?php
namespace tests\fixtures;

use yii\test\ActiveFixture;

class PostFixture extends ActiveFixture
{
    public $modelClass = 'app\modules\Post';
    public $dataFile = '@tests/_data/post.php';
}
```

2. Add a demonstration data set in `test/_data/post.php` file:

```php
<?php
return [
    [
        'id' => 1,
        'title' => 'First Post',
        'text' => 'First Post Text',
        'status' => 1,
        'created_at' => 1457211600,
        'updated_at' => 1457211600,
    ],
    [
        'id' => 2,
        'title' => 'Old Title For Updating',
        'text' => 'Old Text For Updating',
        'status' => 1,
```

```
                  'created_at' => 1457211600,
                  'updated_at' => 1457211600,
            ],
            [

                  'id' => 3,
                  'title' => 'Title For Deleting',
                  'text' => 'Text For Deleting',
                  'status' => 1,
                  'created_at' => 1457211600,
                  'updated_at' => 1457211600,
            ],
      ];
```

3. Activate fixtures support for unit and acceptance tests. Just add `fixtures` part into `unit.suite.yml` file:

```
class_name: UnitTester
modules:
    enabled:
      - Asserts
      - Yii2:
            part: [orm, fixtures, email]
```

Also, add the `fixtures` part into `acceptance.suite.yml`:

```
class_name: AcceptanceTester
modules:
    enabled:
          - WebDriver:
                url: http://127.0.0.1:8080/
                browser: firefox
          - Yii2:
                part: [orm, fixtures]
                entryScript: index-test.php
                cleanup: false
```

4. Regenerate `tester` classes for applying these changes by the following command:

```
composer exec codecept build
```

Writing unit or integration test

Unit and integration tests check the source code of our project.

Unit tests check only the current class or their method in isolation from other classes and resources such as databases, files, and many more.

Integration tests check the working of your classes in integration with other classes and resources.

ActiveRecord models in Yii2 always use databases for loading table schema as we must create a real test database and our tests will be integrational.

1. Write tests for checking model validation, saving, and changing its status:

```php
<?php
namespace tests\unit\models;

use app\models\Post;
use Codeception\Test\Unit;
use tests\fixtures\PostFixture;

class PostTest extends Unit
{
    /**
     * @var \UnitTester
     */
    protected $tester;

    public function _before()
    {
        $this->tester->haveFixtures([
            'post' => [
                'class' => PostFixture::className(),
                'dataFile' => codecept_data_dir() . 'post.php'
            ]
        ]);
    }

    public function testValidateEmpty()
    {
        $model = new Post();

        expect('model should not validate', $model->validate())-
>false();

        expect('title has error', $model->errors)-
>hasKey('title');
        expect('title has error', $model->errors)->hasKey('text');
    }
```

```php
public function testValidateCorrect()
{
    $model = new Post([
        'title' => 'Other Post',
        'text' => 'Other Post Text',
    ]);

    expect('model should validate', $model->validate())-
    >true();
}

public function testSave()
{
    $model = new Post([
        'title' => 'Test Post',
        'text' => 'Test Post Text',
    ]);

     expect('model should save', $model->save())->true();

    expect('title is correct', $model->title)->equals('Test
    Post');
    expect('text is correct', $model->text)->equals('Test Post
    Text');
    expect('status is draft', $model->status)-
    >equals(Post::STATUS_DRAFT);
    expect('created_at is generated', $model->created_at)-
    >notEmpty();
    expect('updated_at is generated', $model->updated_at)-
    >notEmpty();
}

public function testPublish()
{
    $model = new Post(['status' => Post::STATUS_DRAFT]);

    expect('post is drafted', $model->status)-
    >equals(Post::STATUS_DRAFT);
    $model->publish();
```

```
        expect('post is published', $model->status)-
        >equals(Post::STATUS_ACTIVE);
    }

    public function testAlreadyPublished()
    {
        $model = new Post(['status' => Post::STATUS_ACTIVE]);

        $this->setExpectedException('\LogicException');
        $model->publish();
    }

    public function testDraft()
    {
        $model = new Post(['status' => Post::STATUS_ACTIVE]);

        expect('post is published', $model->status)-
        >equals(Post::STATUS_ACTIVE);
        $model->draft();
        expect('post is drafted', $model->status)-
        >equals(Post::STATUS_DRAFT);
    }

    public function testAlreadyDrafted()
    {
        $model = new Post(['status' => Post::STATUS_ACTIVE]);

        $this->setExpectedException('\LogicException');
        $model->publish();
    }
}
```

2. Run the tests:

```
composer exec codecept run unit
```

3. Now see the result:

```
Unit Tests (15) -------------------------------------
✓ ContactFormTest: Email is sent on contact (0.12s)
✓ LoginFormTest: Login no user (0.01s)
✓ LoginFormTest: Login wrong password (0.00s)
✓ LoginFormTest: Login correct (0.00s)
✓ PostTest: Validate empty (0.06s)
✓ PostTest: Validate correct (0.04s)
✓ PostTest: Save (0.04s)
✓ PostTest: Publish (0.03s)
✓ PostTest: Already published (0.04s)
✓ PostTest: Draft (0.03s)
✓ PostTest: Already drafted (0.03s)
✓ UserTest: Find user by id (0.00s)
✓ UserTest: Find user by access token (0.00s)
✓ UserTest: Find user by username (0.00s)
✓ UserTest: Validate user (0.00s)
-------------------------------------------------------
```

That is all. If you deliberately or casually break any model's method you will see a broken test.

Writing functional test

Functional test checks that your application works correctly. This suite prepares $_GET, $_POST, and others request variables and call the Application::handleRequest method. It helps to test your controllers and their responses without running of real server.

Now we can write tests for our admin CRUD:

1. Generate a new test class:

```
codecept generate:cest functional admin/Posts
```

2. Fix the namespace in the generated file and write own tests:

```php
<?php
namespace tests\functional\admin;

use app\models\Post;
use FunctionalTester;
use tests\fixtures\PostFixture;
use yii\helpers\Url;

class PostsCest
{
    function _before(FunctionalTester $I)
    {
        $I->haveFixtures([
            'user' => [
                'class' => PostFixture::className(),
                'dataFile' => codecept_data_dir() . 'post.php'
            ]
        ]);
    }

    public function testIndex(FunctionalTester $I)
    {
        $I->amOnPage(['admin/posts/index']);
        $I->see('Posts', 'h1');
    }

    public function testView(FunctionalTester $I)
    {
        $I->amOnPage(['admin/posts/view', 'id' => 1]);
        $I->see('First Post', 'h1');
    }
```

```php
public function testCreateInvalid(FunctionalTester $I)
{
    $I->amOnPage(['admin/posts/create']);
    $I->see('Create', 'h1');

    $I->submitForm('#post-form', [
        'Post[title]' => '',
        'Post[text]' => '',
    ]);

    $I->expectTo('see validation errors');
    $I->see('Title cannot be blank.', '.help-block');
    $I->see('Text cannot be blank.', '.help-block');
}

public function testCreateValid(FunctionalTester $I)
{
    $I->amOnPage(['admin/posts/create']);
    $I->see('Create', 'h1');

    $I->submitForm('#post-form', [
        'Post[title]' => 'Post Create Title',
        'Post[text]' => 'Post Create Text',
        'Post[status]' => 'Active',
    ]);

    $I->expectTo('see view page');
    $I->see('Post Create Title', 'h1');
}

public function testUpdate(FunctionalTester $I)
{
    // ...
}
public function testDelete(FunctionalTester $I)
{
    $I->amOnPage(['/admin/posts/view', 'id' => 3]);
    $I->see('Title For Deleting', 'h1');
```

```
        $I->amGoingTo('delete item');
        $I->sendAjaxPostRequest(Url::to(['/admin/posts/delete',
'id'
        => 3]));
        $I->expectTo('see that post is deleted');
        $I->dontSeeRecord(Post::className(), [
            'title' => 'Title For Deleting',
        ]);
    }
}
```

3. Run tests with the command:

    composer exec codecept run functional

4. Now see the results:

```
Functional Tests (16) ------------------------------------------------------
--------
✓ ContactFormCest: Open contact page (0.12s)

✓ ContactFormCest: Submit empty form (0.05s)

✓ ContactFormCest: Submit form with incorrect email (0.04s)

✓ ContactFormCest: Submit form successfully (0.09s)

✓ LoginFormCest: Open login page (0.01s)

✓ LoginFormCest: Internal login by id (0.02s)

✓ LoginFormCest: Internal login by instance (0.02s)

✓ LoginFormCest: Login with empty credentials (0.03s)

✓ LoginFormCest: Login with wrong credentials (0.02s)

✓ LoginFormCest: Login successfully (0.02s)

✓ PostsCest: Test index (0.11s)

✓ PostsCest: Test view (0.05s)

✓ PostsCest: Test create invalid (0.07s)

✓ PostsCest: Test create valid (0.07s)

✓ PostsCest: Test update (0.03s)

✓ PostsCest: Test delete (0.07s)
------------------------------------------------------------
```

All tests passed. In other case you can see snapshots of tested pages in `tests/_output` directory for failed tests.

Writing acceptance test

1. Acceptance tester hit the real site from test server instead of calling `Application::handleRequest` method. High-level acceptance tests look like middle-level functional tests, but in case of Selenium it allows to check JavaScript behavior in real browser.

2. You must get the following class in `tests/acceptance` directory:

```php
<?php
namespace tests\acceptance\admin;

use AcceptanceTester;
use tests\fixtures\PostFixture;
use yii\helpers\Url;

class PostsCest
{
    function _before(AcceptanceTester $I)
    {
        $I->haveFixtures([
            'post' => [
                'class' => PostFixture::className(),
                'dataFile' => codecept_data_dir() . 'post.php'
            ]
        ]);
    }

    public function testIndex(AcceptanceTester $I)
    {
        $I->wantTo('ensure that post index page works');
        $I->amOnPage(Url::to(['/admin/posts/index']));
        $I->see('Posts', 'h1');
    }

    public function testView(AcceptanceTester $I)
    {
        $I->wantTo('ensure that post view page works');
        $I->amOnPage(Url::to(['/admin/posts/view', 'id' => 1]));
        $I->see('First Post', 'h1');
    }
}
```

```php
    public function testCreate(AcceptanceTester $I)
    {
        $I->wantTo('ensure that post create page works');
        $I->amOnPage(Url::to(['/admin/posts/create']));
        $I->see('Create', 'h1');

        $I->fillField('#post-title', 'Post Create Title');
        $I->fillField('#post-text', 'Post Create Text');
        $I->selectOption('#post-status', 'Active');

        $I->click('submit-button');
        $I->wait(3);

        $I->expectTo('see view page');
        $I->see('Post Create Title', 'h1');
    }

    public function testDelete(AcceptanceTester $I)
    {
        $I->amOnPage(Url::to(['/admin/posts/view', 'id' => 3]));
        $I->see('Title For Deleting', 'h1');

        $I->click('Delete');
        $I->acceptPopup();
        $I->wait(3);

        $I->see('Posts', 'h1');
    }
}
```

Do not forget to call `wait` method for waiting for page to be opened or reloaded.

3. Run the PHP test server in a new terminal frame:

   tests/bin/yii serve

4. Run the acceptance tests:

   composer exec codecept run acceptance

5. See the results:

```
Acceptance Tests (9)  -----------------------------------------------------
-----
✓ AboutCest: Ensure that about works (0.84s)
✓ ContactCest: Ensure that contact page works (0.36s)
✓ ContactCest: Contact form can be submitted (2.94s)
✓ HomeCest: Ensure that home page works (2.47s)
✓ LoginCest: Ensure that login works (2.67s)
✓ PostsCest: Ensure that post index page works (0.47s)
✓ PostsCest: Ensure that post view page works (0.35s)
✓ PostsCest: Ensure that post create page works (4.11s)
✓ PostsCest: Ensure that post view page works (0.35s)
✓ PostsCest: Test delete (3.61s)
-----------------------------------------------------------
```

Selenium will start Firefox web browser and execute our testing commands.

Creating API test suite

Besides unit, functional, and acceptance suites, Codeception allows to create specific test suites. For example, we can create it for API testing with support of XML and JSON parsing.

1. Create the REST API controller `controllers/api/PostsController.php` for the `Post` model:

```php
<?php
namespace app\controllers\api;

use yii\rest\ActiveController;

class PostsController extends ActiveController
{
    public $modelClass = '\app\models\Post';
}
```

2. Add REST routes for the `UrlManager` component in `config/web.php`:

```php
'components' => [
    // ...
    'urlManager' => [
        'enablePrettyUrl' => true,
        'showScriptName' => false,
        'rules' => [
```

```
        ['class' => 'yii\rest\UrlRule', 'controller' =>
        'api/posts'],
    ],
],
```

and some config (but with enabled `showScriptName` option) in `config/test.php`:

```
'components' => [
    // ...
    'urlManager' => [
        'enablePrettyUrl' => true,
        'showScriptName' => true,
        'rules' => [
            ['class' => 'yii\rest\UrlRule', 'controller' => 'api/
posts'],
        ],
    ],
],
```

3. Add the `web/.htaccess` file with the following content:

```
RewriteEngine On

RewriteCond %{REQUEST_FILENAME} !-f
RewriteCond %{REQUEST_FILENAME} !-d
RewriteRule . index.php
```

4. Check that the `api/posts` controller works:

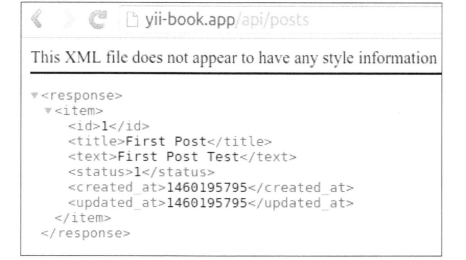

5. Create the API test suite `tests/api.suite.yml` configuration file with the REST module:

```
class_name: ApiTester
modules:
    enabled:
        - REST:
            depends: PhpBrowser
            url: 'http://127.0.0.1:8080/index-test.php'
            part: [json]
        - Yii2:
            part: [orm, fixtures]
            entryScript: index-test.php
```

Now rebuild testers:

```
composer exec codecept build
```

6. Create `tests/api` directory and generate new test class:

```
composer exec codecept generate:cest api Posts
```

7. Write tests for your REST-API:

```php
<?php
namespace tests\api;

use ApiTester;
use tests\fixtures\PostFixture;
use yii\helpers\Url;

class PostsCest
{
    function _before(ApiTester $I)
    {
        $I->haveFixtures([
            'post' => [
                'class' => PostFixture::className(),
                'dataFile' => codecept_data_dir() . 'post.php'
            ]
        ]);
    }

    public function testGetAll(ApiTester $I)
    {
```

```php
        $I->sendGET('/api/posts');
        $I->seeResponseCodeIs(200);
        $I->seeResponseIsJson();
        $I->seeResponseContainsJson([0 => ['title' => 'First
Post']]);
    }

    public function testGetOne(ApiTester $I)
    {
        $I->sendGET('/api/posts/1');
        $I->seeResponseCodeIs(200);
        $I->seeResponseIsJson();
        $I->seeResponseContainsJson(['title' => 'First Post']);
    }

    public function testGetNotFound(ApiTester $I)
    {
        $I->sendGET('/api/posts/100');
        $I->seeResponseCodeIs(404);
        $I->seeResponseIsJson();
        $I->seeResponseContainsJson(['name' => 'Not Found']);
    }

    public function testCreate(ApiTester $I)
    {
        $I->sendPOST('/api/posts', [
            'title' => 'Test Title',
            'text' => 'Test Text',
        ]);
        $I->seeResponseCodeIs(201);
        $I->seeResponseIsJson();
        $I->seeResponseContainsJson(['title' => 'Test Title']);
    }

    public function testUpdate(ApiTester $I)
    {
        $I->sendPUT('/api/posts/2', [
            'title' => 'New Title',
        ]);
        $I->seeResponseCodeIs(200);
        $I->seeResponseIsJson();
        $I->seeResponseContainsJson([
```

```
                    'title' => 'New Title',
                    'text' => 'Old Text For Updating',
            ]);
        }

        public function testDelete(ApiTester $I)
        {
            $I->sendDELETE('/api/posts/3');
            $I->seeResponseCodeIs(204);
        }
    }
```

8. Run application server:

   tests/bin yii serve

9. Run API tests:

   composer exec codecept run api

   Now see the result:

```
Api Tests (6) --------------------------------------------
✓ PostsCest: Test get all (0.12s)

✓ PostsCest: Test get one (0.03s)

✓ PostsCest: Test get not found (0.03s)

✓ PostsCest: Test create (0.04s)

✓ PostsCest: Test update (0.04s)

✓ PostsCest: Test delete (0.04s)
--------------------------------------------------------
```

All tests passed and our API works correctly.

How it works...

Codeception is high-level testing framework, based on the PHPUnit package for providing infrastructure for writing unit, integration, functional, and acceptance tests.

We can use built-in Yii2 module of Codeception which allows us to load fixtures, work with models and other things from Yii Framework.

▶ For further information, refer to:

    ❑ `http://codeception.com/docs/01-Introduction`

    ❑ `https://phpunit.de/manual/5.2/en/installation.html`

▶ The `tests/README.md` file of your basic or advanced application:

    ❑ `https://github.com/yiisoft/yii2-app-basic/blob/master/tests/README.md`

    ❑ `https://github.com/yiisoft/yii2-app-advanced/blob/master/tests/README.md`

▶ The *Unit testing with PHPUnit* recipe

Unit testing with PHPUnit

PHPUnit is the most popular PHP testing framework. It is simple for configuration and usage. Also, the framework supports code coverage reports and has a lot of additional plugins. Codeception from the previous recipe uses PHPUnit for own work and writing unit tests. In this recipe, we will create a demonstration shopping cart extension with PHPUnit tests.

Getting ready

Create a new `yii2-app-basic` application using the Composer package manager, as described in the official guide at `http://www.yiiframework.com/doc-2.0/guide-start-installation.html`.

How to do it...

First, we must create a new empty directory for own extension.

Preparing extension structure

1. First, create the directory structure for your extension:

```
book
└── cart
    ├── src
    └── tests
```

To work with the extension as a Composer package, prepare the `book/cart/composer.json` file like this:

```
{
    "name": "book/cart",
    "type": "yii2-extension",
    "require": {
        "yiisoft/yii2": "~2.0"
    },
    "require-dev": {
        "phpunit/phpunit": "4.*"
    },
    "autoload": {
        "psr-4": {
            "book\\cart\\": "src/",
            "book\\cart\\tests\\": "tests/"
        }
    },
    "extra": {
        "asset-installer-paths": {
            "npm-asset-library": "vendor/npm",
            "bower-asset-library": "vendor/bower"
        }
    }
}
```

2. Add the `book/cart/.gitignore` file with the following lines:

```
/vendor
/composer.lock
```

3. Add the following lines to the PHPUnit default configuration file `book/cart/phpunit.xml.dist` like this:

```
<?xml version="1.0" encoding="utf-8"?>
<phpunit bootstrap="./tests/bootstrap.php"
        colors="true"
        convertErrorsToExceptions="true"
        convertNoticesToExceptions="true"
        convertWarningsToExceptions="true"
        stopOnFailure="false">
    <testsuites>
        <testsuite name="Test Suite">
            <directory>./tests</directory>
        </testsuite>
    </testsuites>
```

```
        <filter>
            <whitelist>
                <directory suffix=".php">./src/</directory>
            </whitelist>
        </filter>
    </phpunit>
```

4. Install all the dependencies of the extension:

    composer install

5. Now we must get the following structure:

```
book
└── cart
        ├── src
        ├── tests
        ├── .gitignore
        ├── composer.json
        ├── phpunit.xml.dist
        └── vendor
```

Writing extension code

To write the extension code, follow these steps:

1. Create the book\cart\Cart class in the src directory:

```php
<?php
namespace book\cart;

use book\cart\storage\StorageInterface;
use yii\base\Component;
use yii\base\InvalidConfigException;

class Cart extends Component
{
    /**
     * @var StorageInterface
     */
    private $_storage;
    /**
     * @var array
     */
    private $_items;
```

```php
public function setStorage($storage)
{
    if (is_array($storage)) {
        $this->_storage = \Yii::createObject($storage);
    } else {
        $this->_storage = $storage;
    }
}

public function add($id, $amount = 1)
{
    $this->loadItems();
    if (isset($this->_items[$id])) {
        $this->_items[$id] += $amount;
    } else {
        $this->_items[$id] = $amount;
    }
    $this->saveItems();
}

public function set($id, $amount)
{
    $this->loadItems();
    $this->_items[$id] = $amount;
    $this->saveItems();
}

public function remove($id)
{
    $this->loadItems();
    if (isset($this->_items[$id])) {
        unset($this->_items[$id]);
    }
    $this->saveItems();
}

public function clear()
{
    $this->loadItems();
    $this->_items = [];
    $this->saveItems();
}
```

```php
    public function getItems()
    {
        $this->loadItems();
        return $this->_items;
    }

    public function getCount()
    {
        $this->loadItems();
        return count($this->_items);
    }

    public function getAmount()
    {
        $this->loadItems();
        return array_sum($this->_items);
    }

    private function loadItems()
    {
        if ($this->_storage === null) {
            throw new InvalidConfigException('Storage must be
            set');
        }
        if ($this->_items === null) {
            $this->_items = $this->_storage->load();
        }
    }

    private function saveItems()
    {
        $this->_storage->save($this->_items);
    }
}
```

2. Create `StorageInterface` interface in the `src/storage` subdirectory:

```php
<?php
namespace book\cart\storage;

interface StorageInterface
{
    /**
```

```
     * @return array
     */
    public function load();

    /**
     * @param array $items
     */
    public function save(array $items);
}
```

and SessionStorage class:

```
namespace book\cart\storage;

use Yii;

class SessionStorage implements StorageInterface
{
    public $sessionKey = 'cart';

    public function load()
    {
        return Yii::$app->session->get($this->sessionKey, []);
    }

    public function save(array $items)
    {
        Yii::$app->session->set($this->sessionKey, $items);
    }
}
```

3. Now we must get the following structure:

```
book
└── cart
    ├── src
    │   ├── storage
    │   │   ├── SessionStorage.php
    │   │   └── StorageInterface.php
    │   └── Cart.php
    ├── tests
    ├── .gitignore
    ├── composer.json
    ├── phpunit.xml.dist
    └── vendor
```

Writing extension tests

To conduct the extension test, follow these steps:

1. Add the `book/cart/tests/bootstrap.php` entry script for PHPUnit:

```php
<?php

defined('YII_DEBUG') or define('YII_DEBUG', true);
defined('YII_ENV') or define('YII_ENV', 'test');

require(__DIR__ . '/../vendor/autoload.php');
require(__DIR__ . '/../vendor/yiisoft/yii2/Yii.php');
```

2. Create a test base class by initializing the Yii application before each test and by destroying the application afterwards:

```php
<?php
namespace book\cart\tests;

use yii\di\Container;
use yii\web\Application;

abstract class TestCase extends \PHPUnit_Framework_TestCase
{
    protected function setUp()
    {
        parent::setUp();
        $this->mockApplication();
    }

    protected function tearDown()
    {
        $this->destroyApplication();
        parent::tearDown();
    }

    protected function mockApplication()
    {
        new Application([
            'id' => 'testapp',
            'basePath' => __DIR__,
            'vendorPath' => dirname(__DIR__) . '/vendor',
        ]);
    }
```

```php
        protected function destroyApplication()
        {
            \Yii::$app = null;
            \Yii::$container = new Container();
        }
    }
```

3. Add a memory-based clean fake class that implements the `StorageInterface` interface:

```php
<?php

namespace book\cart\tests\storage;

use book\cart\storage\StorageInterface;

class FakeStorage implements StorageInterface
{
    private $items = [];

    public function load()
    {
        return $this->items;
    }

    public function save(array $items)
    {
        $this->items = $items;
    }
}
```

   It will store items into a private variable instead of working with a real session. It allows to run tests independently (without real storage driver) and also improves testing performance.

4. Add the `CartTest` class:

```php
<?php
namespace book\cart\tests;

use book\cart\Cart;
use book\cart\tests\storage\FakeStorage;

class CartTest extends TestCase
{
```

```php
/**
 * @var Cart
 */
private $cart;

public function setUp()
{
    parent::setUp();
    $this->cart = new Cart(['storage' => new FakeStorage()]);
}

public function testEmpty()
{
    $this->assertEquals([], $this->cart->getItems());
    $this->assertEquals(0, $this->cart->getCount());
    $this->assertEquals(0, $this->cart->getAmount());
}

public function testAdd()
{
    $this->cart->add(5, 3);
    $this->assertEquals([5 => 3], $this->cart->getItems());

    $this->cart->add(7, 14);
    $this->assertEquals([5 => 3, 7 => 14],
    $this->cart->getItems());

    $this->cart->add(5, 10);
    $this->assertEquals([5 => 13, 7 => 14], $this->cart
    ->getItems());
}

public function testSet()
{
    $this->cart->add(5, 3);
    $this->cart->add(7, 14);
    $this->cart->set(5, 12);
    $this->assertEquals([5 => 12, 7 => 14], $this->cart
    ->getItems());
}
```

```php
public function testRemove()
{
    $this->cart->add(5, 3);
    $this->cart->remove(5);
    $this->assertEquals([], $this->cart->getItems());
}

public function testClear()
{
    $this->cart->add(5, 3);
    $this->cart->add(7, 14);
    $this->cart->clear();
    $this->assertEquals([], $this->cart->getItems());
}

public function testCount()
{
    $this->cart->add(5, 3);
    $this->assertEquals(1, $this->cart->getCount());

    $this->cart->add(7, 14);
    $this->assertEquals(2, $this->cart->getCount());
}

public function testAmount()
{
    $this->cart->add(5, 3);
    $this->assertEquals(3, $this->cart->getAmount());

    $this->cart->add(7, 14);
    $this->assertEquals(17, $this->cart->getAmount());
}

public function testEmptyStorage()
{
    $cart = new Cart();
    $this->
    >setExpectedException('yii\base\InvalidConfigException');
    $cart->getItems();
}
}
```

5. Add a separated test for checking the `SessionStorage` class:

```php
<?php
namespace book\cart\tests\storage;

use book\cart\storage\SessionStorage;
use book\cart\tests\TestCase;

class SessionStorageTest extends TestCase
{
    /**
     * @var SessionStorage
     */
    private $storage;

    public function setUp()
    {
        parent::setUp();
        $this->storage = new SessionStorage(['key' => 'test']);
    }

    public function testEmpty()
    {
        $this->assertEquals([], $this->storage->load());
    }

    public function testStore()
    {
        $this->storage->save($items = [1 => 5, 6 => 12]);

        $this->assertEquals($items, $this->storage->load());
    }
}
```

6. Right now we must get the following structure:

```
book
└── cart
    ├── src
    │   ├── storage
    │   │   ├── SessionStorage.php
    │   │   └── StorageInterface.php
    │   └── Cart.php
```

```
├── tests
│   ├── storage
│   │   ├── FakeStorage.php
│   │   └── SessionStorageTest.php
│   ├── bootstrap.php
│   ├── CartTest.php
│   └── TestCase.php
├── .gitignore
├── composer.json
├── phpunit.xml.dist
└── vendor
```

Running tests

During the installation of all dependencies with the `composer install` command, the Composer package manager installs the `PHPUnit` package into the `vendor` directory and places the executable file `phpunit` in the `vendor/bin` subdirectory.

Now we can run the following script:

```
cd book/cart
vendor/bin/phpunit
```

We must see the following testing report:

PHPUnit 4.8.26 by Sebastian Bergmann and contributors.

. . . .

Time: 906 ms, Memory: 11.50MB

OK (10 tests, 16 assertions)

Each dot shows a success result of the correspondent test.

Try to deliberately break an own cart by commenting the `unset` operation:

```
class Cart extends Component
{
    ...

    public function remove($id)
    {
```

```
        $this->loadItems();
        if (isset($this->_items[$id])) {
            // unset($this->_items[$id]);
        }
        $this->saveItems();
    }

    . . .

}
```

Run the tests again:

```
PHPUnit 4.8.26 by Sebastian Bergmann and contributors.


...F......


Time: 862 ms, Memory: 11.75MB


There was 1 failure:


1) book\cart\tests\CartTest::testRemove
Failed asserting that two arrays are equal.
--- Expected
+++ Actual
@@ @@
 Array (
+    5 => 3
 )


/book/cart/tests/CartTest.php:52


FAILURES!
Tests: 10, Assertions: 16, Failures: 1
```

In this case, we have seen one failure (marked as F instead of dot) and a failure report.

Analyzing code coverage

You must install the XDebug PHP extension from `https://xdebug.org`. For example, on Ubuntu or Debian, you can type the following in your terminal:

```
sudo apt-get install php5-xdebug
```

On Windows, you must open the `php.ini` file and add the custom code with path to your PHP installation directory:

```
[xdebug]
zend_extension_ts=C:/php/ext/php_xdebug.dll
```

Alternatively, if you use the non-thread safe edition, type the following:

```
[xdebug]
zend_extension=C:/php/ext/php_xdebug.dll
```

After installing XDebug, run the tests again with the `--coverage-html` flag and specify a report directory:

```
vendor/bin/phpunit --coverage-html tests/_output
```

After running open the `tests/_output/index.html` file in your browser, you will see an explicit coverage report for each directory and class:

	Code Coverage					
	Lines		**Functions and Methods**		**Classes and Traits**	
Total	95.35%	41 / 43	91.67%	11 / 12	50.00%	1 / 2
storage	100.00%	3 / 3	100.00%	2 / 2	100.00%	1 / 1
Cart.php	95.00%	38 / 40	90.00%	9 / 10	0.00%	0 / 1

Legend

Low: 0% to 50%   **Medium**: 50% to 90%   **High**: 90% to 100%

You can click on any class and analyze which lines of code have not been executed during the testing process. For example, open our `Cart` class report:

```
20      public function setStorage($storage)
21      {
22          if (is_array($storage)) {
23              $this->_storage = \Yii::createObject($storage);
24          } else {
25              $this->_storage = $storage;
26          }
27      }
```

In our case, we forgot to test the creating storage from array configuration.

Usage of component

After publishing the extension on Packagist, we can install a one-to-any project:

```
composer require book/cart
```

Also, enable the component in the application configuration file:

```
'components' => [
    // ...
    'cart' => [
        'class' => 'book\cart\Cart',
        'storage' => [
            'class' => 'book\cart\storage\SessionStorage',
        ],
    ],
],
```

As an alternative way without publishing the extension on Packagist, we must set up the @book alias for enabling correct class autoloading:

```
$config = [
    'id' => 'basic',
    'basePath' => dirname(__DIR__),
    'bootstrap' => ['log'],
    'aliases' => [
        '@book' => dirname(__DIR__) . '/book',
    ],
    'components' => [
        'cart' => [
```

```
            'class' => 'book\cart\Cart',
            'storage' => [
                'class' => 'book\cart\storage\SessionStorage',
            ],
        ],
        // ...
    ],
]
```

Anyway, we can use it as the `Yii::$app->cart` component in our project:

```
Yii::$app->cart->add($product->id, $amount);
```

How it works...

Before creating your own tests, you must just create any subdirectory and add the `phpunit.xml` or `phpunit.xml.dist` file in the root directory of your project:

```
<?xml version="1.0" encoding="utf-8"?>
<phpunit bootstrap="./tests/bootstrap.php"
        colors="true"
        convertErrorsToExceptions="true"
        convertNoticesToExceptions="true"
        convertWarningsToExceptions="true"
        stopOnFailure="false">
    <testsuites>
        <testsuite name="Test Suite">
            <directory>./tests</directory>
        </testsuite>
    </testsuites>
    <filter>
        <whitelist>
            <directory suffix=".php">./src/</directory>
        </whitelist>
    </filter>
</phpunit>
```

PHPUnit loads configuration from the second file if the first one does not exist in the working directory. Also, you can create the `bootstrap.php` file by initializing autoloader and your framework's environments:

```
<?php
defined('YII_DEBUG') or define('YII_DEBUG', true);
defined('YII_ENV') or define('YII_ENV', 'test');
require(__DIR__ . '/../vendor/autoload.php');
require(__DIR__ . '/../vendor/yiisoft/yii2/Yii.php');
```

Finally, you can install PHPUnit via Composer (locally or globally) and use the `phpunit` console command in the directory with the XML configuration file.

PHPUnit scans the testing directory and finds files with the `*Test.php` suffix. All your test classes must extend the `PHPUnit_Framework_TestCase` class and contain public methods with the `test*` prefix like this:

```php
class MyTest extends TestCase
{
    public function testSomeFunction()
    {
        $this->assertTrue(true);
    }
}
```

In the body of your tests, you can use any of the existing `assert*` methods:

```php
$this->assertEqual('Alex', $model->name);
$this->assertTrue($model->validate());
$this->assertFalse($model->save());
$this->assertCount(3, $items);
$this->assertArrayHasKey('username', $model->getErrors());
$this->assertNotNull($model->author);
$this->assertInstanceOf('app\models\User', $model->author);
```

Also, you can override the `setUp()` or `tearDown()` methods for adding expressions that will be run before and after each test method.

For example, you can define own base `TestCase` class by reinitializing the Yii application:

```php
<?php
namespace book\cart\tests;

use yii\di\Container;
use yii\web\Application;

abstract class TestCase extends \PHPUnit_Framework_TestCase
{
    protected function setUp()
    {
        parent::setUp();
        $this->mockApplication();
    }
```

```
    protected function tearDown()
    {
        $this->destroyApplication();
        parent::tearDown();
    }

    protected function mockApplication()
    {
        new Application([
            'id' => 'testapp',
            'basePath' => __DIR__,
            'vendorPath' => dirname(__DIR__) . '/vendor',
        ]);
    }

    protected function destroyApplication()
    {
        \Yii::$app = null;
        \Yii::$container = new Container();
    }
}
```

Now you can extend this class in your subclasses. Even your test method will work with an own instance of the application. It helps to avoid side effects and to create independent tests.

 Yii 2.0.* uses the old PHPUnit 4.* version for compatibility with PHP 5.4.

See also

► For all information about PHPUnit usage, refer to the official documentation at
   https://phpunit.de/manual/current/en/index.html

► The *Testing application with Codeception* recipe

Unit testing with Atoum

Besides PHPUnit and Codeception, Atoum is a simple unit testing framework. You can use this framework for testing your extensions or for testing a code of your application.

Getting ready

Create an empty directory for the new project.

How to do it...

In this recipe, we will create a demonstration shopping cart extension with Atoum tests.

Preparing the extension structure

1. First, create the directory structure for your extension:

```
book
└── cart
    ├── src
    └── tests
```

2. For working with the extension as a composer package, prepare the `book/cart/composer.json` file as follows:

```
{
    "name": "book/cart",
    "type": "yii2-extension",
    "require": {
        "yiisoft/yii2": "~2.0"
    },
    "require-dev": {
        "atoum/atoum": "^2.7"
    },
    "autoload": {
        "psr-4": {
            "book\\cart\\": "src/",
            "book\\cart\\tests\\": "tests/"
        }
    },
    "extra": {
        "asset-installer-paths": {
            "npm-asset-library": "vendor/npm",
            "bower-asset-library": "vendor/bower"
        }
    }
}
```

3. Add the following lines to the `book/cart/,gitignore` file:

    ```
    /vendor
    /composer.lock
    ```

4. Install all the dependencies of the extension:

    ```
    composer install
    ```

5. Now we will get the following structure:

    ```
    book
    └── cart
        ├── src
        ├── tests
        ├── .gitignore
        ├── composer.json
        ├── phpunit.xml.dist
        └── vendor
    ```

Writing the extension code

Copy the `Cart`, `StorageInterface`, and `SessionStorage` classes from the *Unit testing with PHPUnit* recipe.

Finally, we must get the following structure:

```
book
└── cart
    ├── src
    │   ├── storage
    │   │   ├── SessionStorage.php
    │   │   └── StorageInterface.php
    │   └── Cart.php
    ├── tests
    ├── .gitignore
    ├── composer.json
    └── vendor
```

Writing the extension tests

1. Add the `book/cart/tests/bootstrap.php` entry script:

    ```php
    <?php
    defined('YII_DEBUG') or define('YII_DEBUG', true);
    defined('YII_ENV') or define('YII_ENV', 'test');
    require(__DIR__ . '/../vendor/autoload.php');
    require(__DIR__ . '/../vendor/yiisoft/yii2/Yii.php');
    ```

2. Create a test base class by initializing the Yii application before each test and by destroying the application after ones:

```php
<?php

namespace book\cart\tests;

use yii\di\Container;
use yii\console\Application;
use mageekguy\atoum\test;

abstract class TestCase extends test
{
    public function beforeTestMethod($method)
    {
        parent::beforeTestMethod($method);
        $this->mockApplication();
    }

    public function afterTestMethod($method)
    {
        $this->destroyApplication();
        parent::afterTestMethod($method);
    }

    protected function mockApplication()
    {
        new Application([
            'id' => 'testapp',
            'basePath' => __DIR__,
            'vendorPath' => dirname(__DIR__) . '/vendor',
            'components' => [
                'session' => [
                    'class' => 'yii\web\Session',
                ],
            ]
        ]);
    }

    protected function destroyApplication()
    {
        \Yii::$app = null;
        \Yii::$container = new Container();
    }
}
```

3. Add a memory-based clean fake class that implements the `StorageInterface` interface:

```php
<?php
namespace book\cart\tests;

use book\cart\storage\StorageInterface;

class FakeStorage implements StorageInterface
{
    private $items = [];

    public function load()
    {
        return $this->items;
    }

    public function save(array $items)
    {
        $this->items = $items;
    }
}
```

This will store items into a private variable instead of working with the real session. It allows us to run tests independently (without real storage driver) and also improves testing performance.

4. Add the `Cart` test class:

```php
<?php
namespace book\cart\tests\units;

use book\cart\tests\FakeStorage;
use book\cart\Cart as TestedCart;
use book\cart\tests\TestCase;

class Cart extends TestCase
{
    /**
     * @var TestedCart
     */
    private $cart;

    public function beforeTestMethod($method)
    {
```

```php
    parent::beforeTestMethod($method);
    $this->cart = new TestedCart(['storage' => new
    FakeStorage()]);
}

public function testEmpty()
{
    $this->array($this->cart->getItems())->isEqualTo([]);
    $this->integer($this->cart->getCount())->isEqualTo(0);
    $this->integer($this->cart->getAmount())->isEqualTo(0);
}

public function testAdd()
{
    $this->cart->add(5, 3);
    $this->array($this->cart->getItems())->isEqualTo([5 =>
    3]);

    $this->cart->add(7, 14);
    $this->array($this->cart->getItems())->isEqualTo([5 => 3,
    7 => 14]);

    $this->cart->add(5, 10);
    $this->array($this->cart->getItems())->isEqualTo([5 => 13,
    7 => 14]);
}

public function testSet()
{
    $this->cart->add(5, 3);
    $this->cart->add(7, 14);
    $this->cart->set(5, 12);
    $this->array($this->cart->getItems())->isEqualTo([5 => 12,
    7 => 14]);
}

public function testRemove()
{
    $this->cart->add(5, 3);
    $this->cart->remove(5);
    $this->array($this->cart->getItems())->isEqualTo([]);
}
```

```php
        public function testClear()
        {
            $this->cart->add(5, 3);
            $this->cart->add(7, 14);
            $this->cart->clear();
            $this->array($this->cart->getItems())->isEqualTo([]);
        }

        public function testCount()
        {
            $this->cart->add(5, 3);
            $this->integer($this->cart->getCount())->isEqualTo(1);

            $this->cart->add(7, 14);
            $this->integer($this->cart->getCount())->isEqualTo(2);
        }

        public function testAmount()
        {
            $this->cart->add(5, 3);
            $this->integer($this->cart->getAmount())->isEqualTo(3);

            $this->cart->add(7, 14);
            $this->integer($this->cart->getAmount())->isEqualTo(17);
        }

        public function testEmptyStorage()
        {
            $cart = new TestedCart();

            $this->exception(function () use ($cart) {
                $cart->getItems();
            })->hasMessage('Storage must be set');
        }
    }
```

5. Add a separated test for checking the `SessionStorage` class:

```php
<?php
namespace book\cart\tests\units\storage;

use book\cart\storage\SessionStorage as TestedStorage;
use book\cart\tests\TestCase;
```

```php
class SessionStorage extends TestCase
{
    /**
     * @var TestedStorage
     */
    private $storage;

    public function beforeTestMethod($method)
    {
        parent::beforeTestMethod($method);
        $this->storage = new TestedStorage(['key' => 'test']);
    }

    public function testEmpty()
    {
        $this
            ->given($storage = $this->storage)
            ->then
                ->array($storage->load())
                    ->isEqualTo([]);
    }

    public function testStore()
    {
        $this
            ->given($storage = $this->storage)
            ->and($storage->save($items = [1 => 5, 6 => 12]))
            ->then
                ->array($this->storage->load())
                    ->isEqualTo($items)
        ;
    }
}
```

6. Now we will get the following structure:

```
book
└── cart
    ├── src
    │   ├── storage
    │   │   ├── SessionStorage.php
    │   │   └── StorageInterface.php
    │   └── Cart.php
```

```
├── tests
│   ├── units
│   │   ├── storage
│   │   │   └── SessionStorage.php
│   │   └── Cart.php
│   ├── bootstrap.php
│   ├── FakeStorage.php
│   └── TestCase.php
├── .gitignore
├── composer.json
└── vendor
```

Running tests

During the installation of all dependencies with the `composer install` command, the Composer package manager installs the `Atounm` package into the `vendor` directory and places the executable file `atoum` in the `vendor/bin` subdirectory.

Now we can run the following script:

```
cd book/cart
vendor/bin/atoum -d tests/units -bf tests/bootstrap.php
```

Also, we must see the following testing report:

```
> atoum path: /book/cart/vendor/atoum/atoum/vendor/bin/atoum
> atoum version: 2.7.0
> atoum path: /book/cart/vendor/atoum/atoum/vendor/bin/atoum
> atoum version: 2.7.0
> PHP path: /usr/bin/php5
> PHP version:
=> PHP 5.5.9-1ubuntu4.16 (cli)
> book\cart\tests\units\Cart...
[SSSSSSSS_____] [8/8]
=> Test duration: 1.13 seconds.
=> Memory usage: 3.75 Mb.
> book\cart\tests\units\storage\SessionStorage...
[SS_____] [2/2]
=> Test duration: 0.03 second.
=> Memory usage: 1.00 Mb.
```

> Total tests duration: 1.15 seconds.

> Total tests memory usage: 4.75 Mb.

> Code coverage value: 16.16%

Each S symbol shows a success result of the correspondent test.

Try to deliberately break the cart by commenting the unset operation:

```
class Cart extends Component
{
    ...

    public function remove($id)
    {
        $this->loadItems();
        if (isset($this->_items[$id])) {
            // unset($this->_items[$id]);
        }
        $this->saveItems();
    }

    ...
}
```

Run the tests again:

> atoum version: 2.7.0

> PHP path: /usr/bin/php5

> PHP version:

=> PHP 5.5.9-1ubuntu4.16 (cli)

book\cart\tests\units\Cart...

[SSFSSSSS_____] [8/8]

=> Test duration: 1.09 seconds.

=> Memory usage: 3.25 Mb.

> book\cart\tests\units\storage\SessionStorage...

[SS_____] [2/2]

=> Test duration: 0.02 second.

=> Memory usage: 1.00 Mb.

...

```
Failure (2 tests, 10/10 methods, 0 void method, 0 skipped method, 0
uncompleted method, 1 failure, 0 error, 0 exception)!
> There is 1 failure:
=> book\cart\tests\units\Cart::testRemove():
In file /book/cart/tests/units/Cart.php on line 53, mageekguy\atoum\
asserters\phpArray() failed: array(1) is not equal to array(0)
-Expected
+Actual
@@ -1 +1,3 @@
-array(0) {
+array(1) {
+    [5] =>
+    int(3)
```

In this case, we have seen one failure (marked as F instead of dot) and a failure report.

Analyzing code coverage

You must install the XDebug PHP extension from `https://xdebug.org`. For example, on Ubuntu or Debian you can type the following in your terminal:

```
sudo apt-get install php5-xdebug
```

On Windows, you must open the `php.ini` file and add the custom code with the path to your PHP installation directory:

```
[xdebug]
zend_extension_ts=C:/php/ext/php_xdebug.dll
```

Alternatively, if you use the non-thread safe edition, type the following:

```
[xdebug]
zend_extension=C:/php/ext/php_xdebug.dll
```

After installing XDebug, create the `book/cart/coverage.php` configuration file with coverage report options:

```php
<?php
use \mageekguy\atoum;
/** @var atoum\scripts\runner $script */
$report = $script->addDefaultReport();
$coverageField = new atoum\report\fields\runner\coverage\html('Cart',
__DIR__ . '/tests/coverage');
$report->addField($coverageField);
```

Now run the tests again with the `-c` option to use this configuration:

```
vendor/bin/atoum -d tests/units -bf tests/bootstrap.php -c coverage.
php
```

After running the tests, open the `tests/coverage/index.html` file in your browser. You will see an explicit coverage report for each directory and class:

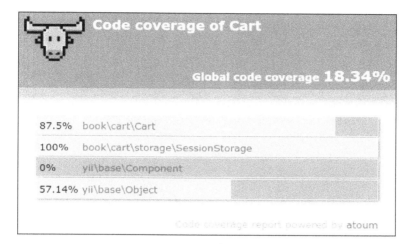

You can click on any class and analyze which lines of code have not been executed during the testing process.

How it works...

The Atoum testing framework supports the **Behavior-Driven Design** (**BDD**) syntax flow, as follows:

```
public function testSome()
{
    $this
        ->given($cart = new TestedCart())
        ->and($cart->add(5, 13))
        ->then
            ->sizeof($cart->getItems())
                ->isEqualTo(1)
            ->array($cart->getItems())
                ->isEqualTo([5 => 3])
            ->integer($cart->getCount())
                ->isEqualTo(1)
```

```
        ->integer($cart->getAmount())
            ->isEqualTo(3);
}
```

However, you can use the usual PHPUnit-like syntax to write unit tests:

```
public function testSome()
{
    $cart = new TestedCart();
    $cart->add(5, 3);

    $this
        ->array($cart->getItems())->isEqualTo([5 => 3])
        ->integer($cart->getCount())->isEqualTo(1)
        ->integer($cart->getAmount())->isEqualTo(3)
    ;
}
```

Atoum also supports code coverage reports for analyzing the testing quality.

See also

▶ For more information about Atoum, refer to `http://docs.atoum.org/en/latest/`

▶ For sources and usage samples, refer to `https://github.com/atoum/atoum`

▶ The *Unit testing with PHPUnit* recipe

Unit testing with Behat

Behat is a BDD framework for testing your code with human-readable sentences that describes code behavior in various use cases.

Getting ready

Create an empty directory for a new project.

How to do it...

In this recipe, we will create a demonstration shopping cart extension with Behat tests.

Preparing extension structure

1. First, create a directory structure for your extension:

```
book
└── cart
    ├── src
    └── features
```

2. To work with the extension as a Composer package, prepare the `book/cart/composer.json` file as follows:

```json
{
    "name": "book/cart",
    "type": "yii2-extension",
    "require": {
        "yiisoft/yii2": "~2.0"
    },
    "require-dev": {
        "phpunit/phpunit": "4.*",
        "behat/behat": "^3.1"
    },
    "autoload": {
        "psr-4": {
            "book\\cart\\": "src/",
            "book\\cart\\features\\": "features/"
        }
    },
    "extra": {
        "asset-installer-paths": {
            "npm-asset-library": "vendor/npm",
            "bower-asset-library": "vendor/bower"
        }
    }
}
```

3. Add the following lines to the `book/cart/.gitignore` file:

```
/vendor
/composer.lock
```

4. Install all the dependencies of the extension:

```
composer install
```

5. Now we get the following structure:

```
book
└── cart
    ├── src
    ├── features
    ├── .gitignore
    ├── composer.json
    └── vendor
```

Writing extension code

Copy the `Cart`, `StorageInterface`, and `SessionStorage` classes from the *Unit testing with PHPUnit* recipe.

Finally, we get the following structure:

```
book
└── cart
    ├── src
    │   ├── storage
    │   │   ├── SessionStorage.php
    │   │   └── StorageInterface.php
    │   └── Cart.php
    ├── features
    ├── .gitignore
    ├── composer.json
    └── vendor
```

Writing extension tests

1. Add the `book/cart/features/bootstrap/bootstrap.php` entry script:

```php
<?php
defined('YII_DEBUG') or define('YII_DEBUG', true);
defined('YII_ENV') or define('YII_ENV', 'test');

require_once __DIR__ . '/../../vendor/yiisoft/yii2/Yii.php';
```

2. Create the `features/cart.feature` file and write cart testing scenarios:

```
Feature: Shopping cart
  In order to buy products
  As a customer
  I need to be able to put interesting products into a cart
```

```
Scenario: Checking empty cart
  Given there is a clean cart
  Then I should have 0 products
  Then I should have 0 product
  And the overall cart amount should be 0

Scenario: Adding products to the cart
  Given there is a clean cart
  When I add 3 pieces of 5 product
  Then I should have 3 pieces of 5 product
  And I should have 1 product
  And the overall cart amount should be 3

  When I add 14 pieces of 7 product
  Then I should have 3 pieces of 5 product
  And I should have 14 pieces of 7 product
  And I should have 2 products
  And the overall cart amount should be 17

  When I add 10 pieces of 5 product
  Then I should have 13 pieces of 5 product
  And I should have 14 pieces of 7 product
  And I should have 2 products
  And the overall cart amount should be 27

Scenario: Change product count in the cart
  Given there is a cart with 5 pieces of 7 product
  When I set 3 pieces for 7 product
  Then I should have 3 pieces of 7 product

Scenario: Remove products from the cart
  Given there is a cart with 5 pieces of 7 product
  When I add 14 pieces of 7 product
  And I clear cart
  Then I should have empty cart
```

3. Add the storage test `features/storage.feature` file:

```
Feature: Shopping cart storage
  I need to be able to put items into a storage

  Scenario: Checking empty storage
```

```
        Given there is a clean storage
        Then I should have empty storage

      Scenario: Save items into storage
        Given there is a clean storage
        When I save 3 pieces of 7 product to the storage
        Then I should have 3 pieces of 7 product in the storage
```

4. Add implementation for all steps in the `features/bootstrap/CartContext.php` file:

```php
<?php
use Behat\Behat\Context\SnippetAcceptingContext;
use book\cart\Cart;
use book\cart\features\bootstrap\storage\FakeStorage;
use yii\di\Container;
use yii\web\Application;

require_once __DIR__ . '/bootstrap.php';

class CartContext implements SnippetAcceptingContext
{
    /**
     * @var Cart
     * */
    private $cart;

    /**
     * @Given there is a clean cart
     */
    public function thereIsACleanCart()
    {
        $this->resetCart();
    }

    /**
     * @Given there is a cart with :pieces of :product
     product
     */
    public function thereIsAWhichCostsPs($product, $amount)
    {
        $this->resetCart();
```

```php
        $this->cart->set($product, floatval($amount));
    }

    /**
     * @When I add :pieces of :product
     */
    public function iAddTheToTheCart($product, $pieces)
    {
        $this->cart->add($product, $pieces);
    }

    /**
     * @When I set :pieces for :arg2 product
     */
    public function iSetPiecesForProduct($pieces, $product)
    {
        $this->cart->set($product, $pieces);
    }

    /**
     * @When I clear cart
     */
    public function iClearCart()
    {
        $this->cart->clear();
    }

    /**
     * @Then I should have empty cart
     */
    public function iShouldHaveEmptyCart()
    {
        PHPUnit_Framework_Assert::assertEquals(
            0,
            $this->cart->getCount()
        );
    }

    /**
     * @Then I should have :count product(s)
     */
```

```php
public function iShouldHaveProductInTheCart($count)
{
    PHPUnit_Framework_Assert::assertEquals(
        intval($count),
        $this->cart->getCount()
    );
}

/**
 * @Then the overall cart amount should be :amount
 */
public function theOverallCartPriceShouldBePs($amount)
{
    PHPUnit_Framework_Assert::assertSame(
        intval($amount),
        $this->cart->getAmount()
    );
}

/**
 * @Then I should have :pieces of :product
 */
public function iShouldHavePiecesOfProduct($pieces, $product)
{
    PHPUnit_Framework_Assert::assertArraySubset(
        [intval($product) => intval($pieces)],
        $this->cart->getItems()
    );
}

private function resetCart()
{
    $this->cart = new Cart(['storage' => new FakeStorage()]);
}
}
```

5. Also, in the `features/bootstrap/StorageContext.php` file, add the following:

```php
<?php
use Behat\Behat\Context\SnippetAcceptingContext;
use book\cart\Cart;
use book\cart\features\bootstrap\storage\FakeStorage;
use book\cart\storage\SessionStorage;
use yii\di\Container;
```

```php
use yii\web\Application;

require_once __DIR__ . '/bootstrap.php';

class StorageContext implements SnippetAcceptingContext
{
    /**
     * @var SessionStorage
     * */
    private $storage;

    /**
     * @Given there is a clean storage
     */
    public function thereIsACleanStorage()
    {
        $this->mockApplication();
        $this->storage = new SessionStorage(['key' => 'test']);
    }

    /**
     * @When I save :pieces of :product to the
       storage
     */
    public function iSavePiecesOfProductToTheStorage($pieces,
    $product)
    {
        $this->storage->save([$product => $pieces]);
    }

    /**
     * @Then I should have empty storage
     */
    public function iShouldHaveEmptyStorage()
    {
        PHPUnit_Framework_Assert::assertCount(
            0,
            $this->storage->load()
        );
    }
}
```

```php
/**
 * @Then I should have :pieces of :product in
 the storage
 */
public function
iShouldHavePiecesOfProductInTheStorage($pieces,
$product)
{
    PHPUnit_Framework_Assert::assertArraySubset(
        [intval($product) => intval($pieces)],
        $this->storage->load()
    );
}

private function mockApplication()
{
    Yii::$container = new Container();
    new Application([
        'id' => 'testapp',
        'basePath' => __DIR__,
        'vendorPath' => __DIR__ . '/../../vendor',
    ]);
}
}
```

6. Add the `features/bootstrap/CartContext/FakeStorage.php` file with a fake storage class:

```php
<?php
namespace book\cart\features\bootstrap\storage;

use book\cart\storage\StorageInterface;

class FakeStorage implements StorageInterface
{
    private $items = [];

    public function load()
    {
        return $this->items;
    }

    public function save(array $items)
    {
```

```
            $this->items = $items;
        }
    }
```

7. Add `book/cart/behat.yml` with contexts definition:

```
default:
    suites:
        default:
            contexts:
                - CartContext
                - StorageContext
```

8. Now we will get the following structure:

```
book
└── cart
    ├── src
    │   ├── storage
    │   │   ├── SessionStorage.php
    │   │   └── StorageInterface.php
    │   └── Cart.php
    ├── features
    │   ├── bootstrap
    │   │   ├── storage
    │   │   │   └── FakeStorage.php
    │   │   ├── bootstrap.php
    │   │   ├── CartContext.php
    │   │   └── StorageContext.php
    │   ├── cart.feature
    │   └── storage.feature
    ├── .gitignore
    ├── behat.yml
    ├── composer.json
    └── vendor
```

Now we can run our tests.

Running tests

During the installation of all dependencies with the command `composer install`, the Composer package manager installs the Behat package into the `vendor` directory and places the executable `behat` file in the `vendor/bin` subdirectory.

Now we can run the following script:

```
cd book/cart
vendor/bin/behat
```

Also, we must see the following testing report:

```
Feature: Shopping cart
  In order to buy products
  As a customer
  I need to be able to put interesting products into a cart


  Scenario: Checking empty cart                   # features/cart.feature:6
    Given there is a clean cart                   # thereIsACleanCart()
    Then I should have 0 products                 #
iShouldHaveProductInTheCart()
    Then I should have 0 product                  #
iShouldHaveProductInTheCart()
    And the overall cart amount should be 0 #
theOverallCartPriceShouldBePs()


  ...


Feature: Shopping cart storage
  I need to be able to put items into a storage


  Scenario: Checking empty storage    # features/storage.feature:4
    Given there is a clean storage     # thereIsACleanStorage()
    Then I should have empty storage # iShouldHaveEmptyStorage()


  ...


6 scenarios (6 passed)
31 steps (31 passed)
0m0.23s (13.76Mb)
```

Try to deliberately break the cart by commenting the `unset` operation:

```
class Cart extends Component
{
    ...

    public function set($id, $amount)
    {
        $this->loadItems();
        // $this->_items[$id] = $amount;
        $this->saveItems();
    }


    ...
}
```

Now run the tests again:

```
Feature: Shopping cart
  In order to buy products
  As a customer
Feature: Shopping cart
  In order to buy products
  As a customer
  I need to be able to put interesting products into a cart

  ...


  Scenario: Change product count in the cart      # features/cart.
feature:31
    Given there is a cart with 5 pieces of 7 prod  #
thereIsAWhichCostsPs()
    When I set 3 pieces for 7 product               #
iSetPiecesForProduct()
    Then I should have 3 pieces of 7 product        #
iShouldHavePiecesOf()
      Failed asserting that an array has the subset Array &0 (
        7 => 3
      ).

  Scenario: Remove products from the cart          # features/cart.
feature:36
```

```
        Given there is a cart with 5 pieces of 7 prod  #
    thereIsAWhichCostsPs()
        When I add 14 pieces of 7 product              # iAddTheToTheCart()
        And I clear cart                               # iClearCart()
        Then I should have empty cart                  #
    iShouldHaveEmptyCart()

    --- Failed scenarios:

        features/cart.feature:31

    6 scenarios (5 passed, 1 failed)
    31 steps (30 passed, 1 failed)
    0m0.22s (13.85Mb)
```

In this case, we have seen one failure and a failure report.

How it works...

Behat is a BDD testing framework. It facilitates writing preceding human-readable testing scenarios to low-level technical implementation.

When we write scenarios for every feature, we can use a set of operators:

```
Scenario: Adding products to the cart
    Given there is a clean cart
    When I add 3 pieces of 5 product
    Then I should have 3 pieces of 5 product
    And I should have 1 product
    And the overall cart amount should be 3
```

Behat parses our sentences and finds the associated implementation of the sentence in the context class:

```
class FeatureContext implements SnippetAcceptingContext
{
    /**
     * @When I add :pieces of :product
     */
    public function iAddTheToTheCart($product, $pieces)
    {
        $this->cart->add($product, $pieces);
    }
}
```

You can create a single FeatureContext class (by default) or create a set of specific contexts for feature groups and scenarios.

See also

For getting more information about Behat refer to the following URLs:

- `http://docs.behat.org/en/v3.0/`
- `https://github.com/Behat/Behat`

And to get more information about alternative test frameworks, see the other recipes in this chapter.

12
Debugging, Logging, and Error Handling

In this chapter, we will cover the following topics:

- ▸ Using different log routes
- ▸ Analyzing the Yii error stack trace
- ▸ Logging and using the context information
- ▸ Displaying custom errors
- ▸ Custom panel for debug extension

Introduction

It is not possible to create a bug-free application if it is relatively complex, so developers have to detect errors and deal with them as fast as possible. Yii has a good set of utility features to handle logging and handling errors. Moreover, in the debug mode, Yii gives you a stack trace if there is an error. Using it, you can fix errors faster.

In this chapter, we will review logging, analyzing the exception stack trace, and implementing our own error handler.

Using different log routes

Logging is the key to understanding what your application actually does when you have no chance to debug it. Believe it or not, even if you are 100% sure that the application will behave as expected, in production, it can do many things you were not aware of. This is OK, as no one can be aware of everything. Therefore, if we are expecting unusual behavior, we need to know about it as soon as possible and have enough details to reproduce it. This is where logging comes in handy.

Yii allows a developer not only to log messages but also to handle them differently depending on the message level and category. You can, for example, write a message to the database, send an e-mail, or just show it in the browser.

In this recipe, we will handle log messages in a wise manner: the most important message will be sent through an e-mail, less important messages will be saved in files A and B, and the profiling will be routed to Firebug. Additionally, in a development mode, all messages and profiling information will be displayed on the screen.

Getting ready

Create a new `yii2-app-basic` application by using the Composer package manager, as described in the official guide at `http://www.yiiframework.com/doc-2.0/guide-start-installation.html`.

How to do it...

Carry out the following steps:

1. Configure logging using `config/web.php`:

```
'components' => [
    'log' => [
        'traceLevel' => 0,
        'targets' => [
            [
                'class' => 'yii\log\EmailTarget',
                'categories' => ['example'],
                'levels' => ['error'],
                'message' => [
                    'from' => ['log@example.com'],
                    'to' => ['developer1@example.com',
                    'developer2@example.com'],
                    'subject' => 'Log message',
                ],
            ],
        ],
```

```
            [
                'class' => 'yii\log\FileTarget',
                'levels' => ['error'],
                'logFile' => '@runtime/logs/error.log',
            ],
            [
                'class' => 'yii\log\FileTarget',
                'levels' => ['warning'],
                'logFile' => '@runtime/logs/warning.log',
            ],
            [
                'class' => 'yii\log\FileTarget',
                'levels' => ['info'],
                'logFile' => '@runtime/logs/info.log',
            ],
        ],
    ],

    'db' => require(__DIR__ . '/db.php'),
],
```

2. Now, we will produce a few log messages in protected/controllers/ LogController.php as follows:

```php
<?php
namespace app\controllers;

use yii\web\Controller;
use Yii;

class LogController extends Controller
{
    public function actionIndex()
    {
        Yii::trace('example trace message', 'example');
        Yii::info('info', 'example');
        Yii::error('error', 'example');
        Yii::trace('trace', 'example');
        Yii::warning('warning','example');

        Yii::beginProfile('preg_replace', 'example');
        for($i=0;$i<10000;$i++){
            preg_replace('~^[ a-z]+~', '', 'test it');
        }
```

```
            Yii::endProfile('preg_replace', 'example');

            return $this->render('index');
        }
    }
```

and view views/log/index.php:

```
<div class="log-index">
    <h1>Log</h1>
</div>
```

3. Now run the preceding action multiple times. On the screen, you should see the Log heading and a debug panel with the log messages number:

4. If you click on **17**, you will see a web log similar to the one shown in the following screenshot:

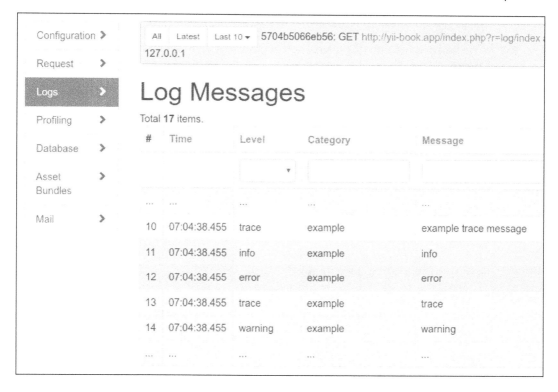

5. A log contains all the messages we have logged along with stack traces, timestamps, levels, and categories.

6. Now open the **Profiling** page. You should see profiler messages, as shown in the following screenshot:

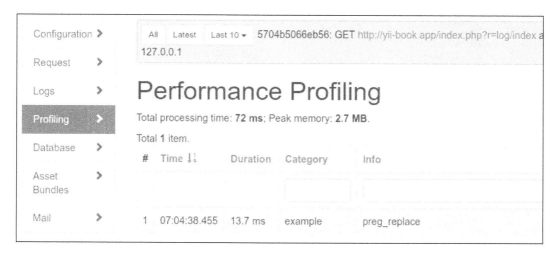

Profiling info displays the total executing duration of own code block.

7. As we just changed the log file names and not the paths, you should look in `runtime/logs` to find log files named `error.log`, `warning.log`, and `info.log`.

8. Inside, you will find the following messages:

```
2016-03-06 07:28:35 [127.0.0.1] [-] [-] [error] [example] error

...

2016-03-06 07:28:35 [127.0.0.1] [-] [-] [warning] [example] warning

...

2016-03-06 07:28:35 [127.0.0.1] [-] [-] [info] [example] info
```

How it works...

When one logs a message using `Yii::erorr`, `Yii::warning`, `Yii::info`, or `Yii::trace`, Yii passes it to the log router.

Depending on how it is configured, it passes messages to one or many targets, for example, e-mailing errors, writing debug information in file A, and writing warning information in file B.

The object of the `yii\log\Dispatcher` class is typically attached to an application component named log. Therefore, in order to configure it, we should set its properties in the configuration file components section. The only configurable property there is targets that contains an array of log routes and their configurations.

We have defined four log routes. Let's review them as follows:

```
[
    'class' => 'yii\log\EmailTarget',
    'categories' => ['example'],
    'levels' => ['error'],
    // 'mailer' => 'mailer',
    'message' => [
        'from' => ['log@example.com'],
        'to' => ['developer1@example.com', 'developer2@example.com'],
        'subject' => 'Log error,
    ],
],
```

`EmailTarget` sends log messages through an e-mail via the `Yii::$app->mailer` component by default. We limit category to example and level to error. An e-mail will be sent from `log@example.com` to two developers and the subject will be `Log error`:

```
[
    'class' => 'yii\log\FileTarget',
```

```
        'levels' => [warning],
        'logFile' => '@runtime/logs/warning.log',
    ],
```

`FileTarget` appends error messages to a specified file. We limit the message level to warning and use a file named `warning.log`. We do the same for info-level messages by using a file named `Info.log`.

Also, we can use `yii\log\SyslogTarget` to write messages into the `Unix /var/log/syslog` system file and `yii\log\DbTarget` to write logs into the database. For the second one, you must apply their migrations:

```
    ./yii migrate --migrationPath=@yii/log/migrations/
```

There's more...

There are more interesting things about Yii logging, which are covered in the following subsections.

Yii::trace versus Yii::getLogger()->log

`Yii::trace` is a simple wrapper around `Yii::log`:

```
    public static function trace($message, $category = 'application')
    {
        if (YII_DEBUG) {
            static::getLogger()->log($message,
            Logger::LEVEL_TRACE, $category);
        }
    }
```

Therefore, `Yii::trace` logs a message with a trace level, if Yii is in the `debug` mode.

Yii::beginProfile and Yii::endProfile

These methods are used to measure the execution time of some part of the application's code. In our `LogController`, we measured 10,000 executions of `preg_replace` as follows:

```
    Yii::beginProfile('preg_replace', 'example');
    for($i=0;$i<10000;$i++){
        preg_replace('~^[ a-z]+~', '', 'test it');
    }
    Yii::endProfile('preg_replace', 'example');
```

`Yii::beginProfile` marks the beginning of a code block for profiling. We must set a unique token for every code block and optionally specify a category:

```
public static function beginProfile($token, $category = 'application')
{ … }
```

`Yii::endProfile` has to be matched with a previous call to `beginProfile` with the same category name:

```
public static function endProfile($token, $category = 'application') {
… }
```

The `begin-` and `end-` calls must also be properly nested.

Log messages immediately

By default, Yii keeps all log messages in memory until the application is terminated. That's done for performance reasons and generally works fine.

However, if there is a console application with long running duration, log messages will not be written immediately. To make sure your messages will be logged at any moment, you can flush them explicitly using `Yii::$app->getLogger()>flush(true)` or change `flushInterval` and `exportInterval` for your console application configuration:

```
'components' => [
    'log' => [
        'flushInterval' => 1,
        'targets' => [
            [
                'class' => 'yii\log\FileTarget',
                'exportInterval' => 1,
            ],
        ],
    ],
],
```

See also

▶ In order to learn more about logging, refer to `http://www.yiiframework.com/doc-2.0/guide-runtime-logging.html`

▶ The *Logging and using the context information* recipe

Analyzing the Yii error stack trace

When an error occurs, Yii can display the error stack trace along with the error. A stack trace is especially helpful when we need to know what really caused an error rather than just the fact that an error occurred.

Getting ready

1. Create a new `yii2-app-basic` application by using the Composer package manager, as described in the official guide at `http://www.yiiframework.com/doc-2.0/guide-start-installation.html`.

2. Configure a database and import the following migration:

```php
<?php
use yii\db\Migration;
class m160308_093234_create_article_table extends Migration
{
    public function up()
    {
        $this->createTable('{{%article}}', [
            'id' => $this->primaryKey(),
            'alias' => $this->string()->notNull(),
            'title' => $this->string()->notNull(),
            'text' => $this->text()->notNull(),
        ]);
    }

    public function down()
    {
        $this->dropTable('{{%article}}');
    }
}
```

3. Generate an `Article` model using Yii.

How to do it...

Carry out the following steps:

1. Now we will need to create some code to work with. Create `protected/controllers/ErrorController.php` as follows:

```php
<?php

namespace app\controllers;

use app\models\Article;
use yii\web\Controller;

class ErrorController extends Controller
{
    public function actionIndex()
    {
        $article = $this->findModel('php');

        return $article->title;
    }

    private function findModel($alias)
    {
        return Article::findOne(['allas' => $alias]);
    }
}
```

2. After running the preceding action, we should get the following error:

> # Database Exception – yii\db\Exception
>
> SQLSTATE[42S22]: Column not found: 1054 Unknown column 'allas' in 'where clause'
> The SQL being executed was: SELECT * FROM `article` WHERE `allas`='php'
>
> ```
> Error Info: Array
> (
>     [0] => 42S22
>     [1] => 1054
>     [2] => Unknown column 'allas' in 'where clause'
> )
> ```

3. Moreover, the stack trace shows the following error:

```
6.  in /work/Dropbox/SERVER/home/yii-book.app/www/vendor/yiisoft/yii2/db/BaseActiv

7.  in /work/Dropbox/SERVER/home/yii-book.app/www/controllers/ErrorController.php


            return $article->title;
        }

        private function findModel($alias)
        {
            return Article::findOne(['alias' => $alias]);
        }
    }


8.  in /work/Dropbox/SERVER/home/yii-book.app/www/controllers/ErrorController.php


    use yii\web\Controller;

    class ErrorController extends Controller
    {
        public function actionIndex()
        {
            $article = $this->findModel('php');

            return $article->title;
        }

        private function findModel($alias)
        {


9.  app\controllers\ErrorController::actionIndex()
```

How it works...

From the error message, we know that we have no alias column in the database, but we have used it somewhere in the code. In our case, it is very simple to find it just by searching all the project files, but in a large project, a column can be stored in a variable. Moreover, we have everything to fix an error without leaving the screen where the stack trace is displayed. We just need to read it carefully.

The stack trace displays a chain of calls in the reversed order starting with the one that caused an error. Generally, we don't need to read the whole trace to get what is going on. The framework code itself is tested well, so the probability of error is less. That is why Yii displays the application trace entries expanded and the framework trace entries collapsed.

Therefore, we take the first expanded section and look for alias. After finding it, we can immediately tell that it is used in `ErrorController.php` on line 19.

See also

▶ In order to learn more about error handling, refer to `http://www.yiiframework.com/doc-2.0/guide-runtime-handling-errors.html`

▶ The *Logging and using the context information* recipe

Logging and using the context information

Sometimes a log message is not enough to fix an error. For example, if you are following best practices and developing and testing an application with all possible errors reported, you can get an error message. However, without the execution context, it is only telling you that there was an error and it is not clear what actually caused it.

For our example, we will use a very simple and poorly coded action that just echoes `Hello, <username>!` where the `username` is taken directly from `$_GET`.

Getting ready

Create a new `yii2-app-basic` application by using the Composer package manager, as described in the official guide at `http://www.yiiframework.com/doc-2.0/guide-start-installation.html`.

How to do it...

Carry out the following steps:

1. First, we will need a controller to work with. Therefore, create `protected/controllers/LogController.php` as follows:

```php
<?php
namespace app\controllers;

use yii\web\Controller;

class LogController extends Controller
{
```

```
public function actionIndex()
{
    return 'Hello, ' . $_GET['username'];
}
}
```

2. Now, if we run the index action, we will get the error message, `Undefined index: username`. Let's configure the logger to write this kind of error to a file:

   `config/web.php`:

```
'components'=>array(
    ...
    'log' => [
        'targets' => [
            [
                'class' => 'yii\log\FileTarget',
                'levels' => ['error'],
                'logFile' =>
                '@runtime/logs/errors.log',
            ],
        ],
    ],
],
```

3. Run the index action again and check `runtime/logs/errors.log`. There should be log information like the following:

   ```
   2016-03-06 09:27:09 [127.0.0.1] [-] [-] [error] [yii\base\
   ErrorException:8] exception 'yii\base\ErrorException' with message
   'Undefined index: username' in /controllers/LogController.php:11
   ```

   ```
   Stack trace:
   ```

   ```
   #0 /yii2/base/InlineAction.php(55): ::call_user_func_array()
   ```

   ```
   #1 /yii2/base/Controller.php(151): yii\base\InlineAction-
   >runWithParams()
   ```

   ```
   #2 /yii2/base/Module.php(455): yii\base\Controller->runAction()
   ```

   ```
   #3 /yii2/web/Application.php(84): yii\base\Module->runAction()
   ```

   ```
   #4 /yii2/base/Application.php(375): yii\web\Application-
   >handleRequest()
   ```

   ```
   #5 /web/index.php(12): yii\base\Application->run()
   ```

   ```
   #6 {main}
   ```

   ```
   2016-03-06 09:27:09 [127.0.0.1] [-] [-] [info] [application] $_GET = [
   ```

```
        'r' => 'log/index'
    ]


    $_COOKIE = [
        '_csrf' => 'ca689043348e...a69ea:2:{i:0;s:...\"DSS...KJ\";}'
        'PHPSESSID' => '30584oqhat4ek8b0hrqsapsbf4'
    ]


    $_SERVER = [
        'USER' => 'www-data'
        'HOME' => '/var/www'
        'FCGI_ROLE' => 'RESPONDER'
        'QUERY_STRING' => 'r=log/index'
        ...
        'PHP_SELF' => '/index.php'
        'REQUEST_TIME_FLOAT' => 1459934829.3067
        'REQUEST_TIME' => 1459934829
    ]
```

4. Now we can give our application to a testing team and check the errors log from time to time. By default, error report log contain values from all the $_GET, $_POST, $_FILES, $_COOKIE, $_SESSION, and $_SERVER variables. If you do not want to display all values, you can specify a custom variable list:

```
'log' => [
    'targets' => [
        [
            'class' => 'yii\log\FileTarget',
            'levels' => ['error'],
            'logVars' => ['_GET', '_POST'],
            'logFile' =>
            '@runtime/logs/errors.log',
        ],
    ],
],
```

5. In this case, the report will contain only the $_GET and $_POST arrays:

```
...
2016-04-06 09:49:08 [127.0.0.1][-][-][info][application] $_GET = [
    'r' => 'log/index'
]
```

How it works...

Yii adds complete information about the execution context and environment in the case of logging error messages. If we are logging a message manually, then we probably know what information we need, so we can set some target options to write only what we really need:

```
'log' => [
    'targets' => [
        [
            'class' => 'yii\log\FileTarget',
            'levels' => ['error'],
            'logVars' => ['_GET', '_POST'],
            'logFile' => '@runtime/logs/errors.log',
        ],
    ],
],
```

The preceding code will log errors to a file named errors. Additionally to a message itself, it will log contents of the $_GET or $_POST variables if they are not empty.

See also

▶ In order to learn more about log filters and context information, refer to `http://www.yiiframework.com/doc-2.0/guide-runtime-logging.html`

▶ The *Using different log routes* recipe

Displaying custom errors

In Yii, the error handling is very flexible, so you can create your own error handler for errors of a specific type. In this recipe, we will handle a 404 not found error in a smart way. We will show a custom 404 page that will suggest the content based on what was entered in the address bar.

Getting ready

1. Create a new `yii2-app-basic` application by using the Composer package manager, as described in the official guide at `http://www.yiiframework.com/doc-2.0/guide-start-installation.html`.

2. Add the fail action to your `SiteController`:

```
class SiteController extends Controller
{
    // ...
```

```
public function actionFail()
{
    throw new
    ServerErrorHttpException('Error
    message example.');
}
}
```

3. Add the `web/.htaccess` file with the following content:

```
RewriteEngine on
RewriteCond %{REQUEST_FILENAME} !-f
RewriteCond %{REQUEST_FILENAME} !-d
RewriteRule . index.php
```

4. Configure pretty URLs for the `urlManager` component in your `config/web.php` file:

```
'components' => [
    // ...
    'urlManager' => [
        'enablePrettyUrl' => true,
            'showScriptName' => false,
        ],
    ],
```

5. Check that framework displays the `Not found` exception for URLs that are not existing:

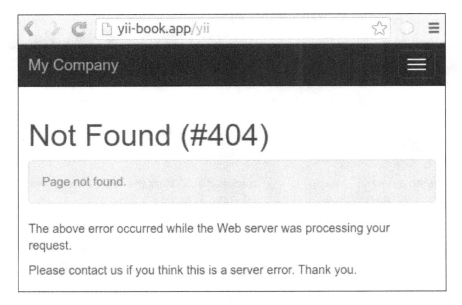

6. Also, check that the framework displays the `Internal Server Error` exception for our `actionFail`:

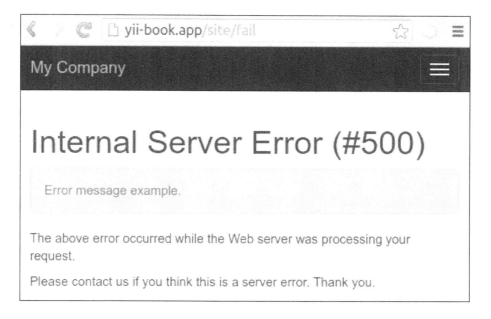

7. Now we want to create a custom page for the `Not Found` page. Let's start it.

How to do it...

Now we need to change the `Not Found` page content, but leave it as it is for other error types. In order to achieve this, follow these steps:

1. Open the `SiteController` class and look for the `actions()` method:

```
class SiteController extends Controller
{
    // ...
    public function actions()
    {
        return [
            'error' => [
                'class' => 'yii\web\ErrorAction',
            ],
            'captcha' => [
                'class' => 'yii\captcha\CaptchaAction',
                'fixedVerifyCode' => YII_ENV_TEST ? 'testme' :
                null,
            ],
```

```
            ];
        }
        // ...
    }
```

2. Remove the default `error` section and leave `actions()` as follows:

```
class SiteController extends Controller
{
    // ...
    public function actions()
    {
        return [
            'captcha' => [
                'class' => 'yii\captcha\CaptchaAction',
                'fixedVerifyCode' => YII_ENV_TEST ? 'testme' :
                null,
            ],
        ];
    }
    // ...
}
```

3. Add the own `actionError()` method:

```
class SiteController extends Controller
{
    // ...
    public function actionError()
    {

    }
}
```

4. Open the original `\yii\web\ErrorAction` class and copy its action content into our `actionError()` and customize it for the render custom `error-404` view for the `Not Found` error with the `404` code:

```
// ...
use yii\base\Exception;
use yii\base\UserException;

class SiteController extends Controller
{
    // ...
    public function actionError()
    {
```

```
if (($exception = Yii::$app->getErrorHandler()->exception)
==
null) {
    $exception = new HttpException(404, Yii::t('yii',
    'Page not found.'));
}

if ($exception instanceof HttpException) {
    $code = $exception->statusCode;
} else {
    $code = $exception->getCode();
}
if ($exception instanceof Exception) {
    $name = $exception->getName();
} else {
    $name = Yii::t('yii', 'Error');
}
if ($code) {
    $name .= " (#$code)";
}

if ($exception instanceof UserException) {
    $message = $exception->getMessage();
} else {
    $message = Yii::t('yii', 'An internal server error
    occurred.');
}

if (Yii::$app->getRequest()->getIsAjax()) {
    return "$name: $message";
} else {
    if ($code == 404) {
        return $this->render('error-404');
    } else {
        return $this->render('error', [
            'name' => $name,
            'message' => $message,
            'exception' => $exception,
        ]);
    }
}
}
}
```

5. Add the `views/site/error-404.php` view file with a custom message:

```php
<?php
use yii\helpers\Html;

/* @var $this yii\web\View */

$this->title = 'Not Found!'
?>
<div class="site-error-404">

    <h1>Oops!</h1>

    <p>Sorry, but requested page not found.</p>

    <p>
        Please follow to <?= Html::a('index page', ['site/index'])
        ?>
        to continue reading. Thank you.
    </p>

</div>
```

6. That is it. Now try to follow to the non-existing URL and see our content from the `error-404.php` view:

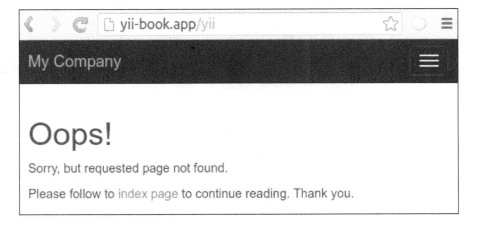

7. However, for a fail action we must see the default content from the `error.php` file:

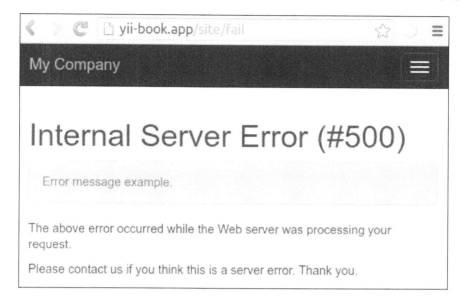

How it works...

By default, in the `yii2-app-basic` application, we configure `errorAction` for the `errorHandler` component in our configuration file `config/web.php` as `site/error`. It means that the framework will use this route for displaying every handled exception:

```
'components' => [
    'errorHandler' => [
        'errorAction' => 'site/error',
    ],
],
```

In the `SiteController` class, we use the built-in standalone `yii\web\ErrorAction` class, which renders the so-called `error.php` view:

```
class SiteController extends Controller
{
    // ...
    public function actions()
    {
        return [
            'error' => [
                'class' => 'yii\web\ErrorAction',
            ],
```

```
                'captcha' => [
                    'class' => 'yii\captcha\CaptchaAction',
                    'fixedVerifyCode' => YII_ENV_TEST ? 'testme' : null,
                ],
            ];
        }
        // ...
    }
```

If we want to override its implementation, we can replace it in an inline `actionError()` method with our own custom content.

In this recipe, we add our own `if` statement for rendering a specific view on the base of error code:

```
if ($code == 404) {
    return $this->render('error-404');
} else {
    return $this->render('error', [
        'name' => $name,
        'message' => $message,
        'exception' => $exception,
    ]);
}
```

Also, we can use a custom design for the `Not Found` page.

See also

In order to learn more about handling errors in Yii, refer to `http://www.yiiframework.com/doc-2.0/guide-runtime-handling-errors.html`.

Custom panel for debug extension

The `Yii2-debug` extension is a powerful tool for debugging own code, analyzing request information or database queries, and so on. Therefore, you can add your own panel for any custom report.

Getting ready

Create a new `yii2-app-basic` application by using the Composer package manager as described in the official guide at `http://www.yiiframework.com/doc-2.0/guide-start-installation.html`.

How to do it...

1. Create the `panels` directory on the root path of your site.

2. Add a new `UserPanel` class:

```php
<?php
namespace app\panels;

use yii\debug\Panel;
use Yii;

class UserPanel extends Panel
{
    public function getName()
    {
        return 'User';
    }

    public function getSummary()
    {
        return Yii::$app->view->render('@app/panels/views/
        summary',
        ['panel' => $this]);
    }

    public function getDetail()
    {
        return Yii::$app->view->render('@app/panels/views/detail',
        ['panel' => $this]);
    }

    public function save()
    {
        $user = Yii::$app->user;

        return !$user->isGuest ? [
            'id' => $user->id,
            'username' => $user->identity->username,
        ] : null;
    }
}
```

3. Create the `panels/view/summary.php` view with the following code:

```php
<?php
/* @var $panel app\panels\UserPanel */
use yii\helpers\Html;
?>
<div class="yii-debug-toolbar__block">
    <?php if (!empty($panel->data)): ?>
        <a href="<?= $panel->getUrl() ?>">
            User
            <span class="yii-debug-toolbar__label yii-debug-
            toolbar__label_info">
                <?= Html::encode($panel->data['username']) ?>
            </span>
        </a>
    <?php else: ?>
        <a href="<?= $panel->getUrl() ?>">Guest session</a>
    <?php endif; ?>
</div>
```

4. Add the `panels/view/detail.php` view with the following code:

```php
<?php
/* @var $panel app\panels\UserPanel */
use yii\widgets\DetailView;
?>
<h1>User profile</h1>
<?php if (!empty($panel->data)): ?>
    <?= DetailView::widget([
        'model' => $panel->data,
        'attributes' => [
            'id',
            'username',
        ]
    ]) ?>
<?php else: ?>
    <p>Guest session.</p>
<?php endif;?>
```

5. Turn on your toolbar in the `config/web.php` configuration file:

```
if (YII_ENV_DEV) {
    $config['bootstrap'][] = 'debug';
    $config['modules']['debug'] = [
        'class' => 'yii\debug\Module',
        'panels' => [
            'views' => ['class' => 'app\panels\UserPanel'],
        ],
    ];
    $config['bootstrap'][] = 'gii';
    $config['modules']['gii'] = 'yii\gii\Module';
}
```

6. Reload the `index` page and look for the **Guest Session** cell at the end of the debug panel:

7. Log in to your site with the `admin` username and the `admin` password. In a success case, you must see your username in the main menu:

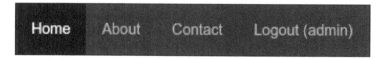

8. Observe the debug panel again. Right now, you will see the `admin` username:

9. You can click on the username in the debug panel and see the detailed user information:

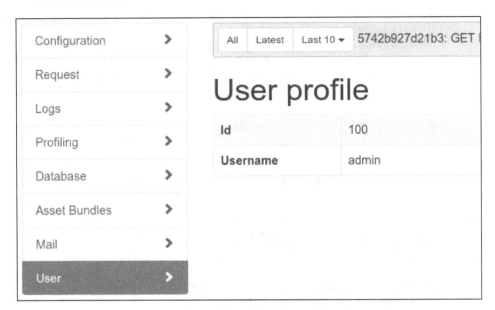

To create our own panel for the `yii2-debug` module, we need to extend the `yii\debug\Panel` class and override its template methods:

- `getName()`: The label for menu item on debug detail page
- `getSummary()`: The debug panel cell code
- `getDetail()`: The detail page view code
- `save()`: Your information which will be saved in debug storage and load back into the `$panel->data` field

Your object can store any debug data and display it on the summary block of panel and on the detail page.

In our example, we store user information:

```
public function save()
{
    $user = Yii::$app->user;
    return !$user->isGuest ? [
```

```
            'id' => $user->id,
            'username' => $user->identity->username,
        ] : null;
    }
```

Display it on summary and detail pages from the `$panel->data` field.

Handling events

You can subscribe to any events of application or any component in the `init()` method. For example, the built-in `yii\debug\panels\MailPanel` panel collects and stores all sent messages:

```
class MailPanel extends Panel
{
    private $_messages = [];

    public function init()
    {
        parent::init();
        Event::on(
            BaseMailer::className(),
            BaseMailer::EVENT_AFTER_SEND,
            function ($event) {
                $message = $event->message;
                $messageData = [
                    // ...
                ];
                $this->_messages[] = $messageData;
            }
        );
    }

    // ...

    public function save()
    {
        return $this->_messages;
    }
}
```

Also, it displays a grid with the list of stored messages on our own detail page.

See also

- In order to learn more about `yii2-debug` extension, refer to `http://www.yiiframework.com/doc-2.0/ext-debug-index.html`

- For more information about creating a views counter panel, refer to `https://github.com/yiisoft/yii2-debug/blob/master/docs/guide/topics-creating-your-own-panels.md`

Index

Symbol

\yii\db\Connection component 142

A

access control and filters
references 216
ActiveQuery class
customizing 114-116
references 117
advanced application template
modifying 430-432
advanced project template
installing 4, 5
AJAX-dependent drop-down list
creating 185-192
AJAX validation
implementing 192, 193
application structures
reference link 428
application templates 6, 7
application webroot
files, placing 429
files, placing in subdirectory 429
moving 429, 430
AR event-like methods
model fields, processing with 117-119
assets
combining 415-420
minimizing 415-420
URL 421

Atoum
code coverage, analyzing 510, 511
extension code, writing 502
extension structure, preparing 501, 502
extension tests, writing 503-507
references 512
tests, executing 508-510
used, for unit testing 500, 511, 512
authentication
about 202
implementing 202-208
URL 208
authentication client
about 271
references 276
using 272-275
working 276
author
setting up, automatically 124-127

B

base controller
reference link 63
using 59-63
basic project template
installing 3, 4
Behat
about 512
references 525
used, for creating shopping
cart extension 512-525

Behavior Driven Design (BDD) 511
behaviors
  URL 326
blocks
  reference link 90
  using 88-90
Bower-to-Composer adapter 3
build-in cache
  reference link 357
built-in components 34

C

cache chains
  using 386-395
cache dependencies
  using 386-395
caching
  reference link 382, 395
Captcha
  customizing 164-166
  references 167
CaptchaWidget
  adding 158-163
  customizing 158-163
CLI commands
  creating 346-350
Closure Compiler
  URL 421
Codeception
  about 457
  references 483
  used, for testing Yii2
    application 457, 458, 461, 482
code generation 27-32
command-line mode 5
compiler.jar file
  URL, for downloading 415
complex forms
  with multiple models 180-184
components
  creating 326-332

existing application components,
  overriding 331
  reference link 332
Composer
  library, installing via 39
Composer package 2
conditional validation
  about 177-180
  URL 180
configuration parts
  moving, into separate files 433, 434
console components
  reference link 34
context information
  logging 538-541
  reference link 541
  using 538-541
controller context
  used, in view 83, 84
controller filters
  using 208-215
controllers
  reference link 54, 337, 342
cron jobs
  cron schedule, setting 447
  custom command, creating 446, 447
  executing 445-447
  Hello command, running 445, 446
  implementing 445-447
  reference link 448
cross-database relations 113
cross-site request forgery (CSRF)
  about 228
  disabling, for all actions 231
  disabling, for specification 231
  extra measures 231
  GET operations, using 232
  POST operations, using 232
  preventing 228-230
  references 232
  validation, for Ajax-calls 231

P

package
URL, for installation 2
packagist
URL 378
pagination
reference link 100
passwords
reference link 247
working with 247
performance tuning
references 382, 386, 403
PHP coding standards
URL 378
PHP framework
advanced project template, installing 4, 5
basic project template, installing 3, 4
installing 2, 6
PHP include
reference link 435
PHP require
URL 435
PHPUnit
code coverage, analyzing 496, 497
component, usage 497
extension code, writing 485-488
extension structure, preparing 483-485
extension tests, writing 489-493
tests, executing 494, 495
used, for unit testing 483, 498-500
Pjax jQuery plugin
about 308
ActiveForm, using 310
custom ID, specifying 309
references 311
using 308
with client-side script 310

R

rate limiting
about 260
implementing 260-264
references 265

read-write splitting
about 139-142
references 143
Redis database driver
about 311
ActiveRecord, using 312
direct usage 312
references 313
using 311-313
regular expressions
used, in URL rules 55-59
rendering view
reference link 88
renderRecords method 108
replication
about 139-142
references 143
RESTful web services
authentication 257-260
error handling 268-270
rate limiting 260-264
REST server, creating 249
versioning 265-268
REST server
content negotiation 254
creating 249-253
references 257
Rest URL rule, customizing 256
reusable controller actions
creating 332-336
reusable controllers
creating 337-342
Role-Based Access Control (RBAC)
about 233
hierarchy 241
RBAC nodes, naming 242
references 242
using 233-241
routing
reference link 54

www.ingramcontent.com/pod-product-compliance
Lightning Source LLC
Chambersburg PA
CBHW081450050326
40690CB00015B/2744